# To Make Our World Anew

National Guardsmen confront marchers on Beale Street, Memphis, in 1968.

# To Make Our World Anew

## Volume Two: A History of African Americans since 1880

edited by

**Robin D. G. Kelley**

and

**Earl Lewis**

OXFORD
UNIVERSITY PRESS

# OXFORD
## UNIVERSITY PRESS

Oxford University Press, Inc., publishes works that further
Oxford University's objective of excellence
in research, scholarship, and education.

Oxford   New York
Auckland   Cape Town   Dar es Salaam   Hong Kong   Karachi
Kuala Lumpur   Madrid   Melbourne   Mexico City   Nairobi
New Delhi   Shanghai   Taipei   Toronto

With offices in
Argentina   Austria   Brazil   Chile   Czech Republic   France   Greece
Guatemala   Hungary   Italy   Japan   Poland   Portugal   Singapore
South Korea   Switzerland   Thailand   Turkey   Ukraine   Vietnam

First published by Oxford University Press, Inc., 2000
198 Madison Avenue, New York, New York 10016
www.oup.com

First issued as a two-volume Oxford University Press paperback, 2005
Vol. 1 ISBN-13: 978-0-19-518134-0
Vol. 1 ISBN-10: 0-19-518134-4
Vol. 2 ISBN-13: 978-0-19-518135-7
Vol. 2 ISBN-10: 0-19-518135-2

Oxford is a registered trademark of Oxford University Press

The Library of Congress has cataloged the one-volume cloth edition as follows:
To make our world anew : a history of African Americans / edited by Robin D. G.
Kelley and Earl Lewis.
p.   cm.   Includes bibliographical references (p.) and index.
ISBN-13: 978-0-19-513945-7
ISBN-10: 0-19-513945-3
1. Afro-Americans—History.   I. Kelley, Robin D. G.   II. Lewis, Earl.
E185 .T68 2000   973'.0496073—dc21   00-021131

1  3  5  7  9  10  8  6  4  2
Printed in the United States of America on acid-free paper

# Contents

# To You

To sit and dream, to sit and read,
To sit and learn about the world
Outside our world of here and now—
    Our problem world—
To dream of vast horizons of the soul
Through dreams made whole,
Unfettered free—help me!
All you who are dreamers, too,
Help me make our world anew
I reach out my hands to you.

                  —Langston Hughes

# Preface to Volume Two

*Robin D. G. Kelley* and *Earl Lewis*

T
he decade of the 1870s ended on the heels of the greatest revolution in American history since the patriots declared their independence from England. In many respects, the revolution of the 1860s and 1870s was more far-reaching than what the Founding Fathers had had in mind a century earlier. Launched in the midst of the Civil War and postwar efforts to reconstruct the South and the nation, ex-slaves, along with radical Republicans and a few poor Southern whites, set out to transform the old plantation oligarchy into a true democracy. Newly freed men and women sought to create a civil society in which the role of government was to provide land for landless ex-slaves, protect all of its citizens from violence and exploitation, make education and basic public services available to all irrespective of race or economic status, ensure that all adult males enjoyed unfettered voting rights, and work actively to achieve full equality for all. As a result of this vision of democracy, Congress passed the 13th Amendment to the Constitution, abolishing slavery, the 14th Amendment granting black people citizenship and fundamental civil rights, and the 15th Amendment enabling black men and poor white men the right to vote without property qualifications. Members of Congress also succeeded in creating free, universal public education. All of this happened, in part, because former slaves ran for political office at the local, state, and national levels, and promoted legislation that continued to expand the definition of democracy.

African Americans did not simply wait for the state or the Republican party to solve their problems. Some freed people left their former masters in search of family members who had been sold away, to find better opportunities, or simply to find out what it felt like to be free. A new group of black leaders emerged out of the war, many of whom had fought for the Union army and saw themselves as liberators. They raised money to build churches and schools, hire teachers, and purchase land. Some former slaves assumed the land of their former masters belonged to them for, after all, "massa" was a war criminal and his wealth was built on the sweat and toil of Africa's children. They were not wrong; indeed, there was some wartime redistribution of land by the Union army and the Freedman's Bureau promised to settle former slaves on plots of their own. Not all former slaves reacted so boldly to the achievement of freedom. Tens of thousands throughout the South stuck close to their old plantations, afraid of starvation and severing deep family and community ties. The transition to freedom revealed that even the most settled families had certain vulnerabilities in the early years of Reconstruction. There were many incidents of planters evicting their former slaves, especially those too old or weak to work.

Despite initial setbacks, black people were indefatigable in their commitment to own land, enjoy citizenship, exercise political power, build institutions, and live in a South where everyone was free and equal. They remained optimistic because of the presence of federal troops and institutions such as the Freedman's Bureau. However, once Andrew Johnson was sworn in as president following Lincoln's assassination, he made his position clear: America is a "white man's nation" and white men shall be the ones to rule the South. Throughout 1866, President Johnson appointed avid racists to positions of power in the Southern provisional government. They, in turn, disarmed the majority of black federal troops at the very moment when planters formed armed terrorist organizations such as the Ku Klux Klan and the Knights of the White Camelia. In 1866, these new office holders dedicated to white supremacy passed a series of laws known as the Black Codes. The Black Codes restricted black freedom of movement, the amount of land blacks could own, whom they could marry (interracial marriages were outlawed), and their right to bear arms. Some of the most draconian of the Black Codes were the apprenticeship laws, which allowed former masters to literally retain ex-slaves under the age of twenty-one under the pretext that they needed a guardian.

Once the radical Republicans in Congress overturned President Johnson's Reconstruction policies in 1866 and passed the 14th and 15th Amendments to the Constitution granting black people citizenship and male suffrage, respectively, the erosion of liberty changed. Throughout the late 1860s and early 1870s, former slaves not only voted, they ran for office and held positions in the state legislature, Congress, and even the Senate. They insisted that free universal public education was a pillar of democracy. Unfortunately, the experiment in democracy was slowly dismantled as Northern industrialists re-established ties to the old planter class and sent black folks back to something akin to slavery. The black militias were disarmed, federal troops were withdrawn, and the Republicans struck a shady deal with the Democrats during the 1876 presidential election that allowed their own Rutherford B. Hayes to win the White House despite having lost in the electoral college, in exchange for withdrawing all federal troops from the South, ending their efforts to reconstruct democracy in the South, and granting the Southern oligarchy more federal appointments and funds for road and bridge construction. The Compromise of 1877 opened the door for the de facto denial of black citizenship, including the right to vote.

During the next fifteen years, things only got worse. It didn't have to be this way. If only poor whites had recognized that their own freedom was tied to the freedom of black people. If they had only understood the power of united action, of blacks and whites working together to overthrow landlords, merchants, and money-hungry factory owners. Instead, tragically, poor white people, barely able to make ends meet, chose allegiance to their race over their class—they identified more with being white than being a worker or a farmer who shared common interests with black workers and farmers. Thus begins what black historian Rayford Logan calls "the nadir" or low point of African-American history.

Low point indeed. During the 1890s and early 1900s, lynchings increased, racial segregation became law, and African-American citizens who had worked so hard for the Republican party in the days of Reconstruction found themselves without the right to vote. Many emancipated black people found themselves with no property working for white landlords under conditions reminiscent of slavery. These rural folk had to rent their land, grow the crops the market demanded, and give half or more of what they produced to their landlords. This system of sharecropping, sometimes called the new slavery, kept most African Americans in debt and in poverty. Yet, it did not destroy their fighting spirit. Africans Americans were more than victims of "Jim Crow" laws and racial violence. They organized, fought back, moved around, thought, wrote, and created works of art. They connected their struggles with the rest of the world, turning to Africa, Europe, and the Caribbean for guidance and inspiration. In many respects they kept a vision of justice and equality born during Reconstruction alive. Some African Americans joined interracial movements such as the Populists or the Knights of Labor; others turned inward and built religious, fraternal, educational, and political institutions that ultimately became sources of power and inspiration for the stony road ahead. Others simply left, finding refuge as far away as Liberia (West Africa), Canada, and Haiti, or as close as Kansas and Oklahoma. African-American men and women founded all-black towns, such as Mound Bayou in Mississippi or Langston and Boley in Oklahoma, and imagined a promised land free of white terrorism. A handful followed the advice of black educator Booker T. Washington, who called on Southern black folk to "cast down their buckets where they are" and carve out a life on the land. He believed proving that African Americans are a productive people, would reduce the terror and eliminate racism. Then there were those, such as Ida B. Wells, who believed blacks should cast down the gauntlet and punch it out with white supremacists. Wells, one of many leading black women activists of that era, declared war on lynching and sexual violence against black women.

If you can't beat them, leave. And this is what over one million Southern blacks did around the time war broke out in Europe. Scores made the move from the countryside to Southern cities such as New Orleans, Houston, Memphis, Birmingham, Atlanta, Durham, Richmond, and Norfolk. With the war-time economy booming and European immigration at a virtual standstill due to the conflict, the demand for labor attracted hundreds of thousands of black folk to the Northern metropolises such as Chicago, New York, Philadelphia, Milwaukee, Cleveland, and Detroit. For some, the move North was a version of Exodus. They sought refuge and possibility in the North; they sought security and safety in the burgeoning ghettoes of the Midwest and Eastern seaboard cities. Many found what they were looking for; others only found more misery. Most experienced a combination of exhilaration and disappointment. And everyone, whether they stayed in the South or joined the Great Migration, confronted a society in flux: The world during and immediately following the Great War was a world marked by destruction, international migrations, rapid industrialization, a wave of anticolonial uprisings in Africa and the Caribbean, revolutions in Russia, Germany, Mexico, Ireland, and elsewhere, and racial violence at home. Black men returned from the war to make the world safe for democracy ready to demand democracy for themselves. For their militancy they paid a dear price—black men were lynched in uniform, black institutions were attacked by racist white mobs, the ranks of black industrial workers that had swelled during the war were rapidly downsized. On the other hand, while the 1920s looked pretty bad for ordinary African Americans, the "artists of the race" experienced a renaissance. Popular fascination with blackness meant that the cultural achievements of African Americans—in literature, music, theater, dance, visual arts—would have an audience.

By the end of the decade, however, things looked bad for everybody. When the Great Depression hit America, African Americans were feeling it even before the stock market crash of 1929. But they had hardly given up hope. On the contrary, the crisis was seen by some as yet another opportunity to "make the world anew." Hope in the midst of crisis is a major theme in the history of the 1930s and 1940s. Alongside images of bank closings, endless soup lines, jobless men selling apples, unemployed workers begging for work, hard-working middle-class Americans losing everything, we find newsreel footage of families glued to radios listening to the president's inspirational speeches, labor leaders declaring victory in the aftermath of militant strikes, radical protesters fighting tenaciously to transform the country. This sense of hope and high expectation was also evident in the many letters ordinary people sent to President Franklin Delano Roosevelt, the man Americans sent to the White House three times in a row beginning in 1932. They believed things would change, that the nation would rise up out of the Depression. Roosevelt himself reinforced their hopes by promising a "New Deal" for all Americans. For African Americans, in particular, the era was simultaneously an inferno and an eden: Black workers had the highest unemployment rate at a time when black leaders held important positions in Roosevelt's Administration; New Deal legislation threw hundreds of thousands of black sharecroppers off the land when the same federal government provided unprecedented opportunities for black writers and artists; dramatic episodes of racist violence against African Americans opened the decade just when Communists and other radicals launched a nationwide campaign against racial injustice.

This sense of hope amid crisis became even more pronounced once the United States entered the Second World War in 1941. For African Americans, the horrors of war provided an opportunity to demand equal treatment. They criticized the United States for fighting for democracy overseas while black people at home were treated like second-class citizens. Unlike the First World War, this time around black leaders called for a "Double Victory"—a victory against fascism abroad and racism at home. The war also created employment opportunities for many black working people, many of whom left the South permanently for the sprawling factories of the urban North. It was *deja vu* all over again. Hopeful that these Northern metropolises would be the "promised land," a good number of these migrants found only frustration and disappointment since a comparatively small proportion of African Americans gained access to industrial jobs and training programs. Those who did obtain good-paying jobs often experienced violent reprisals from disgruntled whites who refused to work with blacks. Thus, throughout the war white workers waged "hate strikes" to protest the promotion of black men and women, and black workers frequently retaliated with their own strikes to protest discrimination. And in many instances, racial tensions spread beyond the workplace, erupting in riots in several major U.S. cities. Spurred by poor housing and living conditions in ghettos, competition between blacks and whites over the use of public parks, and police treatment of black citizens, these riots resulted in several deaths, thousands of injuries, and millions of dollars in property damage. Indeed, it might be said that while U.S. troops invaded Normandy and bombed Okinawa, African Americans in the urban ghettoes fought their own war at home.

It was only the beginning. Despite a long and noble history of black resistance to racism and oppression in the United States, the period from 1945 to 1970 might be described as a protracted war for freedom. Black Americans were determined to be the architects of an inclusive America, one that championed human rights for all. Moreover, they openly linked local efforts to global conditions. The fight for economic and racial justice in Baton Rouge, Montgomery, and other southern towns and cities became part of a worldwide fight for human rights. In song, word, and deed, anti-colonial efforts in Africa were connected to human rights struggles in the United States; opposition to the war in Vietnam became linked to the oppression of Third World peoples everywhere. In that sense the black struggle in the United States became a beacon for the world.

The Second World War had exposed the persistent contradictions between the American ideal and the American reality. Black Americans resolved to eliminate that contradiction. They would not only fight for democracy abroad, they would pursue democracy at home. In communities large and small they organized after the war, often aided by the Second World War veterans who had resolved to return home and change things. They used indigenous institutions such as churches, fraternal orders, and civil rights organizations and created new ones to funnel their efforts. In the lawyerly crafted briefs of attorneys, the cadences of black ministers, the lyrics of gospels and civil rights songs, the energies of college students, the noble dreams of ordinary folk, they plotted their strategies. Victories followed before the Supreme Court in *Brown v. Board of Education* (1954); through the determined actions of Montgomery and Baton Rouge residents; and in the desegregation of military ranks.

Lest it be forgotten, however, it took community mobilization; it took the poor and middle class, the young and old, the college educated and school dropouts to organize the communities for social change. Some resisted, fearing beatings, job loss, and even murder. For good reason—African Americans who organized the Civil Rights movement experienced the range of negative response. After all, the federal government reluctantly backed civil rights workers and aggressively investigated black leaders when they complained about the war in Vietnam and social inequities elsewhere. It is important to understand that while African Americans generally shared a vision of changing the world, they did disagree at times over strategies, procedures, and timing. In time, Southern activists came to realize that the challenges faced by Northern and Western urban dwellers required new emphases. Members of the Student Nonviolent Coordinating Committee (SNCC) publicly and quietly feuded with elders in organizations such as the NAACP and the Southern Christian Leadership Committee (SCLC).

At the same time, women and men turned to a variety of media to capture the world and their place in it. Popular music pulsated with the rhythms and anthems of migrants who had earlier settled in Detroit, Philadelphia, and Memphis, among other locales. A new outpouring of writings probed the inner psyche of black urban and rural folk as well as the ways and folkways of whites. Hollywood tiptoed around the subject of racial inclusion, which television executives readily obliged, while graphically exposing the rawness of segregation and Northern exploitation for evening news viewers. Music, writings, and style played a pivotal role in the affairs of the day.

When the 1960s came to a close most black people were surprisingly optimistic. The Civil Rights movement had made remarkable gains, and many people believed that the Black Power movement might achieve for African Americans the self-determination they had been seeking for the past three centuries. There were some stunning victories, especially in the arena of electoral politics: Several major cities elected black mayors; African-American representation in Congress increased significantly; a black man named Jesse Jackson actually became a serious contender for the presidency. The black middle class expanded, as corporate board rooms became slightly more integrated and black college-educated professionals moved to newly built suburban homes.

However the majority of African Americans were not so lucky. The period after 1970 was marked by massive economic changes that adversely affected black workers: the disappearance of heavy industry, the flight of American manufacturers to foreign lands, and the displacement of millions of workers across the country.

Permanent unemployment and underemployment became a way of life. A few years after the War on Poverty had been declared a victory, the number of black poor grew dramatically. Despite the growing presence of African Americans in political office, city services declined, federal spending on cities dried up, affirmative action programs were dismantled, blatant acts of racism began to rise again (including renewed efforts to disfranchise black citizens), and American cities seemed to experience a constant economic crisis.

Economic decline, poverty, and rising racism in the "post–segregation" age is only part of the story. The final chapters of this book tell yet another story of how black people are still attempting to "make our world anew." It is the same story of how an increasingly diverse and always-complicated black community resisted oppression, struggled for power, dealt with internal tensions, conflicts, and differences, and profoundly shaped American culture. It is the story of the resurgence of black nationalism, the rise of black neo-conservatism, the challenge of black feminism, the impact of Caribbean immigration on African-American communities, the escalation of interethnic tensions, and the roots of rap music and hip-hop culture. It is a story whose final chapters still have to be written by all of us.

*To Make Our World Anew,* volumes one and two, are the product of a truly collective endeavor. We have combined the efforts of eleven leading historians who had authored the original *Young Oxford History of African Americans* to produce the two-volume paperback edition. In this volume, Barbara Bair authored the first chapter, "Though Justice Sleeps: 1880–1900;" James R. Grossman, "A Chance to Make Good: 1900–1929;" Joe William Trotter, Jr., "From a Raw Deal to a New Deal?: 1929–1945;" Vincent Harding, Robin D. G. Kelley, and Earl Lewis produced, "We Changed the World: 1945–1970;" and Robin D. G. Kelley, "Into the Fire: 1970 to the Present." Each of these authors deserves full credit as co-authors of *To Make Our World Anew.*

# To Make Our World Anew

## CHAPTER 1

# Though Justice Sleeps

## 1880–1900

### *Barbara Bair*

In his 1884 book *Black and White*, African-American journalist and activist T. Thomas Fortune analyzed the denial of justice to African Americans and the process of disenfranchisement that characterized the post–Reconstruction era. He observed that the exclusion of African Americans from land ownership and voting were the twin roots of the "great social wrong which has turned the beautiful roses of freedom into thorns to prick the hands of the black men of the South." Despite the promises of freedom, including legal emancipation from slavery and postwar talk of righting economic inequities and providing opportunities, the majority of African Americans faced landlessness, underemployment, and lack of access to political rights or protections. Land, as a symbol of freedom and citizenship, and as a means of independent livelihood, was at the crux of African-American desire in the last two decades of the nineteenth century.

During this period, nine out of ten of the 6.5 million African Americans in the United States made their homes in the South. Eighty percent of these black Southerners lived in rural areas, and most of them were farmers or agricultural laborers. Some were landowners and had their own small farms, but most were tenants. They rented the land where they worked for cash or a share of the crops they raised. Others worked for hire.

It was very difficult for tenant farmers working under sharecropping arrangements to get ahead financially, and having enough to eat and adequate clothing were always worries. Most faced each new year owing money from years before to the white people from whom they rented land and to the merchant who ran the store where they purchased their goods. "We make as much cotton and sugar as we did when we were slaves," one black tenant farmer in Texas observed, "and it does us as little good now as it did then." Laborers who questioned the high prices charged to them, which would invariably be set at a rate that would encompass or exceed the value of their entire year's crop, had little legal recourse. As one black Mississippian testified to the Senate, "Colored men soon learn that it is better to pay any account, however unjust, than to refuse, for he stands no possible chance of getting justice before the law."

Many African-American sharecroppers and farmers sought greater justice by moving to different land. When their contracts were up at one place, they would often pack their belongings and enter into a new arrangement on another tract of acreage, hoping to improve over their last year's experience. One Alabama share-cropper reported the frustration she felt when she went out in the moonlight to plant rosebushes to beautify the plot of land she was renting, never knowing whose yard it would be the next year. Some moved even further than from one plot in the neighborhood to another. They migrated from the South to form new black towns in the West, or dreamed of a life of justice and independence in an all-black Africa.

Leaving, for families already in debt and under white economic control, was no easy matter. It was hard to do without much money, and it could be dangerous. White Southerners did not want black laborers to leave, because their low-paid work made white economic gains possible. Despite the risks involved, thousands of laborers and middle-class people desirous of greater opportunities left for Kansas, Oklahoma, and other areas outside the South. "The word it has been spoken; the message has been sent," wrote Sojourner Truth in verse she composed about the migrations. "The prison doors have opened, and out the prisoners went." For Truth and other older activists who had worked hard to bring about the end of slavery, the post–Reconstruction treks to new lands were seen as one more step in the march toward real emancipation. For other leaders, such as Frederick Douglass, the migrations were a mistake. Douglass felt that African Americans should remain where they were, confront violence, and take a stand for equal rights. This was difficult to do, and while many African Americans did work and speak out to change conditions in the regions where they lived, others, partic-ularly the poor, who lived under harsh circumstances, longed to escape rather than place their hopes in reforming political and economic systems that were so weighed against them.

Some black leaders argued that the federal government should make public lands available to black settlement as compensation for the centuries that Ameri-cans of African descent had spent in slavery. In 1887 William H. Thomas wrote in the African Methodist Episcopal *Church Review* that he saw the involvement of the government in the distribution of land as an issue of morality and legal principle, mandated by the "equity of justice between man and man, and government and citizen." If slavery was wrong, Thomas argued, then "Negroes were illegally held to service; some measure of compensation, therefore, is due them, not only from individuals who were the nominal owners, but from the National Government which was the prime factor in their enslavement and maintenance in bondage. . . . No measure of compensation would work such beneficial results to the free peo-ple, . . . as the ownership of land." Thomas, like many others who had come before and would follow him, proposed the creation of a separate black territory or state within the United States. In Thomas's vision, the government would buy expanses of land in Southern states and divide their acreage into small homesteads that would be made available for black settlement.

The longing for land and political control that beckoned laborers and middle-class investors West also made them think of Africa. Henry Adams and Benjamin Singleton were among the African-American activists who advocated mass black emigration from the South in the late 1870s and 1880s. These advocates contacted organizations founded to provide passage to African Americans who wanted to move to West Africa, including the long-established (and white-dominated) American Colonization Society and several newer enterprises such as the black-administered Liberian Exodus Joint Stock Steamship Company. Gathering support from tens of thousands of rural black Southerners, Adams and other organizers like him viewed Liberia as a potential home for working people with agricultural skills.

Other African Americans, especially middle-class leaders, saw West Africa not so much as a place to escape from white violence or as a land of opportunity for workers with few resources, but as a place where educated blacks of African and African-American origin could develop their own business enterprises and political structures. In the mid-1880s and 1890s, grassroots groups like Benjamin Singleton's United Transatlantic Society, based in Tennessee and Kansas, continued to advocate migration to Africa as a means of racial unity and progress at the same time that they encouraged Southern blacks to move westward.

Bishop Henry McNeal Turner, a leader of the African Methodist Episcopal Church and an advocate of black emigration, had traveled to Liberia and wrote and spoke of its promise. Organizers for the American Colonization Society also toured through the South, speaking at churches and community centers about African heritage and black nationhood in Africa. When African Americans read Turner's letters about Liberia that were published in church newspapers in 1891, they responded. They formed local clubs to encourage emigration, and many wrote to inquire about securing passage or came East in hope of boarding a transatlantic steamer, but the colonization society did not have enough boats to carry them or the funding to promise future voyages. These disappointed travelers became temporary urban refugees. They either returned West or made homes in the city.

While the influence of the colonization society declined as a result of its financial hardships and administrative reorganization after 1892, several independent movements were formed in the 1890s. Emigration remained an important topic of discussion among lower- and working-class African Americans.

Small groups of emigrants successfully left for Africa, but the overwhelming majority of African Americans remained in the United States. Many who wanted to go to Africa could not afford to pay for the passage. If they decided to leave the South, they looked instead for places relatively close to home to secure land and contribute their labor. Since the late 1870s, black people from Kentucky, Missouri, and Tennessee had been establishing new lives in Kansas and in small settlements

*For a fee of five dollars, black settlers of Nicodemus, Kansas, were granted this certificate enti-tling them to any vacant lot in the town. The chance to own their own land was a powerful lure for many African Americans.*

on the Western prairies. Just as national proponents of African repatriation visited churches and schools to teach African Americans about Africa and the possibility of going there, so promoters of migration clubs who wanted to encourage reloca-tion to the West organized through existing black social institutions.

The motivation for going to other states was similar to the idea of going to Africa. "We as a people are oppressed and disfranchised," one westward migrant wrote in a letter in 1891. "We are still working hard and our rights taken from us. [T]imes are hard and getting harder every year. We as a people believe that Affrica is the place but to get from under bondage are thinking of Oklahoma as this is our nearest place of safety."

In 1889–90 portions of what was called the Unassigned Lands in Indian Terri-tory and all of Oklahoma Territory (areas that in 1907 would become parts of the state of Oklahoma) were opened to settlement by non-Indian peoples. Indian Territory had been the home of relocated Indian peoples since federal policy had forcibly moved Native Americans from their traditional homelands in the East in the 1830s. Many blacks and people of mixed race living in the region were former slaves, or the descendants of those who had been held in bondage by Cherokee, Creek, or other Indian peoples for generations. Many of these freedmen and their families were themselves citizens of the Indian nations. In the early 1890s, African

Americans from neighboring Arkansas and other Southern states were attracted to the land grants available in the areas newly opened to settlement by outsiders. More than seven thousand of them moved. They did so with the hope not only for property, but for political independence.

Several all-black towns were established in the territories. These were places where African Americans could form their own municipal governments and protect one another from white incursions and violence. Langston City was one such town. It had its own newspaper, and when black residents across the South read about the plans for the town, they joined dozens of Oklahoma booster clubs that advertised opportunities and promoted migration. A few hundred came to Langston. In 1897 Langston University (also called the Agricultural and Normal University), a college where black teachers were trained, was established in Langston by the territorial legislature. The town's primary promoter, Edward (also Edwin) P. McCabe encouraged emigrants to become involved in Republican party politics and to start businesses. McCabe had earlier helped settle the black town of Nicodemus, Kansas, which was named for an African prince who was brought to the American colonies as a slave and later purchased his own freedom. He hoped enough black people would respond to the Oklahoma Territory land rush that voting majorities of blacks would be created in the territory's local districts. African Americans who came would own land and businesses, and would be able to govern themselves.

Most newly arrived residents in the West and Midwest lived in simple dugouts and took up subsistence farming, much like the African Americans who were already living in the region. A more prosperous middle class also emerged, and these people operated hotels, blacksmith shops, barbershops, saloons, and other service-oriented establishments. Other blacks became deputy marshals or worked on ranches as cowboys and wranglers. Black churches, women's groups, and fraternal orders were founded. By 1900, more than 55,000 African Americans were living in Oklahoma and Indian Territories, and between 1890 and 1910, twenty-five black communities were founded in the Oklahoma region.

Efforts at westward migration and the formation of black towns, like transatlantic emigration to West Africa, were plagued by the relative poverty of the majority of black workers and subsistence farmers. Neither the emigration clubs nor African colonization organizations and companies had funds for long-term investment. Middle-class organizers and developers involved in the black-towns movement and in Liberian colonization schemes tried hard to attract settlers who had the financial capital to start or support businesses, purchase land, and establish long-lasting schools, churches, and civic and social associations. Accomplishing these things was difficult to do for those with little money. Colonists in Africa faced prolonged rainy seasons and types of illnesses and fevers they were not used to, and they often arrived in Africa to find that provisions and resources that had been promised to them were scarce.

Blacks who participated in the westward exoduses purchased more than twenty-thousand acres of land in Kansas in the early 1880s, but at the same time thousands of individuals arrived after difficult journeys, impoverished, undernourished, and in need of help. For them, basics like seeds, clothing, and farming implements were hard to buy. Many took jobs on the railroads or in towns instead of establishing their own small farms as they had hoped to do. Crop failures and droughts made conditions worse. The economic depression of 1893–94 drove down cotton prices and raised interest rates, burying tenant farmers in deeper debt within the credit system, and made cash and jobs even more scarce than before.

Still, there were successes. The presence of a nearby railroad line could make a big difference in a black town's ability to last over time. Mound Bayou, Mississippi, had a railroad depot. Mound Bayou was a town with a majority black population that, like sites further to the West, was founded on the principles of racial pride and economic opportunity. Black citizens there were able to steadily increase the number of acres of land under tillage in surrounding farms. They established several commercial businesses, such as cotton gins and sawmills, whose success was linked to the availability of rail transportation that quickly moved products created or processed by the businesses to the market. In the 1890s, the residents of Mound Bayou replaced dugouts and log cabins with wood houses and built five new churches and a school building. Black people were elected as city aldermen and held office as mayor.

In the 1890s the Langston City, Oklahoma, *Herald* newspaper emphasized the desire of town leaders and promoters to attract middle-class people to their town. Ads called for shoemakers and other artisans, and invited those who could begin new businesses such as a lumberyard and a harness shop. Several grocery stores already existed, as did saloons, blacksmiths, barbershops, feed stores, mills, yeast and soap factories, a bank, hotels, and an opera house. The newspaper's editors also promised black readers that political liberty and justice would be by-products of life in Langston.

But in the same period when this promise was being made, African Americans saw their political rights increasingly under attack. By the 1890s, Jim Crow laws segregated people of different races in public places such as schools, restaurants, and theaters. They also applied different rules that affected blacks' and whites' ability to do things like vote, secure loans, or chose a place to live. The term "Jim Crow" was an old pejorative way of referring to black people. It had been in popular use since the 1830s. The Jim Crow laws made areas of the West and Midwest, which at first had seemed attractive, difficult places for blacks to fulfill their dreams of independent lives free of white control or repression. Despite injustices, people made good lives for themselves and their neighbors. They worked hard, raised families, and looked after one another in their communities. African Americans also had a large presence in the West serving in the U.S. military and working in ranching and the cattle industry. Many experienced black cowboys were born in the West or had served in U.S. Army infantry and cavalry regiments stationed in Western states.

Black cowboys in Texas around 1890. During the last part of the nineteenth century black cowboys played a large role in the development of the Western economy, participating in cattle drives and working on ranches.

With the coming of the railroads and the fencing of the land, the massive trail drives in which African-American cowboys had traditionally found employment gave way to the shipment of cattle by train. In the last part of the nineteenth century, the proportion of cowboys who were black varied from twenty-five to sixty percent in different areas of the West. Many of them worked in Texas and Indian Territory. By the late 1880s and early 1890s, these hands worked for hire on individual ranches, sometimes farming their own homesteads on the side and raising small herds. Other highly skilled cowboys entered the roping contest circuit, turning the work they did on the range into performance art. They competed for prize money as horseback riders and ropers in small town exhibitions, large regional expositions, and state and county fairs. Their presence on the roping circuits set the stage for the later achievements of men like Bill Pickett, a black cowboy at the Miller 101 Ranch who became famous for his performances in rodeo and Wild West shows.

Unlike men who made their living in the cattle industry and its offshoots, women in the West were employed primarily in farming family plots. And many were employed in the service economy, working as cooks, cleaners, and laundresses in households and boardinghouses or hotels, raising other people's children, or for a few, working in black-owned stores.

For most black women who remained in the South, the kinds of domestic chores and farmwork that they did had not changed much since emancipation. They worked long hours scrubbing floors, cooking and preparing food, sewing, washing, mending, and doing dishes. They cared for their children, and they planted, chopped, and picked cotton and helped with wheat, corn, and tobacco crops. They also grew small gardens or sometimes kept a cow in order to add greens, butter, and milk to the regular family diet of cornmeal, salt pork, and molasses. They often would try to do what they could to earn a little cash: raise chickens and sell the eggs, pick wild berries for market, or take in extra laundry.

Most African-American households were headed by a husband and a wife, and on average they had four or five members living under one roof. Men usually were married by the time they were twenty-five years old, and women by age twenty. Hard manual labor, poverty, and poor nutrition among the majority of African Americans who worked as sharecroppers were reflected in low fertility rates, high child mortality rates, and an average life expectancy for black men and women of just thirty-three years. Many families lived near other kin, and as women and men grew older they often took into their households other relatives and boarders from outside their immediate family. In addition to caring for her family, a woman living in the rural South would also be involved in working with other women in her neighborhood.

Some African-American families left agricultural life behind completely. Moving to the city, like migration West and repatriation to Africa, was one of the forms of movement that African Americans engaged in as they searched for a better life. While tenant farmers or sharecroppers would often move from one plot of rented land to another, country people also moved from farms to small towns and from towns to cities. In the 1880s and 1890s, although four-fifths of African Americans still lived in rural areas, the concentration of black populations in the urban parts of the South and of black workers in industries continually increased. For them, it was not land but work that was the focus of their search for equality and rights.

## Labor: "Let Us Put Our Shoulders to the Wheel"

In a letter published in the *United Mine Workers Journal* on July 14, 1892, African-American union organizer Richard L. Davis talked about the rights of working people and addressed some thoughts to those who saw solutions for blacks in migration or back-to-Africa movements. "The negro has a right in this country," Davis wrote, "They are here and to stay."

One of the places that African Americans were staying was in the cities of the South. Some black urban residents had been in the cities since before the Civil War, when they worked either as slaves or as freemen and freewomen. Others came or were born there in the last decades of the 1800s, when the numbers of black people in large Southern urban centers grew. In 1880, for example, the U.S. census showed 16,337 black people living in Nashville, Tennessee. They made up thirty-eight percent of the total population of the city. By the time of the next U.S. census, in 1890, there were 29,395 blacks in Nashville, comprising thirty-nine percent of the city's population. While African-American citizens were still a minority in Nashville in 1890, they made up more than half the populations of other cities, including Montgomery, Alabama, and Raleigh, North Carolina.

Although in this period only a small percentage of the black population of the

United States lived in Northern states, of those who did, most lived in cities. In the great migration movements of the 1900s, many black people moved to major industrial urban centers like Chicago, Detroit, and New York, but in the 1880s and 1890s, Philadelphia had the largest number of black residents of any of the Northern cities. In 1880, 32,000 African Americans were living in Philadelphia, and by 1900, 63,000 black people had made their homes there and accounted for four percent of the city's population as a whole. Proportionately small but significant black populations also lived in the Southern-Northern border city of Washington, D.C., in Baltimore, Maryland, the New England city of Boston, and other urban areas of the North.

For African Americans in the cities, North and South, employment helped determine the way marriages and families were organized. Racism limited black people to a small number of occupations, mostly very poorly paid. Severe racial discrimination also affected where African Americans could live within cities. These conditions made options regarding marriage and family for black people different than those of their white counterparts.

Life was very difficult for the white urban poor also, especially for recent immigrants from Europe who were impoverished and subjected to ethnic prejudice from native-born whites. But while employment options expanded for American-born whites and white-ethnic immigrants, especially in factory and industrial work, opportunities for African Americans in the cities became even more narrowly defined in the 1880s and 1890s.

Earlier in the century, most free black men and male slaves (and, after the Civil War, ex-slaves) who worked in the cities were manual laborers. A significant proportion of men also worked in skilled positions or as artisans and in construction trades such as carpentry and masonry. Richard R. Wright, who became a social scientist, recalled that when he was a young man in Savannah, Georgia, he could walk down the streets and see black carpenters, bricklayers, and wood sawyers at work. Much of the construction of the public works and transportation systems that made Southern cities function, their "railroads and streets . . . sewers and water works," Wright remembered, were "largely constructed by Negroes." Over time, however, black men were increasingly excluded from the trades and the variety of their presence in the city work world was diminished.

The racism that grew more overt in the last two decades of the 1800s meant greater segregation, restriction, and exclusion of black men from apprentice opportunities and from higher-paid skilled types of work. Some black men in the cities continued to work as artisans—as shoemakers, blacksmiths, coopers, bakers, and barbers. Indeed, one of the most famous shoemakers of the era was an African American named Jan Matzeliger who lived in Lynn, Massachusetts. He revolutionized the shoemaking trade when he invented a machine that he patented in 1883. His lasting machine shaped and stitched the upper portion of a shoe to its sole, something that previously had to be done by hand.

Despite their skill and achievement, black artisans and small shopkeepers were increasingly segregated and saw white patronage disappear. They found their customers among the growing number of African Americans coming to the cities, many of whom were very poor. Although there were very successful black businessmen and -women who achieved wealth, it was difficult for most black artisans and shopkeepers to make enough money to achieve middle-class status. Most of the relatively small number of middle-class blacks who made up the elite of African Americans in the cities were professionals—teachers, doctors, or lawyers—or were employed in white-collar government work.

The majority of black men in the urban work force after 1880—about seventy-five percent—were confined to manual labor positions or jobs in personal service. The laborers were stevedores, sailors, hod carriers (who carried supplies like mortar or brick to bricklayers, stonemasons, and others at a construction work site), janitors, and the people who did the heavy labor rebuilding city streets or installing public works such as sewer lines. One-third of the African Americans in Philadelphia in the late 1890s worked as servants. They were house servants, valets, coachmen, porters, hotel help, or waiters. Men made more money in personal service occupations than manual laborers or women in similar service jobs. Given the more strenuous alternatives for employment, they formed a kind of social elite who tended to look down upon those who made a living in ways that involved more dirt and brawn.

Women, too, were restricted in the types of jobs they were allowed to do. The majority of African-American women worked in household service or as laundresses or washerwomen. A few were dressmakers, hatmakers, seamstresses, typists, nurses, or teachers, but it was difficult to get these kinds of work because of white prejudice. White shop girls or office workers would refuse to work beside black women, and white women would not patronize black women who had skills to offer in health care or fashion. Prostitution was also an urban occupation for women. Like live-in personal service, it was a way of making a living that made child rearing difficult.

One out of five African-American residents of cities, men and women combined, worked as domestic servants within white households. Though many went home at night from these jobs, significant numbers lived in the household where they worked, separated from their families. As cities grew, many African Americans found themselves living among networks of friends or kin but outside a formal nuclear family structure. Besides the nature of employment that took them away from their families, many city dwellers were single men and women who had come to the city from the country seeking work. People who were poorly paid in their jobs, or who could not find work, or who were turned away because of prejudice, waited longer to marry. As a result, African Americans in the cities remained single later than those in the country and began having children when they were older. Among the poorest black urban residents—people who suffered most from the strains of overcrowded housing, poverty, and crime—relationships might not be formalized and family arrangements might not last. Because of work conditions that fueled the cycle of poverty, black families tended to be smaller in size in the city than in the country. In the Northern cities, many more black women than those in the rural South remained childless throughout their lives. Whereas all members of a sharecropping family, old and young, worked in the fields and contributed to the family income, in the city it was the individual adult, rather than the family unit, who was most involved in earning support.

A neighborhood survey conducted in 1896 in Philadelphia found that 57 percent of black women and 48.7 percent of men over the age of fifteen were single, widowed, or divorced. These figures included the 85 percent of women over the age of sixty who were either no longer or never married. Black women outnumbered black men in major Southern cities such as Atlanta, New Orleans, Mobile, Richmond, and Savannah. This was true in Philadelphia as well, where an 1896 survey of the black population of the Seventh Ward revealed that there were 1,150 females to every 1,000 males. Of those African Americans who established families, about eight out of ten, in Southern and Northern cities alike, lived in households that were headed by two parents. But about twice as many urban as rural black households were headed by a woman alone.

In 1896–97 the African-American scholar W. E. B. Du Bois interviewed hundreds of black residents about their families in a house-to-house study he conducted with the help of Isabel Eaton in Philadelphia. Their findings were published in a book called *The Philadelphia Negro*. In addition to noting "an abnormal excess of females" among the black people in Philadelphia, Du Bois reported that an African-American "woman has but three careers open to her in this city: domestic service, sewing, or married life." Staying home from work to make married life a woman's "career," although it might have been desired by working-class couples, was mostly just an option for the middle class. While white women of all classes viewed marriage as an alternative to employment, and most endeavored to stop working outside the home when they married, this was not true for black women. Many black women worked for pay throughout their life spans, in spite of marriage, child rearing, and old age.

Residential segregation meant that African Americans were excluded from living in the nicer sections of cities, which were occupied by whites, and were crowded into neighborhoods that had become defined as black. In Washington, D.C., blacks lived in brick or wooden-framed houses in alleyways, built in the middle of blocks behind more stately buildings fronting the main streets and occupied by whites.

In other cities, including Boston and Philadelphia, the backyards of existing buildings were filled with new tenements to accommodate the great need for housing. Theft, violence, and vice were part of black city life, and became more so in the 1890s as black young people who were reared by working parents with little means could often find no jobs for themselves and were welcomed into a developing criminal subculture. Illness also had its impact on black families. Becoming seriously ill was a constant threat for poor city dwellers, who lived in conditions of malnourishment, poor ventilation, and lack of heating in which infectious disease could flourish.

Pay for all African Americans was low. Black men were paid at lower rates than white men or women for equivalent work, and black women made less than black men. In Philadelphia in the late 1890s, according to the Du Bois study, a black man working as a cementer reported that he "receives $1.75 a day; white workmen get $2–$3."

At the same time that pay was lower, rent for African Americans was higher than that paid by whites for the same accommodations. Black Philadelphians living on one street in 1896 reported that African Americans paid "twelve to fourteen dollars and the whites nine and ten dollars. The houses are all alike."

Skin color made a difference in employment. Lighter-skinned women and men of mixed-race heritage were more likely than blacks to be middle class or wealthy, to have inheritances, own property, have acquired skills through education, be involved in the leadership of organizations, and work in professional or entrepreneurial capacities. Clergy, teaching, medicine, and the law were the most common professional occupations among middle-class African Americans in the city. Still, because of the racial prejudice of whites, a majority of mulatto people were restricted to the same narrow range of occupations and opportunities as their darker-skinned sisters and brothers. The bottom level of urban employment was filled with literate and capable African-American men and women who had skills and abilities they were not allowed to use in the workforce and who were vastly overqualified for the work that they were hired to do.

African Americans did many things to counteract job discrimination and to overcome the isolation and family problems that were the social side effects of that form of prejudice. Social status among blacks in cities came from sources other than a person's occupation. As in the country, women who moved to towns and cities often took up residence near kin and friends, so that their household existed not in isolation but in a network of others. They also boarded in the homes of siblings, cousins, or acquaintances, or took in boarders themselves. Black benevolent societies, mutual aid associations, fraternal orders, and church auxiliaries also thrived in the cities, with women's groups very active among them. In places like Petersburg, Virginia, and Atlanta, Georgia, in the 1890s black women's volunteer groups such as the Ladies Union, the Ladies Working Club, the Daughters of Zion, the Sisters of Love, and the Sisters of Rebeccah provided help in the form of food, clothing, medical care, and assistance with funeral arrangements to working women and families in need. They also functioned as social clubs, bringing community activists and neighbors together for fun and friendship. Like these associations, black churches combined social welfare functions and opportunities for socializing. In addition to providing services such as food kitchens and informal employment bureaus, they were key centers for mass meetings and political debates, spiritual renewal, and shared expressions of faith.

The self-reliance and loyalties that were fostered by these group aspects of urban life were also reinforced by the choices that black men and women made about their labor. Although white employers in the cities wanted black women to supply the domestic labor that was necessary to maintain white households (much as white rural landlords wanted black sharecropper families to work the land for white profit), black women preferred the greater autonomy that they had working as independent laundresses instead of as household servants. As isolated live-in maids and cooks, they rarely saw their own children and were never far from their white employer's beck and call. By working in white households but living in their own homes, or taking in washing and ironing and staying at home, domestic workers and laundresses were able to give more time to their own families and social networks.

The Atlanta washerwomen's strike of 1881 is an example of the successful statement black working women could make by standing together. White city boosters in Atlanta organized an International Cotton Exposition to celebrate the New South's embrace of industrialism and Northern capital investment. The washerwomen, meanwhile, spread the word through church congregations that a mass meeting would be held at a certain church, and in July 1881 they met and formed a Washing Society. On July 19 they went out on strike, demanding higher wages to be paid to all members at a standard rate.

The white city council threatened to levy a business tax against the women workers, and landlords punished strikers who were their tenants by raising rents. The August 3, 1881, edition of the *Atlanta Constitution* reported that the strikers countered by announcing that they were willing to pay fees to the city "as a protection so we can control the washing for the city." They also told the council members to make up their minds soon: "We mean business this week or no washing." The influence of the initial mass meeting at the church continued to grow wider, as household workers, asking for higher wages, walked off their jobs and black male waiters at a prominent Atlanta hotel refused service to the dining room until their wages were raised.

In addition to doing service and trade work in the cities, African Americans worked in industries. Sometimes families that were primarily from the country would combine farming with seasonal industrial work. When men would go away for part of a year to work for wages, the women and young people in the family would remain behind to work the farm. Different sorts of wage work were available. In Florida in the 1890s, for example, more than 100,000 black men worked in the forestry industry, felling trees.

Sometimes the pattern of leaving and staying among men and women was reversed: for families who lived along the Atlantic coast, it was often the women, rather than the men, who would leave home to find seasonal work in seafood

While the majority of African-American women found employment as laundresses or in domestic service, a growing number were employed in industry, including those who removed stems and sorted leaves in tobacco processing plants.

processing plants. In rare instances, women would do jobs usually done by men, stepping in, for example, when a husband or brother was unable to work and filling his place in earning wages for the family in industry or manual labor.

Not all labor that African Americans did was voluntary. The convict lease system, in which prison officials collected fees from private employers who contracted with the state for work done by prisoners outside prison facilities, was a source of revenue for the penitentiaries and states that allowed the practice. It also provided industrialists with a steady labor supply otherwise unavailable in the South, where a majority of white as well as black workers were trained in agriculture rather than industry and were used to seasonal or part-time patterns of working.

The Black Codes made black people susceptible to arrest for petty crimes and, once imprisoned, made them available to be assigned to do forced labor. Under these laws, for example, black men who were homeless or unemployed could be arrested by whites and imprisoned on charges of vagrancy or loitering. Once convicted of a crime, they could be made to work under guard for the duration of their prison term rather than spend the time inside a penitentiary or jail.

The states of Alabama, Georgia, and Tennessee all had convict lease systems, and the brunt of the system was borne by African Americans. Eighty to ninety percent of all inmates in Alabama in the 1880s and 1890s were black. In Tennessee, more than sixty percent of the prison population was black, and black convicts made up more than seventy percent of those who were leased out to work in coal mines. Between October 1888 and September 1889, twenty-six convicts died from injuries suffered in the Dade Coal Company mine in Georgia. Others were flogged for rebelling, and two men were shot trying to escape.

In 1891 labor activists in eastern Tennessee challenged the policies of the Tennessee Coal and Iron Company, which was by that time one of the major employers of convict labor in the state. In July 1891 hundreds of miners held a mass meeting. After the gathering they began a series of actions in which they armed themselves and took control of convict camps, freeing the men who were held within them. In the first such action, they freed convicts who were being sent to work in the company's Briceville mine and put them on trains headed for Knoxville or Nashville. Most of the liberated prisoners were black. More than one hundred of them were able to escape, but most were eventually recaptured and returned to prison.

The free laborers were furious that the mining company planned to replace them with less expensive convict workers whose labor they could better control. One observer of the rebellion of the free laborers, H. H. Schwartz, reported in the *United Mine Workers Journal* that "whites and Negroes are standing shoulder to shoulder" in the actions. Their protest sparked surprise investigations of the mines, during which the investigators found many safety and health violations. It also forced the Tennessee State Legislature to hold a special session to reconsider use of the convict labor system. When the legislators decided to continue the system because of the money it made for the state and the contracting companies, the scattered protests became an organized uprising. Support for the Tennessee protestors spread among miners in Kentucky and Virginia. In August 1892 the convict camp at Tracy City, Tennessee, was burned to the ground by protesting miners, and the inmates set free. Hundreds of miners were imprisoned by state militia that had been called out to subdue the protesters, and Jake Witsen, a black miner who was a leader of the free laborers' actions, was shot to death by soldiers. Thousands of opponents of the convict lease system attended his funeral in respect for his leadership and to bring public notice to the injustice of his death. As a result, in 1893 the Tennessee legislature passed a bill abolishing convict leasing as of January 1896, which is when the Tennessee Iron and Coal Company's contract with the state ended.

Several of the activists who led the convict wars in eastern Tennessee were involved in the Knights of Labor or in the United Mine Workers of America. The United Mine Workers was formed in 1890 during a time when mining was expanding as an area of employment for African Americans. By the turn of the century, some ten to fifteen percent of the 400,000 people working in mines were African Americans. They worked mainly in areas bordering between the North and the

South (West Virginia, Kentucky, Tennessee) and in Alabama. In the 1890s some of them also went to work in mines further North—in places like Ohio, Illinois, or Pennsylvania—as did immigrants from eastern and southern Europe, who joined the Irish immigrants and native-born whites who had previously made up most of the workforces in the mines. Instead of organizing these different groups of miners separately, the United Mine Workers attempted to join members of different backgrounds into what were called "mixed" locals. African Americans were an important part of building the union, and by 1900 twenty thousand black miners belonged to it.

Richard L. Davis was a black organizer in Ohio. He was one of the founders of the United Mine Workers and became a national leader of the union. He was born in Virginia at the end of the Civil War and had begun working in a tobacco factory in Roanoke when he was eight years old. At age seventeen he became a coal miner and went to work first in West Virginia and then in Ohio, where he married and had a family. He and other workers in the town of Rendville, Ohio, faced long periods of unemployment in the mid-1890s, when an economic depression caused many of the mines in Ohio to shut down or operate on irregular schedules.

A powerful speaker, Davis was elected to the national executive board of the United Mine Workers in 1896 and again in 1897. He often used verses from the Bible and examples of things that his fellow workers knew well from church to explain the importance of standing together to try to win greater rights, and to look for justice in this world as well as in heaven. "I know that in former days you used to sing 'Give me Jesus, give me Jesus, you may have all the world, just give me Jesus,'" he told his audience of miners in a letter to the *United Mine Workers Journal* on April 18, 1892. "But the day has now come that we want a little money along with our Jesus, so we want to change that old song and ask for a little of the world as well. Don't you think so, friends?"

Davis was involved in the Knights of Labor as well as in the United Mine Workers. The Knights of Labor was organized in 1869 and reached the height of its influence in 1886, when more than seven hundred thousand members belonged. The membership included between sixty thousand and ninety thousand black people, who, like Davis, joined through the locals in their communities. But unlike most traditional unions or the United Mine Workers, which focused on skilled workers or those in a particular trade, the Knights of Labor welcomed all kinds of laborers: farmers, field workers, women, men, black and white crafts workers, and those employed in all kinds of jobs in different industries.

African Americans like Davis were among the organizers who went into neighborhoods, churches, and workplaces to encourage other laborers to join. Many who became involved in the Knights of Labor did so for idealistic reasons. They believed, as Davis wrote in a letter to the mine workers' journal, in the "brotherhood of all mankind no matter what the color of his skin may be" and in the inherent equality of black and white people. Organizers like Davis who believed in these values established a tradition of interracial unionism among lumber workers in Florida, coal miners in Birmingham, Alabama, freight handlers in Galveston, Texas, and male and female tobacco workers in Richmond, Virginia.

Although many white members of the Knights opposed the organization of black workers, the Knights took steps to defy public practices that denied social equality to blacks. In October 1886, for example, they held a convention in Richmond, Virginia, at which a black delegate named Frank Ferrell, who was from New York, spoke to the assembly along with white dignitaries. He did so in defiance of local custom, which barred black people from sitting with whites in public places or from speaking to audiences made up primarily of whites.

Terence V. Powderly, the head of the Knights, believed that white and black workers doing the same kind of work should have equal wages. He also noted that one of the goals of the Knights was to provide education to working-class children, not just to those of the middle and upper classes. In a speech to an assembly in Richmond, Virginia, in January 1885, he explained that in the places where the Knights had become established the "colored men are advocating the holding of free night schools for the children of black and white. . . . The politicians have kept the white and black [working] men of the South apart, while crushing both. Our aim shall be to educate both and elevate them by bringing them together."

For many working-class African Americans, participation in Knights of Labor activities was one way of being treated with the kind of respect that was afforded mainly to middle-class people, and to the working class within their own churches and secret societies. This was especially true for the women. The African-American journalist Ida B. Wells reported on a meeting of the Knights of Labor that she attended in a piece published in the January 22, 1887, issue of the *Cleveland Gazette*. "I noticed that everyone who came was welcomed and every woman from black to white was seated with courtesy usually extended to white ladies alone in this town," Wells observed.

The Knights of Labor also tried to use collective actions to better working conditions. In Louisiana the year after Frank Ferrell spoke in Richmond, some six thousand to ten thousand laborers, mostly black, walked off their jobs in the sugar-cane fields in support of a Knights of Labor strike for higher wages. Like the mine workers who participated in the convict wars in Tennessee, they faced white violence as a consequence of their demands, and several black strikers were killed when companies of state militia were sent in to end the strike.

African-American workers had success organizing in New Orleans, where in 1880 black and white dockworkers who pressed, moved, and shipped bales of cotton on the Mississippi River wharves formed a labor coalition called the Cotton Men's Executive Council. The council coordinated the goals of several dock unions, and covered common laborers as well as men working in the trades. Prior to the formation of the council, black cotton rollers, teamsters, coopers, wheelers, and freight handlers had already created their own separate benevolent or mutual aid associations similar to the Washing Society that black washerwomen had formed in Atlanta. They met together to set uniform wages for their specialties and to help each other in times of need. Demands of the unions involved in the council, which represented some fifteen thousand workers, centered around the need for higher wages. In September 1880 black unionists joined whites in their same industries in a series of strikes that brought wage increases for teamsters, loaders, and other dockworkers.

A year later the unionized waterfront workers struck again, asking for fair wages and for the employers to recognize the union as the representative of the workers. Black unionists kept order until the second week of the general dock strike, when a lone policeman attempted to arrest a black teamster on a city street. The teamster, James Hawkins, was a person that the September 1881 *Weekly Louisianian* described as a "law abiding, peaceful man." He proclaimed his innocence when approached by the policeman and resisted the arrest. The policeman's actions drew the ire of the local African-American women, who threw frying pans and utensils at him from their windows. In the resulting commotion, the police officer drew his gun and shot Hawkins twice, killing him.

Hawkins was murdered, as one of the *Weekly Louisianian* reports of the killing put it, "for no other cause than that a negro has no rights which a police officer is bound to respect." Hawkins's death galvanized the working-class neighborhood.

White unionists joined black dockworkers and their families at Hawkins's funeral, and they emerged determined to defy the powers that would deny them a better standard of living and their desire to have a say in the structure of their own work. They shut down work on the riverfront. Soon all parties involved in the strike met and negotiated a settlement. The strikers succeeded in winning the employers' agreement to standard wages on the docks for each category of labor and some protections for the unions in hiring. More important, they set a standard for biracial working-class unionism that lasted in New Orleans into the 1890s.

The closely related populist and agrarian movements of the 1890s were other ways in which black workers sought to organize both among themselves and, for greater strength, with white working people. Their goals were the defense of racial justice and economic equity in American society. Populism and small farmers' associations were part of a grassroots political movement whose supporters sought to form alliances between poor and working people, especially those who made their living in agriculture.

For example, black farmers in Lovejoy, Texas, formed the Colored Farmers' National Alliance and Cooperative Union in March 1888. Their membership expanded and they joined with white farmers' groups from the Midwest and South. By 1891 the alliance had more than one million members in twelve states. Like the Knights of Labor, the farmers' alliances supported the idea of workers' cooperatives, enterprises in which workers would pool their resources, exchange labor or contribute goods, and share profits. They also wanted to reform wage work to give working people better payment for their labor, and they organized boycotts of merchants who engaged in unfair practices. They sponsored consumer cooperative stores in Southern cities, helped members who were struggling to pay mortgages on their land, and worked to improve the education provided to rural black children.

While the farmers' alliances were being formed, the Populist or People's party emerged as an independent political party in February 1892, when farmers, labor unionists, and reformers met in St. Louis to develop a program to challenge business interests and the low prices being paid for agricultural goods. Populists supported the rights of non-landowning laborers, including black tenant farmers and field workers, and wanted reform of the country's financial system.

In some areas, one of the party's strategies for change was to try to elect black officials to public office. These officials, it was hoped, would be committed to black civil and political rights, including an end to convict lease systems, the right of black people to serve on juries, and what one black delegate from the Colored Farmers' Alliance termed a "free vote and an honest count."

This strategy had some success in North Carolina, where ten black candidates were elected to the state legislature on Populist-Republican tickets in the 1890s, and many more gained county and municipal offices. Racism as well as class differences marred the progressive aspects of the Populist cause over time, as white small farmers who owned land saw their own interests diverge from those of black sharecroppers and tenant farmers who did not own property.

There were many successes in black-white working people's cooperation in farmers' alliances, populist political coalitions, the Knights of Labor, and among unionists. But one of the unresolved questions in black industrial workers' minds at the end of the 1800s was whether it was better to compete against free white labor for jobs or to join in coalition with white workers to collectively demand better wages and conditions. Skepticism about the genuineness of whites' desire for long-range cooperation was rampant. As John Lucus Dennis, a black worker at the Black Diamond Steel Works in Pittsburgh, put it in a letter to the *New York Freeman*: "Our experience as a race with these organizations has, on the whole, not been such as to give us either great satisfaction or confidence in white men's fidelity."

Mining and work in the cities were two areas where the dilemma between competition or attempted coalition continually played out. In the North, mine workers in the late 1800s were almost all white. Mine operators' use of Southern black workers as strikebreakers thus took on more directly racial meanings than it did in the South, where blacks found themselves on both the unemployed and free-labor sides of such conflicts. In both the North and the South, industrialists used racial differences to divide the work force and prevent unionization. They paid black workers less money than white workers for the same labor, and they denied the higher-paid and higher-status positions in industries to blacks. Organized labor often followed these kinds of prejudiced policies. White union members often prevented blacks from becoming apprentices in trades or members of unions, and even unions that claimed biracial principles were dominated by white leadership and weakened by segregated practices, including the organization of separate locals for whites and blacks. African-American experience in unions varied a great deal from industry to industry and from one region or locale to another. It also varied in the same places over time: A successful action in which white and black union members rallied together could be an exceptional event. A long history of exclusion and discrimination might precede and/or follow the period of cooperation. Many black workers were alienated from the very idea of involvement in organized labor because of their association of labor activism with white working-class racism and with union opposition to black industrial employment. At least fifty strikes took place in American industries between 1880 and 1900 in which white workers opposed the hiring of blacks.

Blacks who worked in crafts like carpentry, woodworking, or bricklaying were among those who suffered from white policies of exclusion. This was one reason why the number of black artisans and crafts workers that had once seemed so prevalent in the cities declined, and black men were gradually moved more and more into unskilled areas of labor.

Nonunion white women spinners and weavers in textile factories often spurned working with newly hired black women. Workers who did not have a trade or do skilled work were often excluded from union eligibility of any kind, since craft unions—such as those that represented conductors, locomotive firemen, or engineers in the railway industry—did not accept unskilled or semiskilled workers into their membership.

Black workers also sometimes found themselves in a tug-of-war between industrialists and the unions. In 1890 a leaflet was circulated among black miners in Birmingham, Alabama, that stated "WANTED! COLORED coal-miners for Weir City, Kan., district, the paradise of colored people.... Special train will leave Birmingham the 13th. Transportation advanced. Get ready and go to the land of promise." When the black miners who responded to this call arrived in Kansas, they found the white workers at the mines on strike and manning a stockade barring the entrance to the work site. Some joined the strikers; others returned home to Alabama when the union paid their way. Still others seized the opportunity for employment at higher wages than they earned in Birmingham, but under conditions that hardly constituted a paradise for black people.

What was happening in the places where people worked mirrored the changes that had slowly been occurring on the political front since the end of the political Reconstruction that followed the Civil War. The exclusion from skilled and better-paying jobs and from union representation that African Americans were experiencing in the workplace coincided with the loss of rights to vote, to be elected to office, to live where one chose, or to receive the kind of education that black parents wanted for their children.

### Justice: "They Have Promised Us Law . . . and Given Us Violence"

It was a spring day in May 1884. A young, well-dressed schoolteacher named Ida B. Wells refused to comply with a conductor's request that she move from the first-class "ladies'" section of a Chesapeake, Ohio, and Southwestern Railroad train to a second-class smoking car further back in the train. Ida B. Wells was twenty-one years old. She often took the ten-mile train trip between Memphis, Tennessee, where she lived, and the town of Woodstock, where she taught public school.

But this day was different. On this day the conductor who came to take her ticket tried to enforce a Jim Crow law that had been passed in Tennessee two years before, authorizing separate accommodations for black and white travelers. When the conductor asked her to change cars, Wells protested. Then the conductor tried to pull her from her seat. Soon the two of them were scuffling in the aisle of the ladies' car as he tried to force her off the train and she attempted to keep her seat. Two other railroad employees came running to aid the conductor, and Wells was dragged away, resisting, and removed from the train, which was stopped in a station at the time the incident took place. When Wells chose to resist the trainmen, she turned a corner in her life. She began what would become a lifetime of public activism in which she would use words and deeds to challenge the injustices the American legal system dealt to African Americans.

On that May day she did not stop with standing up for herself inside the train. When she got home after the incident, she sought out a lawyer and filed a lawsuit against the railroad. Legal victory was briefly hers. The judge who heard the case in the local circuit court in December 1884 ruled in her favor. Although he did not question the policy of segregation itself, he found that the smoking car did not constitute accommodations equal to those of the first-class passenger car, and that Wells, having paid for a first-class ticket, deserved first-class conditions of travel. The railroad appealed his judgment, however, and at the beginning of April 1887 the Tennessee Supreme Court reversed the lower court's ruling.

"I felt so disappointed," Ida B. Wells wrote in her diary on April 5, 1887, describing how she reacted to the news of the high-court decision. She went on to explain what she had wanted to accomplish by filing the case. "I had hoped such great things from my suit for my people generally. I have firmly believed all along that the law was on our side and would, when we appealed to it, give us justice." She then voiced her disillusionment in discovering that this ideal was not supported. "I feel shorn of that belief and utterly discouraged," she confessed to her diary, "and just now, if it were possible, would gather my race in my arms and fly away with them." "O God," she continued, "is there no redress, no peace, no justice in this land for us?"

Ida B. Wells's act of defiance and her decision to bring the issue before the Tennessee courts made her a key part of the African-American challenge to a larger legal process that was occurring throughout the 1880s and 1890s. During this time American laws that had been created in the Reconstruction era to guarantee the extension of rights to former slaves were reinterpreted by state and federal courts. As a result, the standard of justice by which black and white citizens lived was altered for decades to come.

These changes in rights came in two important areas. One was in a series of laws and court rulings about the right of blacks to equal access to public places such as inns, restaurants, parks, and—perhaps most important—schools, as well as the ability to travel in the same way as whites on trains, ships, and streetcars. These legal actions raised questions about how the principle of equality should be understood, and also how that principle should be justly applied to society. Most specifically, they created a legal debate about racial integration versus segregation.

The second area where legislation and court cases changed the meaning of racial justice was in regard to political or citizenship rights. In the last decades of the nineteenth century, states began to pass measures that resulted in the loss of political participation by African Americans. The loss of Reconstruction-era protections of the right of African-American men to vote influenced other rights as well, including the ability of blacks to be elected to political office, participate in political parties, and serve on juries. This last loss was doubly harmful, because the exclusion of African Americans from juries interfered with the right of black defendants to have their cases heard by juries of their peers—to be judged, according to the law, by people like themselves.

The most terrible outcome of this erosion of rights was the denial of due process of law: People who committed crimes against African Americans failed to be arrested or prosecuted, and African Americans who were accused of wrongdoing were not assured a fair trial. In the years when statutes were going into effect limiting black people's social and political rights, violence was often directed at African-American citizens. Black men and women were hurt or killed without being tried for alleged misdoings, and the white people who committed atrocities against blacks were not penalized for them. Often the misdeeds for which African Americans were punished outside the law was the simple "crime" of success itself.

Ida B. Wells's case against the railroad fit squarely into the first area in which African-American rights were denied. Her refusal to give up her seat on the train and the lawsuit that stemmed from her action foreshadowed a similar protest that a man named Homer A. Plessy would begin aboard a train in Louisiana in 1890.

Plessy's case, which was heard by the U.S. Supreme Court in 1896, would set the legal precedent by which other similar cases would be judged and made it possible for states to continue to enforce racial segregation laws and practices. Jim Crow laws created between the 1870s and 1910 would remain in force for decades. They would not be overthrown until a successful legal campaign by a new generation of African-American activists led to the U.S. Supreme Court's 1954 ruling in *Brown* v. *Board of Education* and to the Civil Rights movement that followed it.

In filing her suit to protest the railroad's attempt to segregate its passenger cars by race, Wells became the first African American to challenge the U.S. Supreme Court ruling of 1883 that denied access to blacks to transportation, theaters, hotels, or other places regularly used by the public. That case had revolved around the meaning of the 14th Amendment to the U.S. Constitution, which guaranteed that no state could make discriminatory laws or "deprive any person of life, liberty, or property without due process of law, nor deny to any person within its jurisdiction the equal protection of the laws." The justices ruled that this amendment was not meant to be applied to what they called "private wrongs," or the experience of discrimination by individual persons on private property. (The justices included in their definition of such property privately owned theaters, trains, and hotels.)

African-American journalists and politicians were in the forefront of the public outcry against the legal decisions and state laws that endorsed segregation. The newspaper writers and editors who gathered at the Afro-American Press Convention of 1890 denounced the consignment of black people to second-class facilities aboard railroads. Black members of the state legislatures in Louisiana and Arkansas fought against the segregation bills that were introduced in their legislative bodies in 1890 and 1891. Resistance also continued among African-American citizens' groups in cities and towns around the nation.

In Atlanta, Georgia, in 1892 a group of black citizens organized a successful boycott of the city's streetcars after the city council ordered separate cars for white and black passengers. Similar public demonstrations and boycott actions took place in Augusta, Georgia, in 1898, and in Savannah, Georgia, in 1899.

Homer A. Plessy was one of the countless number of African-American activists in cities North and South. The case that carried his name, *Plessy* v. *Ferguson,* was heard in the courts as the result of organized local African-American opposition to the Louisiana Separate Car Act of 1890. The new Louisiana law required what was termed "equal but separate" accommodations for white and nonwhite passengers on railways, with seats to be assigned in segregated cars according to race. In practice, these separate-but-equal regulations actually resulted in segregated and unequal treatment, with whites receiving the best accommodations or services available and blacks given inferior accommodations. According to the Louisiana law, passengers who refused to comply with the rules of segregation could be removed from trains and were permitted no legal recourse.

African-American members of the American Citizens' Equal Rights Association in New Orleans reacted immediately to the threat of the separate car bill. They filed a memorial with the Louisiana legislature on May 24, 1890, protesting that the measure violated the principle that all citizens are created equal before the law. The leaders of the protest action were Dr. Louis A. Martinet, a lawyer and physician who owned the *New Orleans Crusader,* and Rodolphe L. Desdunes, a customs clerk. Both men were prominent middle-class members of New Orleans's mixed-race creole community. They used the *Crusader* as a forum to attack the Separate Car

Act and called for cases to be brought to the courts that would test the constitutionality of the new legislation.

The first major test case was instigated by Homer A. Plessy, a thirty-four-year-old friend of the Desdunes family, who was also a light-skinned member of the elite New Orleans creole community. Plessy was arrested soon after he boarded the East Louisiana Railway on June 7, 1892, and sat down in the coach set aside for whites.

The results, as in Ida B. Wells's case, were not what the African-American activists who planned the test case had sought. Instead of upholding the rights of equity and federal protection guaranteed by the 14th Amendment, as the Citizens Committee activists had hoped, the court in effect dismantled the authority of the amendment's equal protection clause and instead ruled that separation of races on railways was valid. The court also ruled that the passage of separate-but-equal Jim Crow laws was an appropriate and reasonable exercise of state legislative authority. The court thus provided the constitutional basis by which Southern states could enforce the practice of racial segregation.

It was not only the 14th Amendment but the 15th that came under fire by white supremacists in the 1880s and 1890s. The 15th Amendment to the U.S. Constitution guaranteed that the "right of citizens of the United States to vote shall not be denied or abridged by the United States, or by any State, on account of race, color, or previous condition of servitude." Beginning with Mississippi in 1890, South Carolina in 1895, Louisiana in 1898, and North Carolina in 1900, and Alabama and Virginia shortly after the turn of the century, several states amended their constitutions with the intention of denying blacks the right to vote. In other states, the legislatures passed laws that were similarly designed to eliminate black voting. These included laws that required people to pass a literacy test, hold property, or reside on the same property for long periods of time in order to register to vote.

Literacy tests discriminated against all people who were not middle-class or wealthy and who thus did not have the benefit of education. But they had a particularly devastating effect on former slaves who had been barred under bondage from learning to read. Residency and property requirements worked against the majority of African Americans in the South, too, because most of them worked as sharecroppers or tenant farmers. They neither owned property nor stayed on the same land from year to year. Poll taxes, or fees that had to be paid in order to be eligible to vote, were among the most effective means of excluding blacks from the ballot box, because African Americans made up a disproportionate number of the poor who could not afford to pay the taxes.

In many Southern states, grandfather clauses stated that anyone whose father or grandfather had been qualified to vote in 1867 did not have to pass literacy or citizenship tests or be subjected to other hurdles to registration. Since the 15th Amendment enfranchising black men was ratified by Congress in 1870, these clauses virtually excluded African Americans, while making it possible for poor whites who might otherwise not be able to pass the tests to vote without having to take them.

What was called the "white primary," or exclusion of blacks from participation in the Democratic party's primaries, also nullified the black vote. That was because the Democratic party so dominated the South by 1900 that whoever was designated as a Democratic candidate was virtually assured of victory in the subsequent election.

These white supremacist measures were effective in taking the vote away from African Americans. The changes they wrought were dramatic. The promises of citizenship for blacks that had been part of the rhetoric of the federal government during the Reconstruction period were undone by state actions and the failure of the federal government to counteract them. The federal government failed to act in part because of racism and in part because of a desire to heal the divisions between the national government and the power of the states, especially the Southern states, that were still ripe from the Civil War.

Passage of voter restriction laws had a very substantial effect. In Louisiana, where literacy, property, and poll-tax restrictions were enacted, there were 130,344 black registered voters in 1896 and African Americans made up the majority of voters in twenty-six parishes (districts). By 1900, after these laws were passed, there were only 5,320 black registrants and not one parish had a black majority. By 1904 the number of black registered voters had slipped to 1,342. In Alabama in 1900 there were only 3,000 registered African-American voters, out of a potential pool of almost 150,000 black men who were of voting age.

Corruption and intimidation had preceded the passage of these restrictive laws and helped whites control and limit the black vote. Black support for alternatives to the white supremacist platform of the Southern Democratic party was often suppressed by violence. In Virginia in 1883 there was a white backlash against the Liberal Readjuster party, a coalition of radical Republicans who had supported black emancipation and postwar Reconstruction, lower-class white farmers, owners of small businesses, and black farmers, sharecroppers, and factory workers that had gained power in the elections of 1879 and voted in progressive reforms that benefited black people.

In Danville, Virginia, shortly before election day, November 6, 1883, a group of prominent white businessmen issued a circular in the town decrying the idea of black people in positions of authority and claiming that by gaining some political representation, African Americans had become less tractable workers in the white-owned tobacco industry. Blacks were warned not to be on the streets on election day. One conservative proclaimed that the white supremacists would win the election in Danville "votes or no votes" if they had to do it "with double barrel shotguns, breach loading shotguns and Smith and Wesson double-action." White vigilantes took control of the town, forcing campaigning by black and white members of the liberal reform coalition to end. On November 3, they killed three black citizens.

Elsewhere in Virginia, black residents of towns rallied successfully to ensure their ability to get to the polls. In Petersburg, Virginia, African-Americans organized a parade and guarded the polling places in the city precincts.

Mob violence and lynching were an effective tool by which conservative whites controlled all kinds of black behavior, not just the effort to exercise citizenship rights, hold political office, or vote. Lynchings most often happened in rural areas and small towns, but mob riots were the creatures of the cities. Violence or the threat of violence was random and widespread. When a black man named Baker was appointed postmaster in the small town of Lake City, South Carolina, in 1898, a white mob surrounded his house and post office in the night and set the building afire, with him and his family members inside. When Mr. and Mrs. Baker and their children attempted to run from the burning house, they were shot on the threshold, Mrs. Baker with her infant in her arms. In the same year that the Bakers died, whites went berserk in Wilmington, North Carolina, at election time and swept through the black district of the city, setting homes and businesses afire and killing and wounding African Americans whom they encountered.

Between 1882 and 1901 more than one hundred people were lynched each year, the great majority of them blacks living in Southern states. Almost two thousand lynchings of African Americans were officially reported in those two decades. Additional murders by lynching occurred, but they went unreported as such in local records and overall statistics.

Lynchings were attacks motivated by racism during which people were brutally murdered—sometimes in the night, but often in a public way with many witnesses. Lynchings often involved the hanging of victims, but lynch mobs also killed people in other ways. Some victims endured terrible atrocities, such as being dragged behind a wagon, beaten, seeing loved ones harmed, being tied up and burned or having parts of their bodies dismembered, and other forms of torture. These vicious attacks occurred outside any due process of law, and sometimes with the knowledge or participation of law enforcement officials. State and local courts did little to punish lynchers, and if attackers were identified, penalties for killing African Americans in this way were small and considered to be in a different legal category from other kinds of murders. African-American men were the most common targets of lynch mobs, but women were also hurt and killed. Men were the most common members of white mobs or vigilante groups, but white conservative women were among those who supported the practice and participated in it as spectators.

African-American activists were not silent in the face of the injustices of lynching. In 1899 black churches observed Friday, June 2, as a day of fasting and prayer in which parishioners gathered to pray for justice for African Americans in the courts and for freedom from violence. In this unified effort to demonstrate, as the *New York Tribune* described it, "ceasing to be longer silent," ministers were asked to make the following Sunday, June 4, the occasion for sermons on these topics. Refusing to ignore lynching, activists scanned local newspapers and records and compiled and published data on the names of individuals who had been killed and the dates on which they died. Middle-class leaders raised the issue at public meetings and addressed it in editorials. Frances Ellen Watkins Harper, a writer and African-American feminist, spoke out at a meeting of the National Council of Women held in Washington, D.C., in February 1891. "A government which has power to tax a man in peace, [and] draft him in war, should have power to defend his life in the hour of peril," she told her audience.

Anti-lynching crusader Ida B. Wells with Maurine, Betty, and Tom Moss Jr., the family of Memphis grocery store owner Thomas Moss, who was lynched in 1893.

Among all the prominent African-American lecturers and journalists who took a public stand against lynching and worked tirelessly to bring an end to the practice, the most important was Ida B. Wells. Just as her test of the constitutionality of racial segregation laws was sparked by her expulsion from the railroad passenger car, so her campaign against lynching began as the result of a specific incident. This time the incident of discrimination was not just a question of equality and dignity, but one of horror.

Three African-American small businessmen, Thomas Moss, Calvin McDowell, and Henry Stewart, owned and ran a very successful cooperative grocery store called the People's Grocery that was located in an African-American district of suburban Memphis known as the Curve. Moss and his wife, Betty, were the best friends of Ida B. Wells, and Wells was the godmother to their little girl, Maurine. Thomas Moss worked as a letter carrier by day and in the store by night, and he was very active in his church and his lodge. Because of his deep involvement in the community and its functions, everyone in the neighborhood knew him, and he was much beloved.

An economic rivalry soon developed between the People's Grocery and an older, less successful store that had been in the neighborhood longer and was owned by a white man named W. H. Barrett. Barrett had a deep resentment of Moss because of the success Moss and his partners had achieved in their business. That hatred deepened one day when a sidewalk quarrel broke out between black and white boys over a game of marbles. The African-American children bested the white children in the fight, whereupon the white parents, including Barrett, tried to take legal action against the black boys. The case was dismissed after the payment of small fines.

Tensions escalated, and the whites, still vengeful over the success of Thomas Moss's store, which had taken much of the business away from the white-owned grocery, organized a raid on the People's Grocery. They carried out the raid on a Saturday night, just as the store was closing. When they burst in, Moss was busy working on the store's accounts and McDowell was waiting on the last customers. Fearing that threats of violence would be carried out, friends of the partners had stationed themselves in the rear of the shop to guard the store. When the white men broke in through the back of the store, they were met by gunfire, and three of them were wounded.

The next morning there was a general raid of the black households and businesses near the Curve in order to locate the men who might have fired the shots that wounded the white vigilantes. Moss, McDowell, and Stewart were among those picked up and incarcerated in the jail. Black members of the Tennessee Rifles, a local militia that had an armory nearby, guarded the jail against white attacks for the first two nights. But when it was clear that the men who had been shot would recover, they felt that tensions had passed and ceased their watchfulness. On the third night, a mob of white men was given access to the jail. They dragged Thomas Moss and his partners from their cells, loaded them aboard a railroad boxcar, took them outside the city limits, and lynched them. According to an eyewitness newspaper report of the lynching, McDowell tried to struggle with the lynchers and was mutilated before he was killed. Thomas Moss pleaded with his abductors to spare his life on behalf of his wife and children, including his young daughter Maurine and the unborn baby his wife was carrying. His plea was ignored, and when asked for a final statement before he was shot to death, he said: "Tell my people to go West—there is no justice for them here."

Hundreds of black residents of the Memphis area heeded Thomas Moss's last words. As Wells recalled in her memoirs, which were published after her death, the "shock to the colored people who knew and loved both Moss and McDowell was beyond description." And the violence had not ended. Whites rampaged through the black neighborhood the day after the murders, and a white mob looted goods from the People's Grocery and then destroyed the contents of the building. Black reaction was swift. Like the many migrants who had left farms and sharecropping plots before them and moved West or to black towns, many city dwellers sold their property and took their families to Oklahoma Territory. Two leading pastors in the Curve community organized their entire congregations to go. Meanwhile, those that stayed instituted an informal economic boycott of white businesses and stayed off city streetcars.

Ida B. Wells went into action. She had become part owner of the *Memphis Free Speech* newspaper in 1889, and had lost her job as a teacher when she used its pages to protest the inferior quality of schools serving black students. After the murder of her dear friend Thomas Moss, she used the newspaper to encourage the black citizens of Memphis to leave town and went to churches to urge black parishioners to support the consumer boycott of white-owned and -run streetcars. The exodus from the city did more than help African Americans escape from the racist violence that had seized Memphis. It had a very real economic impact upon whites. After the lynching, as Wells recalled in her memoirs, white people discovered a "dearth of servants to cook their meals and wash their clothes and keep their homes in order, to nurse their babies and wait on their tables, to build their houses and do all classes of laborious work."

Wells set out to become an expert on lynching and to dispel some of the myths that were popularly accepted about why lynchings occurred. Thomas Moss was an upstanding citizen who was killed because he had acquired wealth and property. But white newspapers typically claimed that lynchings occurred because of black men's criminality. They especially claimed that lynchings happened because black men sexually assaulted white women. Wells knew that Thomas Moss was neither a criminal nor a rapist, and so she questioned these allegations about lynching in general. She personally investigated every lynching that she heard about in Mississippi in the months after Thomas Moss's death. Then she published an editorial that strongly implied that when the charge behind a lynching was rape, the actual fact of the matter was that in the overwhelming number of cases a black man and white woman had agreed to have a sexual relationship with each other. In short, no rape had occurred. "Nobody in this section of the country believes the old thread bare lie that Negro men rape white women," Wells wrote in her editorial for *Free Speech* in May 1892. The charge of rape was used to cover up the real violence— that of white men against black men. And the reason for this violence was to deprive blacks of political and economic power—to keep them under the thumb of the white establishment.

When the editorial was printed, Wells was traveling in the North. She soon learned of the outcome. The same fate that had met the People's Grocery had been visited upon her newspaper office. Whites had gone to the *Free Speech* office at night, two days after the edition in which the editorial was published, and destroyed the type used to print the newspaper and all the furnishings of the office. They left a note saying that anyone who attempted to publish *Free Speech* again would be killed.

Ida B. Wells was not easily silenced. She was exiled from her home in the South because of her defense of black rights in the face of lawlessness. She took a newspaper job in the North and continued to claim for herself the right of free speech. She wrote editorials under the pen name Iola and prepared pamphlets on the lynching issue that challenged the standard view of lynchings presented in the white press, North and South. Once her writings began to be well known, she traveled widely as a lecturer, speaking on the issue of lynching to women's organizations, churches, and African-American groups.

Wells published her findings in a pamphlet called *Southern Horrors: Lynch Law in All Its Phases* in October 1892. The pamphlet was dedicated to African-American women in Manhattan and Brooklyn, because women's groups in the New York area had raised the funds to make the publication of her work possible. Victoria Earle Matthews, a freelance journalist and women's rights activist who in 1897 established the White Rose Mission, a settlement house that provided social services for black women workers and girls, and Maritcha Lyons, a Brooklyn schoolteacher, were very impressed when they read Wells's articles. They organized a series of small meetings in African-American households and church lecture rooms in which Wells presented information about lynching to groups of women. More than 250 black women attended these meetings and joined in forming a committee that organized a major fundraising event with Wells as the keynote speaker.

Though justice seemed to be sleeping in the last decades of the nineteenth century, African Americans like Wells were wide awake. Many African-American sharecroppers, like the people who had known Thomas Moss in Memphis and who decided to leave the city after his murder, migrated West, away from the lawlessness of the Deep South. Black industrial and farm workers tried forming labor and political coalitions with whites, and other individuals, like Wells and Homer A. Plessy, challenged the reversal of legal protections in court. All over the land people less well known than Wells and Plessy took their own private stands against discrimination, acting in defense of honor when personally confronted by racism. Black intellectuals wrote newspaper articles and books and gave speeches decrying injustices. And black middle-class people set about founding their own schools, churches, businesses, and self-help organizations. If the law offered no guarantee of equal access to existing institutions and services, or protection of black citizens' well-being from violence, then African Americans would create the means for achieving advancement on their own.

## Self-Help: "To Hew Out His Own Path"

Johanna Bowen Redgrey was a midwife and healer who lived on a small farm on the outskirts of Tuskegee, Alabama, in the 1880s. She had been born into slavery near Richmond, Virginia, the daughter of an African-American mother and her mother's Irish-American master. When she was a teenager, her father sold her and her brothers to a white family who had a plantation in Macon County, Alabama. Johanna was a striking woman, six feet tall. She was muscular and strong from the field work she did, with a head of fiery reddish hair and a determined disposition to match her appearance. When the Civil War came, Johanna's brothers joined other young men who escaped from the plantation to try to fight for the North. She assumed they died in the attempt, because she never saw them again nor learned of their fate. She spent the latter part of the war and the early years after war's end working for wages for her former master. Then she met and married Lewis Redgrey.

Lewis Redgrey was a Native American who had spent part of his life in Mexico and spoke Spanish as well as English. He had a fifty-five-acre farm outside Tuskegee, and Johanna went to live with him there. Together they raised hogs and corn and grew a cash crop of cotton. They were both important people in the community. Johanna Bowen Redgrey had gone to school and worked with doctors, and she knew a great deal about plants and herbs and how to make medicines. She delivered babies and nursed both black and white families in times of illness or accident. She was deeply religious. She taught Sunday School and was very active with other women in the neighborhood in her own African Methodist Episcopal Zion church and in the Baptist church located on a nearby hill.

The Redgreys were determined to provide good educations for their son and the other African-American children of Tuskegee. For them, making education available was the key to improving the lives of all African Americans. They were members of a committee of Tuskegee residents who worked to start a school in the town. The committee sought a schoolmaster to run such a school, and sent for one to Hampton Institute, a school in Virginia that trained African Americans for careers in nursing, teaching, farming, and trades, to find a schoolmaster to run it. They were among the group of black townspeople who gathered to greet the young teacher who came from Hampton. His name was Booker T. Washington, and he arrived in Tuskegee in June 1881. Classes in what would become Washington's famed Tuskegee Institute began a few days later, on July 4. The classes met in Johanna Bowen Redgrey's church on Zion Hill.

Church, family, neighbors, and school were at the heart of the Redgreys' lives. These connections between people were avenues for personal fulfillment, community, and mutual care. They also were means of self-expression. Strengthening and cherishing these kinds of social networks and avenues of uplift, and using their voices to present their own points of view, were crucial ways in which African Americans combated the racial injustices of the 1880s and 1890s.

The ability to worship freely, to marry and raise children without having them subject to others' control, and to learn to read and write were all freedoms that had been outside most black people's experience during slavery. This made them all the more precious to African Americans in the decades after emancipation. When it became clear in the post–Reconstruction era that the political rights and protections that had been promised after the end of the Civil War would not be theirs, African Americans set about forming their own separate institutions—schools, churches, hospitals, settlement houses, and newspapers—and making their own way. Through religion, family, and education African Americans built their own brand of freedom, working together for the good of all black people.

In developing separate institutions and systems of self-help, African Americans used the power of words, both those that were written down and those that were spoken aloud. Despite a larger society where blackness was being belittled, souls were exalted through the hymns and sermons of the black church, and children were assured of their self-worth by tales told and passed down within the black family. Black schools gave students the power of literacy, the ability to read and write, and this opened to them new economic and intellectual possibilities. Black newspapers printed the opinions of black journalists, black intellectuals spoke at public events, black writers and poets published novels and books of poetry, and black men and women gathered together in literary societies to read and debate.

People who had not had the opportunity to learn to read could listen and speak. In doing so, they carried on an oral tradition that had long sustained a rich cultural heritage among African Americans from one generation to another. Those who could read passed newspapers and books from hand to hand, or read aloud to others. Black people had a voice, and the words they used gave them hope and strength.

African Americans did not speak in one voice, however. They had many points of view. One of the biggest debates among African Americans at the turn of the century was over the best approach to providing education to black people. Tuskegee Institute and its principal were at the center of this broad discussion.

Many of them supported Booker T. Washington's philosophy of industrial or vocational education, in which students would come to school to learn a trade and find a job. Others criticized it just as strongly. Many African-American intellectuals and political activists saw Washington's vision as a way of appeasing whites who felt that blacks should be manual laborers and not strive for high intellectual achievement— or as Washington himself often put it, that they should live by their hands rather than by their wits. But for these critics, higher education for black people, in which African Americans could enter academic programs in languages and music, the arts and humanities, science and research, or prepare for a profession, was as important as training for a vocation. Thus the debate about the nature of schooling was not only about economics and education, but about how best to react to white racism.

Washington believed that the "power of the mouth is not like the power of the object lesson." That is, he felt that black people could best advance by the quiet example of their cooperation with whites, by self-development, and by their skilled contributions to their mixed-race communities, rather than by overt militancy or protest. This view was scorned by leaders such as Frederick Douglass and Ida B. Wells. Douglass and Wells were among those who used the written and spoken word to confront injustices head-on. "One farm bought, one house built, one home neatly kept, one man the largest tax-payer and depositor in the local bank, one school or church maintained, one factory running successfully, one truck garden properly cultivated, one patient cured by a Negro doctor, one sermon well preached, one office well filled, one life cleanly lived," Washington wrote in 1895, "these will tell more in our favor than all the abstract eloquence that can be summoned to plead our cause."

The academic and vocational philosophies of education developed side by side in the 1880s and 1890s. This is one of the issues on which middle-class black people and poorer African Americans, and African Americans living in the North and in the South, differed. The debate about education and the types of work for which it should prepare students was directly related to ideas about African Americans' proper expectations regarding their status in society. Middle-class and Northern blacks were more likely to identify with and promote academic programs and more intellectual—and therefore elite—types of achievement. Rather than accommodate white views of black people's secondary status, they stressed their desire for equal rights and equal opportunities, including equal access to higher education.

At the same time, less privileged African-American students sometimes rebelled against industrial education curricula because they equated acquiring an education with an escape from manual labor. But others embraced Booker T. Washington's idea that agricultural and industrial labor and other forms of skilled work with the hands should be honored, and they believed that there was dignity in this kind of work. To many blacks living in the South, Washington's brand of education had its own flavor of militancy. Separatism and equality thus became the watchwords in the 1880s and 1890s for two different strategies for black advancement. Both had power, and the two perspectives often intersected in practice.

The story of the creation of the Tuskegee Institute exemplifies this combination of approaches. It is one example of the many separate institutions that were created by or for blacks at the end of the nineteenth century. Within a few weeks of his arrival in Tuskegee, Booker T. Washington was joined by a young teacher named Olivia Davidson. Together, with the help of the Tuskegee townspeople and donations from white Northern philanthropists, they built up the school.

Olivia Davidson had started teaching when she was sixteen. She taught in Mississippi and Tennessee before she graduated from Washington's alma mater, Hampton Institute, and from the Framingham State Normal School in Massachusetts. When she came to Tuskegee in late August 1881, she immediately set about getting to know the people in the community and raising money for the institute. She went door to door and talked to the people of the town about their goals for education. With the aid of black women like Johanna Bowen Redgrey, who were eager to do anything they could to help, she organized bake sales and community potluck suppers where women contributed a dish they had prepared. Long picnic tables were covered with the donated food and the families of the town turned out to celebrate together and support the new school. Soon after classes began, Davidson organized a night of student literary entertainment, in which the students selected and memorized poems and essays and recited them to the black members of the town in an evening performance.

In June 1881 Washington began recruiting students for his new school by speaking at both the Baptist and Methodist churches, inviting anyone who was interested to come see him at his boardinghouse and enroll. He rode around Macon County and familiarized himself with the people in the countryside, reporting in his letters to friends in Virginia his shock at the impoverished conditions of share-cropper families and the lack of books and other materials in the one-room rural schools that were already in operation.

There were thirty students in the first class that began school in the Methodist church on Independence Day 1881. They varied in age from teenagers to middle-aged adults. Most of them were public school teachers who had come to receive better training so they could in turn pass that knowledge on to the rural children who were their pupils.

In time, as the result of Davidson and Washington's efforts, the school acquired land, the former Bowen plantation, and made plans to build a new building. Washington turned his mind to business, and the curriculum of the school soon combined book-learning classes with various manual-labor tasks. The manual labor served two functions. It prepared students for skilled jobs in industry and agriculture, and it earned money immediately for the development of the school.

Students worked hard outside the classroom. They cleared land for a cash crop of cotton. They made bricks that would be used in the construction of Tuskegee Institute buildings or sold to local business owners for use in the town. The prof-its were turned back into expanding the programs and facilities of the school and hiring new teachers. Washington hoped that the kind of business relationships that would be built up between the school and the white townspeople through brick-making and other student enterprises would overcome whites' racist ideas. He also hoped that the influential white residents of Tuskegee would support the school out of self-interest because of the quality products the students produced and the value of the students' skilled employment. Thus the school served, on a small scale, as a model or experiment for Washington's philosophy of race relations, which he felt should be applied to the nation as a whole.

The ceremonies that marked the end of the Tuskegee Institute's first year were symbolic of the combination of forces that had given birth to Washington and Davidson's educational enterprise. People came from all over town, from the countryside, and from as far away as Hampton, Virginia, to meet on Zion Hill in Tuskegee.

When they paraded from the church to the new school grounds, the students and citizens of Tuskegee symbolically moved from the school's past into its future. The church building was soon replaced as the location for the school when class-rooms and dormitories were built. Two years later, there were 169 students study-ing at the school. By 1900, when Washington published his autobiography, *Up from Slavery*, there were fourteen hundred students enrolled, and more than one hundred instructors. The Tuskegee Institute was a thriving school and economic enterprise with its own working farm, sawmill, foundry, brickyard, and blacksmith, machine, woodworking, barrelmaking, and print shops. As Washington's daughter, Portia Washington, wrote in July 1900, the industrial institute had become "really a small village," occupied and run by African Americans, and the goal of "Principal

Washington is to make it an object-lesson, or model community for the masses in general."

By the 1890s, Washington, who made extensive public speaking tours to promote the school, had become a famous and powerful man. White receptiveness to the vocational emphasis of his school had made him into a recognized spokesman on racial matters, and he wielded far-reaching political influence from behind the scenes. The little school that the Redgreys had helped begin had become the center of a social movement, with Washington at its head.

Washington turned to three different well-educated black women to share his work and his private life. During Tuskegee's first year, he married his college girlfriend, Fanny Norton Smith. Their daughter Portia was born in 1883. Fanny Washington died a year later, leaving Washington alone with the little girl. In August 1886 Olivia Davidson became Booker T. Washington's second wife. She had long been his partner in the school, teaching science classes at Tuskegee; acting as the school's lady principal by overseeing the female students; and making fund-raising tours of the North. After their marriage she continued her work with the school. She cared for Portia and gave birth to two sons, Baker and Ernest. But disaster came. Despite her energetic work, Olivia Davidson Washington had always been frail in health. Soon after Ernest was born, the chimney in the Washingtons' house caught fire during the night, burning down the house. Booker T. Washington was away raising money for the school at the time. Olivia and the children escaped the flames, but she had been very ill after childbirth and her condition worsened after the fire. She never recovered. She died in a hospital in Boston in May 1889.

Four years later Booker T. Washington married for a third time. He turned for companionship and help with his children to Margaret (Maggie) Murray, a teacher from Mississippi who had been serving as the lady principal at Tuskegee since May 1890.

Margaret Murray Washington had been educated at Fisk University, in Nashville, where she was associate editor of the school newspaper and president of a campus literary society. She began teaching at Tuskegee in 1889. Like Olivia Washington, Margaret Murray Washington believed strongly in the importance of education for African-American girls and women.

The Tuskegee curriculum combined academic and vocational training for both male and female students, with an emphasis for everyone on preparing for an occupation. Tuskegee students took classes in art, music, and literature, botany, chemistry, and mathematics. In addition, they all enrolled in some program of practical training. All of these training courses were based on gaining skills for employment in occupations that already existed for black people in the South. Within Booker T. Washington's scheme, boys and girls were thought to be suited to different kinds of occupations and thus to separate sorts of classes in their education. Young men trained in agriculture or in trades such as carpentry, blacksmithing, mechanics, or furniture making. Young women were directed toward classes in housekeeping and domestic science. These courses would prepare girls for work in household service, which was the main source of wage employment for black women at the time, and also to run their own homes according to up-to-date Victorian standards. Female students could also learn advanced sewing so they could make a living as dressmakers and hatmakers.

Recognizing that women could do many kinds of agricultural work that could be turned to profit on a family farm, Margaret Murray Washington insisted that female students also be given opportunities to study agricultural methods. The "outdoor work" for women included dairying, raising poultry and livestock, and growing flowers and vegetables for market. Margaret Murray Washington considered these forms of expertise more healthy and independent options for black women in seeking a livelihood than factory work or leaving the rural areas of the South for work in cities.

The agricultural department of Tuskegee Institute as a whole was directed, beginning in 1896, by George Washington Carver. An 1894 graduate of Iowa State University, Carver was a brilliant scientist and teacher who also painted beautiful pictures of fruits and flowers. His experiments in botany and innovations in soil analysis and enrichment made the Tuskegee Institute's experimental farm into a showcase of high-yield crops. He encouraged farmers to grow crops such as sweet potatoes and peanuts in addition to cotton, and to rotate the kinds of crops grown

George Washington Carver (second from right), director of the agricultural department of Tuskegee Institute, with his students in the soil science laboratory.

in their fields to maintain the richness of the soil. He also invented industrial uses for the by-products of these diversified crops, such as the shells of peanuts. In 1899 he began what he called his "Moveable School," a large wagon equipped with farm machinery and exhibits that was drawn by mules around the dirt roads of the countryside. Carver and his assistants used the wagon to bring lessons they taught in their laboratories and classrooms to the African Americans farming throughout the county.

Many students at Tuskegee, both men and women, trained to become teachers, and Tuskegee graduates ran rural schools throughout the South and taught at other colleges. The Tuskegee Institute hospital, opened in 1892, served as a nurses' training school. The hospital and nursing program are representative of a number of black institutions that were founded between 1890 and 1930. Black women like Johanna Bowen Redgrey had long served an important function in their communities as traditionally trained lay healers, nurses, and midwives. At the end of the nineteenth century, black women and men participated in the movement to professionalize nursing, adding clinical training, hospital experience, and basic courses in nutrition, sanitation, and primary care to the kind of practical knowledge and informal apprenticeships that had trained women like Redgrey. The formation of hospitals staffed with black physicians and nurses—like the founding of schools, businesses, and community organizations—was one more important form of African-American institution building in the post–Reconstruction period.

While she oversaw the domestic training, outdoor work, and professional education of women students in teaching and nursing at Tuskegee Institute, Margaret Murray Washington extended the principles that were being taught at the school into practice in the town. Following in the footsteps of Olivia Davidson Washington, she concentrated on ways of organizing the women of Tuskegee, especially those who worked as tenant farmers or sharecroppers and lived outside of town.

In the 1890s she devised a plan for bringing together the middle-class black women who worked as instructors at Tuskegee, or were married to male members of the faculty, and working-class or lower-class women who did not have the benefit of formal education. As she explained in an essay called "Helping the Mothers," which Booker T. Washington printed as part of his 1904 book *Working with the Hands*, the "country women, tired of the monotony of their lives, came crowding into the village every Saturday." On one Saturday, Margaret Murray Washington went into town and sent a small boy around to the women, asking them to come to a room above "a very dilapidated store which stands on the main street of the village." Six came the first night, and thus began the meetings of the Mothers' Union. Held every Saturday of the school year, the meetings attracted more than three hundred women a week by 1900.

When the women came together, Washington wrote, "we talked it all over, the needs of our women, the best ways of helping each other." Women came long

A home economics class at Hampton Institute, Hampton, Virginia. Founded in 1868, Hampton was designed to train young African Americans as teachers and leaders in the black community.

distances on foot to attend the meetings. Among them were Johanna Bowen Redgrey, who brought her young granddaughter along. Many women brought their girls with them, and soon a lending library and classes for the children were organized. Meanwhile, Margaret Washington founded the Tuskegee Women's Club for the instructors and faculty wives on the school campus. The middle-class women founded newspaper reading clubs, staffed the library, and provided Saturday day care. They also visited poor women in their homes in the country, offering advice about improving the standard of living for the farming families.

Much of this advice involved teaching middle-class ways to poor people. The sharecropper women were taught about bathing regularly and wearing more formal apparel, maintaining housekeeping and churchgoing schedules, growing vegetable gardens to supplement a diet of cornmeal and pork, and doing many of the things on the farm that women students were taught to do at the school. The Victorian values passed from middle-class to poor women extended to matters of demeanor. The well-to-do women were judgmental about the working women's conduct and believed they had the right, by their superior social standing, to correct it.

Monthly workshops were held on topics suggested by the country women, with lessons written up in pamphlet form and distributed from home to home. These booklets contained advice on parenting, manners, household repair, and farming, and "also little recipes which any woman may need in her country home, especially when there is sickness in the family." Women students joined in by establishing a house on the grounds of an old two-thousand-acre plantation where seventy-five black families lived in sharecropper cabins. A female student lived in the house and taught reading to the parents and children that were farming the land around it. Sewing, cooking, gardening, and housekeeping classes were soon added.

The kind of outreach and organization among women that Margaret Murray Washington set in motion in Tuskegee was happening among black women all around the nation. Excluded from formal social services, health-care institutions, and charity organizations run by whites, black women served their communities with their own associations.

Benevolent groups in the cities and women's auxiliaries organized through churches had long provided health care to the ill and clothing and food to those who needed it. In the mid-1890s homes for black working women and for the aged, and nurseries and day-care centers for the children of working mothers were established in several cities in the North. Although Margaret Murray Washington began a settlement house in a rural Southern setting, the majority of settlement houses begun in the 1890s by middle-class men and women were located in the North and Midwest. Settlement houses provided classes and job services, including literacy training and information about good nutrition and child care.

One of the most important settlements for black women was the White Rose Mission and Industrial Association, founded in 1897 by Victoria Earle Matthews, one of the women who had organized Ida B. Wells's pathbreaking public lecture in New York. The home was established to help young working women new to the city. The mission offered classes in cooking, laundry, and sewing—teaching the new migrants the city skills that could be converted into jobs in household service. Matthews also established a library of books about black history, and taught neighborhood women to be proud of their heritage.

Black settlement house residents in both the North and the South, including those at the White Rose Mission, also became involved in expanding the kindergarten movement, which in the 1890s was an innovative approach to early childhood education. Settlements and churches served as centers for community forums and lecture tours. Booker T. Washington came to speak to working women and the middle-class women organizers at the White Rose Mission, as did other prominent intellectuals and writers of the day.

In addition to attending public lectures, middle-class men and women formed literary societies that met in members' homes. These societies served a political purpose for middle-class women who were excluded from many of the public functions in which middle-class men participated. They were also one more way in which African Americans exercised the power of the word. The secular benevolent associations, church charity groups, settlement houses, and literary societies were in some ways schools for adults, especially for women. They provided a chance for middle-class women to acquire new speaking and organizing skills. Through their activism in these groups, women learned how to hold meetings, coordinate tasks among people of different backgrounds and interests, organize programs, raise funds, do publicity, to speak with confidence to audiences, and participate in group debate. Many of them would use these skills in broader forums of social and political reform.

Literary society meetings provided a chance for educated middle-class African-American men and women to discuss books and debate the current events of the day, and to give recitations and lectures to one another. The Bethel Literary and Historical Association, for example, was a key literary society in Washington, D.C. It was founded in 1881 by church activists interested in education, and it featured several black women lecturers and debaters. Topics presented at the society meetings ranged from heroes of the anti-slavery movement and other black history topics to discussions of music, social reform, and politics. The separate education of the sexes was one of the frequently debated issues.

The membership of literary societies, churches, and settlement programs often overlapped. One of the leaders of the Bethel Literary and Historical Association was Amanda Bowen, who also directed the Sojourner Truth Home for Working Girls of Washington, D.C., in 1895. The home was supported by the members of the Metropolitan African Methodist Episcopal Church.

The links between the Metropolitan AME Church, the literary society, and the founding of the home for girls in Washington, D.C., or between the AME Zion Church of Tuskegee, the Mothers' Clubs, and the founding of the Tuskegee Institute in Alabama, were not coincidental. These examples are indicative of the way that churches influenced the creation of black social welfare and educational institutions around the country.

The church had long been a mainstay of African-American life. Faith and spirituality were important means of maintaining and building self-worth and group support during the days of slavery. In the post–Reconstruction era, when Jim Crow practices were being made into law throughout the South, the church continued to be the focus of many African-Americans' social and inner lives. The independence of black churches within mixed-race small towns and cities, and the willingness of members to contribute money and volunteer work to their churches, made the church the strongest single institution of African-American self-help in the 1880s and 1890s.

Churches were places of worship. But they were also the primary places that African Americans used as assembly halls and community centers. Many, like the church in Tuskegee that housed the first classes of the Tuskegee Institute, were directly connected to schooling in their communities.

In the same year that Tuskegee Institute was founded in the church buildings in Tuskegee, Spelman College for women began as the Atlanta Baptist Female Seminary in the basement of the Friendship Baptist Church in Atlanta, Georgia. It began as an elementary and secondary school for adult women, offering literacy

Spelman Seminary's missionary training class of 1895. Founded in 1881 with financial help from the women's American Baptist Home Mission Society, Spelman offered education to black women interested in becoming teachers, nurses, missionaries, and church workers.

classes to women who had not had a prior opportunity to learn to read and write, and giving religious instruction. Over the years, it broadened its programs and evolved into a full four-year college. Like Tuskegee Institute and other African-American schools, it offered classes to prepare students for occupations in teaching and household service. A nurses' training program was added in 1886.

African-American women were active as policymakers in education in addition to being students and teachers in the classrooms. The church was an important factor here as well. Beginning in the 1880s, black women church activists organized state conventions where they met to advocate support of black Baptist-owned schools for higher education and missionary work. Conventions were held in Alabama, Arkansas, Kentucky, Missouri, Mississippi, West Virginia, and other states. Many of these state conventions published their own newspapers, and their members also wrote columns on women's and educational issues for general Baptist publications. In 1887 more than forty newspapers were being produced by black Baptists. Most of these were published in the South.

The work of church members was crucial to providing social services to black people who lived nearby. Churches were also places to hold community theater productions, suppers, and programs, and to gather to discuss local issues and current events. In the midst of a larger society that denied leadership roles to African Americans, churches provided opportunities for ministers and members to speak their thoughts and hold positions of authority. Though church activities were spearheaded by the ministers who served them, and the community at large looked to these preachers as spokesmen for their congregations, the social work and fund-raising was done mainly by their women members.

The black church programs, hospitals, newspapers, settlement houses, and schools that were established in the last decades of the nineteenth century left no doubt about the African American's ability to, as Booker T. Washington had put it in 1895, "hew out his [or her] own path."

## Leadership: "Show Us the Way"

One of the most important moments in the life of Booker T. Washington came on the sunny late afternoon of September 18, 1895, when he walked to the front of a stage to give a speech to a huge gathering of business executives and visitors at the Cotton States and International Exposition in Atlanta, Georgia.

The audience at this big commercial event had come to celebrate the emergence of a new post–Civil War South. As Washington recalled in his autobiography, he rose to speak and faced an audience "of two thousand people, composed mostly of Southern and Northern whites." The black people in attendance sat in a separate gallery. The master of ceremonies had just introduced Washington as a great educator, with no reference to his color, but when the audience saw a tall, distinguished black man rise to give the speech, their applause wavered and died out in disapproval. Washington nevertheless strode forward and took his place on the stage.

Washington gave a short and simple oration that expressed opinions he had shared with other audiences many times before. But this time his statement was greeted in a new way. It was publicized, reprinted, and accepted among whites—and damned by some blacks—as a manifesto of black accommodation to white supremacy in the South. In preaching a message that was acceptable to white Southerners—the gradual uplift of blacks in the name of the mutual economic progress of blacks and whites, and thus of the South as a whole—Washington's speech in Atlanta set the tone for race policy and race relations in the United States for decades to come.

The speech also signaled the arrival of a new leader among African Americans. That September day in Atlanta marked the true beginning of widespread recognition of Washington as the most prominent spokesman for African Americans in his time. In his speech Washington displayed the combination of defiance and compromise that would continue to mark his leadership for the rest of his life. The statement of defiance and proclamation of black selfhood and personal authority Washington made silently—by standing up before the Atlanta audience. The compromise could be found in the openly expressed message of his words. Washington's speech symbolizes a time when new black leaders appeared in many fields of political and cultural achievement, and when themes of compromise or accommodation, self-assertion and protest, were found simultaneously in the public life and leadership of black people.

Washington began his oration by telling a story about a ship that had been lost at sea for many days. The crew was thirsty, and when they finally sighted another ship, they called out three times for water. "Cast down your bucket where you are," answered the people on the other vessel. When the thirsty sailors did lower a bucket, they were surprised to draw it back up full of fresh water. Without knowing it, they had drifted near the mouth of a river and the water that flowed under their ship was not undrinkable salt water, as they thought, but good water for drinking.

Washington's story was a metaphor for what he felt black people in the South needed to do. Instead of fleeing and looking for what they needed elsewhere, like those who had gone from Louisiana or Mississippi to Kansas, like those who looked to the North, or trekked from the fields to the cities, he counseled that they remain in the South and find there ways to improve their condition. In his speech, Washington struck a bargain with white Southerners and Northerners in positions of power. According to this deal, black labor would remain in the South and concentrate on developing better agriculture and commerce. White businessmen and landowners would benefit from retaining the hard work and services of African Americans. They would also benefit from the commercial and industrial progress that would come with investment in the education and business enterprises of blacks. In return, both races would act, as Washington said in his speech, in "determination to administer absolute justice, in a willing obedience among all classes to the mandates of law."

The other part of the bargain that Washington suggested was the part that most disturbed black leaders who disagreed with his approach. In exchange for greater future material prosperity and the promise of more evenhanded administration of the law, African Americans, Washington implied, would not make immediate or forceful claims for equal rights and opportunities. Nor would they attempt to share in the social privileges enjoyed by whites in public and private settings. In the most famous line of the speech, which became known as the "Atlanta Compromise," Washington promised that "in all things that are purely social we can be as separate as the fingers, yet one as the hand in all things essential to mutual progress."

This metaphor of the hand and the fingers was greeted with great applause by the white audience, the very same audience that had grumbled when Washington first took the stage. The reaction of the blacks who heard Washington that day was

This montage from an 1896 publication features five of the most prominent black leaders of the era: clockwise, from top left, T. Thomas Fortune, Booker T. Washington, Ida B. Wells, I. Garland Penn, and, in the center, Frederick Douglass.

more cryptic. James Creelman, a reporter for the *New York World,* wrote on the front page of the *World*'s September 19, 1895, edition that at the speech's end "most of the Negroes in the audience were crying, perhaps without knowing just why." Whether they were shedding tears of intense pride in Washington's appearance, or tears of dismay over what his message might mean for African Americans in the future, was not recorded.

We do know how other leaders reacted. The journalist T. Thomas Fortune saw Washington's advice as a triumph of reconciliation and leadership. The black novelist Charles W. Chesnutt saw it in another way. In his 1903 article "The Disfranchisement of the Negro," he observed that "Southern white men may applaud this advice as wise, because it fits in with their purposes." But telling blacks "to go slow in seeking to enforce their civil and political rights . . . in effect, means silent submission to injustice."

Washington explained the philosophy behind his speech when he described the Atlanta event in his autobiography, *Up from Slavery,* which was published in book form in 1901 after being serialized the previous year. The book, like the speech itself, was designed to appeal primarily to a white audience. "I believe," Washington wrote, that "it is the duty of the Negro—as the greater part of the race is already doing—to deport himself modestly in regard to political claims, depending upon the slow but sure influences that proceed from the possession of property, intelligence, and high character for the full recognition of his political rights." This was a policy of appeasement.

Washington's speech symbolized a key change of personalities and techniques in the national leadership of African Americans. The 1880s and 1890s saw the deaths of many members of an older generation of African-American activists, who had led the movement to abolish slavery. The great abolitionist, orator, and women's rights advocate Sojourner Truth died in 1883. The passing of leadership from the militancy of the past to the accommodation of Washington in the present was best signified by the death of Frederick Douglass. Douglass, who had often appeared on the same platform with Sojourner Truth, had long dominated the political stage as an orator and commentator on current events. He died in Washington, D.C., on February 20, 1895, just six months before Washington spoke at the Atlanta Exposition.

In June 1895, W. E. B. Du Bois became the first African American to receive a Ph.D. degree from Harvard University. This, too, was a significant event in shaping the new standard of leadership. The young Du Bois, like Washington, would soon be recognized as one of the leaders of African-American thought.

Because of the erosion of civil rights in the late nineteenth century, black leadership had also declined in party politics and government. Although twenty-two African Americans were elected to the U.S. Congress between 1870 and the turn of the century, the post–Civil War white backlash against an integrated Republican party in the South effectively ended Republican power and Reconstruction reforms by 1877.

In the last three decades of the nineteenth century, twenty African Americans were elected to the House of Representatives. Most of these were elected in the 1870s. Eight represented districts in South Carolina, four were from North Carolina, three from Alabama, and one each was from Virginia, Georgia, Florida, Louisiana, and Mississippi. Two black men—Hiram Revels and Blanche K. Bruce—served as U.S. senators from the state of Mississippi.

Though many of these leaders were ex-slaves, a large proportion of black office-holders (in relation to the overall African-American population) were freedmen before the Civil War. Some were wealthy entrepreneurs or landowners, coming from a business class like that of many white candidates for office. (James T. Rapier of Alabama, Blanche K. Bruce of Mississippi, and Josiah T. Walls of Florida were planters.) But all, regardless of their backgrounds, had an essential political base in the majority black communities in the districts they represented. Many had come to political leadership after gaining experience as leaders in black education or in the black churches in their communities or states.

After the end of Reconstruction in the late 1870s, black Republican politicians saw the need to form alliances with white Democrats and provide patronage to white constituents in order to stay in office. These compromises made it possible for some to retain their positions into the 1880s, but by the 1890s Jim Crow legal disenfranchisement crippled black political influence on the state level.

Because of the effectiveness of the disenfranchisement of black voters, the new leaders who came to the forefront in the 1880s and 1890s were not elected officials. Sometimes they were designated as representatives of African-American opinion by whites, and sometimes they rose to this stature through the esteem with which they were held by fellow African Americans who felt that they spoke what was in their own hearts and minds. The influence of leaders like Booker T. Washington, W. E. B. Du Bois, Ida B. Wells, and T. Thomas Fortune was far-reaching. Each of these leaders was involved in the formation of important organizations that reflected the needs and desires of different segments of the African-American population. And their ideas and chosen methods of activism had an impact upon African-American history well into the twentieth century.

Booker T. Washington's Tuskegee Negro Conference, first held in 1892, is an example of the kind of leadership found in that era. According to the circular advertising the meeting, Washington's aim was to "bring together for a quiet conference, not the politicians and those usually termed the 'leading colored people,' but representatives of the masses—the bone and sinew of the race—the common, hard working farmers with a few of the best ministers and teachers." There were two goals, the circular continued: "First, to find out the actual industrial, moral and educational condition of the masses. Second, to get as much light as possible on what is the most effective way for the young men and women whom the Tuskegee Institute and other institutions are educating to use their education in helping the masses of the colored people to lift themselves up." Washington expected about seventy-five farmers, educators, and preachers to come on February 23. Instead, about five hundred men and women showed up.

They spent the morning sharing with each other information about their lives, describing who owned the land in the regions where they lived, what crops were grown, what their homes were like, where they worshiped, and where their children went to school. In the afternoon they drafted a set of resolutions. The resolutions did not deal with political or civil rights. They were about methods of self-help and ways to climb the socioeconomic ladder to the middle class. They urged all to buy land, build larger houses and schools, "give more attention to the character of their leaders, especially ministers and teachers," and stay out of debt. The desire of women for greater respect and opportunities was reflected in the resolution "to treat our women better."

Tuskegee Conferences were held annually after 1892, and by 1895, the year of Washington's Atlanta Exposition address, so many people were attending that the overall conference was broken into separate conferences for farmers, teachers, and women. Long working hours and domestic violence were among the issues the women brought up as their concerns at the February 1895 conference.

The Tuskegee Negro Conferences represented discussion and change from the bottom up (although it was under the careful stewardship of Booker T. Washington and his colleagues), but the formation of the American Negro Academy represented leadership from the top down. Planned as an elite organization, the academy was founded in Washington, D.C., in 1897 and designed to be the first major learned society for African-American intellectuals. Its first president was Alexander Crummell, long an Episcopal church leader and an inspiration to many of the younger men in the group. Crummell was one of the older generation of leaders, like Frederick Douglass and Sojourner Truth, whose life spanned much of the nineteenth century. He lived and worked in Liberia, West Africa, for many years and was one of the major theorists of the early Pan-African movement, which encouraged political unity among the peoples of the African diaspora. Crummell died the year after the academy was founded.

A person could not just join the academy. Participation was restricted to the select few who were nominated and elected to membership by those who were already members. The founders included Du Bois, sociologist Kelly Miller, and poet Paul Laurence Dunbar. Only one woman, the Washington, D.C., educator and feminist theorist Anna Julia Cooper, was invited to join the men in the academy.

The purposes of the academy included the promotion of scholarly work by black Americans and the refutation of theories and beliefs that stereotyped and demeaned African Americans. In his 1897 speech "The Conservation of Races," Du Bois spelled out the academy's purposes: "It aims at once to be the epitome and expression of the intellect of the black ... people of America, the exponent of the race ideals of one of the world's great races." Du Bois succeeded Crummell as president of the American Negro Academy in 1898.

At the same time that the academy was beginning, Du Bois was busy conducting his survey of African-American urban life in Philadelphia. Soon after finishing the survey, Du Bois became a professor at Atlanta University, where he directed the elite answer to Washington's Tuskegee conferences, the annual Atlanta Conference on Negro Problems. These conferences, held each May at Atlanta University, created a forum for African-American social scientists and other intellectuals. They gathered to exchange their research and ideas and to organize a series of sociological studies about various aspects of African-American life in the South. Studies in the 1890s focused on African-American mortality and life in the cities, and African Americans in business.

Like the Tuskegee conferences, the second Atlanta University gathering included a separate women's meeting, which focused on issues of motherhood, child rearing, and early childhood education. Educators and activists Lucy Laney and Adella Hunt Logan were among the participants who gave papers or addresses there. In 1883, Laney founded a school in Augusta, Georgia, that became the Haines Normal and Industrial Institute. She was a pioneer in kindergarten education and nurses' training. Logan was a teacher at Tuskegee Institute, beginning in 1883, and she worked closely with Olivia Davidson Washington in administering the girls' curriculum at the school. She was a founding member of the Tuskegee Women's Club and a leader in the woman suffrage movement.

The conferences for farmers at Tuskegee and for intellectuals in Atlanta were related to the formation of many new African-American professional societies and social service organizations in the 1880s and 1890s. They were also related to a long-standing method of grassroots political debate—the holding of conventions. Black ministers, editors, business owners, and intellectuals had been holding state and national conventions to address political events since the 1830s. An important national convention was held in Louisville in 1883, and African Americans in many states—including Arkansas, Georgia, Kansas, Maryland, Rhode Island, Texas, and South Carolina—organized conventions in the 1880s and 1890s for regional black leaders to discuss political policies and conditions. Rejecting Washington's tactic of appeasement and silence on political issues, the state leaders who met at these conventions discussed the role of blacks in party politics and demanded that state legislatures and the U.S. Congress respect black people's civil and political rights.

Several rights organizations were outgrowths of the state convention movement. Among them was the National Association of Colored Men, organized at a convention in Detroit in January 1896. In a resolution sent to the U.S. Congress, this group announced, "We aim at nothing unattainable, nothing Utopian, not what the society of the future is seeking, but merely what other citizens of this civilization are now enjoying."

T. Thomas Fortune's National Afro-American League, formed in 1890 and revived in new form in 1898 as the Afro-American Council, was another organization that black leaders joined in order to promote equal citizenship rights.

Fortune was a close friend of Booker T. Washington for many years and he supported Washington's platform on industrial education. Washington in turn gave financial support to Fortune's newspaper, the *New York Age*. Politically, however, Fortune was much more openly militant than Washington, and in the North in the 1890s he was one of the most widely recognized advocates for African-American rights. His National Afro-American League had objectives and approaches to problems facing blacks that would be used again by civil rights organizations in the next century. Fortune made the goals of the league clear in the very first sentence of his address to its founding convention: "We are here to-day," he told the audience, "as representatives of eight million freemen, who know our rights and have the courage to defend them."

The members of the Afro-American League favored public agitation for black rights. At their first convention they demanded an end to lynching and mob violence, the convict lease system, and the suppression of black people's ability to vote in the South. They also pointed out the unfair distribution of funds to black and white schools and discrimination against black people in public transportation and in public facilities. The league emphasized the importance of black solidarity. It favored separate black economic development, including the formation of black banks, job bureaus, and cooperative business enterprises. Local leagues were founded in several states in 1889, most of them in large cities such as San Francisco and Boston, and in other areas of the Northeast and Midwest. Both men and women were urged to participate.

The National Afro-American Council came into being at a convention in Rochester, New York, in September 1898. It was important in large part for its influence and connection to other activist groups that emerged in the years immediately following. Its platform emphasizing civil rights and suffrage, for example, foreshadowed the goals of the Niagara movement, a black intellectual group that W. E. B. Du Bois would help to found in 1905. That, in turn, led to the National Association for the Advancement of Colored People (NAACP), founded in 1910, which would serve as a major source for equal rights advocacy for decades. And, although Booker T. Washington did not participate in the founding sessions of the council, the group's policies and public statements were soon dominated by Washington and his colleagues. The National Afro-American Council remained active until 1906, but its militancy was tempered by Washington's influence, and much of the energy that had gone into its economic programs was diverted to Washington's National Negro Business League, founded in 1900 in Boston.

The need for such a business league, and the importance of black consumers buying goods and services they needed from black-owned businesses, had been voiced a few years before by Du Bois at one of the Atlanta University conferences. Du Bois later became the director of the Afro-American Council's Negro Business Bureau, where he instituted a plan to establish local business leagues around the country. But it was Washington who held more power in the council organization, and thus he who acted upon the idea for a national group to promote black commerce. The late 1880s and 1890s were a time when many new black businesses were started and when growing black urban populations brought increased business to black grocers, barbers, butchers, hotel and retail shop owners, undertakers, and real estate dealers. Black banks and insurance companies, cemeteries, and building and loan companies were also founded.

One of the issues that most concerned T. Thomas Fortune in the first year of the Afro-American Council's activism was the effect of American imperialism on people of color. He was especially concerned about the impact that the United States' war against Spain and its intervention in the Philippines in 1898 and 1899 had on Cubans, Puerto Ricans, and Filipinos.

The Spanish-American War, which began in 1895, was partly a business matter. Spanish control of territory in the New World had been gradually decreased in the late nineteenth century to domination of the islands of Cuba and Puerto Rico. As the end of the century approached, Cubans increasingly desired their political independence. But even as Spanish influence was waning, American business interests had invested many millions of dollars in Cuban plantations and refineries.

When the Cubans revolted against Spanish rule in 1895, the United States had a strong economic interest in controlling the outcome of events. News of the terrible suffering of Cubans who were forced from their homes and faced starvation and disease during the conflict also made many Americans favor U.S. intervention. Many African Americans sympathized with the Cuban rebels, and most cautiously supported U.S. involvement in the war. Others worried that overthrowing Spain and replacing her influence in the Caribbean with that of the United States would only result in the extension of Jim Crow racial discrimination beyond American borders. The coming of the war also raised issues about black patriotism, pointing up the irony of black soldiers serving abroad in the service of a country that did not grant them full citizenship rights at home. Nevertheless, many thousands of African Americans volunteered for service.

The Spanish-American War was one more arena in which African Americans demonstrated leadership in the 1890s. When the war against Spain began in April 1898, Charles Young, a West Point graduate, was the only black commissioned officer in the U.S. armed forces. Young was a friend of W. E. B. DuBois and had taught with him at Wilberforce University. A lieutenant when the war began, he was promoted to the rank of major (in 1916 he became a colonel). Despite severe racial discrimination within the armed services, by war's end there were more than one hundred African-American officers commissioned at the rank of first or second lieutenant. The majority of black volunteer units, including outfits from North Carolina, Massachusetts, and Illinois, had black officers in positions of command. Because the war only lasted a few months (it ended in July 1898), most of these eight thousand to ten thousand black volunteers never left military bases in the United States.

In the years between the Civil War and the Spanish-American War, four regular units of African-American soldiers, including the 9th and 10th Cavalries and the 24th and 25th Infantries, had been active in the U.S. Army in the West. These were the black regiments that were sent to Cuba in June 1898. The soldiers in these units, called "Buffalo Soldiers" by Native Americans in the West, were dubbed "Smoked Yankees" by the Cubans of African descent who met them during the war. They served with distinction in the key battles, most notably at El Caney, Las Guasimas, and San Juan Hill. In the last, they were instrumental in winning the battle for which Theodore Roosevelt and his Rough Riders gained fame. Black sailors also served aboard U.S. Navy ships, and some two thousand black men enlisted in the Navy during the war.

The question of leadership within the military became one of the largest issues of the war for African Americans. John Mitchell, Jr., the publisher of the *Richmond Planet,* a black newspaper in Virginia, coined the phrase "No officers, no fight!" It neatly summed up the African-American demand that blacks be promoted to positions of command and that black units be headed by black officers.

Blacks around the United States were well informed about the war from a black perspective because hundreds of black soldiers wrote home to African-American newspapers about their experiences. Activism through the spoken and written word was often linked through newsprint. For example, Victoria Earle Matthews invited Ida B. Wells to give her landmark speech about lynching because Matthews had read Wells's newspaper articles about lynching. Matthews, like Wells, worked as a journalist. Under the pen name Victoria Earle, she wrote for such papers as the *Brooklyn Eagle* and the *New York Times.* But more importantly, she wrote articles for some of the major African-American newspapers of the day, including the *Richmond Planet,* the *Washington Bee,* and the *Cleveland Gazette.* When she read Ida B. Wells's articles about lynching, she was working regularly for T. Thomas Fortune's *New York Age.* The influence of black newspapers was not restricted to the Northeast and the South. By 1900 more than sixty such newspapers had been founded in the states west of the Mississippi River, including Emmett J. Scott's *Texas Freeman.*

African Americans also emerged as leading figures in sports and the performing arts, and in the writing of fiction and poetry. Some of these cultural leaders achieved stature while accommodating their art to white audiences. Other leading black writers and performers chose to confront the prejudices of white audiences head-on. Some of them reacted to white racism by choosing to perform primarily for black audiences. Others used their art, performances, and writings to educate their mixed audiences about the range of black experience and to dispel negative stereotypes about black people.

Black jockeys dominated the winner's circle at the prestigious Kentucky Derby in Louisville, Kentucky, in the 1880s and 1890s. Isaac Murphy, nationally recognized as America's finest rider at that time, was the first man in history to win the

Kentucky Derby three times—in 1884, 1890, and 1891. At the same time that black athletes were excelling before large crowds in the sport of horse racing, African Americans were emerging as stars in the fields of music and musical theater. Soprano Sissieretta Jones was hailed as the "Black Patti" in tribute to the beauty of her voice, which critics compared to that of the much-acclaimed Italian opera singer Adelina Patti. Jones sang at Madison Square Garden in New York in 1892 and soon after appeared at the White House in a command performance for President Benjamin Harrison. The next year, she made a grand tour of Europe. She returned to the United States and was barred because of her race from performing at the Metropolitan Opera in New York. (The ban against blacks appearing at the nation's most prestigious opera house remained until 1955, when Marian Anderson became the first African American to perform there.)

Jones adapted to the white prejudice that excluded her from major opera houses by forming an all-black concert company called Black Patti's Troubadours. The group, with which Jones appeared as a soloist, presented arias from such operas as *Lucia de Lammermoor* and *Il Trovatore* as well as dancing and selections of popular music. The group went on tour and performed for sixteen years for black audiences in small towns and cities.

New images of blacks were also being presented to white and black audiences in other areas of musical theater and in literature. The lyricism that Sissieretta Jones was famous for portraying with her voice also filled the work of the late nineteenth century's most prominent African-American poet, Paul Laurence Dunbar. Dunbar was an elevator operator in Dayton, Ohio, when he began publishing his poetry. He had been a member of the literary society and editor of the school newspaper at Central High School in Dayton, and his first poems were published in newspapers. His first collection of poems, *Oak and Ivy,* was published in 1892, followed by *Majors and Minors* (1895), *Lyrics of Lowly Life* (1896), and *Lyrics of the Hearth-side* (1899). He also wrote short stories and novels. Dunbar's poetry received great critical acclaim. It also became very popular for African-American schoolchildren to memorize his poems and recite them in public programs, so that he was well known among both the intellectual elite and poorer people. He wrote poems in standard English and using black dialect speech, combining lyrical themes of love and death with depictions of African-American life and tributes to outstanding African-American leaders such as Frederick Douglass and Alexander Crummell.

Although most of Dunbar's work was not political in theme, he wrote what would become one of the most important protest poems in all of African-American literature. Called "We Wear the Mask," the poem talks about the dual nature of African-American existence, in which blacks exhibited a certain code of amiable outer behavior to meet white expectations, while underneath that accommodating outer demeanor, true thoughts and feelings lay hidden. Published in *Lyrics of Lowly Life,* "We Wear the Mask" goes like this:

The team of George Walker (right) and Bert Williams was one of the most popular African-American acts in vaudeville. Despite their celebrity, they faced segregation in the hotels and eating establishments of the cities where they performed. After Walker's death, Williams became the nation's first big-name African-American star as a featured performer with the Ziegfeld Follies.

We wear the mask that grins and lies,
It hides our cheeks and shades our eyes,—
This debt we pay to human guile;
With torn and bleeding hearts we smile,
And mouth with myriad subtleties

Why should the world be over-wise,
In counting all our tears and sighs?
Nay, let them only see us, while
We wear the mask.

We smile, but, O great Christ, our cries
To thee from tortured souls arise.

We sing, but oh the clay is vile
Beneath our feet, and long the mile;
But let the world dream otherwise,
We wear the mask!

In addition to writing poetry, Paul Laurence Dunbar was involved in musical theater as a songwriter. He and composer Will Marion Cook wrote an operetta called *Clorindy* in 1898. When *Clorindy* went on a tour of East Coast cities that September, it starred two of Dunbar and Cook's friends from New York, Bert Williams and George Walker. Bert Williams was born in the British West Indies and went to high school in Riverside, California. He and Walker began their career as a duo in a minstrel company in San Francisco in 1893. They developed their own comedy act, and by the mid-1890s they were leading men in New York variety productions. Walker's wife, Aida Overton Walker, had been a dancer with the Black Patti Troubadours. She appeared in all the Williams and Walker shows and choreographed their major numbers.

Williams and Walker's fame did not come without a price. Their act played to white stereotypes about blacks. Walker was the dandy, appearing in elaborately designed fancy street clothes that made fun of black consumerism and middle-class aspirations. Williams, who had never lived in the American South, played a Southern tramplike figure who sang in dialect and played the banjo. A light-skinned man, he also appeared on stage in blackface, which meant that he rubbed burnt cork on his face to make it look darker and applied makeup to exaggerate his African features. White actors had long been doing the same thing to caricature black people in minstrel and variety shows, and thus Williams's makeup fulfilled white audiences' expectations of what a black person should look like on stage. For Williams, who in real life was a dignified and quiet man, his on-stage persona was one in which he quite literally wore the mask.

The folk dialect that was used in stage by acts like Williams and Walker's, and in popular music like the songs written by Cook and Dunbar, also was used by African Americans who wrote short stories and novels. This was true for the two most prominent African-American authors of the 1890s, Charles Waddell Chesnutt and Frances Ellen Watkins Harper. Both of these writers used dialect when creating dialogue for black folk characters who were illiterate or lacked formal education. For these characters an oral, rather than a written, tradition was paramount. Educated and middle-class characters, by contrast, spoke standard English in these writers' books.

Just as Sissieretta Jones sought to present a new image of black womanhood in music, so Frances Harper's *Iola Leroy* (1892), one of the first novels published by an African-American woman, was written in part to dispel stereotypes that whites had about black women. *Iola Leroy* protested derogatory ideas that whites held about black women's social worth and morality by placing at its center an able and intelligent black woman protagonist whose actions and thoughts were full of virtue. The novel's heroine, Iola Leroy, is a well-educated, middle-class woman who devotes her life to the uplift of her people. Harper also used the story to address a series of injustices in African-American history and demonstrate ways in which elite African Americans in the decades after the Civil War developed systems of self-help.

*Iola Leroy* was published in the same year as two other key works written by African-American women: Ida B. Wells's *Southern Horrors,* an exposé about lynching, and Anna Julia Cooper's *A Voice from the South,* a treatise on the status of women in African-American society. Each of these works, and the lives of each of the women who wrote them, proved that African-American leadership was not just male, but female. Indeed, the 1890s produced so many extraordinary African-American women leaders and organizations that it became known as the "Woman's Era."

## Woman's Era: "Strong in a Love of Justice"

In 1893, a year after her novel *Iola Leroy* was published, the veteran lecturer Frances Ellen Watkins Harper stood on the podium at the World's Congress of Representative Women in Chicago. The Women's Congress, as it was known, was held in conjunction with the World's Columbian Exposition, or Chicago World's Fair. Just as the Atlanta Exposition was held to celebrate the economic resurgence of the American South, so the Chicago World's Fair was organized to laud the industrial and cultural achievements of the Americas in the eyes of the world. Exhibition halls were set up to show advancements in many types of fields, and one hall was devoted specifically to the achievements of women. But the Lady Managers, or the board of women who had organized the women's events at the fair, largely excluded African-American women from participating.

When Harper and other middle-class black women accepted invitations to speak at the Women's Congress, they saw themselves as representatives of all African Americans. They also came to confront the racism that had allowed the Lady Managers of the fair to present only white women's skills and creations as worthy of attention in the Women's Building.

Their speeches, like Harper's novel, Ida B. Wells's pamphlets about lynching, and Anna Julia Cooper's book *A Voice from the South,* represent the bold introduction of black women's voices into the debates within the middle-class African-American community as a whole. Their lectures also represented a defense of black womanhood, answering those who viewed black women as lacking in moral character or as secondary in importance to men. When they appeared in Chicago they challenged white women's racism both by word and example. And they gave voice to principles that they felt black people should hold dear. Among them were the right of young women to educational opportunities equal to those of young men; the right of women—black and white—to vote; and the recognition of the role that women had to play in improving society, both privately within the home and publicly as champions of justice for their race.

At the Women's Congress in Chicago in 1893, Frances Ellen Watkins Harper and the other black women who spoke summed up the issues that were in the minds of many of their sisters. Just as Booker T. Washington's Atlanta speech helped shape race relations well into the twentieth century, Harper's speech in Chicago set the agenda for middle-class black women's activism for years ahead. She also gave a name to the 1890s that reflected the rise of a generation of well-educated African-American women to positions of public leadership. She called it the "Woman's Era."

And so it was. Never before had there been so many African-American women speaking their minds in public forums, founding newspapers and schools, and shaping the world around them. In the Woman's Era, middle-class women working in their own towns and cities on behalf of working-class women and the poor developed a national momentum for positive change. Most important, black women's benevolent associations and mothers' and women's clubs joined together into regional federations, and ultimately into the National Association of Colored Women, which was founded in 1896. But the movement toward the more powerful organization of black women was happening in other ways as well—in the suffrage movement, the temperance movement, and the Baptist church.

In her speech in Chicago, Harper argued that the "world has need of all the spiritual aid that woman can give for the social advancement and moral development of the human race." Women's abilities and contributions were far too valuable to waste, and to talk only of the advancement of men and their greater opportunities was not sufficient. Harper, like her colleague Anna Julia Cooper, believed that women represented a force for good that would counteract men's tendencies toward destructiveness, war, and violence. She also argued, along with Cooper, that women should enter public and economic life. "By opening doors of labor," Harper said of black women trying to broaden the types of work they were allowed to do, "woman has become a rival claimant for at least some of the wealth monopolized by her stronger brother." She called for the "ballot in the hands of woman," which would add direct political power to the already existing influence of women in the home, the church pew, the classroom, and the press. She spoke of the male-led worlds of business and the military, the "increase of wealth, the power of armies," being nothing in contrast to the basic social needs of "good homes, of good fathers, and good mothers." She warned of the effects of heavy drinking upon families, and she castigated lynching.

In presenting this political platform, Harper echoed many of the opinions expressed by Anna Julia Cooper in *A Voice from the South,* published the previous year. Cooper, too, questioned the top-to-bottom structure of power that led one nation to attempt to conquer another, or one race to consider itself superior to another. She compared these attitudes of dominance to the ways that intellectual and political opportunities were open to men but closed to women, and to the fact that white women's prejudices against black women tarnished and limited existing movements for women's political rights. She stated that no civilization could rise higher than its women, and that the key to progress for any society was the development of its women's full rights and opportunities. She argued strongly for women's access to higher education and intellectual achievement, and for the economic independence of women that such training would permit.

Cooper, like Harper, was one of the African-American women who spoke to the international audience at the Chicago Women's Congress. She had taught school in her home state of North Carolina before graduating from the "men's" course of study with A.B. (1884) and M.A. (1887) degrees at Oberlin College—one of the first women students to do so. She headed the modern language department at Wilberforce College in Ohio—the same school where American Negro Academy leader W. E. B. Du Bois and military officer Charles Young taught. Later she moved to Washington, D.C., where she became one of the most important educators of her time. She served as principal of the famed M Street High School. She was also one of the first African-American women to obtain a Ph.D. degree, which she earned from the Sorbonne in Paris in 1925, when she was sixty-six.

At the Women's Congress, Ida B. Wells decided not to speak. Instead she protested white racism by putting together a short book, published in Chicago during the World's Fair. She called it *The Reason Why the Colored American Is Not in the World's Columbian Exposition.* Frederick Douglass, who had long supported women's right to vote and other women's causes, wrote the book's introduction.

The book included chapters about slavery, disenfranchisement, and lynching. It also chronicled African-American achievements, including a list of patents granted to black men and women and biographies of black artists, authors, and musicians. It ended with documentation of black people's exclusion from the fair by the white administrators. Wells raised the money to publish the pamphlet by arranging a series of Sunday afternoon meetings among women at different Chicago-area churches. She printed twenty thousand copies of the pamphlet, and they were distributed throughout Chicago and by mail.

The same year, Wells traveled to England and Scotland to give lectures about lynching. Frederick Douglass encouraged her to go and loaned her the money to make the trip. "It seemed like an open door in a stone wall," she wrote in her memoirs. Excluded from the South because of her newspaper writings, and having trouble getting people in the North to listen to her, she went across the Atlantic Ocean to speak in cities such as Edinburgh, Liverpool, Manchester, and London. In every speech she gave she educated white British audiences about Jim Crow laws in the American South and the realities of lynching. She succeeded in making the anti-lynching campaign international.

Frances Ellen Watkins Harper's speech in Chicago and Ida B. Wells's lectures abroad were both catalysts for more rigorous organization of a national black women's club movement in the mid-1890s. The movement started off with local groups in several different places. Many of these groups began in 1892–93. The Women's Loyal Union had been formed by Victoria Earle Matthews and other middle-class women activists in New York after Wells's Lyric Hall speech in 1892. The Colored Women's League of Washington, D.C., the Women's Era Club of Boston, and the Ida B. Wells Club of Chicago were formed soon after.

Mary Church Terrell, president of the Bethel Literary and Historical Society in Washington, D.C., was one of the founders of the Colored Women's League. The founding statement the league drafted, written in June 1892, summed up the spirit of the middle-class black woman's movement. "Whereas," it read, "in Union there is Strength, and Whereas, we, as a people, have been and are the subject of prejudice, proscription, and injustice, the more successful, because the lack of unity and organization, Resolved, That we, the colored women of Washington, associate ourselves together." The Colored Women's League soon expanded by opening branches in other cities, including Richmond and Norfolk, Virginia, and Newport, Rhode Island.

Journalist Josephine St. Pierre Ruffin headed the Boston Woman's Era Club. Originally called the New Era Club when it was founded in February 1893, it took the name of the Woman's Era that Frances Harper had used in her speech. In March 1894 Ruffin began publishing a monthly journal of opinion called the *Woman's Era*. Black women activists from all over the country—Mary Church Terrell of Washington, Alice Ruth Moore of New Orleans (who later married the poet Paul Laurence Dunbar, and became herself a noted literary figure under the name Alice Dunbar Nelson), Victoria Earle Matthews of New York, and Fannie Barrier Williams of Chicago—contributed to the journal, which served as a forum for the new women's movement.

One of the major concerns voiced in Anna Julia Cooper's *A Voice from the South* and many of the black women's speeches at the World's Fair was whites' habit of questioning black women's sexual morality. Ida B. Wells always made this issue a part of her lectures on lynching. Cooper spoke for the other women activists when she wrote that unwanted sexual advances were typically made by whites, not blacks. Speaking of attitudes about rape, she said that the blame had been misplaced on black people. Historically, whites were primarily responsible for sexual offenses against blacks, not vise versa. "Overtures for forced association in the past history of these two races were not made by the manacled black man, nor by the silent and suffering black woman!" she declared. Black women's outrage over this issue of their alleged immorality was a major impetus to the formation of the national black women's movement.

It happened this way. A white American journalist—a man from Missouri—wrote a letter in which he attacked Ida B. Wells's character because she had spoken out against Southern lynching on her trips abroad, and in which he demeaned the character of black women in general. Copies of the offensive letter were circulated among women activists in the anti-lynching movement in England and passed on to club leaders in the United States. When Josephine St. Pierre Ruffin received a copy of the letter, she decided to take action. She sent out a circular and on the editorial page of the June 1895 issue of *Woman's Era* printed a call for a big meeting of women. "To all colored women of America, members of any society or not," she wrote, "Let Us Confer Together." The result was the First National Conference of the Colored Women of America.

The conference convened in Boston at the end of July 1895. In her keynote speech, Ruffin outlined the many reasons for getting black women from all over the nation together. "In the first place," she said, "we need to feel the cheer and inspiration of meeting each other, we need to gain the courage and fresh life that comes from the mingling of congenial souls, of those working for the same ends." Ruffin also told her audience that they needed to take a united stand and make their voices heard: "Too long have we been silent under unjust and unholy charges," she said, referring to slanderous accusations against middle-class black women. The women delegates decided to form a new organization. They named it the National Federation of Afro-American Women and elected Margaret Murray Washington, the Tuskegee activist, as president.

Meanwhile, other groups were forming. The following summer, in July 1896, the National Federation of Afro-American Women and the National League of Colored Women, based in Washington, D.C., merged with more than one hundred other women's clubs to form a new coalition. It was called the National Association of Colored Women (NACW). Frances Harper was at this historic meeting, a representative of older, former anti-slavery activists, as was the great elderly abolitionist Harriet Tubman. Frederick Douglass's only daughter, Rosetta Sprague, participated. Ida B. Wells, who had recently married and changed her name to Ida B. Wells-Barnett, came with her new baby son to chair one of the conference committees. Mary Church Terrell was elected president of the new national organization. When the NACW met for its second annual conference in 1897, it moved its meeting south to Nashville, Tennessee, and began publication of a periodical, *National Notes*.

Mary Church Terrell had graduated from Oberlin College with Anna Julia Cooper and, like Cooper, lived in Washington, D.C. She grew up in Memphis, Tennessee, and like Ida B. Wells, had been a close friend of Peoples' Grocery owner Thomas Moss. Her husband, Robert Terrell, was a close associate of Booker T. Washington and from the well-to-do Terrell family. Mary Church Terrell's election as president was questioned by some. To some of the more progressive delegates she represented an overly conservative approach to social issues and, as a very rich

The National Association of Colored Women was formed in 1896 by the merger of the National League of Colored Women and the National Federation of Afro-American Women. Representing more than a hundred women's clubs, the new coalition proved to be a powerful promoter of self-help, equity, and justice for black women.

woman, she had a sensibility that was very remote from the lives of the masses of black Americans. Nevertheless, she headed the National Association of Colored Women from its inception in 1896 until 1901.

The motto of the NACW, "Lifting As We Climb," reflected the perspective of the middle-class women who made up the movement. They saw themselves improving the conditions and behavior of lower-class women as they instituted social reforms and defended the respectability of women like themselves. The activities of the NACW were similar to the kinds of outreach that was already being done in local areas through churches, settlement houses, and women's neighborhood groups. Under Terrell's leadership the NACW members emphasized early childhood education, especially the establishment of kindergartens and day nurseries. They also actively supported the major women's progressive movements, including suffrage, temperance, self-help, and moral reform.

In a time when most black Americans lived in the South and made their living in agriculture, the leadership, and much of the membership, of the NACW was largely based in the North and among urban women. The middle-class clubwomen had economic opportunities and lifestyle choices that were not available to a majority of black women. There were also internal splits among the ranks of NACW leaders. Ideological rivalries existed between women such as Mary Church Terrell, who was often compared to Booker T. Washington in politics and temperament, and more fiery and militant members such as Ida B. Wells-Barnett. Geographic rivalries also existed between the various NACW leaders from different Northern cities, whether Boston, Chicago, Washington, D.C., or New York, each of whom had a claim to the leadership of the original club movement. But despite these internal differences, the NACW functioned as a clearinghouse for black women's community action until the 1930s.

Black women's involvement in the temperance movement straddled the line between the secular politics of the women's club movement and the religious convictions that led black women of all classes to work in their communities through their churches. The movement to moderate or ban the use of alcohol was part of the self-help aspect of black institution building. The misuse of alcohol, temperance leaders argued, drained families of needed income, took attention away from children, and led to domestic violence. Women and children often paid the emotional and physical price of men's drinking, and men who socialized at bars and pool halls were not turning their attention to more constructive things. They also helped feed white stereotypes about nonproductive black men.

As president of the NACW, Mary Church Terrell was a widely sought-after speaker. Her conservative views on social and racial issues placed her at odds with other more militant members of the group such as Ida B. Wells.

When the African Methodist Episcopal church sponsored a symposium about temperance in 1891, it was Frances Harper who gave the keynote address. Harper had long worked with the Women's Christian Temperance Union (WCTU). She was a city, state, and eventually, national WCTU organizer for temperance in black communities. In her poetry in the 1880s, she wrote about the destructive effects on families caused by the abuse of alcohol, and in 1888 she wrote an essay called "The Women's Christian Temperance Union and the Colored Woman." She told of moral influence women could have in the home and of the direct-action tactic in which "saloons were visited, hardships encountered, insults, violence and even imprisonment endured by women, brave to suffer and strong to endure."

Harper's relatively positive experience in regional chapters of the WCTU contrasted with that of Josephine St. Pierre Ruffin and Ida B. Wells, both of whom found the white leadership of the WCTU intolerably racist. Wells in particular was appalled at WCTU president Frances Willard's acceptance of the white Southern practice of lynching and negative stereotypes of both black women and men. Despite such prejudices, black women joined black auxiliaries to the white women's union. By 1898, five independent black women's state temperance unions had been founded in the South—in Arkansas, Georgia, North Carolina, Tennessee, and Texas.

The racism and the opposition of white Southern women to integration that characterized the temperance movement also limited the ability of black women to participate in the organized woman suffrage movement. Black women leaders found their own ways of furthering the cause of women's right to vote. Mary Ann Shadd Cary, a Washington, D.C., lawyer and a graduate of Howard University, founded the Colored Women's Progressive Franchise Association as an auxiliary of the predominantly white National American Woman Suffrage Association (NAWSA) on February 9, 1880. Cary's self-help group supported equal rights for women and made lobbying for suffrage its first priority. Adella Hunt Logan, who led women's sessions at the annual Tuskegee conferences and participated in the Atlanta University conferences, was a very light-skinned black person. She used this to her advantage in "passing" as white in order to attend National American Woman Suffrage Association conventions in the segregated South. She then related what had happened in the meetings to fellow black activists in Southern states. Mary Church Terrell was a life member of NAWSA in the North and appeared as a speaker at many of the organization's national meetings, including those in 1898 and 1900. Terrell was among those who used her upper-class, college-educated status as an argument for the right of others like her to vote, arguing that the franchise should not be withheld from black women of culture and learning.

While Mary Church Terrell and other conservative clubwomen were advocating the rights of privileged black women, Lucy Parsons championed the cause of working people and the poor. Parsons moved in entirely different circles from the black reformers who united into women's organizations in the 1890s. Parsons was born in Waco, Texas, of mixed African, Indian, and Mexican ancestry. She married a white man named Albert Parsons, and together they entered a life of political activism. Just as the anti-lynching and women's movements foreshadowed many of the issues and approaches of the Civil Rights and women's liberation movements of the twentieth century, Lucy Parsons's kind of activism set an example for black people's involvement in the various movements of the American Left.

Lucy Parsons was an anarchist and socialist. She and her husband lived in primarily white-ethnic, working-class neighborhoods in Chicago, where she worked as a seamstress. Albert Parsons was a leader in the International Working People's Association, and both he and Lucy were members of the Knights of Labor. Lucy Parsons wrote revolutionary essays about homelessness, violence, unemployment, and working people's rights for her husband's newspaper, *Alarm,* and she became an organizer for the Chicago Working Women's Union.

She was known for her electrifying speeches, and as part of her work with the Knights of Labor she organized mostly white Chicago women in the sewing trades in support of an eight-hour workday. In 1891, Lucy Parsons joined the ranks of black women editors when she began publishing her own newspaper, *Freedom.* Unlike the periodicals of the black women's movement, *Freedom* put class, rather than race or gender, at the forefront of the fight for justice.

Nannie Helen Burroughs bridged the worlds between the working women whom Parsons championed and the middle-class realm of the black women's club movement. Much of her activism took place within the black church. Most of the African-American women who became involved as activists in the Woman's Era had experience as community workers through their churches, and much of the spirit of reform that filled the 1890s emerged originally from self-help messages within the church. It is fitting, then, that women's organization building and feminist thought in the last decade of the nineteenth century also had an impact on the way women were viewed within the black church. The growing awareness about women's abilities that had sprung from the church and blossomed in middle-class, secular organizations was plowed back in to enrich the soil of religious institutions. Nannie Helen Burroughs was only twenty-one years old when she gave a speech called "How the Sisters Are Hindered from Helping" at the annual National Baptist Convention in Richmond, Virginia, in September 1900. Her plea for a more powerful and united presence for black women within the Baptist church led to the founding of the Woman's Convention, an auxiliary to the National Baptist Convention. The Woman's Convention, with more than one million members, proved to be the largest black women's organization in America. Through it, church women set their own policies and provided their own national leaders.

In 1893, Frances Ellen Watkins Harper spoke of being on the threshold of a Woman's Era. In 1900, black men and women stood together on the cusp of a new century. They had as their foundation the many churches, schools, and organizations they had built, and a legacy of leadership that would carry them into the next decades. The message that the African-American activists of the 1880s and 1890s left for those in the twentieth century was a clear one. Frances Harper said it at the Chicago Women's Congress in 1893: "Demand justice, simple justice, as the right of every race."

## CHAPTER 2

# A Chance to Make Good
## 1900–1929

*James R. Grossman*

In 1900, ninety percent of all African Americans lived in the South; three-fourths of these eight million people inhabited rural communities. The 880,771 black Northerners, on the other hand, were decidedly urban; seventy-one percent lived in cities.

History and personal experience taught African Americans that their position in U.S. society could not be understood without understanding racism. But race was not the only basis for discrimination in American life. Nor was it the only way Americans defined themselves. Class and gender, along with religion, ethnicity, and age, also shaped lives, ideas, and dreams.

Perhaps, indeed, "the problem of the Twentieth Century is the problem of the color line," as W. E. B. Du Bois declared in 1903. But the significance and the composition of that line cannot be reduced to the biology of skin pigmentation. The meaning of race, and the practice of racism, were tightly intertwined with labor systems, ideas about family life, and assumptions about the relationship between manhood and citizenship. Du Bois recognized that it was impossible to understand the meaning of race without also understanding class. The place of African Americans in society was inseparable from their place in the economy.

In African-American history, images of victimization spring to mind as readily as notions of progress. Hope has most often bred disappointment and frequently disillusionment as well. In the early twentieth century, black Americans shared in the aspirations and expectations of their fellow citizens but did so as a people with a unique history and set of barriers to overcome.

African Americans argued among themselves as to what those barriers were made of; exactly where they were situated; how permanent they were; and whether they should be destroyed, circumvented, or hurdled. During the first three decades of the twentieth century, thousands of black men and women obliterated, removed, tiptoed around, climbed over, and even passed through these barriers. Others ignored them. Some resigned themselves to the limitations and pain these barriers produced, without accepting the notion that such obstacles were either natural or just. And still others suffered from the costs of pounding the barriers at times and in places where they were too deeply embedded in the social fabric to be breached.

## Making a Living

At the dawn of the twentieth century the color line, or the separation between whites and blacks, was most clear and most rigid in the South. With ninety-five percent of African Americans living south of the Ohio River and east of central Texas, this was also where the overwhelming majority of black people lived. Before the Civil War, the Ohio River and the Mason–Dixon line (separating Pennsylvania from Maryland) had marked the line between slavery and freedom—even though "freedom" in the North was limited by employment discrimination, barriers to voting and officeholding, and racial segregation.

In 1900, thirty-five years after emancipation, this boundary remained particularly meaningful to African Americans. South of the line, citizenship guaranteed little. To describe the condition of blacks in the South, both whites and blacks used a phrase first articulated by the United States Supreme Court in the 1857 case of *Dred Scott* v. *Sanford* to limit the scope of African-American citizenship before the Civil War: Blacks had "no rights which the white man was bound to respect." That was still the case in the South in 1900.

In the North, black men and women enjoyed the same legal rights as whites, but an informal color line set the races apart, limiting where blacks could work, live, and send their children to school. In the West, patterns somewhat resembled the North. In both regions African Americans lived mainly in cities. Because the black populations in Western states remained small, however, there tended to be greater flexibility and fewer restrictions. Indeed, blacks not only were barely visible in the West, but in many cases attracted less hostility than Asian and Mexican immigrants. Despite these significant variations, however, racism had become a part of American national culture. African Americans everywhere were likely to earn less than whites, work longer hours at less desirable jobs (or be unemployed), and confront limitations on where they could go and what they could do. The story of the twentieth century begins where the restrictions were the most concrete and wide ranging, and where most African Americans lived and worked: in the South.

As the century opened, four-fifths of all black Southerners lived in rural communities. Most were members of families who earned their living from the land. What they planted depended largely on where they lived. Tobacco remained important in Virginia, North Carolina, and Kentucky. Sugarcane continued to be grown in Louisiana. Through most of the South cotton still reigned. But whatever they grew and wherever they lived, most African Americans across the South worked, worshiped, rested, and partied around cycles of labor—the long hours required to plant, cultivate, and harvest a cash crop. And most operated within a system of land ownership and rental that varied considerably in its details but little in its basic framework.

By 1900, approximately one-fourth of all black Southerners who operated farms owned the soil they tilled. The number of black farm owners—and their total acreage—increased each year. Southern black leaders frequently pointed to these accomplishments as evidence of a strong work ethic among their people and of the great potential that lay in the rural South.

But the story was more complicated and less encouraging than the tale told by these statistics. Impressive increases in total acreage owned by black Southerners did testify to hard work and frugality. Many lived according to the work ethic later articulated by Alabama farmer Ned Cobb: "I didn't come in this world to rust out. If I need anything done in my field I ought to be there if time will admit it, on time. I got to work. I'm born to work."

In the opening decades of the twentieth century Cobb clawed his way up the ladder from wage laborer to sharecropper, cash renter, and finally owner. But he never was able to accumulate much, and more than once he was cheated out of his assets by white landlords or merchants. For him, as so many others, prosperity—even mere independence—remained a difficult goal to achieve and maintain.

These farms were small and seldom grew any larger. Moreover, even farmers who had not borrowed money to purchase their farms still needed some form of credit to meet a year's expenses before their crop could be harvested in the fall. Partly because the land worked by black farmers tended to be worth less than the crop that could be grown on it, local merchants and bankers would secure loans by taking a lien on the crop, guaranteeing they would have first rights to the sale of the crop, rather than a mortgage on the land. Instead of repossessing the land if a farmer failed to repay, the lender took what was due out of the sale of the crop. The farmer got what was left, and sometimes that was very little.

The holder of the lien could (and often did) require that the farmer put most of his fields into a cash crop in order to increase the likelihood of the farmer repaying his debt. Families who owned land thus had to purchase food that they otherwise might have grown themselves—and often from the same merchant who demanded that as a condition of their loan they plant most of their fields in cotton or tobacco.

With little money to invest, and working on land that was less productive than that available to renters, most black farm owners maintained an unstable grip on their independence. One or two years of bad weather or low prices for their crops could hurl them back into tenancy. The symbolic value of ownership, and the extent to which it permitted members of the family to go about their lives without thinking about a white landlord, could only multiply the pain of losing one's land.

The vast majority of black farmers rented their land, either as cash renters or sharecroppers. Most black tenants were sharecroppers, especially where cotton was the main crop. Because most sharecroppers had no source of money until the

Children provided an essential supplement to their parents when it came time to pick cotton. Schools for African-American children in the South closed when the bolls ripened.

end of the year, they had to borrow—either from the landlord or from a local merchant—in order to meet normal family expenses. These loans (often called "furnish") would be repaid after "settlement." Settlement took place at the end of the year, when the landlord (or merchant) would compare the value of the tenant's portion of the crop with the sum "advanced" to the tenant during the preceding twelve months.

Almost invariably the sharecropper came out either behind or barely even. Even the thousands of sharecroppers who were illiterate and therefore unable to challenge the accounting suspected that they seldom received their due. In 1919, for example, George Conway of Keo, Arkansas, raised twenty bales of cotton, worth thirty-five hundred dollars Although he knew that he had not purchased more than three hundred dollars worth of merchandise on credit from his landlord that year, he was told at settlement that he still owed forty dollars. His demand for an itemized accounting earned him only a beating. Still claiming a debt of forty dollars, the landlord seized Conway's household goods and drove him off the plantation.

The inevitability of the unfair settlement became a staple of African-American humor, with innumerable variations of a joke that has a tenant secretly withholding a bale or two of cotton at settlement time. As William Pickens, whose family sharecropped in South Carolina and Arkansas, later observed, "Who could deny it? The white man did all the reckoning. The Negro did all the work."

To complain or to threaten legal action was useless; no court would rule in favor of a black sharecropper against a white landlord. A sharecropper could carry over a debt into the next year; move to another farm with the debt built into the next contract; or quietly try to leave—to skip out on an obligation that most black Southerners considered a complete sham anyway.

Indeed the debt was even worse than a sham. By law the tenant was actually a wage laborer; the crop belonged to the landlord. But the landlord had it both ways. The sharecropper family worked, yet received no regular wages. They were paid nothing until the crop had been harvested and sold. Thus the landlord was actually the one who should have been considered the debtor. The cash—or wage—that was being withheld from the laborer was a debt, cash that the landlord owed the tenant but did not have to pay until December.

To satisfy the basic needs of their families, sharecroppers thus had to borrow at high interest rates, generally ranging from forty to seventy percent in an era when rates elsewhere generally fluctuated between four and eight percent. Even at these outrageous prices, sharecroppers could get credit to buy only what the landlord (or furnishing merchant) deemed appropriate.

Those basic needs were quite modest. The standard of living among black sharecroppers in the South was generally lower than that of mid-nineteenth-century westward pioneers. But where the pioneers' log cabins suggest to us images of upwardly mobile families clearing homesteads and carving out a living from the land, sharecroppers' log cabins represent a very different reality. These cabins, which could be constructed out of rough boards rather than logs, were dark, sometimes without windows. Where there were openings they generally lacked glass panes, and often even shutters. Screens were virtually unknown. Keeping the house clean, considered to be women's work, was virtually impossible.

With only three rooms or fewer, it was equally impossible to create specialized spaces for such activities as eating, sleeping, or memorizing one's school lessons. Several members of a family slept in a single room, with five or more not at all uncommon. At a time when middle- and upper-class Americans had come to expect divisions between "private" and "public" spaces in their homes, the tenant's cabin afforded no such luxury. There was no such thing as a room that had only one purpose or was the domain of a single family member.

For many sharecroppers, family life was different from that idealized by a "mainstream" middle-class family. Black families in the rural South resembled the two-parent households common elsewhere in the United States at the time, but were more likely to include older relatives as well. Perhaps the presence of other adults left husbands and fathers with less authority than their counterparts elsewhere. Many definitely had to share authority with their landlords, who drew contracts that permitted them to require family members to work the fields. Black men thus came to value their ability to relieve their wives and children of field work. Moreover, by controlling the furnish, a landlord could influence relations within a sharecropper's family by defining the range of purchasing options—how much of each kind of clothing, how many luxuries, or what kind of food.

The sharecropper's diet was dull and often sparse. A garden could yield plenty of food, but many landlords required their tenants to grow cotton almost to the door. The Delta Farm Company, owner of 35,000 acres of land in Mound Bayou County, Mississippi, for example, prohibited its tenants from raising anything other than cotton. No chickens or vegetables were permitted. Generally, tenants tended small gardens, supplemented by what they could afford at the local store. The result was a lot of cornmeal and poor cuts of pork, all prepared with generous quantities of animal fat—another challenge to women who increasingly were being told by agricultural reformers (black and white) to be better housewives by preparing more healthful food.

Indeed, the growing movements for better farming methods and more efficient rural housekeeping bore little relevance to the realities of sharecropping. There was no incentive for tenants or owners to improve either the farm or the dwelling. Landlords were steeped in a culture committed to an agricultural economy based on cheap labor. They also were steeped in a culture that assumed black people would have difficulty learning advanced farming methods or how to operate and maintain machinery. Landlords considered mules and cabins appropriate to the aptitudes and productivity of African Americans. A greater investment in equipment or living conditions, they thought, would neither raise the value of their property nor increase output. Moreover, the landlord would receive only a portion of any increased yield that might result from improvement.

On the tenant's side, improving the farm made even less sense. Why invest sweat or money into a home or farm that was owned by someone else? What little cash a family might accumulate was best spent in moveable items that could increase one's share of the crop next time around: a wagon, a mule, or a plow. And why accumulate household goods when in all likelihood the family would move within a few years? Little surprise that housekeeping technology seldom went far beyond water pail, washtub, and cooking kettle.

Having no investment in home or farm, and encountering constant frustration regardless of how hard they worked, sharecroppers were bound to remain alert to other possibilities. Although many families remained on a single farm for years, William Pickens's parents were more typical. By the time he had reached his nineteenth birthday in 1900, he had known more than twenty buildings that he could call "home."

At first they moved locally, from farm to farm within their rural South Carolina community. Their big chance seemed to strike in the late 1880s, when a visitor told them about Arkansas, where planters were clamoring for men to work land being brought under cultivation. The man was a "labor agent," one of many recruiters who in the late nineteenth century traveled through those parts of the South where years of growing cotton or tobacco had worn the land thin.

These agents worked for planters further south in Florida or—more frequently—further west in the Mississippi Delta or in Arkansas. With no prospects in South Carolina, Pickens's parents were prepared to listen. "The agent said that Arkansas was a tropical country of soft and balmy air, where coconuts, oranges, lemons, and bananas grew. Ordinary things like corn and cotton, with little cultivation, grew an enormous yield."

So they went. During the last two decades of the nineteenth century and the first decade of the twentieth, the system stabilized but people moved. The South's black population churned as rural people moved from plantation to plantation, county to county, state to state in quest of the holy grail of land ownership. Some, like the Pickenses, were lured by labor agents. Others, especially in hilly areas where whites already outnumbered blacks, were pushed out in a process known as "whitecapping," a term that referred to the practice of night riders pushing African Americans off their land through threat of violence. At least 239 instances of whitecapping were recorded during the two decades beginning in the late 1880s, with Mississippi the most common site. The term seems to have originated in Indiana, where night riders invading a small community or threatening an individual African-American resident would wear white caps as part of their disguise.

Despite its origins in the Midwest, whitecapping was mainly a Southern rural phenomenon. Successful black farmers were the most likely target of this kind of eviction because of the common assumption among whites that the success of some blacks might unleash unrealistic (and dangerous) aspirations among the local black population. A farmer in Alpharetta, Georgia, recognized that he "better not accumulate much, no matter how hard and honest you work for it, as they—well, you can't enjoy it." In some cases, whole communities were forced from their homes.

In areas more heavily populated by African Americans, especially the "Black Belt" stretching across the cotton-growing region of South Carolina, Georgia, Alabama, Mississippi, Louisiana, and East Texas, nature took its toll as well. The boll weevil, which devoured cotton, entered the United States from Mexico toward the end of the nineteenth century.

Some landlords responded by diversifying their farms, especially after 1910, when the weevil's impact interacted with a growing agricultural reform movement. Corn required only one-fifth as much labor as cotton, which meant that many black tenants and wage hands were suddenly thrown out of work. In other cases black farmers confronted with a weevil-infested crop headed for areas rumored to be untouched, or abandoned farming altogether.

This constant movement vexed landlords, but it was virtually built into the system. Indeed, contrary to conventional opinion among whites, the proclivity to move had little to do with what whites called "Negro character." Black Southerners did move more frequently than whites, but mainly because they were more likely to be sharecroppers—the most mobile category of farmers. Among all sharecroppers in the early-twentieth-century South, African Americans had the lowest rates of mobility; black cash renters and owners were each more stable than their white counterparts.

Moving was, in fact, the American way. The movement of labor toward opportunity is essential to the efficient operation of labor markets in a growing economy. Free labor implies the ability of workers to move from depressed locales to areas of expansion, liberating both the worker to take advantage of opportunity and the employer from any responsibility for supporting former employees.

But the rural South, especially where cotton or sugar cultivation dominated patterns of employment, was committed to a different type of economy—one dominated by the plantation, a form of production that required a tightly controlled labor force. Except in areas where new lands were being brought into cultivation, a stable labor force seemed essential to both the prosperity of individual landowners and the stability of the system itself. Complaints about a "chaotic" labor market and "restless" and "unreliable" black labor abounded. White landowners lamented the inclination of their tenants to be "controlled far more by their fancies than by their common sense."

In response, nearly all Southern states, and many localities as well, attempted to immobilize black labor by erecting legal and economic barriers to movement. Although enmeshed in a capitalist economy based on the ability of the employer to purchase—and control—only the *labor* of workers, and not the workers themselves, Southern landlords insisted on their right to limit the ability of people they called "their negroes" to change employers.

Control over land and credit provided the basis for one set of barriers to mobility. Many landowners limited the amount of land they would rent to each tenant in order to ensure that the sharecropper would cultivate the land intensively. Moreover, tenants with small plots were less likely to earn enough to permit them to advance into the ranks of landowners.

The goal was to keep black Southerners as dependent as possible on white landowners and merchants. Where the sharecropper was not dependent he could be tied down by contract. In most Southern states a sharecropping contract differed from most other contracts in that it was enforceable in criminal rather than civil courts. A sharecropper who skipped out after planting a crop would not be sued (he was not likely to have any assets anyway), but arraigned on criminal charges.

What really mattered, however, was not whether a tenant remained on a particular farm so much as whether a locality's total labor force remained stable. Local movement was expected and tolerated. Indeed, local movement provided frustrated and discontented tenants with an apparent choice of options, a reason to hope that a new chance might yield a better crop and brighter future. What was crucial was to limit the threat to the local labor supply, to ensure that come picking time there would be enough black men, women, and children to drag heavy sacks through the fields.

Assuming (incorrectly) that long-distance movement was largely the result of smooth-tongued recruiters, Southern landlords and employers went to considerable lengths to curb the "labor agent menace." States and localities across the South put considerable effort into keeping "their negroes" ignorant of outside opportunities. In 1900 the United States Supreme Court for the first time upheld the constitutionality of the laws requiring labor agents to pay licensing fees that were so high as to make it impossible to legally entice away a community's black workers. A flood of legislation followed, as state and local governments determined to protect their labor force from recruiters.

Recruitment laws had little effect, however. They were extremely difficult to enforce. Even more important, they ignored the influence of informal networks across the black South that carried information—and misinformation—about opportunities in developing sections of the region. What really kept black Southerners in place kept them not in particular communities, but in the regional economy as a whole: There were few alternatives—at least for men—beyond seasonal farm work. As the *Pee Dee Watchman,* a South Carolina black newspaper, explained in 1917, since the end of Reconstruction in the 1870s, "thousands desired to leave but could find no haven, no place where the demand for negro labor was greater than the supply."

Moreover, within the rural economy opportunities existed for employment during the slack season. A cotton crop requires spurts of intense activity—preparing the field, planting, hoeing, and harvesting—punctuated by intervals of monitoring. These intervals permitted family members who did not have primary responsibility for a crop to seek other employment.

Turpentine camps, sawmills, cottonseed-oil mills, and other industries tied to the rural economy provided young men with opportunities to earn cash wages. Young women ventured into cities and towns to earn extra cash washing, cooking, or cleaning. In most cases these individuals moved back and forth between town (or less frequently, city) and farm, with the longest interval coming after picking in the late fall and before planting time in March.

Leaving the countryside permanently, however, was a more daunting matter, especially for men. The new, expanding industries of the early-twentieth-century South offered few opportunities to black workers. Textiles, furniture, oil and gas, paper, chemicals—each contributed to the growth of Southern cities and Southern factories, each was interested only in white people as machine tenders.

Skilled positions in such new urban sectors as electrical production and streetcar transportation remained equally off-limits, while at the same time white workers were displacing blacks from nineteenth-century footholds in the skilled construction trades. Black men could find jobs in coal mines and in the iron and steel mills in the area of Birmingham, Alabama. But these represented exceptions to the general pattern of casual employment known as "negro labor." The urban economy thus meshed effectively with the rural. The plantation needed a stable labor force that could find outlets during slack periods; town and city employers looked to black workers to fill temporary needs usually involving a shovel or a broom.

Black women, on the other hand, had little difficulty finding urban employment as long as they were willing to work for a pittance. Middle- and upper-class white southerners expected black women to do their domestic chores. Wages for domestic workers were so low that even many white workers considered the availability of black "help" a part of their birthright. In contrast to Northern cities, where black servants were part of a labor market that included a large component of white European immigrants, Southern households invariably employed African Americans. And in contrast to a widespread pattern of live-in service among those immigrants, black women generally insisted on living at home. "They seem to think that it is something against their freedom if they sleep where they are employed," observed one employer whose dismissal of this sentiment stands in stark contrast to its accuracy. Nevertheless, in addition to a customary twelve- to fourteen-hour day, black women domestic workers often had to respond to demands for extra hours.

The servant's day was not only long, it was physically and emotionally difficult. Only servants for the wealthiest families could specialize as cook or nurse. "I'm looking for a nurse for my children," usually implied cleaning, cooking, and serving as well. That nurse also had to fight for her dignity in a household where as one woman noted, "The child I work for calls me girl." The man of the house could (and often did) present a very different kind of threat to a servant's dignity—pressure for sexual favors. One servant explained that she lost a job when "I refused to let the madam's husband kiss me. . . . He walked up to me, threw his arms around me, and was in the act of kissing me, when I demanded to know what he meant, and shoved him away." When the black woman's husband filed a complaint against her employer, he was arrested and fined twenty-five dollars.

Resistance to the regimen and the disrespect, however, was often more subtle than a generally useless formal complaint. Taking advantage of whites' assumptions about black women's carelessness, servants would appear to be careless. A hot iron purposely left too long on a garment could provide a fitting revenge against an employer who refused to permit a servant to take a quick trip home to visit her own children. Similarly, servants would invent holidays that their employers would grudgingly acknowledge. Whites chalked the festival up to "negro character" (they would never have used the word "culture")—something which they could never understand and felt was not worth figuring out anyway.

A woman who wanted a little more control over her time, especially to take care of her own family, would clean other people's clothes rather than their homes. The work was hard, and only slightly more remunerative than domestic service. And taking in laundry carried risks: One ruined or lost garment could bring a refusal to pay for a whole load. Like the sharecroppers whose landlord refused to pay a proper settlement, a laundress had no recourse to the courts when a dispute arose. Remarkably, washerwomen and domestics did strike, in some cases maintaining considerable solidarity. But the deck was stacked against any permanent shift in the balance of power between these women and their employers. Most women even preferred picking cotton to domestic work (it paid better), and white women in towns and cities across the "cotton belt" complained—or raised wages—when ripening cotton bolls attracted their servants to the countryside.

Residents of towns and cities were unlikely to find the countryside unfamiliar. Many had come from farms in the first place. Moreover, black urban neighborhoods in the South showed little evidence of the outpouring of services undertaken by cities of this era. African Americans generally lived on unpaved streets where such standard urban services as police, fire protection, garbage collection, and sewers were rare. As late as the mid-1920s Monroe Work, director of research at Tuskegee Institute in Alabama, could describe most of the Southern urban black population as living under "country conditions . . . just beyond the zones for water, lights, and other conveniences." Infant mortality was high, as were stillbirths. In this, as in so many other ways, the black South remained a rural world even as the proportion living in cities rose gradually from fifteen percent in 1890 to twenty-one percent twenty years later.

By the second decade of the twentieth century, cotton cultivation still employed more black Southerners than any other single activity. Men awoke at dawn and headed to the fields. Women awoke even earlier to prepare breakfast—sometimes eaten in the cabin and sometimes in the fields, where women often worked alongside their husbands. The two major slack periods in the cotton cycle—July and August, when the weeds had been hoed and the plants could be left with minimal attention, and the last two months of the year, after the cotton bolls had been picked—provided rural black Southerners with opportunities for leisure.

The first of these periods coincided with food harvests. Barbecues, religious revivals, and other community gatherings were common summer activities. The later months followed "settlement"; what little cash was realized from a year's labor could be devoted to generally secular Christmas celebrations, shopping either in town or from a mail-order catalog, and contemplating a change of scenery. Well into the 1920s, the rhythms of the black South synchronized with the patterns of cotton cultivation.

The black North and West, on the other hand, were distinctly urban. Cities housed seventy percent of all black Northerners and sixty-seven percent of black Westerners at the turn of the century. By 1910 the urbanized portion of the black population in both regions was close to eighty percent. As they did in the South, women were most likely to find work as domestic servants. Men occasionally had access to industrial jobs, but usually only as temporary strikebreakers replacing white unionists.

A small business class, complemented by an even smaller group of professionals, constituted the upper class in these communities. Craftsmen had difficulties finding employment, especially in cities with strong unions in the building trades, which generally excluded African-American workmen. In some cities, most notably on the West Coast, black men in such occupations as hotel waiters and bellmen were losing their jobs to immigrants from abroad. For most men, the tools of the trade all too often remained the familiar shovel, broom, or mop.

In many cities these workers lived in all or mostly black areas. In the largest cities, such as New York, Philadelphia, and Chicago, ghettos already had begun to emerge. But even where African Americans lived in racially mixed neighborhoods the trend was toward increased segregation. Blacks generally did not have access to housing elsewhere in the city, even if they earned enough to be more selective. Newcomers were immediately steered to districts known as "Little Africa" or the "Black Belt." African Americans who managed to circumvent efforts by real estate agents to keep blacks out of "white" areas were met with bombings or personal threats.

Black communities were diverse and included small business and professional classes. The middle class also included certain service workers. In Chicago, one of the most important judges of social standing in the black community was Julius Avendorph, whose job as personal assistant to businessman George Pullman entailed duties generally performed by a valet or a messenger. Only slightly further down the ladder stood the Pullman porters, men who worked the railroad sleeping and dining cars operated by Pullman's company. Their high status resulted in part from their relatively high job security and because many of them had high school—and in some cases even college—education.

Unlike their white counterparts, however, the black middle class—and even the minuscule black upper class—could not take advantage of the new housing available along transportation lines emerging from the city center. In a period when American cities were becoming increasingly segregated by class, African Americans remained residentially segregated by race instead.

## The "White Problem"

James Weldon Johnson remembered well his introduction to the full implications of what it meant to be a black man in the United States. As a student at Atlanta University in the 1890s he recognized that "education for me meant, fundamentally, preparation to meet the tasks and exigencies of life as a Negro, a realization of the peculiar responsibilities due to my own racial group, and a comprehension of the application of American democracy to Negro citizens." The future songwriter, diplomat, writer, and civil rights leader did not learn this in the classroom; rather, he learned it on campus and around town.

Johnson, of course, already knew that he was "a Negro," and that race mattered. He had grown up in Jacksonville, Florida, after the overthrow of Reconstruction.

Although his family was better off than most African Americans (his father was a headwaiter at a hotel, his mother, a teacher), they experienced the same exclusions, acts of discrimination, and affronts to their dignity that other black Southerners suffered as white Southerners began to reestablish white supremacy. The task for black Southerners was to teach their children how to accommodate the system without accepting either the system or their place in it as natural, just, or inevitable.

In the North things were not entirely different; they simply carried a different twist. W. E. B. Du Bois described a social snub he received in the 1860s in Great Barrington, Massachusetts, at the tender age of six:

> Something put it into the boys' and girls' heads to buy gorgeous visiting–cards—ten cents a package—and exchange. The exchange was merry, till one girl, a tall newcomer, refused my card,—refused it peremptorily, with a glance. Then it dawned on me with a certain suddenness that I was different from the others; or like, mayhap, in heart and life and longing, but shut out from their world by a vast veil.

One had to learn where the color line was, what it meant, how and when to cross it, and how to maintain one's self-respect when it could not be crossed. Thousands of African Americans would spend a good part of their lives trying to destroy that line.

By the 1890s a new generation of African Americans was reaching adulthood. These young men and women had never experienced slavery. They had experienced the violent overthrow of Reconstruction only as children. Unaccustomed to timidity toward whites and without vivid memories of the disillusion and despair following Reconstruction, they did not readily settle in places defined by the racial etiquette that had emerged during the previous two decades. This was especially true in cities and towns, where black populations were increasing despite the lack of regular employment for black men.

In an era when white Southerners were writing, reading, and reminiscing about a mythical antebellum South characterized by harmony between the races brought by slavery, these seemingly rootless young African Americans could seem threatening indeed. "The negroes are being overbearing and need toning down," declared one Louisiana newspaper in 1896.

Most white Southerners continued to believe that the descendants of Africans remained at a lower stage of civilization than Europeans and their descendants. In the early twentieth century, Southern historian Ulrich B. Phillips would describe the slave plantation as a school, and most white Southerners were certain that emancipation had freed a people who had been dismissed from the school of slavery too early. Black people who did not know their place, did not acknowledge their subordinate status, and did not recognize the folly of trying to reach too high were considered dangerous.

This notion of one's "place" was central to the role of African Americans in Southern life. Place referred partly to where "the Negro" could fit in the Southern economy: mainly in agriculture. Blacks were to grow the cotton. Jobs in the industries processing the cotton into cloth were generally reserved for whites. Where the "Negro's place" was not agricultural, it was servile.

Place also referred to the location of African Americans in Southern culture, a subordinate role that was enacted and reenacted on the street, in the store, and elsewhere in the daily lives of Southerners.

The prevailing ideas about race, coupled with the inheritance of the plantation economy, contributed to the development of a legal system that left blacks peculiarly vulnerable to domination by their employers and landlords. "What could we do?" declared a black Georgian forced to work without pay to settle a fraudulent debt. "The white folks had all the courts, all the guns, all the hounds, all the railroads, all the telegraph wires, all the newspapers, all the money, and nearly all the land."

A white attorney in Mississippi explained in 1914 (six years before taking office as a judge) that "an important branch of the law here in Mississippi" was "Negro law." This law was unwritten, and at its center was the premise of African-American powerlessness.

Given how easy it was for white landlords and employers to call the shots, they considered it essential that African Americans remain in the South at the bottom of the heap—available for work that nobody else would do. Any education black Southerners received should not, as one Southern governor put it, give them aspirations "beyond the sphere of negro life."

The concern with blacks not accepting their place reveals a lasting tension within Southern white culture. On the one hand, early-twentieth-century white Southerners tended to be confident that their black workers, tenants, and servants were "amiable." African Americans thus constituted the perfect labor force: easily coerced, unlikely to organize, and readily available because they supposedly lacked the ambition and aptitude to do anything else.

Existing side by side with this confidence, however, was a set of fears. Those whites who saw blacks as a race teetering on the edge of barbarism worried about the aggressions lurking beneath the thin veneer of amiability. Moreover, white Southerners either remembered Reconstruction or had grown up hearing the recollections of their parents—recollections enveloped in myths of evil white Northerners bent on revenge and profit and allied with illiterate black legislators intent on legalizing racial intermarriage.

These memories were furthered poisoned by the myths of corruption and incompetence that hid the accomplishments of the relatively rational, clean, and progressive state governments of the Reconstruction period. But they also included accurate images of black men voting, carrying guns, and taking their landlords to court. The danger of black political participation was clear to white Southerners who wished to learn from history rather than repeat it.

White Southerners had perfectly good reason to fear that African Americans did not accept things the way they were. Black men were moving around more, finding employment in the expanding seasonal turpentine and lumber industries. Less tied to the land than their parents, young African Americans were increasingly moving to the city, especially after the depression of the 1890s sent cotton prices cascading downward. Women were welcomed as domestics but men had no settled place in the urban economy. Strikes by black domestic workers, longshoremen, lumber workers, and railroad men were unusual events, but point to an increased unwillingness among black workers to accept their place.

Black men and women were also determined to become educated. Between 1870 and 1910, the literacy rate among black Southerners increased from nineteen percent to sixty-one percent.

By the last decade of the nineteenth century, many white Southerners were growing increasingly concerned that their black neighbors, employees, servants, and tenants would not accept their place. It seemed that protocol and custom no longer held behavior in check. Even intimidation required more effort.

In cities reports of blacks resisting arrest had been on the rise since the late 1880s. Complaining of black servants referring to one another as "Miss Johnson" or "Mr. Jones," one Louisiana newspaper identified the nub of the issue: "The younger generation of negro bucks and wenches have lost that wholesome respect for the white man, without which two races, the one inferior, cannot live in peace and harmony together."

To some white Southerners the answer to this apparent threat to white supremacy lay in increased levels of intimidation. The result was an epidemic of lynching in the South, beginning in 1882 and rising to a peak a decade later.

But lynching was a disorderly way to go about maintaining order. Southern white elites—men who published newspapers, owned plantations, sat on the boards of banks and railroads, and pulled strings behind the scenes in the Democratic party—recognized that violence outside the legal system undermined the majesty of the law. Politically, however, it was unwise to condemn lynching more forcefully than a gentle chiding after each grisly murder of an African American. Lynchings, after all, were community events, festivals that parents attended with small children, holding them high in the air to afford a better view of the victim twisting in a noose or burning at the stake.

Lynchings were not only disorderly. They also gave the region bad press in the North. This was the early heyday of "yellow journalism," a new kind of newspaper publishing that attracted readers by appealing largely to their emotions. Lurid tales of Southern violence provided good copy, especially when tinged either with accusations of sexual violence or with a crowd's determination to cut off a victim's

A twin lynching in Marian, Indiana, on August 8, 1930. The Ku Klux Klan had moved to the urban North and West during the 1920s and gained its greatest influence in Indiana.

sexual organs. White Northerners, drawing on a long tradition of satisfying their consciences by expressing sympathy to black victims of Southern racism, seized on vivid descriptions of lynchings as continued evidence of Southern backwardness.

These twin threats posed by lynching—disregard for legal procedures and the possibility of federal intervention generated by outrage from the North—roused the Southern white establishment. White disorder had to be curbed, a task that required eliminating the instability and uncertainty in race relations that underlay that disorder. Blacks had to be kept in their place by other means. Across the South, state constitutions, state legislation, and city ordinances were rewritten to enshrine in law the subordinate place of black people in Southern life. Black male Southerners would no longer vote or serve on juries. Separation of the races would be required by law.

Poll taxes, property and literacy qualifications for voting, and the institution of the "white primary" were effective measures. In Mississippi, the president of the 1890 constitutional convention straightforwardly declared that "we came here to exclude the Negro," and the delegates did their job. Only black men who were economically independent or regarded by whites as "good" or "safe" Negroes remained on the voter rolls. By the turn of the century, only 10 percent of black men in Mississippi were registered to vote. Forty years later that proportion had dwindled to 0.4 percent (2,000 registered voters out of approximately 500,000 possible voters). Among Alabama's 181,471 African American men of voting age in 1900, only 3,000 were registered to vote. Across the South, the proportions were similar, and black voting remained insignificant until the 1960s.

Disfranchisement, or the stripping of people's right to vote, was an attack not only on black political influence—of which there was precious little by the turn of the century—but also on black manhood. Nineteenth-century Americans tied manhood and citizenship closely together. Both hinged on independence. Cast as naturally docile, unable to control their sexual passions, and economically dependent, black men were labeled as unfit for citizenship. Denying them the ballot reinforced their exclusion from the civic community.

The logical next step was to minimize disorder by minimizing contact between the races. Between 1890 and 1915, legislators across the South, as far west as Texas and Oklahoma, enacted Jim Crow laws that ensured, regardless of how interdependent the races might be in the South, they would not inhabit the same public spaces. In the most ordinary and yet meaningful way African Americans in the South would constantly be reminded—especially in cities and towns—that they were people without social honor, people whose dignity had no official existence, people who were not a part of mainstream society.

In most cases the trains and railroad stations were the first targets of Jim Crow laws. One waiting room was marked "colored," the other "white." Next, rules of conduct were passed for streetcars—whites were seated from front to back, blacks from back to front. Some streetcar companies considered this a foolish business practice, expensive and needlessly antagonizing their large black clientele. But the laws required segregation. For the races to sit alongside each other was to imply equality; front to back versus back to front reminded one and all who belonged in front and who belonged in the back.

The legislation quickly extended to nearly all aspects of public life. Anything worth doing or building outside people's homes was worth a segregation ordinance: hotels, restaurants, restrooms, drinking fountains, parks, schools, libraries, saloons, telephone booths, theaters, doorways, stairways, prisons, cemeteries, and brothels. In some communities the ordinances even specified the size of the ubiquitous "whites only" or "colored" signs. Florida required separate storage facilities for school textbooks. In Georgia, courtrooms had two Bibles for swearing in witnesses.

This obsession with race, which reached its apex in the first decade of the twentieth century, was not unique to the South. Throughout the United States, the concept of race had become an increasingly important way of categorizing people and cultures. World atlases published during this period were less interested in economies or social systems than in the particular races inhabiting one place or another. Relying on the dominant theories in the social and physical sciences, powerful decision makers in government and industry divided the American population into a staggering array of "races": Armenians, Gypsies, Ruthenians, Jews, Syrians, Greeks, Italians, Africans. Each was a separate race, and each had its own distinct characteristics.

Northern industrialists devised hiring policies reminiscent of eighteenth-century Southern slaveholders who had been certain that Africans from one area made better slaves than men and women from another part of the continent. Thus Poles and Slavs were presumed to be suited to tasks requiring great physical exertion; Jews, Italians, and Portuguese supposedly had an aptitude for lighter, repetitive tasks that required a keen eye or nimble finger. Italians were unstable and untidy "but not destructive," noted one Milwaukee industrialist, who lamented that they drank too much (though less than the Greeks), quarreled, and did not understand modern machinery. Hungarians, although "thrifty and honest" in the view of another employer, were not clean. In most variations of this complex scheme, "Africans" were considered inefficient, incapable of mechanical labor, emotional rather than rational, oversexed, and in general a cut below everyone else.

The South differed from the rest of the country in the relative simplicity of its racial roster. There race remained largely a question of black and white. White Northerners and Westerners, although equally inclined to think in racial terms, were less likely than their Southern counterparts to translate those ideas into a system of rigid distinctions embodied in the law. They shared white Southerners' assumptions about the capabilities of the descendants of Africans, but the diversity of the population in these regions complicated the equation.

In the West, "Asiatic races," especially the Chinese, seemed a more threatening presence than the small black population. There was, of course, considerable variation. James Weldon Johnson, a performer traveling with his brother in 1905, could secure no hotel accommodations in Salt Lake City. They had considerable difficulty even finding a place to eat. A few days later in San Francisco they easily secured a room and dined without incident. Yet even in San Francisco patterns were uneven. The manager of a leading hotel there explained at the turn of the century

At the peak of its power in the 1920s, the Ku Klux Klan marches down Pennsylvania Avenue in Washington, D.C., in 1926. Its members hid behind masks and robes as they terrorized black citizens. Catholics and Jews also attracted Klan hatred during the 1920s.

that incidents seldom occurred, largely because "the colored people who travel . . . do not often place themselves or us in embarrassing positions."

In the North, race was complicated by the multiplicity of European nationalities. Blacks were not essential to the labor market. Their ability to vote generally aroused little concern because their numbers were relatively small until the 1920s. Few whites considered their presence a threat to social stability. This would begin to change in the 1920s, as social theories increasingly reduced "race" to a triad of black/white/yellow (with American Indians either a fourth race or thrown in as descendants of Asians), and as a growing black population came to play a major role in urban culture and politics. Until the First World War, however, "race" as a division between two groups was largely a Southern way of thinking.

Because most Southern states by the first decade of the century had passed laws governing race and social interaction from marriage to public transportation to circus entrances and exits, it was essential to create usable definitions. How did one decide who was "a Negro"? Skin tones, after all, could suggest only so much in a society in which Africans, Europeans, and Indians—none of whom were uniformly tinted to begin with—had mingled over the centuries.

In New Orleans, for example, the population was considerably more diverse than elsewhere in the South. Because of a long history of sexual relations between people of European and African descent, skin hues ranged infinitely. A streetcar official explained why the new segregation law required clear, if arbitrary, definitions: "Our conductors are men of intelligence, but the greatest ethnologist the world ever saw would be at a loss to classify streetcar passengers in this city."

Apparently the only possible solution was to "eyeball" passengers and rely on conventional assumptions about the physical characteristics that distinguished "black" from "white." Indeed, this was the approach of the United States Bureau of the Census, which instructed its enumerators until 1920 to categorize an individual by estimating the proportion of African blood according to color and other features.

This might work for the census, but racially segregated institutions needed more exact ways of determining inclusion and exclusion. The color line had to be defined to regulate such important civic activities as school enrollments, marriage, and jury service. A question with serious social implications everywhere in the United States also had wide-ranging legal implications in the South.

Southern states divided roughly equally in how their laws defined race. Approximately half defined "a Negro" as anyone with "a trace of black ancestry." Nearly all the rest identified anyone with at least one-eighth "Negro blood" (one great-grandparent) as "colored." Yet this solution to the problem of categorization was neither inevitable nor "natural." Why should a child with one parent of European descent and one parent of African descent be a "Negro"? How much genealogical research was to be required to define someone's legal status?

Elsewhere in the Western hemisphere, societies used a broad variety of categories. Even in the United States the terms *mulatto* (half and half), *quadroon* (three white grandparents, one black), and *octoroon* (one black great-grandparent, seven white) were frequently used, both in popular speech and even (at least in the case of "mulatto") in the United States Census until 1920. Indeed, the decision to drop "mulatto" as a category that year resulted from bureau estimates that seventy-five percent of all African Americans were of "mixed blood," and eyeballing the difference between "Negroes" and "mulattoes" was impossible. Anyway, the only categories that mattered were those required by the Southern laws. "One drop" of Negro blood sullied the purity of whiteness, pushing an individual across the color line.

The legal existence and meaning of these categories was ratified by the United States Supreme Court in 1896, when it ruled in the case of *Plessy* v. *Ferguson* that state laws requiring racially segregated facilities were permissible under the Constitution as long as the facilities were "equal." They never were. But it would take nearly sixty years for American law to recognize that inequality. Not until 1954 would the Supreme Court begin dismantling Jim Crow by ruling in *Brown* v. *Board of Education* that "separate educational facilities are inherently unequal."

## Building Communities

The Independent Order of St. Luke was in trouble. Founded in Maryland in 1867 to provide sickness and death benefits to dues-paying members, the order had flourished for two decades, rapidly expanding to New York and Virginia. But in 1899, in part because of the deepest economic depression the nation had yet experienced, the organization was virtually bankrupt. After thirty years in office its chief executive resigned, leaving his successor $31.61 in cash and $400 in debts.

The new Grand Worthy Secretary, Maggie Lena Walker, assumed her position at a fraction of her predecessor's salary. Under her leadership the Order of St. Luke not only survived but flourished. From 57 councils with 1,080 members, it grew to 2,020 councils with more than 100,000 members in 28 states. Guided by Walker's commitment to expanding economic opportunities for African Americans, the order established programs for black youth, an educational loan fund, a weekly newspaper, a department store, and a bank. Walker and her colleagues in St. Luke led a boycott against segregated streetcars in Richmond, Virginia, in 1904. The *St. Luke Herald*, the organization's paper, took positions opposing segregation, lynching, and discrimination against black job seekers.

Maggie Lena Walker was the first woman in the United States to serve as president of a bank. Born in Richmond, Virginia, in 1867, Walker graduated from that city's Colored Normal School (a teachers' college) sixteen years later. By then she already had shared the work experience of most urban African-American women, helping her widowed mother with child care and with the laundry taken in to make ends meet. Her degree qualified her to teach in Richmond's segregated black schools, but she was forced to resign when she married.

Walker had joined the Independent Order of St. Luke when she was fourteen and by 1899 had held numerous leadership positions in the organization. During the next three decades she would supplement her leadership of the Order of St. Luke with active involvement in the woman suffrage movement, Richmond Council of Colored Women, Virginia State Federation of Colored Women, National Association of Wage Earners, International Council of Women of the Darker Races, National Training School for Girls, Richmond Urban League, and the National Association for the Advancement of Colored People.

Maggie Lena Walker's career suggests both the challenges faced by African-American communities in the early twentieth century and the diversity of initiatives fashioned by black leadership to meet those challenges. Although she was speaking of women in particular, Walker effectively described where African Americans as a group stood and where they had to go: "To avoid the traps and snares of life," they would have to "band themselves together, organize . . . put their mites together, put their hands and their brains together and make work and business for themselves."

Walker was calling for what her biographer has termed a "community of struggle." This community could be diverse, encompassing men, women, and children; businesspeople and domestic servants; preachers and sinners. It also could accommodate differences of opinion. But to be a community capable of moving forward it would have to encompass a people aware of their common past and shared future. The long agenda suggested by Walker's career meant that no single approach, no focus on any single organization, could define African-American leadership or purpose.

For African Americans in the early twentieth century this struggle had two related and mutually supportive components. One was to build community institutions such as schools, churches, businesses, clubs, and lodges within the African-American world. The other was to fight for integration into American institutional life, to integrate schools, workplaces, residential neighborhoods, public accommodations like hotels and restaurants, and especially councils of government. Even today these goals are often presented as alternatives, warring strategies competing for the loyalty of people forced to choose one path or the other.

Presenting these alternatives as a harsh choice is misleading. Although particular leaders and institutions did express competing visions and emphases, activism took place simultaneously at many levels. When rural black Southerners banded together to build a school, they were engaging in self-help while at the same time yielding to segregation. But they also were resisting white assumptions about the appropriate form of education for their children. They were insisting on a literacy that defied Southern white definitions of their "place." To build a school was to participate in the struggle for equality.

Yet the quest for integration did not always reflect a desire to mix with white people. Despite the ruling of the U.S. Supreme Court in *Plessy* v. *Ferguson* that separate institutions were constitutional only if they were equal, African Americans recognized that in practice separate always meant unequal. Thus blacks frequently fought for integration into white institutions in order to gain access to better services or commodities. By living among whites, a Los Angeles journalist observed, black Californians could secure "the best fire, water, and police protection."

Robert and Mary Church Terrell made the same judgment in Washington, D.C. As the first president of the National Association of Colored Women, Mary Terrell was one of the most prominent women in the United States. Robert Terrell was an attorney and eventually a federal judge. They did not necessarily want to live among white neighbors, she later recalled of their search for a house. But housing in "white" neighborhoods was "more modern" (in other words, better equipped and in better condition). It also was less expensive. Real estate agents selling homes in "Negro" neighborhoods could price properties higher because African Americans had access to only a small portion of the city's housing market. For the Terrells and others, the struggle for integration did reflect sentiment for increased contact across the color line. But even many integrationists were wary of whites, seeking integration only because the color line divided the powerful from the powerless.

Whether building community institutions or battering the walls of racial separation and discrimination, African Americans had to mobilize limited resources. These resources included a long history—dating from slavery—of community life built on families and religion. In the rural South the other major institution to emerge after emancipation was the school. In towns and cities these institutions joined with women's clubs, fraternal societies, businesses, and social service organizations to shape African-American community life and provide the basis for activism.

Other than the family, the oldest African-American institution was the church. By the beginning of the twentieth century the church brought together African Americans as no other institution possibly could. In 1906 more than half of the nearly seven million African Americans ten years or older belonged to churches, a proportion comparable to patterns among white Americans. Much more striking is the number of African Americans united in a few particular organizations. The National Baptist Convention, the largest black institution in the United States, claimed more than 2.2 million members. The African Methodist Episcopal (AME) church constituted the second largest denomination, with nearly 500,000 members.

Like most white Southerners, African-American Christians tended to be fundamentalists, men and women who read their Bibles literally and worshiped energetically. Especially in the rural South and in working-class urban churches, black Americans demanded that their ministers evoke emotional responses with powerful sermons. A pastor's ability to "shout" his congregation (to arouse a vocal expression of passion during the sermon) measured his leadership as well as his spiritual credentials.

The greatest heights of ecstasy were often reached in Holiness and Pentecostal churches, which emphasized the importance of a worshiper's personal experience with the Holy Spirit. At first attracting both black and white Southerners, Holiness and Pentecostal sects grew most rapidly after 1910. Subsequently, as Southerners moved north and west these sects expanded, especially into the urban Midwest.

African-American churches were not, however, merely places where people went for relief from the burdens of everyday life. "The social life of the Negro centres in his church," W. E. B. Du Bois observed in his 1899 study, *The Philadelphia Negro*. "Baptism, wedding and burial, gossip and courtship, friendship and intrigue—all lie within these walls." Many ministers and deacons (lay leaders) complemented their inspirational roles with political activity, or served as community spokesmen. In middle-class churches, where emotional behavior was rejected as "undecorous," a pastor might provide intellectual leadership as well.

In rural areas and small towns, churches often were the only gathering places available outside of small business establishments. People would come together in the church to discuss building a school or respond to a threatened lynching. They would share information and opinions about migration to the new "black towns" being established in Oklahoma, to agricultural areas touted by labor agents, or to Northern cities.

Although Southern cities had other gathering places, churches still functioned as one of the most important community institutions. Social services and emergency support were especially common because so many black Southerners could secure only irregular employment. A strong sense of extended family helped, providing a network of support during periods of unemployment. Beyond the family lay the church, whose members gave freely when they could and received without shame when in need.

In Atlanta, most black churches took an "after collection" each Sunday, to be distributed to members in financial distress. Fifth Street Baptist in Louisville collected and distributed clothing, paid for funerals of members unable to afford proper burial, awarded an annual college scholarship, and held annual fundraising drives for an orphanage, a home for the elderly, and a local black college.

Northern churches were likely to add to this traditional form of charity with programs influenced by early-twentieth-century progressive reform movements. Under the leadership of Reverend Reverdy Ransom, the Institutional AME Church in Chicago resembled a settlement house, providing a wide variety of social services to the neighborhood. After finding a job through Institutional's employment bureau, a black worker could leave her child at its kindergarten or day nursery. Classes in sewing, cooking, stenography, and typing taught useful skills. Leisure opportunities included concerts, lectures, a reading room, and a gymnasium.

More typical in its less ambitious program was Antioch Baptist Church in Cleveland, which sponsored boys' and girls' clubs, choral groups, and a recreation center located in two adjacent houses. Destitute members received cash assistance. North and South, black churches and denominational associations published newspapers, provided social welfare services, helped congregants find jobs, and provided recreational facilities.

These activities required time and money. In most black churches the greatest energy came from the volunteer labor of the women who raised money from communities that had little cash to spare. The role of women as church activists was particularly evident in the National Baptist Convention, where they constituted two-thirds of the membership. In 1906, forty-three percent of all female African Americans who had reached their tenth birthday belonged to the National Baptist Convention. Men, however, dominated the organization's leadership, occupied the pulpits, and controlled the finances.

Just as African Americans in general looked to the church as an institution independent of white domination, black women determined that they needed an organization within the church that would provide them with a similar degree of independence. Founded in 1900, the Woman's Convention of the National Baptist Convention quickly grew to one million members, providing many women with their introduction to community activism.

This experience in local churches and in the Women's Convention brought many black women into the emerging women's club movement. The National Association of Colored Women grew quickly, from five thousand members in the late 1890s to fifty thousand in the 1910s and one hundred thousand a decade later.

Membership in the NACW came mainly from the urban elite—generally teachers and wives of professionals, ministers, and businessmen. These women shared with their white peers a concern with upholding traditional standards of morality and respectability amid the turmoil of movement from country to city and changes in employment from farm to factory. And, like black men, they organized to challenge the increasing level of racism at the turn of the century.

Black clubwomen recognized that their destiny was inextricably intertwined with less-privileged African Americans. If they could elevate other black women to their standards of morality and manners, then the black masses would be lifted up from the gutter of poverty and degradation. At the same time they would win from white America the acceptance they deserved by dint of their middle-class values and position.

Although the NACW did achieve recognition as an affiliate of the largely white National Council of Women in 1901, black women generally encountered difficulties with major women's reform organizations at the turn of the century. As the suffrage, temperance, and women's club movements moved toward national organization, they had to consider the sensibilities of white Southerners.

The urge to participate in "white" clubs and in "white" feminist organizations did not necessarily signal a desire to turn away from the black community toward a largely white social environment. White women who worried that black women seeking to join their suffrage organizations or the Women's Christian Temperance Union sought "social equality" deluded themselves. Black women simply recognized that these larger, more broadly based organizations could provide stronger backing and more visible platforms.

Indeed, like other black institutions, black women's clubs and reform societies owed their existence only partly to exclusion from white institutions. Black communities faced problems different from those confronted by white reformers. Like their white counterparts, NACW affiliates sponsored kindergartens, day nurseries, training schools, orphanages, and clubs for mothers. But they did so in response to a community with unique needs and limited resources.

Black women's clubs represented a type of institution whose roots lay in African-American fraternal societies (lodges) and mutual benefit associations. The distinctions between the two kinds of voluntary organizations were not always clear. Generally lodges were places for recreation for their members, and membership in a lodge was considered a badge of social respectability. Mutual benefit associations, by contrast, were likely to focus more on insurance functions, especially death benefits.

By the end of the century, these organizations had increasing overlapping functions. Nearly all provided members with burial and life insurance. Some, like the Independent Order of St. Luke, which was unusual in that it included both men and women, operated small businesses or banks. Nearly all provided opportunities for leadership.

Membership in a fraternal order could provide African-American men with a badge of respectable manhood within the community. A black man denied civic recognition in the Jim Crow South was somebody when he wore the uniform of the Elks, Knights of Pythias, Masons, Oddfellows, or any one of a number of other lodges. The largest order was the Oddfellows, with more than 300,000 members by 1904.

North and South, fraternal and sororital organizations were an integral aspect of urban culture among the mass of working-class black men and women. In the North, lodge membership provided men with political connections and stature. Robert R. Jackson, who was elected to the Illinois legislature in 1912 and was a major player in Chicago politics for two decades, belonged to approximately twenty-five fraternal orders.

There was no clear line between clubs and fraternal societies. But clubs were more likely to be exclusive and perhaps have reform or political orientations; fraternal societies were more likely to be national organizations with broad memberships. Fraternal societies were also more likely to perform business functions. Like the Order of St. Luke, most lodges took their burial and life insurance functions seriously. The first African-American insurance companies grew out of these and similar activities among church-related mutual benefit societies. Because companies controlled by whites charged blacks higher premiums—supposedly because they had higher mortality rates—black companies had a ready market for their products. So did African-American banks, since white banks seldom solicited business in the black community. Significantly, black banking and insurance companies first developed in the South, where black communities were larger and the color line was clearest.

The most dramatic example of how fraternal orders could evolve into financial institutions can be seen in the history of the Grand United Order of the True Reformers. William Washington Browne, an ex-slave and Union Army veteran, founded the organization in Richmond, Virginia, in 1881, with the intertwined goals of building a business and advancing the race. Secret ritual, regalia, a grand annual convention with a colorful parade: Each provided members with opportunities for camaraderie and ceremony within an organization also dedicated to community service. At the same time, Browne's wife found a way to earn profits with a regalia factory that she established in the True Reformers' building.

From the beginning the order's mission included mutual benefit activities. The insurance business grew so rapidly that by 1888 Browne saw an opportunity in the need to deposit and invest the cash it generated. By the turn of the century, the True Reformers counted 100,000 members and had expanded into real estate, printing, and undertaking in addition to operating an old-age home and a hotel. All catered to a black clientele.

North and South, there was a noticeable rise in black business enterprise at the beginning of the twentieth century. To a considerable extent this bustling business activity was the result of the increasing segregation of African Americans into urban ghettos. But it also was part of a broader change in the social and economic life of urban black America.

In the nineteenth century black businessmen and even professionals had enjoyed a small white clientele in many cities. These men constituted an elite, an "upper crust," within their communities. Their social networks were generally distinct from those of other African Americans. In many cities, especially in the North, they worshiped at black churches (or in a few cases even predominantly white churches) affiliated with "white" denominations: Episcopalians, Presbyterians, Congregationalists. This group would remain the "upper crust" of black America, but by the turn of the century it was giving way to a new business and professional class, men and women who made their living serving an African-American clientele.

This transition in community leadership was personified in the career of John Merrick, a former slave who accumulated savings as a barber and owner of six barbershops in Durham, North Carolina. Merrick also sold insurance for the True Reformers. His prosperity, however, was due in large part to the stability and status provided by his position as personal barber to the white tobacco magnate James Buchanan Duke. He parlayed this stake into a much larger fortune during the first decade of the twentieth century, when he drew on his experience with the True Reformers to join with two other African-American entrepreneurs to form the North Carolina Mutual Life Insurance Company.

Southern cities like Durham led the way in the growth of an African-American business class catering to African-American consumers. The largest enterprises were insurance companies and banks, but small shops were the most common form of black enterprise. What mattered to the mainly black clientele was how they were treated—with respect and in a businesslike fashion. A woman could not try on a hat in a Southern downtown store; once it sat on her head it was a "Negro hat" (or worse, a "nigger hat") that the white shop owner could not in good conscience sell to a white customer. At the pharmacy a black druggist did not expect his customers to bow and scrape, or to stand aside until all the white customers were served.

Making a virtue out of necessity, many influential black Southerners declared that the race's future lay in a "group economy." Black businesses catering to black

# THE GIFT OF THE GOOD FAIRY

ONCE upon a time there lived a Good Fairy whose daily thoughts were of pretty little boys and girls and of beautiful women and handsome men and of how she might make beautiful those unfortunate ones whom nature had not given long, wavy hair and a smooth, lovely complexion. So she waved her magic wand and immediately gave to those who would be beautiful a group of preparations known from that time, fifteen years ago, until to-day and at home and abroad as

## MADAM C. J. WALKER'S SUPERFINE PREPARATIONS FOR THE HAIR AND FOR THE SKIN

Wonderful Hair Grower
Glossine
Temple Grower
Tetter Salve
Vegetable Shampoo

Vanishing Cream
Cleansing Cream
Cold Cream
Antiseptic Hand Soap
Complexion Soap

Superfine Face Powder (white, rose-flesh, brown)
Floral Cluster Talcum Powder
Antiseptic Dental Cream
Witch Hazel Jelly

Results from the use of our preparations especially noticeable in the hair and skin of children.

*Very liberal trial treatment sent anywhere upon receipt of a dollar and a half.*

## THE MADAM C. J. WALKER MFG. CO.

**640 North West Street**    *Dept. 1-X*    **Indianapolis, Indiana**

Madam C. J. Walker was probably the first African-American woman to become a millionaire.

customers would employ black men and women, creating a racial self-sufficiency rather than the individual self-sufficiency envisioned by so many rural black Southerners since emancipation.

In most cases, however, such businesses were precarious enterprises whose owners had little extra cash for emergencies or to tide them over during occasional slow months. The limited clientele had little to spend and often needed short-term credit to weather bouts of unemployment. Retail shops sold small items, more likely to be priced in cents than in dollars. Corner groceries, barber shops, beauty parlors: All were unstable operations. Retail businesses were especially risky because whites (often European immigrants with few other business opportunities) could open stores in black neighborhoods and compete, largely because they had greater access to borrowed money and supplies. Barbering, undertaking, and beauty shops, on the other hand, did not face competition from white entrepreneurs reluctant to deal with black bodies.

One of the manufacturing opportunities open to black entrepreneurs lay in supplying cosmetics to African-American beauticians. Among the earliest of these manufacturers was Madam C. J. Walker, a St. Louis laundress who in the 1890s developed the first commercially successful hair-straightening process. The daughter of ex-slaves, she grew up in Mississippi as Sarah Breedlove; she later took her name from her second husband, Charles Joseph Walker. By the 1910s the Madam C. J. Walker Manufacturing Company stood at the center of an empire of approximately twenty thousand managers, sales agents, clerks, and factory workers. Walker, who died in 1919, was probably the first African-American woman to join the ranks of American millionaires.

Walker's business success was unusual, but not unique. Other African Americans accumulated fortunes in the cosmetics business, in some cases opening schools to train beauticians in their particular method and, of course, tying that method to a particular line of products. Anthony Overton established the Overton Hygienic Manufacturing Company in Kansas City, Kansas, in 1898 and moved the company to Chicago in 1911. Sales of such products as High Brown Face Powder provided him with sufficient resources to diversify into real estate development and journalism. But all of this remained within a black world. Overton developed property in Chicago's South Side ghetto, known to many as "Bronzeville"; his newspaper, the *Chicago Bee,* had few white readers or advertisers.

This business class, however, remained small. With an even smaller professional class, and many businessmen barely holding on, the top of the class structure of urban black communities was extremely limited. Except at the very highest levels, status tended to depend less on wealth or on white definitions of occupational prestige than on notions of "refinement" and "respectability" maintained by the upper and middle classes. The few professionals tended to dominate the highest rungs, with the more secure businessmen (most were, in fact, men) close behind.

In northern cities, postal workers, porters serving railroad travelers in luxurious

Pullman cars, and servants employed by the best hotels and wealthiest white families constituted much of the solid middle class. Other workers with stable incomes and some education could also claim middle-class status. What often mattered most was property ownership, preferred leisure activities, and membership in an appropriate club, lodge, or church.

This group, based in black businesses and social institutions, seized the mantle of African-American leadership in most urban black communities around the turn of the century. They replaced the older elite whose commitment to integration sometimes led them to oppose building separate institutions to serve the community. In many cities, for example, it was clear that if blacks wanted a YMCA it would have to be a segregated institution. Banks, hospitals, professional baseball teams, social service institutions, political organizations—North and South, their existence often depended on the willingness of black communities to accept segregated institutions.

Baseball provides a typical example of the shift from blacks' slight access to white institutions to the establishment of a segregated black world. In the nineteenth century, a handful of black players joined white athletes on professional diamonds. By the early twentieth century they had been driven out, relegated to all-black barnstorming tours and marginally successful leagues.

Only after the First World War, under the tenacious and imaginative leadership of Rube Foster, owner-manager of Chicago's American Giants, would the Negro National League establish a stable setting for black baseball. Black players flourished in this new arrangement, but they did so under conditions far inferior to those of their white counterparts. Yet the teams constituted a source of pride to the black communities that they represented. Whatever their individual team loyalties, black fans pulled together on the few occasions when Negro League stars competed against white major leaguers.

These separate black institutions caused mixed feelings among black Americans. On the one hand, segregated institutions owed their existence to the exclusion of blacks from "mainstream" American life. In some cases African Americans even paid taxes for public facilities from which they were excluded. Finally, separate was almost never equal. African-American institutions such as schools, clubs, businesses, and athletic leagues nearly always lacked the facilities, money, and equipment available to their white counterparts.

At the same time, however, segregated institutions permitted community control over important cultural activities. A baseball team, a YMCA, a hospital, a retirement home—black communities could proudly claim these as their institutions maintained by and for African Americans.

## Schooling for Leadership

In the early twentieth century, education was one area in which African Americans confronted the tension between the high price of segregation on the one hand and the advantages of community control on the other. Descended from slaves denied by the law any access to literacy, twentieth-century African Americans recognized the importance of education in the advancement of both individuals and the race as a whole. Black children needed schooling, and black Americans needed those schools to teach the values and skills required of a new generation of men and women who would lead the march toward equality and full citizenship.

Before the Civil War most Northern states had either excluded black children from public education or shunted them into separate schools. In some cities black communities and white abolitionists established private schools for black children. During the 1870s and 1880s, however, Northern state legislatures reversed legislation requiring segregation and even went so far as to prohibit the exclusion of children from their local school on the basis of race.

By the early twentieth century, many of the emerging ghettos in Northern cities were not yet sufficiently compact to enable white city officials to draw school district lines that would segregate neighborhood schools. In such cases black children attended schools that were predominantly, but not exclusively, African American. They were not the best schools their cities had to offer. They were housed in older buildings, often were overcrowded, and many of the white teachers looked down on their students. But they were decent schools, capable of providing students the opportunity to graduate from a high school that met the academic standards of the time. The schools were fully supported by tax dollars and taught by instructors with appropriate academic credentials.

Black Northerners valued these schools, and their children were less likely than the children of European immigrants to drop out as teenagers. They also valued integration, rising in protest whenever pressures emerged from segments of the white citizenry to segregate the schools. Most African Americans assumed, wisely, that the presence of whites guaranteed a certain degree of commitment from city politicians.

At the same time, however, Northern black communities had little control over what was taught or who stood in front of the classrooms. Nearly all school officials were white; so were the teachers, most of whom assumed that black children could not perform as well as their white peers. Some teachers simply assumed that the "white race" was more intelligent and more disciplined. Others who were more liberal extended sympathy to black children who they thought were crippled by the cultural heritage of African backwardness combined with the traumas of slavery. The cost of full integration into the system, even if not into completely integrated schools was clear: These were institutions *for* African Americans; but they were not African-American institutions.

By contrast, in most of the South black children went to schools staffed by black teachers and black principals. But the facilities varied from inadequate to abysmal. By the early twentieth century most Southern black children had some access to a public school, but in rural areas that school was likely to be open for less than six months of the year—even as little as two months in some cases. White planters wanted black children in the fields, not wasting their time sitting on the crude benches of a one-room schoolhouse.

In 1915, only fifty-eight percent of all black school-age children in the South were enrolled in school at all, compared with eighty percent of whites. City kids were the most likely to be in school. Attendance rates of black urban children lagged only slightly behind rates for whites, a remarkable comparison because few cities provided public high schools for black children.

In most Southern cities, especially in the Deep South, white civic leaders considered the education of black children an extravagance, a decision consistent with school systems that readily placed as many as sixty-five black children in dilapidated classrooms headed by a single teacher. The *Atlanta Constitution* left little doubt as to its idea of how much schooling black children needed, defending black education on the basis of its ability to "make a better cotton picker and a more efficient plowman."

By 1915, following a decade of unprecedented expansion in high school education in the South, neither Georgia, Louisiana, Mississippi, North Carolina, nor South Carolina had yet built a high school for black teenagers. The enlightened officials of Delaware, Florida, and Maryland had established a single black high school in each of these segregated states. During this period most American communities were transforming high school from a privilege available to those who could afford private school to a right funded by the taxpayers. Southern black youth were denied that right.

Tragically, black adults were among the taxpayers who supported the very school systems that allocated them only crumbs from an expanding pie. To provide better opportunities for their children, black Southerners had to mobilize their communities and do the work themselves. In effect, they paid twice—once for a public school system that allocated them a fraction of the money available to white schools and a second time to supplement those meager resources or pay tuition at a private black high school.

In many cases the additional burden was paid with labor rather than dollars, as many black Southerners had little more than their hands, tools, and skills to spare. Thousands of black public schools in the rural South were erected in the early twentieth century through donations from Chicago philanthropist Julius Rosenwald (the president of Sears, Roebuck & Company), who required that each community match his contribution dollar for dollar. In most cases public funds from white-controlled sources—that is, from taxes—amounted to less than the hard-earned cash generated within the black community.

In addition to contributing to the construction of public schools, black Southerners built private schools, especially at the high-school level. At the turn of the century three-fourths of all Southern black high-school students attended a private school. Coming from grossly inadequate grammar schools, many of these students required remedial classes, further straining the already precarious budgets of these institutions.

Neither public nor private schools in the South were controlled by African Americans. Public school teachers and principals had to answer to white officials, most of whom cared less about whether black children were being educated than whether they were learning anything that threatened social stability. In Palmetto, Georgia, a teacher was dismissed for merely expressing his approval when President Theodore Roosevelt invited the exceedingly moderate black leader Booker T. Washington to dinner at the White House.

African-American private schools owed a different kind of allegiance. Although by the early twentieth century nearly all of these were headed by African Americans, they still depended on the contributions of Northern white philanthropists for a considerable portion of their budget. And in rural areas they remained vulnerable to white public opinion, which tolerated a black private school only if it clearly was not educating its students out of their place. Northern philanthropists, in part because they envisioned an increasingly industrialized South with a black work force, aimed for a considerably higher level of literacy than most white Southerners thought black children would ever need.

In spite of these limits on the independence of Southern black educators, many black schools were, in fact, community institutions. Black children were taught by black teachers partly because black parents had demanded this change during the closing decades of the nineteenth century. White officials had given in to this demand for financial reasons: Black teachers earned less than their white counterparts. But the large-scale entrance of African Americans into the teaching profession is significant nevertheless. These men and women played active roles in their communities, organizing women's clubs, farmers' clubs, boys' clubs, school improvement leagues, and various other self-improvement efforts.

African Americans looked upon schooling as a privilege—one that carried with it an obligation to use one's learning on behalf of the entire community. And teachers joined lawyers, social workers, librarians, nurses, doctors, and newspaper reporters and publishers as leaders of their community.

These educational institutions stood at the center of major divisions among black leaders about the role of African Americans in American society. All the schools taught the same basic values of industry, thrift, and service to the community. They recruited similar types of students. But curriculum and school leadership reflected different notions of how black Americans could attain full citizenship in a nation seemingly committed to their subordination. To what kinds of jobs should they aspire? How should they respond to the rising tide of segregation? Where should they look for allies? How hard should they push for immediate equality when few whites even considered African Americans capable of eventual equality?

Booker T. Washington's gospel of hard work, landownership, self-help, and success through small business struck genuine chords among most black Americans. To some, however, his accommodationist philosophy and the Atlanta Compromise conceded too much. John Hope, a young Southern educator and future college president, considered it "cowardly and dishonest for any of our colored men to tell white people or colored people that we are not struggling for equality."

William Monroe Trotter, editor of the *Boston Guardian* (founded in 1901), was even more scathing. Washington's willingness to accommodate to Jim Crow, along with his success in forging alliances with white businessmen, proclaimed Trotter, exposed him as "a coward" and a "self seeker." He was "the Benedict Arnold of the Negro race, the Exploiter of Exploiters, the Great Traitor," Trotter wrote.

In 1903 a more measured—and eventually more influential—challenge to Washington emerged in the form of a book, *The Souls of Black Folk*, by W. E. B. Du Bois. Du Bois, Trotter, and Hope stood out as spokesmen for a more militant response to the rising tide of racism, but they hardly stood alone. Residents of Southern cities, many of them people who admired Washington and acknowledged his distinction, participated in boycotts of Jim Crow streetcars between 1898 and 1904. In a few instances black Southerners even filed unsuccessful court suits challenging the legality of segregation ordinances.

In the North, where nineteenth-century black elites had developed ties to prominent whites and participated in a handful of integrated institutions (including high schools, colleges, political organizations, and an occasional club or philanthropic society), an older generation refused to abandon the goal of integration. The younger men and women of this class were less influential within the community than the rising class of black business and professional people catering to a black clientele. Nonetheless, many of this younger black middle class remained loyal to their parents' ideals and emerged as some of Washington's most articulate critics.

Moreover, despite Washington's ability to influence the editorial policies of most black newspapers, Trotter's was not the only militant editorial voice. Harry T. Smith, editor of the *Cleveland Gazette,* not only assailed any evidence of racial discrimination but he denounced the establishment of black facilities meant to provide services that comparable white institutions refused to provide to African Americans. He and others of like mind in Northern cities insisted that to build a black facility made it easier for the whites to maintain their policies of exclusion. Chicago's black leadership had rejected a segregated YMCA in 1889 on these principles. Smith dismissed Washington's Atlanta Compromise as a "doctrine of surrender."

For much of the African-American leadership at the beginning of the century, politics involved more than a choice between racial integration or self-help, protest or accommodation, liberal or vocational education. Alliances shifted. Lines were never neat and clean. Du Bois broke with Washington eight years after the Atlanta

Compromise speech. Mary Church Terrell publicly supported Washington while fighting for suffrage—for African Americans and for women.

Robert Abbott, editor of the *Chicago Defender,* was a graduate of the vocationally oriented Hampton Institute who believed that all black children should learn a trade and advised black Southerners to "stick to the farm." He admired Washington and praised Tuskegee as a great black institution. At the same time his headlines offered very un-Washingtonian advice to black Southerners: "WHEN THE MOB COMES AND YOU MUST DIE TAKE AT LEAST ONE WITH YOU."

Yet there were occasions when black people felt they had to line up, to take a particular position. Led by Du Bois and Trotter, a small group, nearly all from the North and mostly urban college graduates, met in 1905 to form the Niagara movement. The movement was named for its meeting place on the Canadian side of Niagara Falls, a major terminus of the Underground Railroad. Du Bois had encountered difficulty arranging hotel accommodations on the American side. The following year the group met at Harpers Ferry, West Virginia, the site of John Brown's famous raid on behalf of abolitionism.

The Niagara movement denounced white racism and demanded full citizenship for blacks and the abolition of all racial distinctions. At the same time it underscored the increasingly significant double bind facing African-American workers: Industrial employers hired them only as temporary strikebreakers, and most unions excluded them from membership.

Two events in 1906 underscored the immediacy of the Niagara movement's agenda, while at the same time pointing to the ineffectiveness of black protest up to this point. In August of that year President Theodore Roosevelt ordered the dishonorable discharge of three companies of black soldiers after they were accused of inciting a riot in Brownsville, Texas. Evidence of their responsibility was thin at best. They were more likely victims of violence than instigators. Their mistake, apparently, was in fighting back.

Roosevelt's "executive lynching" demonstrated that black Americans had few friends in high places. They had even fewer in the streets. In Atlanta, a month after the Brownsville incident and following a spate of local newspaper articles that fictitiously reported assaults on white women by black men, a mob of more than ten thousand white citizens freely attacked African Americans. The attacks continued for five days, and the police generally refused to interfere. The city's white establishment blamed the riot on irresponsible journalism and overreaction by lower-class whites. Nevertheless, most white Atlantans shared the mayor's conclusion that the bottom line was "black brutes [who] attempt rape upon our women." Once again, whites associated lynching with rape when in fact there had been no rape.

By 1908, the Niagara movement's weakness was as obvious as its astute analysis of the crisis of American race relations. Few of the movement's four hundred members bothered to pay dues; most of the black press ignored it as a handful of cranky elitists hurling manifestos. Whites paid even less attention.

The Niagara movement represents a turning point because of its view of race relations in the United States and its militant agenda for change. Its collapse coincided with an event that shocked the small portion of the Northern white population that considered racism a major "problem" in American life: lynchings and mob attacks on African Americans in Springfield, Illinois. The violence was ignited by a spark recognizable to anyone familiar with the behavior of Southern lynch mobs: A white woman had accused a black workman of rape (she later recanted, admitting that a white man whom she refused to name had beaten her). When the authorities removed the accused man from town to protect him from enraged white citizens, a mob gathered, determined to make the black community pay a price for its supposed tolerance of such criminal behavior. Five thousand soldiers were required to restore order after whites attacked black businesses, homes, and individuals.

White Northerners had condemned the Atlanta riot but had explained away the terrorism by blaming it on the peculiar backwardness of the South. But in Abraham Lincoln's hometown, on the centennial of the great emancipator's birth? This event pushed the minority of white reformers who already had begun to question Booker T. Washington's accommodationist agenda to consider the views of Du Bois and the "radicals."

In 1910, the remnants of the Niagara movement joined with a small group of reformers—mostly white—who had met the previous year in response to the Springfield riot. Their new organization, the National Association for the Advancement of Colored People (NAACP), began with a straightforward agenda: to secure the basic citizenship rights guaranteed by the 14th and 15th Amendments to the United States Constitution. Most specifically this meant the end of all segregation laws, a right to equal education, and a guarantee of the right to vote.

The NAACP would publicize discrimination whenever and wherever it occurred, lobby legislatures and Congress for civil rights legislation, and file lawsuits grounded in constitutional law. It also launched a campaign against lynching, which used research and on-site reports to undermine the standard Southern defense of lynching—that its real cause was black criminality and uncontrolled sexuality. Tame by twentieth-century standards, the NAACP departed significantly from Washington's accommodationism.

Like the Niagara movement, the NAACP was led mainly by elites. But it also sparked enthusiasm among two groups that the Niagara radicals had not tapped: the black middle and working classes, and white liberals. Although Du Bois was the only African American in the original "inner circle" of the organization, African Americans dominated the membership from the beginning. By 1918 the NAACP monthly magazine, *The Crisis* (founded and edited by Du Bois), claimed a circulation of 100,000. In the rural South many enthusiasts read and circulated the journal at considerable risk.

As African Americans like James Weldon Johnson and Walter White moved into more leadership roles after 1916 and local branches multiplied, the organization

This cartoon, entitled "The Next Colored Delegation to the White House," appeared in *The Crisis* in 1916. It ridiculed the racist views of President Woodrow Wilson, a native of Virginia.

solidified its place at the center of the African-American protest movement for the next half-century.

Equally crucial—and more controversial—was the level of white involvement, especially in the early years. Disdainful of efforts that depended on white goodwill, William Monroe Trotter remained skeptical of the organization's potential and kept his distance. Men and women at the other end of the social spectrum from the Harvard-educated Trotter were probably equally skeptical.

But the great portion of black leadership was moving toward a position best articulated by Ida B. Wells. Wells identified power as the bottom line. Washington was right in arguing that it was useless to wait for whites to help. Blacks should build whatever economic power they could. And he was right, she said, to argue that it was foolish to forget that power lay in white hands and that any strategy had to recognize that blacks were playing a weak hand. But Wells took this analysis a step further. She insisted that militant protest was both possible and effective if it could reach an audience of potentially sympathetic whites. America did not have a "Negro problem," she explained. It had a white problem.

### The "Second Emancipation"

On August 25, 1893, Frederick Douglass stood wearily before a large audience at the World's Columbian Exposition in Chicago. The former abolitionist, journalist, and Republican politician had been chosen to deliver the principal address on the occasion of "Colored American Day" at the fair. The "Day" itself was controversial among African Americans. Many viewed the gesture as token recognition insufficient to compensate for their exclusion from planning and presenting exhibits. Separate, unequal, and subordinate, the special day smacked of Jim Crow.

Ida B. Wells advised African Americans to stay away from the exposition completely. Douglass shared Wells's anger, but the aging orator was reluctant to pass up the chance to expose American hypocrisy on an international stage. He denounced the nation that, proud of its own freedom, denied meaningful freedom to many of its own citizens. "There is no Negro Problem," Douglass proclaimed, only the problem of Americans refusing to "live up to their own Constitution."

Douglass's long career was coming to a close in 1893. With the approach of a new century he was passing the mantle of leadership to a new generation. Wells, Booker T. Washington, and W. E. B. Du Bois had already claimed roles in this African-American vanguard. They would eventually be joined by a member of Douglass's audience, a young Georgian who would emerge as the voice of hope for tens of thousands of black Southerners, a "Black Moses," in the words of his biographer. His name was Robert Sengstacke Abbott.

Abbott came to the fair not to agitate but to entertain. Taking his place on the stage with the other three members of a vocal quartet from Hampton Institute, the twenty-five-year-old tenor was as captivated by the Windy City itself as he was by the inspiring words of Douglass and the excitement of performing at the great exposition. Like thousands of other fair visitors Abbott sensed that the future lay in Chicago.

After learning the printer's trade at Hampton, Abbott returned to Chicago in 1897, hoping to begin a career as a journalist. Ida B. Wells had resettled in Chicago two years earlier, resuming her career as a journalist and a crusader against lynching. That two ambitious young African Americans would share this interest is not surprising. The African-American press stood at the center of black American urban life and politics in the early twentieth century. Even in the rural South, religious newspapers permitted communication across county and state lines, connecting African-American communities to one another.

In the South, black newspapers filled columns with brief, but revealing, articles, usually noting when a woman—or occasionally a single man—was visiting relatives. A reader of the *Norfolk Journal and Guide,* for example, would learn that "Mr. Lonnie Jones, Norfolk, visited his parents, the Rev. and Mrs. Jones in Durham, North Carolina." These items were more than "filler"; readers wanted to know

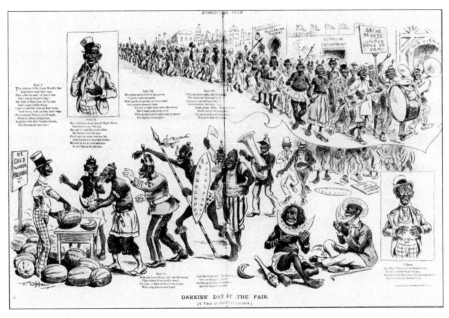

The cartoon "Darkies' Day at the Fair" appeared in the British humor magazine *Puck*. It satirized the display of Africans at the World's Columbian Exposition in Chicago in 1893, which Frederick Douglass and other African Americans found extremely offensive.

where people came from and who they visited. The linkage of family life, generation to generation, across distances great and small had become an important part of African-American culture.

The idea of movement itself, an important theme in American history in general, has held special significance to the African-American experience. Upon emancipation many former slaves had tested their freedom by moving, if only a few miles to the next plantation. The impulse and its significance were so powerful that sixty-five years later, a woman declared an end to an interview about her early years as a slave by asserting her freedom to come and go. "I can go when I please and come back when I please. I'll come to see you, I must go home now. I am a free rooster."

Merely thinking about moving could boost the endurance of black workers who recognized that limited opportunities meant that moving along—rather than moving up—would eventually provide relief from their toil—at least until they began work someplace else.

For men, sawmills, turpentine camps, phosphate mines, and coal mines provided endless opportunities to move from place to place. Some were merely looking for work during breaks in the agricultural routine. Others sought liberation from farm life entirely. Cities promised more community life but fewer jobs, except in places like Birmingham, Alabama, where the steel mills provided unusual (though still limited) industrial opportunities. Women, always in demand as servants and laundresses, could more easily find stable employment. Families could, and did, move to the coal towns stretching across Appalachia south toward Birmingham. Some sought agricultural opportunities farther south in Florida, or—more often—west to the Mississippi Delta, Arkansas, and Texas. These destinations within the South drew African Americans who either persisted in their hopes to attain independence through landownership or whose frustration kept them on the move but with no other apparent alternative.

Frustration and alienation, however, could also provide the foundation for hope, for faith in the ability of black people to turn their backs on their "white problem" and build their own alternatives. Some were attracted to a growing movement to establish "black towns," mainly in Oklahoma, but also as far west as Allensworth, California. The most common, and most enduring destination for potential black emigrants was Liberia, which had come to be considered a haven from American racism.

For most black Southerners, however, leaving the South meant moving north. And moving to the North meant the city. Northern farmland was expensive and most Northern rural communities expressed sympathy for oppressed blacks only as long as they remained oppressed *Southern* blacks.

Even in cities, as Robert Abbott learned, opportunities varied from nonexistent to scarce. Like other African-American craftsmen, most of whom had been trained in the South, this skilled printer found it impossible to find regular employment in a Northern city. Abbott took short-term printing jobs while attending Kent College of Law at night—the only African American in his graduating class. But the Chicago bar was no more hospitable to blacks than most of the city's neighborhood bars.

The rapidly growing metropolis of nearly two million people needed plenty of attorneys, but African-American legal business for the most part had to be generated by the small black community of thirty thousand people. An established core of black attorneys left little space for outsiders. Even within that community, Abbott found that his skin color put him at a disadvantage. A prominent African-American lawyer once curtly informed him that he was too dark to be effective in a courtroom.

Abbott returned to irregular employment as a printer, but with a larger goal in mind. On a May evening in 1905, he appeared on the streets of black Chicago selling the four-page *Chicago Defender,* which on its front page proclaimed itself "The World's Greatest Weekly." He began with virtually no money; the publisher and editor was also the reporting staff, business manager, and sales force. His landlady's kitchen table doubled as his desk.

Although the obstacles facing Robert Abbott illustrate the difficulties confronting black newcomers to Northern cities in the early years of the century, his actual experience was unusual. Black Southerners struggled mightily to provide their children with a decent education, but few young men or women reached the heights of a secondary or college degree. Moreover, Hampton, Tuskegee, and their offshoots encouraged graduates to remain in the South, to assume positions of leadership in their communities.

Black Southerners did move North during the early years of the twentieth century, but they did so in small numbers. Most came from the border states rather than such Deep South states as Abbott's native Georgia. Educated or uneducated, urban or rural, male or female, black Southerners who thought about the possibility of a better life elsewhere had to face the reality that earning a decent living in the North was close to impossible.

After building the *Defender* into a stable business, Abbott turned to the region of his birth and advised black Southerners that they should confront Southern racism rather than try to escape it. "The only wise thing to do," he declared in 1915, "is to stick to the farm." By then, however, increasing numbers of black Southerners were finding this advice difficult—if not impossible—to follow. A series of natural disasters during the preceding decade had struck with particular force in the cotton belt. In addition to boll weevils who "eat up all de cotton," drought followed by flood plagued Southern farmers. Consecutive years of poor crops in some counties had made it difficult for farmers to obtain credit, a necessity for tenants and owners of small farms. Hard times, however, were nothing new for black Southerners. They had endured Jim Crow for a generation. Most knew no life other than one of hard work with poverty as its reward. It is unlikely that a substantial number would have left the South as a result of these setbacks.

Something new was happening, however, in the North. The beginning of the First World War in Europe in 1914 sent shock waves across the Atlantic, stimulating the American economy while shutting off its traditional source of industrial labor. American manufacturers could earn astronomical profits, selling first to the European combatants and, by 1916, to a domestic market on the verge of conversion to a wartime economy. But where would the additional workers be recruited? The war had stopped immigration from Europe. Within a year American entry into the war would divert thousands of men from the labor force to the armed forces. New sources of labor would have to be found.

Labor shortages hit first on the railroads, which were traditional employers of large numbers of casual laborers. By 1916 these men could find more secure and lucrative jobs in factories. Before railroad companies would turn to African Americans, however, they had to exhaust other alternatives. Some railroad executives assumed that they could recruit Mexicans to perform the regular track maintenance required every spring in the Northeast and Midwest. Other railroad executives looked to a different labor source. "By starting track work early," one executive explained, it would be possible to complete this chore with "American labor. The American hobo caught in the spring of the year will work."

Leaving aside this common assumption that the category "American" did not include African-American workers, such approaches reveal that employers considered the shortage temporary, requiring little rethinking of traditional assumptions about the ability of black men to do a "white man's job." Referring to employment patterns in Northern cities, the magazine *New Republic* observed in mid-1916 that "the Negro gets a chance to work only when there is no one else."

The notion of "no one else" depended not only on ideas about race, but also about gender. Many employers first reconsidered whether white man's work was necessarily man's work. During the First World War thousands of white women moved into meat packinghouses, munitions and chemical factories, electrical industries, and other workplaces previously reserved for their husbands, fathers, and brothers. But stereotypes about gender were powerful, and employers generally considered women unsuitable for most types of industrial work.

In the packinghouses, for example, women could stuff and pack sausages but they were considered incapable of such tasks as herding animals, butchering, or lugging meat. To keep the production lines running, therefore, industrialists were forced to experiment with employing black men, generally referred to as "the Negro." The experiment spread to black women when new opportunities for white women left jobs open at the bottom of the hierarchy of female work. For the first time in American history, the nation's basic industries offered production jobs to African Americans. From New York, Boston, and Philadelphia to Pittsburgh, Chicago, Detroit, and to a lesser extent Los Angeles, factory gates opened.

Work in railroad yards, steel mills, food-processing plants, garment shops, and other industries paid wages far beyond what was available in the rural or urban South. But it was more than the money that attracted black Southerners north. These jobs also represented portals into the industrial economy. These opportunities promised a new basis for claims to full citizenship—a promise that a previous generation of black Southerners had envisioned in the possibility of landownership.

Approximately 500,000 black Southerners moved between 1916 and 1919, with twice that many following during the 1920s. This movement, known as the "Great Migration," would ebb and flow until the 1970s, shifting the center of gravity of African-American culture from the rural South to the urban North. Southern cities drew increasing numbers of men and women from surrounding counties, many of whom stayed only long enough to earn enough money to move to the relative prosperity of the North. Employment in the coal mines of Appalachia drew thousands of others north as well. Smaller numbers headed west, especially toward Los Angeles, which by 1900 had surpassed San Francisco as the largest African-American community in that region. But the best opportunities and the highest wages lay in the North. What the North offered was a new start; Robert Abbott called the Great Migration a "second emancipation."

The men and women who translated the opening of new opportunities into a vast population movement had good reason for their optimism. These were not refugees blown across the winds of historical change. Rather, this was a movement of men and women who first sought information and then traveled established routes to destinations already inhabited by friends or relatives.

In the earliest months of the Great Migration—the fall and winter of 1916–17— recruiters working for Northern industry attracted attention in the South with stories of high wages and better living conditions in the North. Many of these recruiters were actually black workers visiting "home" with instructions (and cash incentives) from employers to recruit "reliable" friends and relatives.

In other cases black Southerners readily accepted offers of jobs and even free transportation only because they had already heard from other African Americans about the new opportunities and the differences in race relations. Men working in railroad yards and on trains, for example, could readily spread information along the tracks.

Chicago enjoyed a special reputation, because it was the home of the best-selling black newspaper in the South, the *Chicago Defender*. Fearless, sensational, and militant, Robert Abbott's newspaper expressed a perspective that was dangerous, if not impossible, for black Southerners to maintain in the presence of whites. Red ink announced lynchings, and readers were encouraged to fight back.

Abbott's advice shifted focus when jobs became available in Northern cities. Like other business leaders in Northern black communities he recognized that migration from the South promised opportunity not only for migrants, but also for African-American businesses and political interests. He became the primary cheerleader for "The Exodus," at one point fueling the bandwagon by setting a specific date for people to participate in a "Great Northern Drive."

Innumerable other links joined North and South, city and country. Fraternal organizations and church conventions met in different cities each year, providing opportunities to visit, see the sights, and listen to hosts brag. Returning home for weddings, funerals, or just to show off their accomplishments, migrants flaunted city clothes and spoke of voting, going to big league baseball games, and passing white people on the street without having to step into the gutter.

Alighting in a train depot downtown could stimulate exhilaration, which writer Richard Wright recalled feeling when he looked around the station for the familiar "FOR WHITE" and "FOR COLORED" signs that hung over water fountains, bathrooms, snack bars, and elsewhere in Southern terminals. He paused at a newsstand, feeling a tinge of anxiety as he exchanged coin for newspaper, "without having to wait until a white man was served."

For some, this sense of liberation was tempered by a combination of uncertainty, anxiety, and even fear. The famed musician Louis Armstrong later recalled his terror upon disembarking in a Chicago train station in 1922. He scanned the crowd, unable to locate his mentor Joe Oliver, who had made the same journey from New Orleans a few years earlier:

I saw a million people, but not Mister Joe, and I didn't give a damn who else was there. I never seen a city that big. All those tall buildings. I thought they were universities. I said, no, this is the wrong city. I was fixing to take the next train back home—standing there in my box-back suit, padded shoulders, double-breasted wide-leg pants.

Armstrong's anxiety, one that characterized millions of immigrants to American cities decades before and after he made his move, was very different from Wright's. Armstrong worried about city life. Wright pondered the difficulty of making the transition from a region where the rules of interaction (and separation) were spelled out and inflexible to the more ambiguous patterns of the North.

## The Promise of the Cities

The Thomas family arrived in Chicago in the spring of 1917. Like thousands of other black Southerners moving north at the time, their first task was to find a home. For a week they pounded the pavements of the South Side ghetto. To look elsewhere would have been futile. In Chicago the "black belt," along with a few other scattered neighborhoods, provided the only housing available to African Americans. The parents, their nineteen-year-old daughter, and a son two years younger crowded into a five-room apartment—cramped, but probably larger than the farmhouse they had left behind in Alabama.

The second task was to find work. The men went off to the stockyards; the women turned to the familiar trade of wringing the dirt out of other people's clothing. Optimistic about the future, the teenagers spent their evenings in night school, hoping to improve on the grade-school education they had brought with them from a rural Southern schoolhouse. In their free time the family explored the leisure activities available on Chicago's South Side, carrying picnics into the park and venturing into theaters and ice-cream parlors.

This family's experience hardly invokes the idea of a "second emancipation." The Thomases struggled with the mundane aspects of everyday life that confront anyone who leaves home to begin a new life elsewhere. For poor people this was a particularly daunting challenge. For African Americans in the first half of the twentieth century, most choices also were limited by racial discrimination. By 1918 migration chains linking South and North enabled thousands of Southerners to choose destinations where they had friends or relatives to offer a welcoming hand. A Southern town, city, or county might develop links to many Northern cities, but a particularly strong connection usually reached toward one or two potential destinations.

In most cases these patterns conformed to lines of longitude, largely because of railroad routes. North and South Carolinians went to New York, Philadelphia, and other eastern seaboard cities. Pittsburgh's African-American newcomers were likely to hail from Alabama, Georgia, or Kentucky. From Mississippi, Louisiana,

Tennessee, and parts of Georgia and Alabama, people headed for Chicago—an especially popular destination because of the influence of the *Chicago Defender* and the long tentacles of the Illinois Central Railroad.

Arriving during a wartime housing shortage, most migrants encountered difficulty finding a home. Choices were limited. In the largest cities, emerging African-American ghettos provided obvious starting points, with New York's Harlem and Chicago's South Side especially well known among Southerners. In medium-sized cities like Cleveland, Milwaukee, and Buffalo, the process of ghettoization had begun before the Great Migration, but there was not yet a district so dominated by black residents that the neighborhood seemed segregated. In Los Angeles most blacks lived in an area that stretched thirty blocks along Central Avenue, but as late as 1919 their neighbors included Mexicans, Italians, and Russian Jews.

In some cases local geography was a crucial factor. Pittsburgh's hills and hollows, breaking toward the rivers, contrasted sharply with Chicago's flat prairie or the unbroken expanse of Manhattan Island. African-American steelworkers in the Pittsburgh area did not inhabit a single district, instead congregating in a series of steel mill communities with the largest concentration in Pittsburgh itself. Still, however, they tended to live in enclaves, in neighborhoods that became increasingly segregated during the First World War and the 1920s.

In general northbound migrants entered cities where housing segregation had proceeded far enough to exclude them from most neighborhoods. But the state of flux was such that in most cases a black Northerner in 1920 was likely to have at least a few white neighbors within a couple of blocks. By 1930, that likelihood had diminished considerably, with African Americans segregated into ghettos—neighborhoods dominated by a single group excluded from other parts of the city.

Ghettos are not, however, necessarily slums. Harlem, in particular, was not a slum on the eve of the Great Migration. A middle-class neighborhood barely a decade earlier, it suffered from overcrowding during and after the war. Most urban black neighborhoods were less fortunate at the outset, with aging housing stock ill suited to the rapid influx of newcomers beginning in 1916.

Segregation by itself did not cause a decline in either housing standards or the quality of a neighborhood. What segregation meant was that neither black newcomers nor established residents could move beyond the borders of the emerging ghettos, except for gradual expansion at the fringes of these neighborhoods. The result was overcrowding and a strain on the physical capacity of buildings.

This strain was also a result of the economics of ghettoization. Contrary to popular belief, property values have not always declined as neighborhoods shifted from "white" to "black." During the Great Migration and throughout much of the twentieth century the process was more complicated. As Southerners, most of them poor and unaccustomed to urban life, moved into the least expensive and oldest neighborhoods, established residents tended to seek better housing in less crowded districts. But ghettos could expand only slowly, and only at their edges.

Real estate speculators purchased homes in these border districts, often by frightening white homeowners with the prospect of "Negro invasion." Known as "blockbusting," this tactic yielded generous profits, as the investor could sell the properties to black home buyers at inflated rates. In Los Angeles, for example, the markup (in essence a race tax) went as high as one hundred percent. African-American purchasers had nowhere else to go because of the limitations defined by a dual housing market: one set of choices for whites, one (more limited) for blacks. In Northern and Western cities, African Americans generally paid more than whites would pay for equivalent living space.

At the same time, however, black workers earned less than their white counterparts. What this meant was that African Americans spent an inordinate proportion of their income on shelter. In Harlem, rents generally commanded nearly half of the earnings of African-American residents, placing a considerable burden on family budgets. There and elsewhere, the solution often lay in transforming a home into a commercial enterprise. Families rented out rooms to lodgers, often relatives or former neighbors recently arrived from the South.

Lodging, however, constituted only one type of residential overcrowding. In the long run, the deterioration of buildings probably owed more to a different way of crowding more people into limited spaces—the division of houses and apartments into smaller units by landlords eager to squeeze out more rent. Real estate investors who operated in the "white" market made profits by developing what are known as "subdivisions," large tracts of land divided into individual lots for residential construction. Building a subdivision increased the value of the land and its environs.

On the African-American side of the dual housing market, a very different kind of "subdivision" took place, one that was equally profitable but that eventually drove values down rather than up. An investor would purchase a single-family home or an apartment building and divide the structure into a rabbit warren of small apartments, known in some cities as "kitchenettes" and in others as "efficiency units." These spaces were efficient because their inhabitants (often families) slept, cooked, ate, socialized, and relaxed in a single room. The rental income from these converted buildings yielded a quick profit, thereby increasing the value of the property. But these buildings deteriorated equally rapidly, due to shoddy renovation and inadequate maintenance.

The dual housing market contributed to the deterioration of some African-American neighborhoods in other ways as well. With a captive market for their properties, landlords collected rents more assiduously than they maintained their buildings. Tenants who demanded proper maintenance (and many of them did) would usually be replaced with newcomers who either knew little about what to expect or took what they could get because choices were few.

African Americans who purchased homes often overpaid because of their inability to shop throughout the city. In some cases this left homeowners without enough money to maintain their houses adequately. Despite the continuing presence of middle-class African-American neighborhoods, invisible to whites who blithely equated slum with ghetto, the trend was downward.

During the First World War and sporadically during the 1920s it was easier for black newcomers to find places to work in Northern cities than to find places to live. The Great Migration itself was catalyzed by the opening of thousands of new railroad jobs, mainly laying track and performing manual tasks around rail yards. By 1917, although still largely excluded from industrial work in the West, African Americans were working in heavy industry across the Northeast and Midwest.

On the whole these black men and women were relegated to jobs disdained by their white counterparts, who took advantage of wartime opportunities to advance into more skilled positions. Most of these jobs in steel mills, auto plants, packing-houses, and rubber factories required little skill and could be learned quickly. The hardest part for many migrants from the South was probably the adaptation to a different approach to time—an adjustment confronted by generations of rural workers around the world upon their introduction to industrial employment.

In the rural South, as in other agricultural societies, the calendar and the weather determined the rhythm of work. Planting, cultivating, and harvesting were performed at the same time each year, but with variation according to the weather. Cotton cultivation was characterized by one planter as "a series of spurts rather than by a daily grind."

But this would not work on an assembly line in Detroit. By the early twentieth century, workers in most Northern factories were punching time clocks. Arrive ten minutes late and your pay was docked one hour. On the "disassembly lines" of the packinghouses, conveyer belts moved carcasses from worker to worker, each of whom would make a single cut. Tardiness or absence could disrupt the whole process. Moreover, once the line began moving, the newcomer had no control over the pace of work.

Newcomers to industrial labor also had to accustom themselves to repeating a single task rather than completing an operation from start to finish. A man who formerly butchered a whole hog now performed only a single task among more than a hundred. A woman accustomed to picking up dirty laundry from customers and dropping it off cleaned and ironed might take a job in one of the many mechanized laundries employing thousands of black women in Northern and Southern cities. There she could spend hour after hour, day after day, only pressing cuffs, yokes, or sleeves.

Most migrants, however, not only stayed with these jobs but encouraged their friends and relatives to join them. The hard work produced rewards during the war years and the 1920s. In interviews and in letters back home, migrants spoke enthusiastically of sending their children to school, voting, sitting where they pleased on the streetcars, and other accomplishments.

Migrants to Southern cities encountered a somewhat different employment picture. With fewer basic manufacturing industries than Northern cities, places like

Louisville, Norfolk, Nashville, and Mobile provided fewer opportunities. Industries directly related to war production, especially shipyards in coastal cities, provided most of the new jobs. But where black men in the North generally held onto their foothold at the bottom of the industrial ladder until nearly the end of the 1920s, their Southern counterparts suffered the fate of black women: When the war ended most were pushed back into menial service employment.

Northern employers were willing to permit black industrial workers to keep their positions in part because they had learned during the war that these men could do the job. But the decision drew equally on two other factors: immigration restriction and the threat of unionization. Beginning in 1921 federal legislation limited immigration from nations outside the Western hemisphere to a trickle, once again forcing industrialists to look beyond European immigrants for a supply of new workers.

At the same time, union organizing campaigns in major industries during the war had convinced Northern employers that maintaining racial divisions within their work force was a strong weapon against unionization. When African-American workers passed through factory gates to their new jobs during the war, they had a reputation among white workers and employers as instinctively anti-union. This image was not entirely accurate. Black Southerners had joined unions as early as 1872 on the New Orleans docks. In cities across the South, black carpenters and bricklayers had joined segregated union locals around the turn of the century.

On the whole, however, few black workers did belong to unions, largely because most unions either excluded them from membership or simply made no attempt to organize them. In addition, most unions at the time organized mainly skilled craft workers such as carpenters, bricklayers, plumbers, printers, and cigar makers, showing little interest in the agricultural and service occupations in which most African Americans worked. Only the United Mine Workers (UMW) and the Industrial Workers of the World (IWW) systematically organized unskilled workers.

The IWW had little presence in areas populated by African Americans, although it did have some success among black dockworkers in Philadelphia and timber workers in the Louisiana forests. The UMW stood alone among major national unions in its willingness and ability to enlist African-American members. But even among the mine workers, racial divisions frequently hampered the ability of the union to maintain solidarity. Thus when white union workers went on strike, employers could—and occasionally did—tap a substantial pool of underemployed and nonunion African Americans to replace the strikers. In coal mines and packinghouses, on the railroads and in hotel restaurants, African-American workers had filled the places of white unionists on strike since the closing decades of the nineteenth century.

Between 1917 and 1921, unions undertook major organizing campaigns most notably (in terms of the role of black workers) in steel, meat packing, and coal. Except in the Appalachian coal mines these campaigns made little headway in the

South, but in major industrial centers across the Northeast and Midwest workers joined by the thousands. What made a difference was that for the first time, unions in steel and meat packing organized by *industry*, as coal miners did, rather than by *craft*, or specific occupation, as workers did in the building trades. In addition union leadership recognized that black workers were now part of the industrial labor force and would have to be included if an organizing campaign were to succeed.

Many black industrial workers did join unions during and immediately after the war, but more either dropped out quickly or never joined at all. Some black workers had difficulty appreciating the sincerity of the unions' welcome, given the record of racial exclusion and the continuing hostility among white workers and local union leadership in some areas. Others were reluctant to risk the jobs that had provided the path out of the Jim Crow South. Perhaps most important, however, was the difference in how black and white workers saw the relationship between their community and their workplace.

White industrial workers often lived in neighborhoods near the plant; unions were as much community institutions as workplace institutions. In most cities, however, African Americans lived in increasingly segregated neighborhoods away from their workplaces, which tended to be lumped with a white world dominated by white institutions. Except for the handful of African-American unions, most notably the Brotherhood of Sleeping Car Porters, founded in 1925, unions were likely to be perceived as white organizations, unable or unwilling to understand the needs of black workers.

Even though black workers identified strongly with their community and its institutions, the class differences that preceded the Great Migration remained. Indeed, these Northern urban black communities now experienced even deeper divisions. Newcomers were more likely than established residents to come from the Deep South and to work at industrial jobs that previously had played no role in the black class structure because blacks had been excluded from these workplaces. They also encountered African-American communities that encouraged migration yet held the migrants themselves at arm's length. "They didn't seem to open-arm welcome them," recalled a porter at one of Chicago's busy railroad stations, "but they seemed to welcome them."

People who called themselves "Old Philadelphians" ("O.P.'s") in one city, or "Old Settlers" in others, generally considered northbound migration to be "good for the race." The wages workers carried home increased the flow of dollars into black businesses. The votes of newcomers, most of them loyal to the Republican party, increased the clout of black politicians. Moreover their departure from the South dealt a blow to Jim Crow and proclaimed to the nation that black Southerners were not the "happy Negroes" depicted by Southern white spokesmen. The *Cleveland Gazette*, echoing other African-American newspapers, cheered the exodus as evidence that black Southerners understood the folly of "depending

The future of the Negro lies in his Health.

**WAR, DISEASE, FAMINE Now a MEMORY**

Reconstruction in 1919 must begin with toning up the health of the individual and comunity.

The War's backwash caused Pittsburgh's death rate to increase 43% last year.

Negroes suffered greatly. The amount of sickness was appalling.

7,320 deaths in Pittsburgh from **Pneumonia** and **Influenza** last year. 630 were Negroes.

To YOU, who have recovered, Specialists say that "the after effects are as bad or worse than the disease."

Watch that weakened Heart or those Kidneys or Lungs. If in doubt —see your Doctor.

Tuberculosis kills relatively almost twice as many Negroes as white people;—if treated in time, it can be cured. Consult the Tuberculosis Dispensary at once.

Bad teeth means a bad stomach, which cause indirectly 75% of all sickness.

The Medical examination of our draftees—your sons, husbands and sweethearts has shown the alarming prevalence of Venereal diseases.
Read that Literature.

**ARE YOU MOVING? READ**

A Negro family moved into a house vacated by a foreigner in the East End one month ago. One week afterward the whole family, man, wife and three children were seriously ill from germs left in the house—one child died. "Nuf Sed."

Fully half of all the sickness and deaths are preventable, this means that 45 out of every 100 Negroes who died last year ought to be living.

BABIES D O N O T HAVE TO HAVE Measles, Scarlet Fever, Whooping Cough, etc.

Twice as many Negro babies die before they reach one year of age than babies of all other races in the City.

Find the nearest Baby Health Station and take your baby regularly.

The League Office will give you information on request.

**IMMEDIATE STEPS.**

See that your garbage and waste is moved promptly.

Don't live in or over damp basements.

In 1919, the Urban League of Pittsburgh ran its second annual Negro Health Education Campaign. It advised African Americans to seek medical attention for infectious diseases, to see their dentists regularly, and to practice good sanitation.

upon the people [white southerners] who have destroyed them in the past to aid them in the future." Instead, migrants could depend on black leadership in Northern communities to represent their interests and ease the transition to their new homes.

Black Southerners arriving in cities encountered an array of agencies committed to helping them find places in the city. The most systematically active and professionalized of these were the local branches of the National Urban League. Founded in 1911, the Urban League added dozens of branches during the decade after 1916, in a wide variety of cities across the country.

Although services varied from city to city, the Urban League developed a reputation among black Southerners preparing to leave home as an organization "that cares for Southern emigrants." This care came in the form of job and housing registries, which often dispensed advice on work habits, housekeeping, and coping with landlords and city officials. Urban League officials in Pittsburgh proudly referred to their instructions to women on "the use of gas, electricity, marketing of foods, how to purchase and prepare cheap cuts of meat."

Black branches of the Young Men's and Young Women's Christian Associations initiated cooperative programs with employers and established room registries and recreation programs. In some cases community centers, churches, and women's clubs developed day-care programs, a crucial service given the unusually high level of married African-American women who held paid jobs. The husbands of black working women earned less than white men. Thus it was not unusual for these women to add wage labor to the customary housekeeping burdens of wives and mothers.

The assistance of clubs and groups like the Urban League, however, came with a double edge. Clubwomen concerned about the availability of child care for domestic workers were equally concerned about respectable housekeeping habits and public appearance. Newcomers were told not to wear head rags, scarves that Northern black women saw as symbols of servility and second-class citizenship. On a front porch shoes were a must, aprons a no-no. Like the settlement houses in white immigrant neighborhoods, YMCAs and YWCAs tried to compete with the streets and saloons for workers' leisure hours. And like the settlement houses, their efforts, though well meant, were often insulting and only partly successful.

Black newspapers printed lists of "do's and don'ts" similar to the lectures printed on Urban League brochures. Most of these lessons dealt with public behavior, reflecting anxieties about the impact of the migrants' Southern and rural habits on white images of African Americans. When newcomers were lectured not to "allow children to beg on the streets," encourage gambling, congregate in loud crowds, or "act discourteously to other people in public places," they sensed they were being talked down to. And they were.

In the North, even among African Americans, Southerners encountered a contempt for rural Southern culture. At the same time, however, these instructions reflected realistic concerns about Northern race relations and the differences between North and South. Northern whites did see African Americans as belonging to a single, unchanging, unified culture. Whatever black Northerners had accomplished in developing a community reputation could crumble under the onslaught of the new images conveyed by newcomers.

W. E. B. Du Bois recognized the dilemma of streetcar behavior in terms of the prevailing etiquette that required a male passenger to offer his seat to a female. This was something that migrants supposedly did not do, reflecting poorly on African-American manners and gentility. Southern black men were not by nature rude, observed Du Bois. But they had learned in the South to avoid interaction with white women. Even eye contact at the wrong time and place could provoke a lynching. Offering a seat to a white woman implied a social grace, a statement of manhood that was acceptable in the South only if accompanied by the kind of shuffle and deference that had no place in the North. Many black men who had recently arrived from the South took the safe—if "discourteous"—route. When a white woman boarded, they averted their glance and kept their seats.

Many newcomers responded to what they considered a cool reception by distancing themselves, especially on Sunday morning. Thousands left the big urban churches they had initially found so exciting and established smaller congregations in storefronts, often sending back home for their minister. Yet they continued to read the local black newspaper and align themselves politically with the established leaders of their communities.

This identification with the community, with the "home sphere," reflected the ways in which African Americans fit into early-twentieth-century American cities. Where they could (and could not) live related closely to race. Their children sat in classes filled mainly with other black children but with a white teacher standing in front. Whites owned the big stores; blacks, the small shops. And nearly all bosses were white. For white workers, race was taken for granted and class divisions often seemed to explain injustices and inequalities. But for black workers—and most African Americans earned working-class incomes—injustice and inequality had a distinctly racial cast. Class differences mattered, especially when thinking about the internal workings of their own community. But "their own community" was defined mainly by race.

Black Southerners who moved north hoping to leave behind the color line and racial hostilities quickly learned a harsher reality. The rules were unwritten in the North, but they were rules nevertheless. These neighborhoods were off-limits; those restaurants "don't serve Negroes." Sit where you want on the streetcar but don't be surprised if a white passenger moves away. Many teachers made no secret of their belief in the inability of black children to learn as quickly as their white peers. And there was violence.

In 1917, less than a year after industrial jobs first opened in the North, black workers in East St. Louis, Illinois (across the Mississippi River from St. Louis, Missouri), learned how dangerous their new homes could be. Thousands of black Southerners had come to work in aluminum factories, many of them recruited by employers seeking to replace striking white workers. The combination was explosive: cynical industrial managers using race to divide their workers, union organizers who raised the familiar cry of "nigger scab," corrupt white politicians, irresponsible journalists, and police inclined to look the other way when whites attacked blacks. The result was a race riot.

Nine whites and at least thirty-nine African Americans were killed; it was impossible to establish the number of black victims because their dead bodies were allegedly thrown into ditches and never recovered. The coroner was more concerned with white fatalities. Thousands of black residents were left homeless by fires set by white arsonists. Three weeks later, Du Bois, James Weldon Johnson, and other NAACP officials led a protest march down New York's Fifth Avenue. Following muffled drums, ten thousand men and women marched from Harlem through the heart of Manhattan in complete silence, with only their signs expressing their outrage.

Two years later violence erupted once more, this time in twenty-five cities and towns during a six-month period. James Weldon Johnson called it the "Red Summer," referring to the blood that flowed from racial conflict. Attacks occurred in rural Arkansas; small-town Texas; Tulsa, Oklahoma; Charleston, South Carolina; Knoxville, Tennessee; Washington, D.C.; and Omaha, Nebraska. Only the West was spared, probably because black populations were not yet large enough to pose a threat to the stability of white neighborhoods or to white men's jobs.

The worst riot was in Chicago, where black and white Chicagoans battled in the streets for five days in July, with occasional attacks punctuating an uneasy calm the following

A triumphant group of young rioters celebrates outside a damaged home during the 1919 Chicago riots.

week. Catalyzed by an attack on a black teenager who had floated onto a "white" beach, the violence was initiated by white street gangs fighting to secure their turf, their community's jobs, and their political patrons' power against the threat posed by the influx of African Americans into the city. The police stood by as blacks passing through white neighborhoods were beaten. In response black Chicagoans set upon whites as well, usually inside the boundaries of the black ghetto. Only a timely rainstorm and the Illinois National Guard restored order.

No silent marches this time. In many of these conflicts the protest had come immediately and on the field of battle. Nineteenth-century "race riots" had generally consisted of attacks on black communities while authorities looked the other way. Blacks sometimes defended themselves but seldom counterattacked. But in Longview, Texas, in 1919, blacks responded to an attempt to drive the local *Defender* agent out of town by taking out their rifles. In Chicago white peddlers and merchants in the "Black Belt" were attacked after the initial assaults on African Americans. Claude McKay's poem, "If We Must Die," published in July 1919, articulated the mood:

> If we must die, let it not be like hogs
> Hunted and penned in an inglorious spot,
> While round us bark the mad and hungry dogs,
> Making their mock at our accursed lot.

Members of the 369th Colored Infantry arrive home in New York in 1919. Every member of this unit—the first of the African-American troops to see action—received the Croix de Guerre for gallantry.

> If we must die, O let us nobly die,
> So that our precious blood may not be shed
> In vain; then even the monsters we defy
> Shall be constrained to honor us though dead!
> O kinsmen! we must meet the common foe!
> Though far outnumbered let us show us brave,
> And for their thousand blows deal one deathblow!
> What though before us lies the open grave?
> Like men we'll face the murderous, cowardly pack,
> Pressed to the wall, dying, but fighting back!

### "New Negroes"

On February 17, 1919, less than two years after the dramatic "silent protest" parade from Harlem to downtown Manhattan, another set of disciplined marchers walked Fifth Avenue in the opposite direction. The men of the 369th Infantry Division of the United States Army had returned home from the war. They had fought hard, losing hundreds of men on the battlefield. They had fought well, becoming the only American unit to win the prized Croix de Guerre from the French, who had dubbed the unit the "Hell Fighters."

The French knew these Americans well, because the regiment had been attached to the French Army—"owing to the need for replacements in French units," according to U.S. government documents prepared after the war. The truth, however, was more complicated. Four National Guard units fought with the French. The troops were black; the officers an interracial group headed in three cases by a white colonel. Only the Illinois regiment, the pride of African Americans across the United States because of publicity from the *Chicago Defender,* had an African American in command.

Combining these regiments with white units was unthinkable to American military leaders. Nor were these generals prepared to combine the African-American units into a fully equipped all-black combat division. With the French clamoring for replacements, American commanders loaned to their allies the men they preferred not to lead into battle themselves. Appropriately, the war heroes stepped uptown in American uniforms but in French drill formation.

The decision of the United States government to enter the First World War in April 1917 received a mixed reception among the American public. Many Americans opposed participation. Ethnic loyalties played a part in this opposition, as did criticism of European imperialism and a sense that Europe's troubles need not consume American lives or tax dollars. Many African Americans, questioning their role in a "white-folks' war," shared this skepticism. Most black voices, however, supported W. E. B. Du Bois's call for African Americans to "close ranks" behind the war effort. Military service, Liberty Bond purchases, diligent labor on the home front, and vocal support for the war would provide a basis upon which the black community could expect increased recognition and acceptance. As one black teacher in the South explained, his people were "soldiers of freedom. . . . When we have proved ourselves men, worthy to work and fight and die for our country, a grateful nation may gladly give us the recognition of real men, and the rights and privileges of true and loyal citizens of these United States." Democracy at home would be the reward for supporting democracy abroad.

The American military, however, had difficulty determining a potential role for black soldiers. First the army turned away black candidates for enlistment. Next, draft boards discriminated against black men seeking exemption. Grudgingly the War Department established a facility to train black officers, but the selection process weeded out many of the most qualified candidates in favor of men less likely to succeed. Black soldiers were "loaned" to the French army, whose officers were warned by American authorities that such men were potential rapists who had to be kept away from civilian populations.

In the end, 380,000 black men served, nearly half of them in Europe. Only 42,000 of these served in combat units. The rest were relegated to digging, cleaning, hauling, loading, and unloading.

Despite efforts to insult black soldiers and to remind black civilians that a war fought to "make the world safe for Democracy," as President Woodrow Wilson put it, did not necessarily mean making America itself any more democratic, African Americans drew their own lessons from the war. Writing in *The Crisis* in May 1919, Du Bois made the point:

> We *return*
> We *return from fighting.*
> We *return fighting.*
> Make way for Democracy! We saved it in France, and by the Great
> Jehovah, we will save it in the United States of America or know the
> reason why.

White Southerners wasted little time casting doubt on whether democracy had been saved at home. They lynched seventy African Americans during the year after the war. Ten of these were soldiers, some murdered in their uniforms. The riots of 1919 both punctuated this epidemic of publicly sanctioned homicide and dispelled any notions that racism and violence were unique to the South.

The riots also, however, provided a clue to an increasingly assertive sensibility spreading across black America. In some Southern cities the violence itself was sparked by white outrage at the sight of armed black veterans in uniform. In the North the riots were linked to the impact of the Great Migration, itself a statement of bold ambition and a commitment to a new role in American life. Everywhere the heightened tensions were related to an impatient mood working its way across black America. Black soldiers epitomized this sense of anticipation, this expectation that things were changing, that things had to change. Men who had fought for their country abroad had little tolerance for continued appeals to "wait" for recognition of their rights as citizens at home. This sense that they were entitled to the full rewards of American life combined with the ambition and excitement of the Great Migration to form the heart of what came to be called the "New Negro" movement.

The idea of the "New Negro" took hold in many influential black publications in the 1920s, and the term itself was used as the title of a book edited by Howard University Professor Alain Locke in 1925. In his introduction Locke proposed two complementary principles underlying this new perspective. New Negroes insisted on the rights embodied in "the ideals of American institutions and democracy." They also promoted "self-respect and self-reliance" among African Americans, with a distinct emphasis on race pride.

This perspective was not as new as Locke claimed. Instead it brought together strands of Booker T. Washington's gospel of self-reliance, deep traditions of

African-American protest, ranging from abolitionism to the founding of the NAACP in 1910, and the hopes and aspirations underlying the Great Migration. What was new was a sense of expectation unequaled since emancipation and an odd combination of disillusionment, anger, militancy, and euphoria dramatized by the parades of returning veterans.

Nor was the New Negro represented by a single approach to African-American culture or the problems defined by the American color line. New Negroes moved into the arts and literature, social work and social activism, politics, the union movement, and a variety of organizations claiming to offer the solution to the dilemma of black life in a nation seemingly committed to white supremacy.

The most enduring expression of the New Negro was the literary and artistic flowering often referred to as the Harlem Renaissance. The term encompasses the work of a broad variety of novelists, poets, essayists, artists, and musicians. Their work displayed a diversity of form and content that defies simple categorization. Some, like poet Langston Hughes and folklorist and novelist Zora Neale Hurston, took street life or rural folk culture as their subject. This approach differed from older African-American literary traditions, which tended to emphasize respectability.

Others, like novelist Jessie Fauset, stuck with high culture and the black elite. Some explicitly protested against American racial oppression; others adopted racial themes but avoided overt political statements. What mattered, declared Hughes, was the inclination to write from inside the experience and to be true to one's creative muse.

By the 1920s Harlem had emerged as the cultural capital of black America, in much the same way that New York City stood at the center of mainstream American high culture. This was not an accident. The diversity of the population—a yeasty mix of New Yorkers, recent migrants from the South, and immigrants from the West Indies and Africa—played a part.

So did the efforts of Charles Johnson, an African-American sociologist who at the time was the editor of the Urban League publication *Opportunity*. Johnson, along with *The Crisis* literary editor Jessie Fauset, envisioned their journals as vanguards of social change. Through the publication of short stories, poems, and essays, and the awarding of cash prizes, these two journals promoted the work of Hughes, Hurston, Countee Cullen, Jean Toomer, and countless others. Perhaps as important, the journals also provided a bridge across which African-American culture could be presented to white audiences.

And indeed, white Americans did discover African-American culture during the 1920s. A small group of white political activists, literary figures, editors, and intellectuals read the books, went to art exhibits, and even donated money for literary prizes. Few tackled the more difficult work, like Toomer's *Cane,* a series of fictional portraits connected by poetic interludes. But then again, few blacks read *Cane* either; it sold only five hundred copies. Toomer's deft manipulation of literary form to explore the rural roots of black culture and consciousness would become a classic, but it would take nearly a half-century for it to be rediscovered.

Jessie Fauset's genteel aristocrats, every bit as proper as their white counterparts but not nearly as affluent, posed a different challenge. "White readers just don't expect Negroes to be like this," explained one white editor in rejecting her manuscript. The street hustlers of Claude McKay's *Home to Harlem,* the love poems of Countee Cullen, the blues rhythms of Langston Hughes: These were easier. Charles Johnson's vision of a cultural terrain that provided a common ground for black and white Americans overestimated the interest of whites in black culture, history, or sensibilities. Whites were mainly interested in something called "The Negro," an exotic neighbor who was not bound by the narrow conventions of social morality.

It was not the literature or the art that brought white people and their money to Harlem or the South Side of Chicago. It was the nightclubs. White urbanites crowded into the clubs to listen to a new kind of music called jazz, which had emerged in the South earlier in the century. Some of these nightspots, owned and operated by whites, employed black musicians and chorus girls to entertain mainly white audiences who saw Harlem and its smaller counterparts in other cities as places where they could cast aside their inhibitions and enjoy exotic entertainment. Other clubs resembled Chicago's "black and tan" cabarets, where the white downtown theater crowd mingled with the black middle class. In some cities these integrated establishments were the most likely nightspots to attract police in the mood to enforce legislation enacted in the 1920s as part of the outlawing of liquor sales during Prohibition. Apparently alcohol was more dangerous when imbibed interracially. The appeal of ghetto glitz reached its apex at Harlem's Savoy Ballroom, where integrated crowds of up to four thousand danced to music provided by the most famous dance bands of the era.

Few of Harlem's residents, however, could afford the Savoy. The world of cabarets, concerts, and publication contracts that swirled around the notables of the Harlem Renaissance meant little to the majority of women who toiled daily as domestic workers, or to men carrying home a few dollars each day for pushing a broom or tending a machine. They caught their music at rent parties, all-night affairs in tightly packed apartments where a quarter at the door purchased food, drink, and live entertainment, with the proceeds used to pay the rent. Or they got music through a new phenomenon known as "race" records.

By mid-decade the strong economy had brought enough secure employment in most cities to permit many black families in cities across the country to purchase phonographs. After Okeh Records took the plunge in 1920 and issued Mamie Smith's *Crazy Blues* (which sold thousands of copies), other recording companies jumped into the market. Race records brought substantial profits to white record company owners. Black Swan Records, whose advertisements truthfully trumpeted "The Only Genuine Colored Record," enjoyed only brief success, in part because of its commitment to maintaining a catalogue of more respectable (but not profitable) classical music in addition to blues recordings.

Sustaining an African-American voice in film proved more difficult. The first attempt came in 1915 with the establishment of the Lincoln Motion Picture Company. Noble Johnson, an actor with experience at Universal Studios, made the films in Los Angeles. His brother George took care of the marketing after finishing his shift at the Omaha, Nebraska, post office. They drew support from both communities, especially in Los Angeles, with its pair of African-American hotels, a black baseball league, an "African cafe," and an active NAACP branch.

Drawing on the emerging Watts ghetto for his screenplays, Noble Johnson sought "to picture the Negro as he is in his every day life, a human being with human inclination, and one of talent and intellect." George Johnson developed strong relationships with black newspapers, and Lincoln films were able to take advantage of the wartime migration to cities to build an audience.

The story of the Johnson brothers, however, also reveals the difficulties of black enterprise and the obstacles faced by African Americans committed to using the new tools of mass culture (at that time, radio, newspapers, and motion pictures) to provide honest depictions of black life. Lack of money and restricted access to distribution networks and credit undermined the company's ability to compete with white-owned film companies.

Nor did the Johnsons reach beyond a black audience; whites showed no interest in their films. The Lincoln Motion Picture Company folded in 1921. Another independent black filmmaker, Oscar Micheaux, would continue working through the 1920s and 1930s, but on the whole the film industry would be dominated by large studios turning out films with either no black characters or African Americans appearing in stereotypical and demeaning comical roles.

Surveying the state of black America in 1925, one young African-American scholar concluded that the business of producing culture was less indicative of the power and potential of the New Negro than the culture of the black businessman. E. Franklin Frazier, at the beginning of a long career as a distinguished sociologist, stated his minority opinion in one of the essays of Alain Locke's anthology, *The New Negro*.

He urged his readers to look beyond Harlem toward Durham, North Carolina, where African Americans owned thriving insurance companies and banks. "Durham offers none of the color and creative life we find among Negroes in New York City. . . . It is not a place where men write and dream, but a place where men calculate and work." His essay pointed to black economic dynamism, not cultural achievement, as the truly important change in the 1920s. Black financiers and businessmen along with a growing industrial working class would eventually merge black America with white America. When this happened race would cease to be important; what would matter was class.

A small group of young activists argued that class already was the division that mattered. The challenge was to convince black Americans that as workers their interests were best represented not by the middle-class NAACP and National Urban League, but by the labor and socialist movements, which claimed to speak for all workers. At the same time white workers would have to be convinced that black workers were allies, rather than rivals.

Calling itself the voice of the "New Crowd Negro," a new magazine called *The Messenger* was launched in 1917 by A. Philip Randolph and Chandler Owen. Both men were college educated and had migrated from the South to Harlem. Their notion of a "New Negro" had less to do with culture than with politics—in particular socialist politics. Randolph and Owen opposed American involvement in the First World War. Dismissing the war as a battle among European imperialists, they tied the oppression of African Americans to colonialism in Africa (the political and ecomonic control of most of Africa by European nations) and to the oppression of the working class around the world.

Both union activity and socialist politics were becoming increasingly visible in African-American communities in the early part of the twentieth century. The leading black socialist of that time was probably George Washington Woodbey. Born a slave in Tennessee in 1854, Woodbey educated himself after the Civil War, despite less than two years of formal schooling. He moved to San Diego in 1903 (like so many other migrants, part of a family chain—he first went there to visit his mother), where he served as a minister and as a socialist orator and pamphleteer.

Woodbey's visibility in the movement in some ways highlights socialism's weakness among African Americans. He stood out among socialists for the attention he gave in his speeches to the relationship between racial oppression and class conflict, a link that many socialists either ignored or treated superficially. Although generally less committed to white supremacy than most other white Americans, the socialists seldom directly challenged prevailing notions about race. Moreover, Woodbey's status as a minister was important. Most African Americans were likely to look within, rather than outside the black community for leadership—to their preachers, editors, business owners, lawyers, and educators.

By the end of the 1910s radical politics was developing deeper roots in some black communities, most notably Harlem. Hubert Harrison, a leading street-corner orator and Socialist party activist before the First World War, broke with the party in 1917. He proclaimed the need for a combination of black nationalism and socialism, with "race first" as the cornerstone.

Harrison frequently crossed paths with Cyril Briggs, founder in 1917 of the African Blood Brotherhood. Briggs described his organization as "a revolutionary secret order" dedicated to armed resistance to lynching, opposition to all forms of racial discrimination, and voting rights for black Southerners. He also sought the unionization of black workers and African-American control of political institutions in parts of the United States where they were a majority of the population.

The brotherhood also opposed American participation in the First World War and linked the struggle for black liberation in the United States to the battle against European colonization in Africa. The organization never grew beyond a few thousand, but by the early 1920s had expanded from its Harlem base to places as diverse as the West Indies and West Virginia. Like Hubert Harrison and George Washington Woodbey, the African Blood Brotherhood is significant because of its place in the broad range of African-American thought in the early twentieth century. It also is an example of the participation of black Americans in international debates about colonialism, politics, and race.

Organizing in Harlem for the nearly successful Socialist candidate for mayor in 1917, Randolph and Owen managed to attract thousands of black voters to the socialist banner. But success was short-lived and localized. In general the Socialist party failed to attract black voters, in part because it was unwilling to take a strong stand against Jim Crow.

The Communist party attracted few African Americans during the 1920s. These were mainly intellectuals impressed with its forthright stands against colonialism in Africa and racism in the United States. The party would win many black supporters for the help it lent to African Americans in civil rights and economic issues during the Great Depression of the 1930s. But in the 1920s attempts by the Communist party to organize black workers were so unsuccessful that A. Philip Randolph dismissed black Communists as a group that could meet in a phone booth.

Not that Randolph, Owen, or other African-American labor organizers had done much better. Several attempts had been made to organize unions with mainly black membership. All had failed, mostly because of resistance from white unions. By 1925, the *Messenger* was barely surviving after dropping from its peak circulation of 26,000 in 1919. Chandler Owen left to work for another publication in Chicago, and Randolph began to rethink his attitudes toward the American Federation of Labor (AFL).

The only route to black unionization seemed to be inclusion in existing labor organizations. The NAACP and the National Urban League had tried this route in 1918–19, urging black workers to join unions wherever they were accepted on an equal basis. But few unions would take blacks on an equal basis with their white members. In his earlier years as a radical Randolph had viewed the AFL as not only racist, but also too willing to accept the class structures created by capitalism. Now he decided that the AFL's approach to unionism—accepting the system and trying to secure workers a larger share of corporate profits—was the best way for black workers to move toward the standard of living that unionized white workers had attained.

Randolph began organizing an all-black union whose agenda resembled that of mainstream white craft unions: higher wages, job security, and collective bargaining. The Brotherhood of Sleeping Car Porters and Maids struggled against the Pullman company for a decade, winning partial victories in 1926 and 1929 and complete recognition in 1937. Despite considerable opposition and only after tireless insistence on Randolph's part, the Brotherhood also became the first African-American union awarded a full charter by the American Federation of Labor. Its organizing battles and its grassroots leadership would eventually provide the basis for a half-century of civil rights struggles in cities across the United States.

For most black Americans in the 1920s, however, unionization did not represent an option. The Harlem Renaissance was a distant phenomenon, not very important even to many Harlemites. What captured the imagination of the black masses was another movement rooted in Harlem, the Universal Negro Improvement Association (UNIA). The organization was inseparable from its founder, chief spokesman, and strategist, Marcus M. Garvey.

Garvey founded the UNIA in 1914 on his native West Indian island of Jamaica, at the time still a British colony. He attracted little support for his organization and brought his vision of a liberated Africa and a fully emancipated black population to the United States two years later. That vision and Garvey's expression of it drew heavily on the rhetoric surrounding the First World War, which had been justified by the United States and its allies as a fight for "self-determination." Garvey compared his cause to that of the Irish revolutionaries fighting for independence and the Zionists struggling for a Jewish state in Palestine. His version called for the self-determination of Africans across the globe—"Africa for the Africans."

"A race without authority and power is a race without respect," declared Garvey. Criticizing the NAACP's strategy of seeking justice through lawsuits and legislation, he observed that "there is not justice, but strength." Blacks, therefore, had to compete. They had to establish independent nations in Africa, independent businesses in the United States, and a framework of black institutions independent of white influence.

The UNIA would provide that framework. Its newspaper, the *Negro World*, attained a circulation of fifty thousand to sixty thousand in the mid-1920s. Among African-American newspapers, only the *Chicago Defender* reached a wider audience. The UNIA established businesses, especially laundries and groceries, retail operations that could rely on a black clientele and employ UNIA members. Most visibly, Garvey founded the Black Star Line Steamship Company, funded by sales of stock to UNIA members. To buy shares was to invest in the race. Garvey promised profits, employment for black seamen, and transportation for African-American passengers traveling to Africa to lead that continent's struggle against European colonial domination.

At its height between 1923 and 1926 the UNIA counted more than seven hundred branches in thirty-eight states, in addition to a substantial body of support in the Caribbean and Central America. Some of these branches probably consisted of a handful of enthusiasts, or perhaps even a single household. Others, in large cities, numbered in the thousands. Perhaps most striking is the geographic diversity, as the UNIA ranged across country and city and from the Northeast to the Midwest,

The charismatic Marcus Garvey promoted racial pride and economic self-sufficiency for blacks. In 1919 he founded the Black Star Line to provide black Americans with jobs, transportation, and profits.

South, and Pacific Coast. The organization claimed six million members, but five hundred thousand is probably a more realistic estimate. At least another half-million supporters never paid dues but counted themselves among Garvey's followers. The UNIA was easily the largest African-American mass movement the United States had ever seen.

The moment, however, was brief. The Black Star Line was a financial disaster, due in part to bad luck associated with calamitous weather on its initial freight run and in part to weak management. The company's bankruptcy provided ammunition to Garvey's enemies, a list that included nearly all of the established African-American leadership. To radicals like A. Philip Randolph and Cyril Briggs, Garvey had too much faith in capitalism. To the moderates in the NAACP he was too inflammatory. Respectable middle-class community leaders found his advice to look to Africa for salvation as foolish (actually, this was a minor part of the Garvey agenda, but one that has remained most visible in the public mind).

Editor Robert Abbott of the *Chicago Defender,* an unyielding opponent of racism but a firm believer in American institutions, hated Garvey so much that he banished mention of the UNIA from his newspaper. His readers learned absolutely nothing about the active Chicago chapter, even though it had nine thousand members. In 1922 Garvey confirmed his opponents' worst fears. He attended a meeting of the Ku Klux Klan and declared that the Klan was more honest about race in the United States than the NAACP and other black organizations. At Abbott's urging Garvey was indicted for fraud in 1923 in connection with the sale of shares in the Black Star Line. Most likely he was less guilty of fraud than of incompetence. Nevertheless, he was convicted and jailed until his deportation from the United States in 1927.

Garvey remained a hero to thousands of black Americans, especially small businesspeople and working-class men and women. Years later Malcolm X would recall accompanying his father to UNIA meetings during the 1930s, long after the movement's decline. In his autobiography, he recalled the dozen or so people packed into a living room and was struck by

> how differently they all acted, although they were the same people who jumped and shouted in church. But in these meetings both they and my father were more intense, more intelligent and down to earth. It made me feel the same way. . . . I remember how the meetings always closed with my father saying, several times, and the people chanting after him, "Up, you mighty race, you can accomplish what you will."

## CHAPTER 3

# From a Raw Deal to a New Deal?

## 1929–1945

### Joe William Trotter, Jr.

L ong before the stock market crash in October 1929, African Americans had experienced hard times. The "last hired and the first fired," African Americans entered the Great Depression earlier and more deeply than other racial and ethnic groups. Sociologists St. Clair Drake and Horace R. Cayton believed that the black community served as a "barometer sensitive to the approaching storm." Months before the stock market crash, the *Chicago Defender* warned, "Something is happening . . . and it should no longer go unnoticed. During the past three weeks hardly a day has ended that there has not been a report of another firm discharging its employees, many of whom have been faithful workers at these places for years."

The depression brought mass suffering to the country as a whole. National income dropped by nearly fifty percent, from $81 billion in 1929 to $40 billion in 1932; unemployment rose to an estimated twenty-five percent of the labor force; and nearly twenty million Americans turned to public and private relief agencies to prevent starvation and destitution. Still, African Americans suffered more than their white counterparts, received less from their government, and got what they called a "raw deal" rather than a "new deal."

The depression took its toll on virtually every facet of African American life. As unemployment rose, membership in churches, clubs, and fraternal orders dropped. Blacks frequently related the pain of this separation from friends and acquaintances. "I don't attend church as often as I used to. You know I am not fixed like I want to be—haven't got the clothes I need."

Blacks in the rural South faced the most devastating impact of the Great Depression. As cotton prices dropped from eighteen cents per pound to less than six cents by early 1933, an estimated two million black farmers faced hard times. The number of black sharecroppers dropped from nearly 392,000 in 1930 to under 300,000 as the depression spread. All categories of rural black labor—

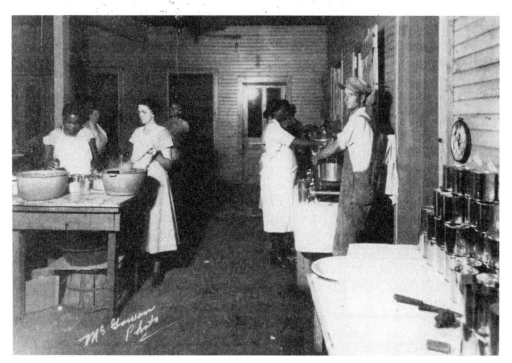

The Great Depression forced growing numbers of white women to enter the work force, where they competed with black women for jobs. Here, blacks and whites work side by side at a cannery in North Carolina.

landowners, cash tenants, sharecroppers, and wage laborers—suffered from declining incomes. Mechanical devices had already reduced the number of workers needed for plowing, hoeing, and weeding, but planters now experimented with mechanical cotton pickers as well. As one black woman put it, many jobs had "gone to machines, gone to white people or gone out of style." Public and private relief efforts were virtually nonexistent in the rural South, forcing farm families to continue their trek to the city.

Despite declining opportunities to work in southern and northern cities, black migration continued during the depression years. The percentage of urban blacks rose from about forty-four percent in 1930 to nearly fifty percent during the depression years. The black population in northern cities increased by nearly twenty-five percent; the number of cities with black populations of over one hundred thousand increased from one in 1930 to eleven in 1935. Public social services played an increasing role in decisions to move. As the Swedish economist Gunnar Myrdal noted in his classic study of black life during the period, "It was much harder for Negroes who needed it to get relief in the South than in the North."

The increasing migration of blacks to cities intensified the poverty of established residents. Before the stock market crash of 1929, urban blacks had already faced the impact of increasing mechanization, declining demand for manufactured goods, and loss of employment to whites. The stock market crash further undercut the economic position of African Americans. By 1932, black urban unemployment reached well over fifty percent, more than twice the rate of whites. In northern and southern cities, black workers faced special difficulties trying to hold on to their jobs. In Pittsburgh, for example, some black workers were fired when they refused to give kickbacks to the foreman for being permitted to keep their jobs. At the same time, unemployed whites made increasing inroads on the so-called "Negro jobs," lower-level positions that blacks had occupied during good times. Not only in factories but in street cleaning, garbage collection, and domestic service work, whites competed for the traditionally black jobs.

As the depression intensified, many white women entered the labor force for the first time. They competed with black women for jobs as maids, cooks, and housekeepers. In northern cities, unemployment and destitution forced many black women to participate in the notorious "slave market." Congregating on the sidewalks of major cities, these women offered their services to white women, who drove up in their cars seeking domestic help. Some of the employers were working-class women themselves and paid as little as five dollars weekly for full-time household workers. The work was difficult indeed. One young black woman, Millie Jones, offered a detailed description of her work for one family for five dollars a week.

> Each and every week, believe it or not, I had to wash every one of those windows [fifteen in a six-room apartment]. If that old hag found as much as the teeniest speck on any one of 'em, she'd make me do it over. I guess I would do anything rather than wash windows. On Mondays I washed and did as much of the ironing as I could. The rest waited over for Tuesday. There were two grown sons in the family and her husband. That meant that I would have at least twenty-one shirts to do every week. Yeah, and ten sheets and at least two blankets, besides. They all had to be done just so, too.

In urban factories and commercial laundries, black women also faced difficult times. In a New York laundry, black women worked fifty hours each week. According to one employee, "it was speed up, speed up, eating lunch on the fly." Women working in the starching department stood on their feet for ten hours each day, "sticking their hands into almost boiling starch." When the employees complained, the boss threatened to fire and replace them with workers from the large pool of unemployed women. But black women did not accept these conditions without a fight.

Racism and job competition helped to narrow the margin between bare survival and destitution. Evidence of racism abounded. In the South, white workers rallied around such slogans as, "No Jobs for Niggers Until Every White Man Has a Job" and "Niggers, back to the cotton fields—city jobs are for white folks." The most violent efforts to displace black workers occurred on southern railroads, where the white brotherhoods, as their unions were called, intimidated, attacked, and murdered black workers in order to take their jobs. By early 1933, nearly a dozen black firemen had lost their lives in various parts of the country. Although the Ku Klux Klan had declined by the mid-1920s, it now renewed attacks on African Americans.

The discriminatory policies of employers and labor unions also affected African Americans in northern cities. Employers maintained their views that African Americans were fit only for dirty, unpleasant, low-paying, and heavy work. As blacks sought employment, employers again frequently claimed that, "We don't have a foundry in our plant and that's the kind of work Negroes are best suited for." In Milwaukee, one firm justified its exclusion of black workers in familial and paternalistic terms: "We just sort of work like a family here and to bring in Negro workers would cause confusion and cause white workers to feel that their jobs had lost in dignity if being done by Negroes." White workers reinforced and frequently demanded such policies. Twenty-four unions, ten of them affiliates of the American Federation of Labor (AFL), barred blacks completely and others practiced other forms of discrimination and exclusion. Thus, disproportionately large numbers of African Americans entered the bread lines, sold their belongings, and faced eviction from their homes.

It was a difficult time, but the Republican administration of Herbert Hoover did little to relieve the suffering. Hoover resisted proposals for aiding the nation's poor and destitute. Instead, he pursued a policy of indirect relief through the establishment of agencies like the Reconstruction Finance Corporation, which provided loans to relieve the credit problems of huge corporations like railroads, banks, and insurance companies. By "priming the pump" of big business, Hoover believed that federal aid to corporations would stimulate production, create new jobs, and increase consumer spending—that is, that wealth would "trickle down" to the rest of the economy and end the depression. Unfortunately, these policies provided little help to African Americans.

Despite their suffering under the Hoover administration, African Americans rallied to the slogan "who but Hoover" in the presidential election of 1932. Hoover had not only failed to advance effective policies for dealing with the depression; he had also offended African Americans in a variety of ways, including refusing to be photographed with black leaders. Still, he received about sixty-six percent of the black votes. Only in New York and Kansas City, Missouri, did the majority of blacks vote for Franklin Delano Roosevelt. The Republican party of Abraham Lincoln was still seen as the party of emancipation.

From the black vantage point Roosevelt looked little better than Hoover. As assistant secretary of the navy during the First World War, he had supported the racial segregation of the armed forces. He had also adopted Warm Springs, Georgia, as his home and accepted the system of racial segregation in that state. Moreover, during its national convention, the Democratic party rejected an NAACP proposal for a civil rights plank that called for an end to racial discrimination.

Unemployed blacks line up outside the State Employment Service in Memphis, Tennessee, in 1938. During the depression blacks received far less aid than their white counterparts.

Once in office, FDR did little to build confidence among African Americans. The new president depended on Southern segregationists to pass and implement his "New Deal" programs. FDR saw the depression as an economic disaster that required massive federal aid and planning. The president formulated his New Deal programs accordingly, giving close attention to the needs of big business, agriculture, and labor. Roosevelt opposed federal anti-lynching legislation, prevented black delegations from visiting the White House, and refused to make civil rights and racial equity a priority. FDR repeatedly justified his actions on the grounds that he needed Southern white support for his economic relief and recovery programs. In a conversation with an NAACP official, he confided that, "If I come out for the anti-lynching bill now, they will block every bill I ask Congress to pass to keep America from collapsing. I just can't take that risk."

African-American rights were placed on hold. Each piece of New Deal legislation failed to safeguard African Americans against racial discrimination. The National Recovery Administration (NRA), Agricultural Adjustment Administration (AAA), the Works Progress [later Projects] Administration (WPA), the Tennessee Valley Authority (TVA), the Civilian Conservation Corps (CCC), and the Federal Energy Relief Administration (FERA), to name only a few, all left blacks vulnerable to discriminatory employers, agency officials, and local whites. Despite the initiation of

New Deal relief measures, African Americans repeatedly complained of their inability to secure relief. When a father of six lost his job and sought relief in the city of Pittsburgh, relief officials denied his request. Only when he deserted his family, his wife reported, did she and the children receive aid. According to the woman's testimony: "He told me once that if he wasn't living at home the welfare people would help me and the kids, and maybe he just went away on that account." Southern state and local officials disregarded federal guidelines and paid African-American relief recipients less than their white counterparts. In Atlanta, blacks on relief received an average of $19.29 per month compared to $32.66 for whites. In Jacksonville, Florida, about five thousand whites received forty-five percent of the relief funds, while the fifteen thousand blacks on relief received the remaining fifty-five percent. Southern politicians defended the practice, arguing that the low living standard of blacks enabled them to live on less than whites.

The local Federal Emergency Relief Administration was not alone in discriminating against blacks. The Agricultural Adjustment Act paid farmers to withdraw cotton land from production, create a shortage, and drive up the price of cotton on the market. Set up to administer the law at the local level, AAA county committees excluded African Americans from participation. By depriving African Americans of representation white landowners were able to institute policies that drove black landowners into the ranks of sharecroppers and forced growing numbers of sharecroppers off the land altogether. During its first year, for example, the AAA encouraged farmers to plow under cotton that was already planted. Landowners took government checks, plowed up cotton, and denied tenants a share of the government income.

At the same time that planters removed increasing acres of land from cultivation, the largest landowners turned increasingly to scientific and mechanized farming. Tractors and cotton-picking machines rendered black labor more and more dispensable. Although their numbers dwindled, the remaining black sharecroppers earned less than their white counterparts. White sharecroppers received a mean net income of $417 per year compared to only $295 for blacks. Whites receiving hourly wages made $232 per year, compared to only $175 for blacks.

Lower earnings aggravated other forms of racial inequality. In his survey of 612 black farm families in Macon County, Alabama, the sociologist Charles S. Johnson found that more than half lived in one- and two-room weatherworn shacks. When asked if her house leaked when it rained, a black woman said, "No, it don't leak in here, it just rains in here and leaks outdoors." Another tenant complained that the landlord refused to provide lumber for repairs: "All he's give us . . . is a few planks. . . . It's nothin doin'. We just living outdoors." Food was also difficult for farm families to come by. Black tenants had good reasons to view these early years of the New Deal with skepticism.

The National Recovery Act also discriminated against black workers. Partly by exempting domestic service and unskilled laborers from its provisions, the NRA removed most blacks from its minimum wage and participatory requirements. Since over sixty percent of African Americans worked in these sectors, the measure had little meaning for most blacks, especially women. Nonetheless, other blacks who held on to their precarious footing in the industrial labor force, despite hard times, faced new pressures from employers and white workers. In 1934, the Milwaukee, Wisconsin, Urban League reported a strike at the Wehr Steel Foundry. The chief aim of the strike, the League reported, was the "dismissal of Negroes from the plant." When black workers decided to cross the picket line, police joined strikers in attacks on them. The Milwaukee Urban League reported that: "The first few days of the strike brought considerable violence between the Negroes who attempted to continue on the jobs and the white pickets.... Police had been summoned [by management] to protect those who cared to enter but in turn joined with the strikers in overturning an automobile filled with Negro workers."

Even on construction projects for black institutions, white workers rallied to bar African American workers. In St. Louis, for example, when the General Tile Company hired a black tile setter on the $2 million Homer Phillips Hospital for blacks, all the white AFL union men quit and delayed construction for two months. In Long Island and Manhattan, the Brotherhood of Electrical Workers and Building Service Employees' Union pursued similar practices. When African Americans were brought under the provisions of the law in southern textile firms, employers reclassified African American jobs, in order to remove them from the protection of the NRA codes. Some firms simply argued that blacks were less efficient than whites and thus deserved low wages. In Atlanta, for example, the Scripto Manufacturing company told black workers, "This company does not base wages on color but entirely on efficiency. Our records show that the efficiency of colored help is only fifty percent of that of white help in similar plants."

Where the codes did upgrade the pay of black workers, many firms replaced their African American workforces with white employees. It is no wonder that blacks frequently called the NRA, the "Negro Run Around," "Negroes Ruined Again", and "Negro Rarely Allowed." In short, NRA legislation (particularly section 7a, which gave workers the right to collective bargaining with employers) enabled labor unions to strengthen their hand at the expense of blacks in the North and South. As late as 1935, organized white labor also blocked the inclusion of a non-discrimination clause in the National Labor Relations Act, sponsored by Senator Robert Wagner of New York. The new Wagner law gave workers and their unions extended protection in their effort to bargain collectively with management.

African Americans not only faced discrimination in industrial, agricultural, and relief programs but confronted racial bias in federal housing, social security, and regional planning and youth programs as well. The Federal Housing Administration refused to guarantee mortgages (homeloans) in racially integrated neighborhoods; the Social Security Act excluded farm laborers and domestic service employees; and the TVA and CCC developed along segregationist and unequal lines.

Established in 1933, the Tennessee Valley Authority was promoted by the Roosevelt administration as a model of social planning to improve the lives of millions of Americans in seven states in the Tennessee River Valley. It was hoped that the TVA would stimulate economic development and reduce poverty by establishing a massive program of rural electrification at dramatically reduced rates. African Americans comprised eleven percent of the two million residents of the region, and the project promised "nondiscrimination" in its official design.

African Americans took heart at the promise of benefits from TVA. Yet, the project soon accepted the racial status quo for black workers and their families in the valley. The agency barred blacks from skilled and managerial positions, excluded them from vocational training programs, and reinforced patterns of segregation in housing. When queried about the exclusion of blacks from its model town of Norris, Tennessee, TVA chairman Arthur Morgan referred to a long "lilly white" waiting list and suggested that it was unlikely that blacks would be able to move to Norris. Even more important, African Americans received inadequate benefits from the reduced rates for electrical power for their homes. In an essay on the "Plight of the Negro in the Tennessee Valley," the NAACP magazine *The Crisis* reported: "For Negroes the introduction of cheaper electric rates into Lee County as result of the TVA power policy has meant nothing. Landlords, whether of Negro slum dwellers in Tupelo or of Negro tenant farmers in the rural section of the county, have not found it to their advantage to wire their Negro tenants' homes at the cost of $15 to $25, when already they are squeezing all the rent possible from these tenants."

In the face of blatant forms of discrimination during the early New Deal, African Americans found little to praise in the government's relief efforts. They were acutely aware that they suffered disproportionately from unemployment, but faced the greatest discrimination and received the least benefits from government relief, work, housing, and social security programs. All Americans gained increasing assistance from the federal government, but such assistance would only slowly reach African Americans and help to reverse the impact of hard times on their families and communities. By the mid-1930s, however, a variety of new forces would gradually transform the "raw deal" into a "new deal."

## A New Deal, 1935–1939

Between the stock market crash of 1929 and the early years of the New Deal, the condition of African Americans moved from bad to worse. Neither the Hoover administration nor the first efforts of the Democratic regime of Franklin Roosevelt did much to lessen the suffering of African Americans. By 1935, however, a variety of forces helped to transform the relationship between blacks and the New Deal. Changes in American attitudes toward race and class, the emergence of new interracial alliances, and the growing political mobilization of African Americans themselves all put pressure on the federal government to address the needs of African Americans. In a nationwide radio broadcast, President Franklin D. Roosevelt symbolized the shift. In a speech before a conference of the Churches of Christ in America, he condemned lynching as murder: "Lynch law is murder, a deliberate and definite disobedience of the high command, 'Thou shalt not kill.' We do not excuse those in high places or low who condone lynch law." Following the president's pronouncement, the NAACP's *Crisis* magazine exclaimed that FDR was the only president to declare "frankly that lynching is murder. We all knew it, but it is unusual to have a president of the United States admit it. These things give us hope."

As the federal government increasingly affirmed its responsibility for the social welfare of all Americans, it helped to change the context of the African-American struggle for social justice. By 1939, African Americans had gradually gained a larger share of New Deal social programs and improved their economic situation. African-American income from New Deal work and relief programs—Public Works Administration, Works Progress Administration, and Civilian Conservation Corps—now nearly equaled their income from employment in agriculture and domestic service. On CCC projects, African Americans increased their percentage from less than six percent in 1935 to eleven percent in 1939. African Americans also occupied about one-third of all low-income PWA housing units, obtained a rising share of Federal Farm Security Loans, and access to a variety of new WPA educational and cultural programs. Because the government spent more money on education, including the building of new facilities, black illiteracy dropped ten percent during the 1930s. The number of African Americans on relief and the amount of money available to them rose steadily. African Americans increasingly hailed such New Deal social programs as "a godsend." Some even suggested that God "will lead me" but relief "will feed me."

The changing relationship between blacks and the New Deal was not merely a matter of the government's shifting attitude toward the social welfare of all Americans. The Roosevelt administration also responded to the growing importance of the black vote on national elections, the emergence of an interracial alliance of black and white New Dealers, and especially a rising core of black federal appointees. Roosevelt acted to the growing importance of the black vote by appointing increasing numbers of African Americans to federal posts. By the mid-1930s, some forty-five blacks had received appointments in various New Deal agencies and cabinet departments. The "Black Cabinet," as these black advisers were called, included Robert L. Vann, editor of the *Pittsburgh Courier,* in the office of the Attorney General; William H. Hastie, a civil rights attorney, in the Department of the Interior; Robert C. Weaver, an economist, also in the Interior Department; Lawrence A. Oxley, a social worker, in the Department of Labor; Edgar Brown, president of the United Government Employees, in the Civilian Conservation Corps; and Mary McLeod Bethune, founder of Bethune-Cookman

President Franklin Roosevelt responded to the growing importance of the black vote in national elections by appointing increasing numbers of blacks to federal posts. Members of the "Black Cabinet," as these appointees came to be called, gathered for a photograph in 1938.

College, head of the Negro Division of the National Youth Administration. The "Black Cabinet" enabled African Americans to improve their position in a variety of New Deal programs.

The first lady, Eleanor Roosevelt, played a key role in helping these black New Dealers improve the federal response to the needs of African Americans. Although Mrs. Roosevelt had little contact with African Americans before early 1933, she soon befriended Walter White of the NAACP and Mary McLeod Bethune. Through her frequent interactions with black leaders Eleanor Roosevelt gradually increased her support of civil rights issues. Following the election of 1936, for example, she endorsed legislation designed to abolish the poll tax, make lynching a federal offense, and increase aid to black institutions, particularly schools. Historians credit Mrs. Roosevelt with helping to push FDR's position on civil rights from one of caution and aloofness to one of significant support. FDR eventually allowed himself to be photographed with black leaders, conferred with civil rights delegations at the White House, and sent greetings to African American organizations.

As the White House seemed to escalate its support for racial justice, other New Dealers took heart and advanced the cause of African Americans. The policies of Harold Ickes, Secretary of Interior and administrator of the PWA; Harry Hopkins, head of the WPA; and a few others exemplified the growing support that African Americans received in some New Deal agencies. Before taking his post as Secretary of the Interior, Ickes had served as president of the Chicago chapter of the NAACP. Upon assuming his duties, he ended segregation in the department's rest rooms and cafeteria. Although local whites often ignored his policies, Ickes advocated the employment of skilled and unskilled black laborers on PWA construction projects. The secretary insisted that all PWA contractors agree to hire blacks in proportion to their percentage in the 1930 occupational census.

Under the leadership of Harry Hopkins, the WPA established policies making it illegal for any relief official to discriminate "on account of race, creed, or color." FDR had strengthened his hand, by issuing Executive Order 7046, which mandated that the WPA would assign persons "qualified by training and experience" to work projects without discrimination "on any grounds whatsoever."

Under Hopkins's leadership, the WPA also promoted black adult education, hired unemployed black professionals, and stimulated the arts within the black community. The WPA Education program employed over 5,000 blacks as leaders and supervisors, taught nearly 250,000 blacks to read and write, and trained many for skilled jobs. The Federal Music Project staged concerts involving the works of black composers; the Federal Art Project employed hundreds of black artists; and, under the direction of Hallie Flanagan, the Federal Theater Project (FTP) established an African American unit.

Supplementing the artistic work of the FTP was the Federal Writers Project. Young writers and scholars like St. Clair Drake, Horace R. Cayton, Richard Wright, and Ralph Ellison gained opportunities and early training on the Federal Writers Project. Both the FWP and FTP developed activities designed to increase interracial understanding, which provoked an investigation by the U.S. House of Representatives Un-American Activities Committee (HUAC). The HUAC helped to undercut the growth of their programs by charging them with "conspiracy and subversion" of American ideas, beliefs, and institutions.

Although most southern New Dealers resisted equal treatment for blacks, others supported efforts to improve the status of African Americans. Born in Alabama, Aubrey Willis Williams, served as Deputy Works Progress Administrator and head of the National Youth Administration (NYA). At the NYA, Williams resisted the establishment of racial differentials in wages paid to blacks and whites. He repeatedly stated the belief that African American youth should be prepared for jobs that would move them beyond the usual categories of maid and janitor. Will Alexander, director of the Farm Security Administration (FSA), was another Southern white who befriended African Americans during the period. Under his leadership, the FSA appointed a larger percentage of black supervisors than any other agency and gradually improved benefits for African Americans.

There were other reasons why federal policies toward blacks began to change for the better. Across the land, American attitudes toward race and class had begun to change. This was reflected in the emergence of new intellectual, cultural, and political currents. Increasing numbers of Americans criticized industrial elites—corporate executives, bankers, and Wall Street financiers—for eliminating their jobs and placing them in bread lines. Working Americans launched mass movements for

# FARM SECURITY ADMINISTRATION AIDS THE NEGRO FARMER

## THE NEGRO FARMER'S PROBLEM IS THE SOUTH-ERN FARMER'S PROBLEM

95 PERCENT OF NEGRO FARMERS ARE IN THE SOUTH. 47 PERCENT OF THESE ARE SHARECROPPERS. 32 PERCENT ARE TENANTS. —

## ONLY 21 PERCENT ARE OWNERS .

## FARM SECURITY HELPS THROUGH ...

1. REHABILITATION LOANS FOR EQUIP-MENT, LIVESTOCK, SEED, FERTIL-IZER .

2. TENANT PURCHASE LOANS TO MAKE OWNERS OUT OF CROPPERS AND TENANTS .

3. DEBT ADJUSTMENT TO REDUCE INTEREST, RE-SCALE PAYMENTS TO THE FARMER'S CAPACITY.

4. CO-OPERATIVE COMMUNITIES TO ENABLE SMALL FARMERS TO COM-PETE WITH LARGE, MECHANIZED FARMS.

The Farm Security Administration highlights its efforts to aid black farmers in this 1939 poster. The FSA sought to increase the number of black farmers who owned the land they worked.

greater government support of their interests during the 1930s. This increased activism could be seen in the rise of the Communist party, the resurgence of organized labor, and increasing efforts to attract African Americans to the ranks of both of these types of organizations.

An unpopular minority, the Communist party was especially eager to attract black members. Although the party often used the race issue to foster its own specific ideological attacks on capitalist institutions, such as the two-party system, it nonetheless played a key role in publicizing racial injustice and placing civil rights before the nation.

Few blacks joined the Communist party, but its activities on behalf of African Americans soon got their attention. The party's most famous campaigns centered on efforts to free one of its own members, the black communist Angelo Herndon, from a Georgia chain gang and the attempt to win aquittal on rape charges for nine blacks held in Scottsboro, Alabama, known as the Scottsboro Boys.

The case of the Scottsboro Boys was perhaps the most infamous instance of racial injustice in the courts of the 1930s. During the depression years, blacks and whites routinely "hoboed" the nation's freight trains, traveling from place to place looking for work and the means to survive. In March 1931, a group of black and white youths boarded a freight train, southbound from Chattanooga, Tennessee, to Alabama. A fight eventually broke out and the blacks forced the whites off the train.

The white youths reported the incident to local authorities who stopped the train near Scottsboro, Alabama. Nine young black men and two white women were removed from the train by the local sheriff. Fearing arrest, the young women accused the black youths of rape at knife point. Although the black defendants pleaded "not guilty," the court failed to appoint proper legal representation for the young men. An all-white jury ignored the different versions of events on the train given in the testimony of the two women and found the defendants guilty of rape and the court sentenced all but the youngest to death in the electric chair.

The Communist party soon took up the case. The party's Central Committee issued a statement describing the sentence as a "legal lynching," and within a few days, launched a national and international crusade to save the young men. As protest rallies emerged in major cities across the nation, non-Communist organizations like the NAACP soon joined communists in demanding justice. At the same time, the party's International Labor Defense pressed the legal case through the Alabama Supreme Court, which upheld the convictions. On two separate occasions the party carried the case forward to the U. S. Supreme Court, which overturned the convictions and ordered retrials, which in both cases, *Powell* v. *Alabama* (1932), and *Norris* v. *Alabama* (1935), led not to release but to new death sentences. However, the execution dates kept being postponed and eventually all defendants were cleared of the charges brought against them. After having spent more than fifteen years in jail for a crime he did not commit, the last defendant was released after the Second World War.

The Communist party not only staged demonstrations and legal actions to free blacks like Herndon and the Scottsboro boys, it also carried out day-to-day activities designed to improve the economic status of African Americans. The party organized hunger marches, unemployed councils, farm labor unions, and rent strikes to aid unemployed and destitute workers. In Chicago, when families received eviction notices, mothers would sometimes shout to the children, "Run quick find the Reds!" On one occasion, when communists attempted to prevent the eviction of a black family in Chicago, police shot and killed three African Americans. The Communist party responded by distributing nearly five thousand leaflets, urging black and white workers to unite and demand justice for the deceased.

During the 1930s the Socialist party also campaigned against racial injustice. In 1929, the party established the United Colored Socialists of America. Socialist party head Norman Thomas appointed a special black organizer for the South and supported a resolution condemning racial discrimination by trade unions. By 1933 the Socialist party endorsed federal anti-lynching and anti-poll tax legislation; the party also organized sharecroppers unions, and elevated blacks to leadership positions.

Launched in 1934, the Southern Tenant Farmers Union (STFU) represented the Socialist party's strongest effort to organize workers across racial lines. Founded near the town of Tyronza, Arkansas, the STFU resolved to organize black and white tenant farmers in the same union. Under the leadership of H. L. Mitchell, a white associate of Norman Thomas, and two ministers, Howard Lester and Claude Williams, the organization advocated both economic justice for all sharecroppers and racial justice for African Americans. A white organizer for the STFU emphasized the futility of separate organizations and appealed to what he called "belly hunger" to help erase the color line among farmers. "If we organize only a Union of Negro sharecroppers then the Negroes will be evicted and white sharecroppers from the hill country or the unemployed in Memphis will take their places. If on the other hand we organize only a Union of white sharecroppers then the white men will be evicted and Negro sharecroppers from Mississippi and the unemployed in Memphis will take their places." Although the organization failed to bring landowners to the bargaining table, it demonstrated how the American Left pushed the Roosevelt administration to create a "new deal."

The economic slump of the 1930s and the Roosevelt administration's liberalized labor laws energized the organized labor movement. However, the movement split over the issue of whether to organize workers along broad industrial lines or on a narrow, craft-by-craft basis. Impatient with the exclusionary policies of the American Federation of Labor (AFL), the Committee for Industrial Organization broke from the AFL at the 1935 convention. Under the leadership of John L. Lewis, head of the United Mine Workers of America (UMW), the CIO (renamed the Congress of Industrial Organizations in 1938) embarked upon an aggressive organizing drive. This change was especially significant for blacks because they were disporoportionately represented in mass production industries.

Learning from its failure to organize southern black miners in the coal strikes of 1927, the UMW made a firm commitment to organize black and white workers. Following the "UMW formula," the CIO soon launched the Steel Workers Organizing Committee (SWOC), the Packinghouse Workers Organizing Committee (PWOC), and the United Automobile Workers (UAW). In each case, the union appealed to black organizations like the NAACP and the National Urban League; employed black organizers; placed African Americans in key union offices; and advocated an end to racially biased pay scales. Under the prodding of black labor leaders like A. Philip Randolph, competition from the emerging CIO, and the growing influence of blacks in the New Deal political coalition, the AFL also modified its position on organizing black workers. AFL President William Green eventually supported the move to free Angelo Herndon and the Scottsboro Boys, to obtain federal anti-lynching legislation, and to abolish poll taxes that disfranchised black voters. By 1939, African Americans had moved into the meeting rooms of the "house of labor."

Reinforcing the lowering of racial barriers in the Labor movement were new intellectual and cultural perspectives on race in American society. Scholars, artists, and the popular media gradually changed their views on race. Social scientists rejected the notion of the inborn inferiority of races and developed a new consensus. Most intellectuals and social scientists agreed that African Americans were not inferior to whites, that racism injured its victims both psychologically and socially, and that racism itself was a mental illness that damaged the health of the individual and the nation as a whole. These views gained currency in the ongoing research of Columbia University anthropologist Franz Boas, his students, and associates, who questioned the long-held assumption that racial and ethnic group differences were inherited through the genes. Boas and his associates challenged the racists to prove that African Americans suffered a lower plane of living because they were intellectually inferior to their white counterparts. In short, he forced the social scientific community, which prided itself on attending to the "facts," to recognize that it had little evidence to support some of its most cherished theories. As one scholar put it, "We do not yet know scientifically what the relative intellectual ability of the various races is. Some different tests, equally valid, might give the Negro a higher score that the white. Until we do know, probably the best thing is to *act* as if all races had equivalent mental ability."

The intellectual assault on racism reached its high point in 1937 when the Carnegie Corporation invited the Swedish economist Gunnar Myrdal to the United States to head "a comprehensive study of the Negro." The Myrdal study resulted in the publication of the monumental *An American Dilemma: The Negro Problem and Modern Democracy* (1944). Myrdal brought together numerous scholars to work on different aspects of race relations. All defined the "Negro problem" as a problem of white racism, immorality, and inequality. *An American Dilemma* concluded that "The American Negro problem is in the heart of the [white] American. It is there that the interracial tension has its focus. It is there that the decisive struggle goes on. This is the central viewpoint of this treatise. Though our study includes economic, social, and political race relations, at bottom our problem is the moral dilemma of the American—the conflict between his moral valuations on various levels of consciousness and generality."

Although legal change came only slowly, the U.S. Supreme Court also issued rulings that weakened the hold of racism in American society. As early as 1935, legal opinions on race started to change, Donald Murray, a black graduate of Amherst College in Massachusetts, applied for admission to the University of Maryland Law School. When the school denied him admission based upon his race, he took the case to court and challenged racial discrimination in graduate education. Like most southern states, Maryland set up a tuition grant program that "assisted" blacks who sought graduate study and professional training by steering them elsewhere. But the Maryland Court of Appeals ordered the University of Maryland to set up a separate law school for blacks or admit them to the white one. Rather than contesting the court's decision, university officials quietly admitted blacks to the law school. In the case of *Missouri ex rel. Gaines* v. *Canada* (1938), the U.S. Supreme Court reinforced the Maryland precedent by ruling that law schools in the various states had to admit blacks or establish separate law schools.

The courts reinforced these decisions with others that slowly began to help blacks achieve full protection under the law. On two occasions (1932, 1935), the U.S. Supreme Court overruled the Alabama Supreme Court in the Scottsboro Case and insisted on due process of law for black defendants. In the case of *Hale* v. *Kentucky* (1938), the court noted the systematic exclusion of blacks from jury service and overturned the conviction of a black man accused of murder. Over the next three years, the U. S. Supreme Court also strengthened the economic position of African Americans. It upheld the right of African Americans to boycott businesses that discriminated in their employment practices; struck down a Georgia peonage law that permitted the virtual enslavement of blacks as sharecroppers; and upheld the elimination of unequal salaries for black and white teachers in Norfolk, Virginia. In short, by 1939 the court slowly undermined the historic *Plessy* v. *Ferguson* decision of 1896 that permitted a "separate but equal" society for blacks and whites.

Despite shifting conceptions of race and the New Deal's growing response to the needs of blacks, by 1939 poverty, unemployment, and racial discrimination continued to affect the African American community. Even the most egalitarian programs experienced a huge gap in policy and practice. The Farm Securities Administration, which secured homeloans for farm families, for example, operated with limited funds and used a tough credit-rating system that disqualified most

Despite the many opportunities offered to blacks by the New Deal, this sign for a "colored waiting room" at a bus station in Durham, North Carolina, attests to the racial discrimination that was still a part of daily life for the majority of blacks.

black tenants and sharecroppers from qualifiying for loans. Low-income federal housing programs reinforced the racial segregation of urban communities, adding federal policy to the ongoing historical forces—discriminatory real estate agents, restrictive covenants (regulations in many suburban neighborhoods that required resale of properties only to whites), and white neighborhood opposition—in the rise and expansion of the black ghetto.

The Works Progress Administration established regulations ending racial discrimination in its programs, but southern whites continued to evade the rules and made it more difficult for blacks than whites to gain adequate public works jobs and relief. Black women faced special forms of discrimination on WPA projects in the South. They were often forced to perform "men's jobs" at a time that white women received jobs defined as "clean" or "easy." In a South Carolina town, a local physician reported, "The Beautification project appears to be 'For Negro Women Only.' This project is a type of work that should be assigned to men. Women are worked in 'gangs' in connection with the City's dump pile, incinerator and ditch piles. Illnesses traced to such exposure as these women must face do not entitle them to medical aid at the expense of the WPA."

By the late 1930s, as whites returned to full-time employment in private industry in growing numbers, most blacks continued to depend on public service and relief programs. Despite the various interracial alliances and growing sensitivity to the destructive impact of class and racial inequality, white Americans continued to insist that their needs be met first. While the CIO helped to organize blacks who were fortunate enough to maintain their jobs during the depression years, as the country lifted itself out of the depression it did little to promote the equitable return of employment of black and white wokers in equal numbers. For their part, although the socialists and communists helped to change attitudes toward interracial cooperation, the benefits of these efforts remained largely symbolic rather than material. Blacks continued to suffer racial injustice. African Americans, in short, would have to attend to their own interests, unite, and wage an even stronger offensive against the barriers of racial and class inequality.

## Family, Community, and Politics, 1933–1939

A variety of factors shaped the experiences of African Americans during the Great Depression. The impact of economic hard times, the emergence of New Deal social programs, and changing perspectives on race and class helped to define the black experience. Despite widespread deprivation and suffering, African Americans developed a variety of strategies for coping with the depression on their own. They deepened their connections with family, friends, and the African American community. At the same time, they strengthened their links with organized labor and broadened their participation in the political process, particularly the New Deal coalition of the Democratic party. As early as 1932, Robert Vann, editor of the *Pittsburgh Courier* had urged African Americans to abandon the party of Lincoln. "My friends, go turn Lincoln's picture to the wall. That debt has been paid in full."

As the depression took its toll on their lives, African Americans developed a variety of strategies for making ends meet. For many black women the depression was an old experience with a new name. As black men lost jobs in increasing numbers, African-American women helped keep their families in tact by relying on black kin and friendship networks.

African-American families took in boarders, cared for each other's children, and creatively manipulated their resources. In rural areas, they maintained gardens, canned fruits and vegetables, fished, hunted, and gathered wild nuts and berries. And blacks adapted these rural responses to the realities of life in cities. In small urban spaces, for example, some continued to maintain gardens to supply certain southern staples, particularly collard greens, cabbage, potatoes, and tomatoes. Under the impact of the depression, such activities became even more important.

Since the threat of eviction weighed so heavily on the minds of urban blacks, the "rent party" represented a significant source of income. Sometimes described as "chittlin's struts," these parties had deep roots in the rural South. "Down home" food—chittlins, corn bread, collard greens, hogmaws, pig feet, and so on—was on the menu. Sponsors charged a small admission fee and sometimes offered printed or handwritten tickets.

A key component in the survival of urban blacks during the 1930s, the rent parties also served as a training ground for the next generation of black blues artists—

the blues men who followed in the wake of such classical blues recording artists as Bessie Smith, LeRoy Carr, Jimmy Yancey, Cripple Clarence Lofton, Big Maceo Merriweather, Sonny Boy Williamson, and Big Bill Broonzy among others moved to the fore with lyrics familiar to the house parties.

> How Long, how long has that evening train been gone
> How long, how long, baby, how long?
> Standing at the station, watch my baby leaving town
> Feeling disgusted, nowhere could she be found.
> How long, how long, baby, how long?

Such parties became even more lucrative when sponsors added gambling and liquor to food, music, and dancing. The "policy" or numbers game was also an adaptation to poverty that African Americans brought to the city and used to help weather the storm during the depression years. The game had its roots in the mid-nineteenth century, but it gained increasing popularity among the poor because it allowed bets as low as a penny. On the South Side of Chicago, one black resident tried to imagine a world without policy. It was so important to Chicago's black community that without it he believed, "seven thousand people would be unemployed and business in general would be crippled, especially taverns and even groceries, shoestores, and many other business enterprises who depend on the buying power of the South Side."

The church provided another arena in which African Americans sought to make ends meet. Established Baptist, Methodist, and Holiness (Church of God in Christ) churches struggled to assist their parishioners to survive hard times. New religious movements also increased their following, partly as a result of their success in feeding their parishioners. For example, the Peace Mission of Father Divine (George Baker) whose efforts on behalf of the unemployed started during the 1920s, expanded dramatically during the depression. In 1932, he moved the mission from New Jersey to Harlem and gained credit for feeding the masses and offering hope in a time of widespread despair.

At the same time, Bishop Charles Emmanuel Grace, known as "Daddy Grace," established the United House of Prayer of All People with headquarters in Washington, D.C. The organization spread to more than twenty cities and provided thousands of people respite from hard times.

Black religious services featured music that sometimes resembled the music of the "rent party." It was in 1932 that the Gospel pioneer Thomas Dorsey broke from his growing reputation as a blues pianist and dedicated himself to Gospel song writing, which led to his most popular tune, "Precious Lord." Dorsey's swinging, rocking, and blueslike melodies eventually caught on and stirred the entire world. Over and over again, whether in religious or secular settings, black children of the depression recalled how their families struggled, to place food on the table and clothing on their backs.

The pastor of the Church of God in Christ in Washington, D.C., preaches during a service in 1942. Black churches also featured music that mirrored the growing influence of urban life.

In order to improve the circumstances of their families and communities, African Americans also moved increasingly toward the Labor movement, which had dramatically expanded under the impact of New Deal legislation. The new CIO increasingly displaced the older, more racially restrictive AFL. Under these new conditions, African Americans took the initiative to expand their place within labor's ranks. In Milwaukee, for example, LeRoy Johnson, a black butcher and packinghouse worker, became a major figure in the organization of the local United Packinghouse Union. Described by an associate as an "aggressive sort of guy and quite articulate," Johnson helped to make the CIO campaign in the city a success.

Perhaps more than any other single figure during the 1930s, however, A. Philip Randolph epitomized the persistent effort of black workers to organize in their own interest. During that decade, when new federal legislation (the Railway Labor Act of 1934) recognized the rights of workers to organize, Randolph and the Brotherhood of Sleeping Car Porters and Maids (BSCP)—which he had helped form in 1925—increased their organizing drive among black porters. Randolph's rhetoric and actions inspired the rank and file during the hard days of the depression. At one convention, he exclaimed, "The lesson that Pullman porters in particular and Negroes in general must learn is that salvation must and can only come from within."

Black pullman porters rallied to the BSCP, which, by 1933, claimed to represent some 35,000 members. Two years later the BSCP defeated a Pullman company union and gained the right to represent porters in negotiations with management, which, in 1937, signed a contract with the union. In the meantime, the AFL had grudgingly approved a full international charter for the brotherhood, placing it upon an equal footing with other member unions. The BSCP victory had extraordinary significance: It not only helped to make blacks more union conscious, but increased their influence on national labor policy, and the larger civil rights struggle.

As black workers increased their organizing activities, the major civil rights organizations also moved toward a sharper focus on the economic plight of African Americans. In 1933, the NAACP, the Urban League, and other interracial organizations formed the Joint Committee on National Recovery (JCNR). Although underfunded and ill staffed, the JCNR lobbied in Washington, D.C., on behalf of blacks and helped to publicize the plight of African Americans in the relief and recovery programs. The Urban League also formed Emergency Advisory Councils and Negro workers councils in major cities across the country and played a major role in promoting closer ties between blacks and organized labor. Although the League had earlier supported black strikebreaking activities and emphasized amicable relations with employers, it now urged black workers to organize and "get into somebody's union and stay there." For its part, the NAACP formed a Committee on Economic Problems Affecting the Negro; invited representatives of the CIO to serve on its board; and worked with organized labor to gain housing, wages, hours, and Social Security benefits for black workers.

The major civil rights organizations also supported the "Don't Buy Where You Can't Work" campaign. Aimed at white merchants who served the African American community but refused to employ blacks, "Don't Buy Where You Can't Work" galvanized the black urban community. In New York, Chicago, Washington D.C., and other cities, blacks boycotted stores that refused to hire African Americans, or hired them only as low-paying domestic and common laborers.

New York launched its "Don't Buy Where You Can't Work" campaign under the leadership of Reverend John H. Johnson of St. Martin's Protestant Episcopal Church. When white Harlem store owners refused to negotiate, Johnson and his supporters formed the Citizens League for Fair Play, which set up picket lines around Blumstein's Department Store, took pictures of blacks who crossed the line, and published photos in the black newspaper, the *New York Age*. After six weeks, the store gave in and hired black clerical and professional staff. As a result of such actions, New York blacks obtained the nation's first black affirmative action plan—a pattern of hiring that gave preference to previously excluded groups. In 1938, the New York Uptown Chamber of Commerce negotiated with the Greater New York Coordinating Committee for Employment and agreed to grant African Americans one-third of all retail executive, clerical, and sales jobs. The businesses would not fire whites to make room for blacks, but agreed to give blacks preference in all new openings.

Although African Americans expressed their resentment toward discrimination in formally organized and peaceful group actions, they sometimes despaired and adopted violent responses. On March 25, 1935, a race riot broke out in Harlem, when a rumor spread that a black youth had been brutally beaten and nearly killed by the police. Flyers soon appeared: "Child Brutally Beaten—near death," "One Hour Ago Negro Boy Was Brutally Beaten," "The Boy Is Near Death." Although the youth in question had been released unharmed, outrage had already spread and African Americans smashed buildings and looted stores, in a night of violence that resulted in at least one death, more than fifty injuries, and thousands of dollars worth of property damage.

In the volatile climate of the 1930s, some blacks gravitated toward the Communist and Socialist parties. They perceived radicalism as the most appropriate response to the deepening plight of African Americans. In 1931, aided by the Communist party, blacks in rural Alabama founded the Alabama Sharecroppers Union. The organization developed an underground network of communications that enabled them to maintain secrecy. Meetings took place in black churches, where their plans were disguised as religious undertakings. The union's membership increased to an estimated three thousand in 1934. Its efforts soon attracted the attention of local authorities and violence broke out when law officers tried to confiscate the livestock of union members, who allegedly owed money to landowners. In 1932, Ned Cobb (referred to as Nate Shaw in the published oral history of his life) joined the sharecroppers union and fought the system that oppressed him. As he recalled, he had to act because he had labored "under many rulins, just like the other Negro, that I knowed was injurious to man and displeasin to God and still I had to fall back." One cold morning in December 1932, Shaw refused to "fall back." When deputy sheriffs came to take his neighbor's livestock, he took part in a shootout with local law officers.

Nate Shaw's action underscored the increasing militancy of rural black workers. Despite violence and intimidation, black workers also took an active part in the formation of the socialist Southern Tenant Farmers Union (STFU). A black farmer helped to inspire the organization when he spoke up at the initial meeting of the group: "For a long time now the white folks and the colored folks have been fighting each other and both of us has been getting whipped all the time. We don't have nothing against one another but we got plenty against the landlord. The same chain that holds my people holds your people too. If we're chained together on the outside, ought to stay chained together in the union." When white landowners evicted sharecroppers in Arkansas, the black STFU vice president, Owen H. Whitfield, led some 500 black and white farmers onto the main highway between Memphis and St. Louis and vowed to remain there until the federal government intervened. The Missouri State Highway patrol soon moved in and loaded families and their possessions on trucks and scattered them on back country roads. Although these radical actions produced few results, they highlighted the increasing activism of rural black workers in their own behalf.

A small number of blacks joined the Communist party and played a role in the party's League of Struggle for Negro Rights (LSNR). According to a recent study of the party in depression-era Alabama, blacks made up the majority of the party's membership during most of the period. The party's fight on behalf of the Scotts-boro Boys attracted local black workers.

Most African Americans, however, shunned membership in radical parties and worked hard to broaden their participation in the New Deal coalition. In 1936, African Americans formed the National Negro Congress (NNC). Spearheaded by Ralph Bunche of Howard University and John Davis, executive secretary of the Joint Committee on National Recovery, the organization aimed to unite all exist-ing organizations—political, fraternal, and religious—and press for the full socio-economic recovery of the black community from the ravages of the depression. Nearly six hundred organizations attended the founding meeting, which selected A. Philip Randolph as its first president.

The National Negro Congress demonstrated a new level of African-American political organization and mobilization. Because of the dramatic growth of the black population in most cities, black voter registration drives picked up momen-tum during the 1930s. The proportion of the black population that had registered to vote had risen rapidly in the major industrial cities—from less than thirty percent to sixty-six percent in Detroit. In Philadelphia the number of registered black voters rose by more than ninety percent. In Chicago the rate of black voter registration exceeded the percentage of white. In the South as well—Durham, Raleigh, Birmingham, Atlanta, Savannah, and Charleston—African Americans formed political clubs to fight for the franchise and increase the number of black voters in that region.

As Republicans continued to ignore the pleas of black voters, blacks increasing-ly turned toward the Democratic party. In the election of 1936, African Americans voted for the Democratic party in record numbers, giving Roosevelt seventy-six percent of the Northern black vote. Following that election, African Americans used their growing support of the Democratic party to demand greater considera-tion from federal policymakers.

African Americans placed justice before the law high on their list of priorities. In 1933, the NAACP organized a Writers League Against Lynching and launched a nationwide movement to secure a federal anti-lynching law. Sponsored in the House of Representatives by Edward Costigan of Colorado and in the Senate by Robert Wagner of New York, the anti-lynching bill gained little support from FDR and failed when Southern senators killed the measure in 1934, 1935, 1937, 1938, and 1940. Despite its failure, the campaign against lynchings produced results. The number of lynchings dropped from eighteen in 1935 to two in 1939. Under the lead-ership of black attorneys William Hastie, Charles Hamilton Houston, and Thurgood Marshall, African Americans won important cases before the U.S. Su-preme Court: selection of blacks for jury duty; admission to previously all-white law schools; and greater access to employment, housing, and public accommodations. Houston, Marshall, and Hastie carefully planned an overall strategy, emphasizing test cases with broad implications for dismantling the entire segregationist system.

*Missouri ex rel. Gaines* v. *Canada* (1938) was one of the most celebrated of these cases. Houston's decision to take the case represented a tactical manouver to dismantle the separate but equal principle that the Court established in an earlier case, *Plessy* v. *Ferguson* (1896). Lloyd Gaines, a black graduate of Lincoln University in Missouri, was denied admission to the University of Missouri Law School because the school did not accept blacks. The university advised Gaines to take advantage of state funds provided to support black legal training in other states. Supported by the St. Louis chapter of the NAACP, Gaines sued, demanding access to training at the all-white law school. Houston argued the case in the Missouri courts where Gaines lost. Then Huston argued the case to the U.S. Supreme Court, where Gaines won a major victory. The Court's decision outlawed the practice of giving blacks subsidies to receive legal training at out-of-state schools. It also supported the admission of blacks to all-white schools in the absence of fully equal facilities for blacks.

As black lawyers attacked the system of legalized racial segregation, black social scientists and artists assaulted its intellectual underpinnings. E. Franklin Frazier, W.E.B. Du Bois, Carter G. Woodson, and other black social scientists and historians had worked for years counteracting racist stereotypes. Under the leadership of Carter G. Woodson, the Association for the Study of Negro Life and History (founded in 1915) continued to promote the study of African-American history, emphasizing the role of blacks in the development of the nation. While the organization continued to publish the scholarly *Journal of Negro History* founded in 1916, in 1933 it added the *Negro History Bulletin* as a publication designed for broader circulation. Launched in 1926, Negro History Week also became a regular feature of African-American community life across the country.

E. Franklin Frazier conducted seminal studies of black community and family life, which culminated in the publication of his *The Negro Family in the United States* (1939). Although he underestimated the role that poor and working-class blacks played in shaping their own experience, Frazier emphasized environmental over racial factors in explaining poverty. In his scholarship on African-American history, W.E.B Du Bois also called attention to the impact of class and racial discrimination in his massive reinterpretation of the emancipation period, *Black Reconstruction in America, 1860–1880* (1935). Gunnar Myrdal's *An American Dilemma* built upon the scholarship of some thirty black scholars, including young men like Charles S. Johnson, St. Clair Drake, Horace R. Cayton, and Ralph Bunche among others.

Reinforcing the work of black social scientists and historians were the contributions of black artists. Concert singers Roland Hayes, Paul Robeson, and Marian Anderson frequently appeared on stage and on national radio broadcasts. Born to a working-class family in Philadelphia in 1902, Marian Anderson had pursued advanced musical training in Europe and had performed widely in Sweden, Norway, and Denmark. As a result of her growing success in Europe, Anderson returned to the United States in 1935. *The New York Times* reported, "Marian Anderson has returned to her native land one of the great singers of our time."

In 1939 the Daughters of the American Revolution, who owned Constitution Hall in Washington, D.C., barred Anderson from giving a concert there. For her part, Eleanor Roosevelt resigned from the DAR over the incident. In her popular newspaper column, "My Day," she explained that she could no longer belong to an organization that maintained the color line. African Americans and their white allies formed a committee of protest and got permission from Secretary of the Interior Harold Ickes to hold the concert at the Lincoln Memorial. Nearly 75,000 people stood in the cold open air to hear her sing, and millions more heard her on radio. Her repertoire included Negro spirituals, bringing them to a wide audience for the first time, along with the works of classical European composers.

Richard Wright, Langston Hughes, William Attaway, and others expressed the experiences of African Americans through novels and plays. In 1938, Richard Wright won a WPA writing prize for his book *Uncle Tom's Children,* a collection of short stories on black life in the rural South. Two years later he published his most famous novel *Native Son,* which characterized the Great Migration of blacks to American cities and the destructive impact of racism on their lives. One observer later recalled, "The day *Native Son* appeared, American culture was changed forever." Wright's book was a phenomenal success. It set a sales record for Harper and Brothers and soon surpassed John Steinbeck's *The Grapes of Wrath* on the best-seller lists. Born on a plantation near Natchez, Mississippi in 1908, Wright later wrote that his head was "full of a hazy notion that life could be lived with dignity, that the personalities of others should not be violated." The Mississippi-born writer William Attaway expressed similar sentiments in his powerful portrayal of black site workers in his novel, *Blood on the Forge* (1941).

Adding to the artistic portrayal of black life were the dramatic productions of black theater groups like the Rose McClendon players, the Harlem Players, and the Negro People's Theatre; the music of jazz artists like Fletcher Henderson, Duke Ellington, Bessie Smith, and Jimmie Lunceford; the paintings of Romare Bearden; and the films of the pioneer black filmmaker Oscar Micheaux. African Americans also gained greater access to mainstream radio and film and gradually used these media to project more positive images of themselves than was previously possible. The blues singer Ethel Waters had her own radio show and the film industry broke new ground by giving Paul Robeson the lead role in the movie version of the stage play *The Emperor Jones,* with whites serving as supporting cast.

African Americans developed a variety of responses to life during the Great Depression. The depression offered different problems and prospects for educated black professional people on the one hand and the masses of working-class and poor people on the other. Yet all were linked to each other through the persistence of racial inequality. The emergence of prizefighter Joe Louis as a folk hero for all African Americans is perhaps the most potent evidence of their sense of a common

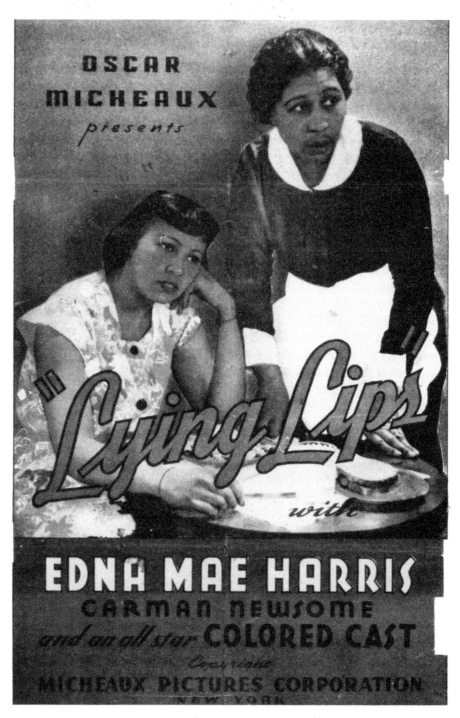

*Lying Lips,* a 1939 movie produced and directed by the pioneering black filmmaker Oscar Micheaux, featured an all-black cast.

plight, kinship, and future. Indeed, Joe Louis helped to unify black people during the period and gave them hope that they could topple the segregationist system. When he lost they cried, as in his first bout against the German Max Schmeling in 1936. They were especially heartbroken because Hitler preached the doctrine of Aryan supremacy, which claimed the physical and intellectual superiority of all white people, and the German people in particular.

On the other hand, when Joe Louis won, black people celebrated. After he knocked out Schmeling in the first round of their rematch, black people everywhere applauded, celebrated, and danced in the streets. Similarly, when Louis knocked out the Italian heavyweight Primo Carnera, black people were also elated and felt that they had to some degree avenged Benito Mussolini's invasion and bombing of Ethiopia in 1935. The singer Lena Horne offers a powerful statement on Joe Louis as a black folk hero: "Joe was the one invincible Negro, the one who stood up to the white man and beat him down with his fists. He in a sense carried so many of our hopes, maybe even dreams of vengeance."

The depression, New Deal, and social change sent a mixed message to African Americans. On the one hand, they experienced the gradual growth of new and more egalitarian ideas and practices on race; on the other, they suffered persistent economic deprivation and discrimination. Because they faced a dual process of poverty and progress, African-American responses were likewise complex and varied. At times, they despaired and exploded into violence, as in the Harlem riot of 1935. At other times, they gave up on mainstream institutions and turned toward alternative visions and strategies, as reflected in their growing connections with the Communist and Socialist parties. Their music also reflected a similar range of responses—blues, gospel, and jazz. Above all, however, as symbolized in the boxing career of Joe Louis, they deepened their struggle to break down barriers to their full participation in American society. They launched movements to break the back of Jim Crow and broaden their access to the larger economic, political, social, and cultural life of the nation. Their struggle would gain even greater fruits during the crisis of the Second World War, another epic fight that lay only a few years ahead.

## The Second World War, 1940–1945

Under the impact of the Second World War, African Americans gained new industrial opportunities as the nation mobilized for war and called men into the military in rising numbers. It was during this period that African Americans regained a foothold in the industrial economy and broke the unskilled "job ceiling," moving into semiskilled and skilled jobs. Yet, the movement of African Americans into defense industry jobs was a slow process. Employers, labor unions, and government agencies, all discriminated against blacks and undermined their participation in the war effort. The *Chicago Defender* captured the frustrations of many African Americans in an editorial. "Why die for democracy for some foreign country when we don't even have it here?"

Most African Americans nonetheless supported the nation's declaration of war against Germany and Japan. Black servicemen and women fought in the European, Pacific, and Mediterranean theaters of war. Unlike the First World War, however, African Americans refused to simply "close ranks" and postpone their own struggle for full citizenship and recognition of their rights at home. They now used the war emergency, as well as their growing influence in the Democratic party and the new unions, to wage a "Double V" campaign—for victory at home as well as abroad. Their campaign received its most powerful expression in the militant March on Washington, which led to the federal Fair Employment Practices Committee. By war's end African Americans and their white allies had set the stage for the emergence of the modern Civil Rights movement.

As the nation edged toward war in the years after 1939, African Americans continued to face a pattern of racial discrimination. Despite growing U. S. protests against the racism of Nazi Germany, African Americans confronted racial injustice at home and abroad. In the defense industries and armed services, African Americans complained of racial bias. In 1940 blacks made up less than two percent of employees in the nation's expanding aircraft industry, and management officials in that industry often stated overtly their determination to keep blacks out. At the large North American Aviation firm, for example, the company's president reported that black applicants would be considered only for janitorial jobs. In Milwaukee, the A. O. Smith Company, producer of auto frames and tanks for the military, stated that they "never did and didn't intend to employ Negroes." Black women confronted even greater difficulties gaining defense jobs than black men did. Employers expressed the belief that black women were peculiarly suited for domestic service but not for industrial jobs. Thus many African-American men and women believed that it was a waste of time to seek work in all-white defense plants.

Craft unions reinforced discrimination against black workers in defense work. Skilled black workers—plumbers, bricklayers, carpenters, electricians, cement finishers, and painters—faced exclusion from labor unions either by provisions of their bylaws or by some form of "ritual," or gentleman's agreement that blacks would not be proposed for membership. In a resolution introduced at the 1941 convention of the AFL, A. Philip Randolph pinpointed labor union discrimination against black workers in a broad range of jobs in different parts of the country. He cited the International Association of Machinists (IAM) as the union with the most conspicuous record of labor union discrimination against African Americans. By accepting only white members, the IAM reinforced the exclusion of blacks from the metal trades and the aircraft industry, including the huge Boeing Aircraft Corporation in Seattle.

Since many defense industry jobs required additional training for large numbers of white as well as black workers, the U. S. Office of Education financed such programs under the Vocational Education National Defense (VEND) Training Program. In his study of black labor during the period, economist and New Dealer Robert Weaver documented racial discrimination in the implementation of such

Blacks continued to struggle against racial discrimination at home, even as African-American soldiers fought and died overseas during the Second World War.

programs. According to Weaver, such discrimination had deep roots in earlier patterns of discrimination in federal educational programs. During the 1930s, the federal government had established a precedent for discrimination, by awarding blacks less than $4.75 per capita of federal funds, compared to $8 for whites. When the government established VEND, it continued the same practices. As Weaver put it, "This discrimination was in reality a projection of past practices. Most vocational education officials at the national, state, and local levels were not prepared

Cadets in the U.S. Army's first all-black air unit, the 99th Pursuit Squadron, were trained at Tuskegee Institute in Alabama. More than 600 black pilots were trained there during the war.

to champion new policies relative to minority groups' training." Vocational training programs reinforced a vicious cycle of black exclusion from defense jobs. When asked why blacks were not trained and employed in defense industry jobs, training school supervisors, unions, and employers conveniently blamed each other, thus passing the buck back and forth and assuring that nothing was done about their discrimination practices.

African Americans fared little better in the armed services. During the early 1940s, as the government trained white pilots to fly warplanes, the War Department barred African Americans from the U. S. Air Corps. Blacks were admitted to the U. S. Army in large numbers, but were placed in segregated service and labor units, responsible for building, maintenance, and supplies. In 1940, there were an estimated five thousand blacks in the Army, but only four black units were up to full strength and there were fewer than twelve officers in a corps of over twenty-three hundred thousand enlisted men and officers. At the war's outset, the Marine Corps and Air Corps barred blacks completely, while the Department of the Navy and Coast Guard accepted them only as messmen or laborers.

Despite the existence of racial discrimination in the defense program, African Americans played a key role in the war effort. The number of blacks selected for military service increased from 2,069 in 1940 to about 370,000 in 1942, following the

Japanese attack on Pearl Harbor on December 7, 1941, and the official entry of the United States into the Second World War. By the end of the war, nearly one million black men and women had served in the armed forces, nearly three-quarters in the U. S. Army, followed in numbers by the Navy (and Coast Guard), Marine Corps, and the Air Corps, in which only a few blacks served. At the same time, black civilians supported the war effort by purchasing war bonds and launching vigorous bond campaigns in their churches, schools, and community organizations. Despite the poverty of many, they also cooperated with the government's food conservation program and staffed United Service Organizations (USO) to boost the morale of black service men and women. The USO coordinated the social service activities of a wide range of organizations, including the YWCA, YMCA, and the Salvation Army, to name a few. In addition, African Americans served as nurses' aides, drivers in motor corps, and other voluntary but vital jobs in the Red Cross.

Nearly 500,000 African Americans saw service overseas. Most served in transportation corps, port battalions, and construction units. They moved troops and supplies, built and repaired roads and fortifications, and cleared battle zones of debris and dead and wounded soldiers. They also engaged the enemy in combat in the European, Mediterranean, and Pacific theaters, and gained recognition for their outstanding services. The 761st Tank Battalion, which served in six European countries and fought in the Battle of the Bulge, received several commendations for its bravery on the battlefield. By war's end, many of these units received the Presidential Citation for their contributions to winning the war. The Air Corps awarded the Distinguished Flying Cross to eighty-two African American pilots and several blacks received the Navy Cross. Messman Dorie Miller became perhaps the most renowned of these seamen. "Without previous experience [he] ... manned a machine gun in the face of serious fire during the Japanese attack on Pearl Harbor, December 7, 1941, on the Battleship *Arizona* shooting down four enemy planes."

The significant number of Distinguished Flying Crosses was made possible by the training of black airmen at segregated institutions, like Tuskegee Institute. Although some black leaders resisted the training of blacks in segregated facilities, others accepted the arrangement as an opportunity to expand their war-and-peace-time opportunities. Tuskegee trained some six hundred black pilots who flew missions in Africa, France, Italy, Poland, Romania, and Germany. Colonel Benjamin O. Davis, a graduate of the U.S. Military Academy at West Point, became the highest ranking black officer. He flew sixty missions and won several medals for distinguished service. Other African Americans received medals of honor from the governments of France, Yugoslavia, and the Soviet Union.

African Americans served and achieved against great odds. On and off military bases, black service personnel often did not receive courteous treatment and recognition of their human and civil rights. In Durham, North Carolina, for example, a local jury acquitted a white bus driver who murdered a black soldier

African-American women service a truck at Fort Huachuca, Arizona. During the war, black women, perhaps even more so than white women, performed traditionally male jobs.

following an altercation on his route. When German prisoners of war arrived in the United States, they often received service in white establishments that denied service to African Americans.

No less than black men, black women in the military were also subject to brutality in the Jim Crow South. When they failed to move along fast enough, three black Women in the Women's Army Corps (WACS) were brutally assaulted by civilian police in a Kentucky railroad station. When African Americans resisted such treatment, racial violence erupted at Fort Bragg, N.C., Fort Dix, N.J., and other military bases.

Racial discrimination in the military was part of a broader pattern of hostility toward blacks in American society. Attracted by new jobs created by the war effort, nearly 1.6 million blacks moved into the nation's cities. The percentage of blacks living in urban areas rose from less than fifty percent in 1940 to nearly sixty percent in 1945. Western cities like Los Angeles, San Francisco, and Seattle now joined established northern and southern cities as major centers of black urban population growth. Between 1940 and 1945, the black population of Los Angeles county rose from about 75,000 to 150,000. Seattle's black population leaped from 3,800 to nearly 10,000. At the same time, established midwestern and northeastern cities attracted large numbers of new blacks. In the three year period between 1940 and 1943, Detroit's black population increased by fifty thousand. As the black urban population increased, race relations deteriorated and violence broke out in several cities. One example was the so-called "zoot suit" riots in which white sailors and civilians attacked African Americans and Latino residents. Marked by their dress as well as their color—broad felt hats, pegged trousers, and pocket knives on gold chains—African American and Latino youth were assaulted in Los Angeles, San Diego, Long Beach, Chicago, Detroit, and Philadelphia.

Racial violence went well beyond the "zoot suit" confrontations. The most serious conflicts occurred in Harlem and Detroit. In 1943, a policeman shot a black soldier and touched off the Harlem riot, which resulted in at least five deaths, five hundred injuries, hundreds of arrests, and five million dollars in property damage. The actor Sidney Poitier later recalled his experience of the riot: "In a restaurant downtown where I was working I heard that there was trouble in Harlem. After work I took a train uptown, came up out of the subway, and there was chaos everywhere—cops, guns, debris and broken glass all over the street. Many stores had been set on fire, and the commercial district on 125th Street looked as if it had been bombed."

The confrontation in Detroit left behind even more deaths, injuries, and arrests. On June 20, 1943, more than 100,000 Detroiters crowded the city's Belle Isle Amusement Park to escape the sweltering summer heat. Before long, violence between blacks and whites broke out at the park's casino, ferry dock, playgrounds, and bus stops. The violence soon spilled over into the black Paradise Valley area. At a local club, a patron took the microphone and announced: "There's a riot at Belle Isle! The whites have killed a colored lady and her baby. Thrown them over a bridge. Everybody come on! There's free transportation outside!" Although the report of the death of a black woman and her child was false, by early morning African Americans had smashed windows and looted numerous white-owned stores on Hastings Avenue. Only the arrival of federal troops put down the violence, which resulted in 34 deaths, 675 injuries, nearly 1,900 arrests, and an estimated $2 million in property damage. In both the Harlem and Detroit riots, most of those killed, injured, or arrested were blacks, while the damaged property belonged almost exclusively to whites.

Racial violence in Detroit and elsewhere was intertwined with the growing residential segregation of African Americans in the urban environment. As it had during the depression years, federal housing policy reinforced patterns of residential segregation. For example, in 1941, the Federal Public Housing Authority (FPHA) approved the Sojourner Truth Housing Project. Although the project was designated for black occupancy, it was located in a predominantly white working-class neighborhood. When local residents protested, federal authorities rescinded its decision and handed the project over to whites. Only the vigorous protests of the black community, organized in the Sojourner Truth Citizens Committee and supported by the United Auto Workers union, regained for African Americans their right to live in the project.

On the other hand, the federal government soon established an all-white project at the Ford Motor Company's new Willow Run factory. Although blacks and their CIO allies tried to persuade federal officials to permit blacks and whites to occupy the units, the FPHA insisted on a policy of racial segregation. Such housing policies, along with restrictive employment practices and discrimination in the military, embittered black-white relations in the city of Detroit and fueled the underlying forces leading to the 1943 race riot.

African Americans did not passively accept racial discrimination in the defense program. They waged a militant "Double V" campaign against social injustice at home and abroad. Popularized by the *Pittsburgh Courier,* the "Double V" campaign enabled African Americans to declare their loyalty to the war effort without abandoning their thrust for equal rights at home. As early as summer 1940, the NAACP criticized the navy's policy of recruiting blacks as messmen only. The organization emphasized the injustice of using black tax dollars to finance opportunities for whites, while denying such opportunities to blacks.

The fight against discrimination in the military was not limited to male branches of the service. Under the leadership of Mabel K. Staupers, executive director of the National Association of Colored Graduate Nurses, African Americans waged a vigorous fight to integrate the Army and Navy Nurse Corps. The army established a quota on the number of black women accepted for service, while the navy barred them altogether. In her campaign to end such discrimination, Staupers tried to enlist the support of white nurses groups. Only the acute shortage of white nurses by early 1945 helped to end the army's quota system and break the barriers on black women in the navy.

African Americans also attacked racial discrimination in war industries with government contracts. On its July 1940 cover, the NAACP's *Crisis* featured an airplane factory marked, "For Whites Only," with the caption, "Warplanes—Negro Americans may not build them, repair them, or fly them, but they must help pay for them."

The African-American quest for social justice gained its most potent expression in the emergence of the militant March on Washington Movement (MOWM). Spearheaded by A. Philip Randolph, the MOWM was launched in 1941 following a meeting of civil rights groups in Chicago. The critical moment came when a black woman angrily addressed the chair: "Mr. Chairman ... we ought to throw fifty thousand Negroes around the White House, bring them from all over the country, in jalopies, in trains and any way they can get there, and throw them around the White House and keep them there until we can get some action from the White House." Randolph not only seconded the proposal but offered himself and the Brotherhood of Sleeping Car Porters as leaders: "I agree with the sister. I will be very happy to throw [in] my organization's resources and offer myself as a leader of such a movement."

By early June, the MOWM had established march headquarters in Harlem, Brooklyn, Washington, D. C., Pittsburgh, Detroit, Chicago, St. Louis, and San Francisco. The movement spread through the major rail centers and soon joined forces with local NAACP and Urban League chapters, churches, and fraternal orders.

The MOWM helped to mobilize the masses of black working people as well as the middle and upper classes. According to Randolph, "It was apparent ... that some unusual, bold and gigantic effort must be made to awaken the American people and the President of the Nation to the realization that the Negroes were the victims of sharp and unbearable oppression, and that the fires of resentment were flaming higher and higher." Although the MOWM welcomed liberal white support, Randolph insisted that African Americans lead the movement. Randolph was wary of the labor movement, the major political parties, and the growing Communist influence in black organizations like the National Negro Congress (NNC). When the Communist party gained control of the NNC in early 1940, for example, Randolph resigned from the presidency and soon left the organization.

Although Roosevelt resisted the movement as long as he could, the threat of a march on Washington finally produced results. Roosevelt met with leaders A. Philip Randolph and Walter White of the NAACP on June 18, 1941. A week later, on June 24, 1941, FDR issued Executive Order 8802, banning racial discrimination in government employment, defense industries, and training programs. The order also established the Fair Employment Practices Committee (FEPC) to implement its provisions. The FEPC was empowered to receive, investigate, and address complaints of racial discrimination in the defense program.

Executive order 8802 proved to be a turning point in African-American history. It linked the struggle of African Americans even more closely to the Democratic party and helped to transform the federal government into a significant ally. African Americans used the FEPC to broaden their participation in the war effort, but it proved to be a slow process. Although an estimated 118,000 blacks were trained for industrial, professional, and clerical jobs in 1941, by the end of 1942 only a small percentage had obtained employment in defense industries. Industrial firms in the North and South dragged their feet on the putting of fair employment practices into effect. In January 1942, the FEPC cited five Milwaukee firms for racial discrimination against the city's black workers, and directed them "to give written notice" that they would end such practices. Shipyard companies in Houston, Galveston, Mobile, New Orleans, and Tampa widely advertised for white women and boys to pursue training as welders, but they resisted the FEPC's push to place black welders. Southern colleges also barred blacks from training programs supported by federal money, forcing African Americans to travel to a limited number of black training centers. In Mobile, when the FEPC pressured the Alabama Drydock and Shipbuilders Company to upgrade some black workers to the job of welder, the company supported the walkout and a riot of some twenty thousand white workers, who quit in protest against the employment of black workers.

Southeastern railroads offered even stronger evidence of white resistance. In 1940, with the support of the National Mediation Board, the southeastern railroads and the exclusively white unions signed the notorious "Washington Agreement," designed to eliminate black firemen from employment. Black workers soon challenged the Washington Agreement under the new FEPC guidelines. The FEPC ordered the companies and unions to adjust their policies "so that all needed workers shall be hired and all company employees shall be promoted without regard to race, creed, color or national origin." When the roads and unions defied the order, African Americans took their case to court, but nothing was determined until 1944 when a U.S. Supreme Court ruling, *Bester William Steele* v. *The Louisville and Nashville Company Brotherhood of Locomotive Firemen and Engineers,* upheld their claims. Every year, at the annual meetings of the AFL, A. Philip Randolph exhorted white workers to end racial bias.

Despite the persistence of discrimination, as the wartime labor shortages increased, the FEPC played a key role in helping black workers find jobs in defense plants. The number of blacks in war production increased from less than three percent in March 1942 to over eight percent in 1944. And unlike what happened during the First World War, substantial numbers now moved into semiskilled and skilled positions. As St. Clair Drake and Horace R. Cayton noted in their study of Chicago during the period, "The Second World War broke the ceiling at the level of semiskilled work and integrated thousands of Negroes as skilled laborers in the electrical and light manufacturing industries, from which they had been barred by custom, and in the vast new airplane-engine factories . . . They also began to filter into minor managerial and clerical positions in increasing numbers."

While the AFL unions and the railroad brotherhoods did much to hamper this process, the unions of the Congress of Industrial Organizations often supported the FEPC claims of black workers and helped them to break the job ceiling. At its annual convention in 1941, for example, the CIO denounced racially discriminatory hiring policies as a "direct attack against our nation's policy to build democracy in our fight against Hitlerism." A year later, the organization established its own Committee to Abolish Racial Discrimination and urged its affiliates to support national policy against discrimination. Although black workers faced ongoing obstacles in their struggle for skilled, managerial, and clerical positions, by the end of the Second World War they claimed the CIO, the Democratic party, and the federal government as important allies in their struggle for social change.

The "Double V" campaign for victory at home and abroad, the March on Washington Movement, and the growing use of the federal government to secure their aims helped to write a new chapter in the history of African Americans and set the stage for the modern Civil Rights movement of the postwar years.

## CHAPTER 4

# We Changed the World

## 1945–1970

*Vincent Harding*

*Robin D. G. Kelley*

*Earl Lewis*

N ear the end of the Second World War, Adam Clayton Powell, Jr., one of
black America's most internationally conscious spokesmen, tried to place
the ongoing African-American freedom movement into the context of
the anticolonial struggles that were rising explosively out of the discontent of the
nonwhite world. Already, movements for independence had begun in British
colonies in West Africa and French colonies in West and Equatorial Africa. Later,
colonies in North Africa and British East Africa joined the freedom struggle.
Powell, who was both a flamboyant and effective congressman from Harlem and
the pastor of that community's best-known Christian congregation, the Abyssinian
Baptist Church, declared:

> The black man continues on his way. He plods wearily no longer—he is
> striding freedom road with the knowledge that if he hasn't got the world in
> a jug, at least he has the stopper in his hand.... He is ready to throw him-
> self into the struggle to make the dream of America become flesh and blood,
> bread and butter, freedom and equality. He walks conscious of the fact that
> he is no longer alone no longer a minority.

Although they might not have been able to express it in Powell's colorful language, many black Americans were quite aware of the changes taking place. There
were glaring differences, for instance, between where they grew up in the South
and the Northern cities where they were trying to establish themselves for the first
time.

Most of the new arrivals realized that the North was not heaven, but they
believed that it was a place where they could escape some of the most hellish
aspects of their life in the South. For instance, they did not expect ever again to
have to see the bodies of men hanging from trees after they had been riddled with

A member of the 12th Armored Division stands guard over Nazi prisoners who were captured by U.S. forces in 1945.

bullets and often mutilated. They did not expect that women would be vulnerable to rape and exploitation simply because they were black and defenseless. In the Northern cities they did not expect to have to teach their children to move out of the path when white people were approaching.

Blacks also migrated to the West and settled in cities such as Los Angeles and Seattle. One of the most exciting gifts that these new locales offered was the opportunity for black people to vote as free men and free women for the first time in their lives. Registering to vote in Philadelphia, Detroit, or Oakland did not mean risking your life and the lives of your family, risking your job or your home. In those postwar years, black people took significant advantage of this new freedom and became voters in even larger proportions than white Southerners who had migrated North. As a result, black voters in some Northern cities like Chicago and New York held the balance of power in close municipal elections.

This new political involvement brought with it another change. In most of the Northern cities where the black Southerners settled, the political structures were largely dominated by the Democratic party. Generally, the men who controlled these tightly organized political machines were eager to add the newly arrived black people to their voting tallies as long as they thought they could control their votes. And, in fact, millions of African Americans eventually broke away from their generations-long allegiance to the Republican party, the party of Lincoln, the Great

Emancipator. Ironically enough, this transfer of allegiance meant that Northern blacks were now aligned with the same Democratic party that had long been dominated on the national scene by the white racist sons of the slaveholders, men who kept their control of the party largely through terrorist acts to deny black voting rights in the South. In the North, black voters were now part of that Democratic party structure and were in a position to begin to challenge its worst traditions.

Despite such rewards as finding better jobs and educational opportunities, and gaining the right to vote, this liberating movement into the Northern cities carried some clear penalties. Racism lived in many white urban neighborhoods and postwar suburbs. The rising black middle class, anxious to buy property in a "nice" neighborhood with good schools and efficient services, often bumped up against a threatening white mob and its racist rhetoric. Sometimes white resistance to black neighbors turned deadly. In Chicago, Los Angeles, Detroit, and several other cities (in both the North and the South), newly purchased homes were burned, vandalized, or had crosses burned on their lawns—a common tactic adopted by white supremacist organizations, notably the Ku Klux Klan.

Of course, there were real estate agents and white residents who insisted that their form of segregation was not racist but driven by economic realities. They claimed to have nothing against black people but were simply worried about their homes declining in value. Sadly, their arguments were tacitly backed by the federal government, notably the Federal Housing Administration (FHA), the agency that insured homeowners' loans to low-income Americans and set housing standards. Indeed, after the Second World War, the FHA refused to provide mortgages to blacks moving into white neighborhoods and claimed that African Americans were regarded as poor risks for loans. The FHA also claimed that the future value of homes owned by blacks was uncertain.

Most of the new migrants could not afford to buy homes immediately, especially in the sprawling suburbs. No matter where they ended up, however, primarily the inner areas of urban centers like Chicago and Detroit, they sought to create the rich sense of community they had left behind. For even in the midst of harsh white oppression and poverty, black people, nurtured by their extended families and by their churches, had managed to build astonishing reservoirs of love, faith, and hope in the South. Such support was not readily available in the North.

Reflecting on his own Harlem childhood in *Nobody Knows My Name* (1961), James Baldwin caught some of the perplexing dilemma of a city block in the long-anticipated "Promised Land" of the North.

> They work in the white man's world all day and come home in the evening
> to this fetid block. They struggle to instill in their children some private
> sense of honor or dignity which will help the child to survive. This means,
> of course, that they must struggle, stolidly, incessantly, to keep this sense
> alive in themselves, in spite of the insults, the indifference, and the cruelty

they are certain to encounter in their working day. They patiently browbeat the landlord into fixing the heat, the plaster, the plumbing; this demands prodigious patience, nor is patience usually enough.... Such frustration so long endured, is driving many strong, admirable men and women whose only crime is color to the very gates of paranoia....

It required the sensitivity and skills of gifted artists to capture the complexities of the changes that millions of black women, men and children were experiencing in their movement North. Baldwin was only one of the writers who tried to explain that complexity to the world. Ann Petry provided a painfully honest account of a young woman's encounter with the Northern urban reality in her novel *The Street*. Ralph Ellison's classic novel *Invisible Man* reflected the humor, anger, hope, and the search for new beginnings that the urban experience represented for the transplanted black Southerners. Ellison's protagonist discovers a major difference between the South and the North when he first arrives in Harlem and begins to mingle with the evening crowds who have gathered to listen to the street-corner teachers and lecturers. Most of the rousing speeches eventually turn to the injustices of white people against people of color at home and abroad, and the young man in the novel, who has come North from Alabama, says, "I never saw so many Negroes angry in public before."

The expanding ability to be angry in public was a major part of the change that black people found in the North. In his novels, short stories, and essays, Richard Wright, who had originally gone to Chicago from Mississippi in the twenties, expressed this anger and its consequences more vividly and consistently than anyone else in his novel *Native Son* (1940).

Still, there were emotions and experiences that could never be captured by the written word. The music surging out of black communities became a powerful vehicle for communicating these feelings. The blues that had come up with the solitary old guitars from Memphis and the Mississippi Delta took on the new electricity and complexity of the cities, eventually becoming the music of small combos and big bands, pressing on toward what would soon be known as rhythm and blues. At the same time, out of the familiar settings of classic African-American jazz, piercing new sounds began to break through, offering unexpected, unresolved, and often jagged tonal edges in place of the smoother flows of the music from which it sprang. This was called "bebop" or "bop" for short. The names of its practitioners—Thelonious Monk, Dizzy Gillespie, Charlie ("Yardbird") Parker, and the young Miles Davis—and the boldness of their lifestyles soon became as well known in the black community and among white jazz fans as their predecessors Lester Young, Louis Armstrong, and Coleman Hawkins.

Whatever else bop was, it was the music of change. Everything in it sounded protest, marked a determination to break out of the older, predictable harmonies. Based in places like Minton's Playhouse in Harlem, the 52nd Street jazz strip further downtown in New York City, and Los Angeles's famed Central Avenue, the irrepressible music grew out of the urgency of a postwar generation to sing its new songs, to wail and scream when necessary.

Nowhere were the songs more important than in the thousands of black churches in the Northern cities. Following the lead of vibrant women vocalists such as Mahalia Jackson, Sallie and Roberta Martin, and Sister Rosetta Tharpe, supplied with a stream of songs by the prolific gospel songwriter Rev. Thomas A. Dorsey, the churches were filled with resounding, rhythmic witness to the new time, as gospel singers shouted, "There's been a great change since I been born."

In the decade following the Second World War, more than sixty percent of the black population was still living in the South, however. And the nation's attention focused on that region as the African-American community won a series of significant battles in the courts and at the executive level of the federal government. In 1946, for example, the Supreme Court ruled that segregation on buses was unconstitutional. Two years later, the Court outlawed the use of "restrictive covenants"—codicils added on to a deed to limit the sale of a home to specific racial groups. Restrictive covenants were generally used to keep African Americans from buying homes in all-white neighborhoods. Although these gains were long overdue, they were partial outgrowths of national and international circumstances that forced President Harry S. Truman and the Democrats to pay attention to blacks.

First, Truman, his cabinet, and Congress were all concerned about America's image abroad, especially now that the United States was competing with the Soviet Union for influence over the new nations in Asia and Africa, for example, created by the collapse of European colonialism. They could not promote their version of democracy abroad as long as the United States treated its own black citizens so badly. Second, Truman's reelection in 1948 depended on black votes more than ever. This time around, the Democratic party was in utter disarray. On one side stood former Vice President Henry Wallace, who decided to run for president as a member of the newly formed Progressive party. Wallace was highly regarded in the black community; his civil rights record was impeccable, and he sought to bring the Cold War with the Soviet Union to an end through cooperation rather than military threats.

On the other side were the Southern Democrats led by South Carolina senator Strom Thurmond. Their break from the Democrats further divided the vote, creating a situation in which black voters would have a decisive role in the elections. Calling themselves the States' Rights party (also known as the Dixiecrats), these Southern Democrats believed Truman's civil rights agenda had gone too far.

Because Truman had to respond to African-American and international pressure, he and his cabinet contributed to the Southern white flight from the Democratic party. The main catalyst was Truman's decision to create the first Civil Rights Commission. The commission's report, *To Secure These Rights* (1947), proposed some specific ways in which the federal government might respond to the demands of the postwar black community. For example, the report called for the establishment of a permanent federal civil rights commission—a bold and progressive proposal in those days. The report urged an end to segregation in the U.S. armed forces and pressed for laws to protect the voting rights of black people.

*To Secure These Rights* provided solid evidence to black people that their needs were finally being dealt with at the highest level of U.S. political life. Meanwhile, almost every year in the crucial postwar decade seemed to produce new, affirming responses from the federal courts to the dozens of challenges to segregation and disenfranchisement that the NAACP and thousands of black plaintiffs were pressing in the courts.

One of the most important of these cases, *Morgan* v. *Virginia,* was heard by the U.S. Supreme Court in 1946. Irene Morgan had firmly refused to move to the back of a Virginia-to-Baltimore Greyhound bus, as Virginia law required. She was convicted of a misdemeanor. The Court declared that the practice of segregated seating in interstate public transportation was unconstitutional and that black people traveling across state lines could not be legally forced into segregated rear seats when they arrived in a Southern state. The "back of the bus" experience was one of the most humiliating and widely known manifestations of legalized white supremacy, so word of the decision was welcomed in the nation's black communities. Irene Morgan became a hero among black Americans. But a Supreme Court decision did not guarantee change. Neither the bus companies nor the Southern states leaped to comply with the ruling. So others had to take up Irene Morgan's initiative and move it forward.

That was precisely what happened in the spring of 1947 when a group of sixteen men, evenly divided between black and white, began what they called a Journey of Reconciliation. The trip was organized by a Chicago-based interracial organization known as the Congress of Racial Equality, or CORE. A relatively new offshoot from the Fellowship of Reconciliation (FOR)—a Christian pacifist organization, founded during the First World War, that advocated nonviolent social change through civil disobedience—CORE was deeply committed to nonviolent direct action. Its members took inspiration from the spirit of the Indian nationalist leader Mahatma Gandhi in their quest for racial justice and reconciliation. At the same time, with the black members of the team sitting in front and the whites in back of the two Greyhound and Trailways buses that they rode from Washington, D.C., to stops in Virginia, North Carolina, and Kentucky, they were testing compliance with the recent *Morgan* decision and urging federal enforcement of the ruling. The major immediate result of the journey was that some other black passengers felt encouraged to move toward the front of the buses. In one incident during the fifteen-city trip through the South, three members of the CORE team were arrested and sentenced to twenty-one days of hard labor on a North Carolina prison farm. The Journey of Reconciliation provided the model for the later Freedom Rides in 1961.

Probably no legal victory of the immediate postwar years could match the overall significance of the 1944 Supreme Court decision in *Smith* v. *Allwright.* This decision essentially destroyed one of the major legal obstacles to black political participation in the South—the white primaries of the Democratic party.

Earlier in the twentieth century, having claimed that their party primary voting process was the activity of private associations, Democrats managed to exclude African Americans from participating in this "private" activity. As a result, black citizens were left with little voice in government, since the Southern Democratic primaries often determined the outcome of the general elections. African Americans refused to accept this situation, and in state after state they brought lawsuits challenging these exclusively white primaries.

In July 1940, Lonnie Smith, an African-American resident of Harris County, Texas, was stopped from voting in the Democratic party's primary election. Though he met all the legal requirements to vote, Smith was forbidden to vote because of his race. With the assistance of an NAACP legal team that included attorney Thurgood Marshall, Smith sued election judge Allwright. Finally, in *Smith* v. *Allwright*, the Supreme Court responded to the black challengers with a judgment outlawing the white primary process. When that happened, everyone knew that a new era was beginning: blacks across the South took that decision regarding the Texas primary as a signal to expand and intensify their voter registration activity.

With the help of a ruling by a South Carolina federal judge, J. Waties Waring, black plaintiffs won a crucial victory in that state. When South Carolina attempted to circumvent the *Smith* v. *Allwright* decision by removing all statutes relating to primaries—on the assumption that without state involvement, the Democratic primaries would be a private matter—George Elmore challenged the state's move. In the case of *Rice* v. *Elmore* (1947), Waring ruled that as long as the Democratic primary constituted the only real election in the state, blacks were entitled to participate in it.

In many places this was a dangerous resolve to take, especially in the rural South's "Black Belt"—a line of counties stretching from North Carolina to Texas, where the flat and fertile land had been dominated by cotton plantations. There, the legacy of plantation-based slavery had created counties where black people outnumbered whites in proportions of three-, four-, and five-to-one—sometimes more. The obvious implications of this human arithmetic were clearly stated by one distressed white cotton-gin owner. Speaking to a *New York Times* reporter, he tried to imagine what would happen if black people gained full access to the ballot box in his Tennessee county: "The niggers would take over the county if they could vote in full numbers. They'd stick together and vote blacks into every office in the county. Why you'd have a nigger judge, nigger sheriff, a nigger tax assessor—think what the black SOB's would do to you."

Ever since the days of slavery such fears were common to many white Southerners who wondered what black people would do if the racial tables were turned. Many whites found it easy to rally around the virulently racist rhetoric of a politician like Theodore G. Bilbo, U.S. senator from Mississippi. He voiced the fears of many Southern whites, especially the poorer ones, when he declared that the

Second World War "and all of its great victories will not in any way or in any manner change the views and sentiments of white America on the question of social equality . . . of the negro and white race." In a time when so much was changing, Bilbo and his fellow white supremacists were seeking guarantees that they would continue to dominate.

Throughout the South, white supremacists were desperate to preserve an old world that was coming to an end. They had no intention of giving up their control of the region and would use all legal means of undermining the constitutional defenses on which black people increasingly depended. Many also conspired to use illegal means, from economic coercion to acts of terrorism, to keep their black fellow Southerners "in their place."

Nowhere was this new world more evident than in the ranks of the thousands of African Americans who returned from the battlegrounds of the Second World War. They were the ones who seemed most ready to demonstrate the truth of Adam Clayton Powell's statement that black people were "ready to throw [themselves] into the struggle to make the dream of America become flesh and blood." A recently discharged army corporal from Alabama spoke for many of his black comrades in 1945 when he declared, "I spent four years in the army to free a bunch of Dutchmen and Frenchmen, and I'm hanged if I'm going to let the Alabama version of the Germans kick me around when I get home. No sirree-bob! I went into the Army a nigger; I'm comin' out a man."

Among those determined to win voting rights for blacks in the South was a solid core of veterans who felt like they had earned the right to vote after risking their lives for democracy overseas. In 1946, brothers Charles and Medgar Evers returned home from the war to their town of Decatur, Mississippi, determined to vote. But they were driven away from the registrar's desk, and one of the white men predicted that there would be "trouble" if these black citizens persisted in their attempts to register and vote. But he could never have guessed the nature of the coming trouble. For the Evers brothers and thousands like them would return all over the South to challenge the keepers of the old terror.

The powerful thrusts of postwar change were not confined to politics. A remarkable change in the world of sports captured the attention of the rest of the nation. Jackie Robinson, another veteran of the war and a baseball player with the Kansas City Monarchs of the segregated Negro Leagues, was signed by the Brooklyn Dodgers in 1945. The action broke the racial barrier in major league baseball, the "national pastime." An outstanding athlete who had lettered in baseball, basketball, track, and football at the University of California at Los Angeles, an outspoken critic of America's racial betrayals of democracy, the twenty-eight-year-old Robinson spent a year with the Dodgers' farm team in Montreal before finally joining the Brooklyn lineup in the spring of 1947. Black people were ecstatic.

The black community followed local and national developments in civil rights by reading African-American newspapers such as the *Pittsburgh Courier,* the

*Chicago Defender*, the *Baltimore Afro-American*, and the *Norfolk Journal and Guide*. These papers were circulated through many hands in households, barbershops, beauty parlors, churches, and restaurants. In the hands of Pullman car porters, they found their way into the Deep South as well.

By reading the papers, black people followed the anticolonial, independence-oriented exploits of the darker-skinned majority of the world in places like India, Africa, and China. There were constant references to Gandhi, who had spent decades challenging his people in India to wage a nonviolent struggle for independence against the great British Empire that governed them. Repeatedly, the black newspapers carried letters and editorials contending that Gandhi's movement offered a model for black America, especially in the South. Mordecai Johnson, president of Howard University in Washington, D.C.; Howard Thurman, mystically oriented preacher and dean of Howard University's chapel; and Benjamin Mays, president of Morehouse College in Atlanta, were some of the best-known black Americans who had made the pilgrimage to the ashrams, the humble communal villages where Gandhi based himself.

Gandhi's life and teaching mirrored some of the best African-American traditions. Like the nineteenth-century abolitionists David Walker and Frederick Douglass, like W. E. B. Du Bois, Ida B. Wells-Barnett, and Howard Thurman, Gandhi believed that the despised of the earth actually carried within their own lives and history the seeds of healing transformation for themselves, their oppressors, and their world. So when black Americans identified their struggle as part of a larger, worldwide movement, it was not simply the idea "that [we are] no longer alone" that compelled them. It was also the vision that as the rising children of their enslaved forbears, they—like Gandhi's masses—might have some liberating gift to offer to the world.

While blacks were developing an understanding of worldwide repression, the U.S. government seemed to be, in some instances, supporting that repression. On the one hand, U.S. foreign policy appeared to link the United States with the interests and points of view of its white, Western allies, such as England, France, Portugal, and white South Africa, countries still identified with colonial domination. On the other hand, as part of the deepening Cold War against the Soviet Union, the United States was also projecting itself as "the leader of the free world," avowedly concerned for the rights of oppressed people everywhere, especially people of color who might be tempted to turn to the Soviet Union and to other socialist and communist movements for assistance in their freedom struggles.

So when black leaders with socialist sympathies, such as W. E. B. Du Bois and the politically active actor, singer, and scholar Paul Robeson, spoke out on behalf of the nonwhite peoples and their freedom struggles, when they articulated too positive a view of the Russian Revolution's social and economic ambitions, when they sharply criticized U. S. foreign and domestic policy, the U.S. government considered them un-American and dangerous. The passports of both men were confiscated to prevent them from traveling and speaking abroad on behalf of the anticolonial movements and against the reign of white supremacy in America. Still, both men continued to speak out. But the price they paid was very high. Robeson essentially lost his lucrative concert career, and ultimately his health. Du Bois, in the fearful climate of anticommunism in America, found himself deserted by many people who had benefited from his decades of unstinting service to the cause of freedom, justice, and democratic hope, and he moved permanently to Africa.

Anticommunist fervor virtually crushed these two intellectual giants, but it could not crush the movement. In the streets and in the courts, black activists forced the federal government to admit that segregation was wrong and must be remedied. By 1954, it became evident to all that African Americans, like their counterparts in the colonial world, would no longer wait for the birth of a new freedom.

## Jim Crow Must Go!: The Road from Brown to Montgomery

Revolutions always exact a price from their participants. People have lost their livelihoods, lost friends and family, lost their connection to community, even lost their lives. The movement to end segregation and press America to live up to its creed of justice for all was no different. Nowhere was this personal cost more obvious than in the five legal cases that would force their way into the U.S. Supreme Court and become known collectively as *Brown* v. *Board of Education*. The case known as *Briggs* v. *Elliott* provided the legal bedrock on which the entire set of *Brown* cases was built.

The setting for this initial drama was Clarendon County, South Carolina, known for its bitter resistance to any attempts at changing the brutal traditions of white supremacy. There, love for their children drove black parents to take the simple but dangerous risk of confronting the school board with their children's need for bus transportation to their segregated school. The white children had several buses, while the black children, who outnumbered the others, had no buses at all. Of course, the black parents and their supporters were also aware that the all-white school board spent more money on each white child in the county than on each black one. What the adults had to figure out was how to deal with the rude and repeated rebuffs from the school board and its chairman, R. W. Elliott, who said at a meeting with black people, "We ain't got no money to buy a bus for your nigger children."

Then Rev. J. A. Delaine, a local black pastor and school superintendent in Summerton, met Rev. James A. Hinton, a regional representative for the NAACP, at a meeting at Allen College, one of the black colleges in Columbia, about sixty miles from Summerton. Hinton told the gathering that the NAACP was trying to find men and women to become plaintiffs in a case that would challenge the legality of the segregated schools. Delaine knew after the meeting that he had to become the bridge between the unrelenting but frustrated neighbor parents and the national organization.

Delaine and his wife worked for the school board they were suing, and both lost their jobs. They also lost their home and their church when the buildings were burned to the ground. Meanwhile, in Farmville, Virginia, in 1951, a courageous sixteen-year-old high-school junior organized her fellow students to fight for equal facilities for black schools. Under Barbara Rose Johns's dynamic leadership, the black students at the woefully inadequate Moton High not only went on strike but arranged with the NAACP to file a desegregation lawsuit in their county. That suit was eventually tied to the one initiated by Oliver Brown of Topeka, Kansas, on behalf of his daughter Linda and all the black children of their city.

The Topeka school board had denied Linda Brown admission to a school just five blocks from her home, forcing her to make a long commute across town, because her neighborhood school was for whites only. Charles Houston and Thurgood Marshall of the NAACP Legal Defense and Education Fund were the attorneys for the Browns. In his Supreme Court argument, Marshall presented evidence that separating black and white students placed the blacks at a great disadvantage. Marshall's strategy was to force the Supreme Court to overturn the 1896 *Plessy* v. *Ferguson* ruling, which upheld the legality of segregation as long as states provided "separate but equal" facilities to African Americans. Such practices, he said, violated the 14th Amendment to the Constitution, which guarantees equal protection of the laws. Once he was able to get the Court to overturn *Plessy,* Marshall did not have to prove that facilities set aside for "colored only" were unequal to those set aside for whites. To buttress his argument, Marshall brought in pioneering black psychologists Mamie and Kenneth Clark, whose research demonstrated that African-American children in inferior, segregated schools had a negative self-image and generally performed poorly as a result.

When the Supreme Court handed down its unanimous decision in *Brown* on Monday, May 17, 1954, it was a stunning accomplishment. All eyes focused on the solemn announcement that "in the field of public education the doctrine of 'separate but equal' has no place." After more than half a century of determined struggle, black people and their allies had finally turned the Supreme Court around. Two days after *Brown,* the *Washington Post* declared, "It is not too much to speak of the court's decision as a new birth of freedom."

Perhaps it was only the opening of a new chapter in the long black struggle for authentic democracy in America. But it forced individual men and women to make hard, exciting choices about how they would lead their own lives. In Boston, Martin Luther King, Jr., and his new bride, the former Coretta Scott, had been facing such choices together ever since their marriage in June 1953, and his completion of the coursework for his doctorate in theology at Boston University. Soon Coretta would complete her three years of work in music education at the New England Conservatory of Music, and the choices they had been wrestling with were now leading to a move from Boston to Montgomery, Alabama.

Born in Atlanta in January 1929, Martin was the beloved first son of Martin Luther King, Sr., one of that city's leading Baptist ministers, and his wife, Alberta

Williams King, whose father had been the founding pastor of Ebenezer Baptist Church, the congregation now headed by King Senior. The younger King entered Morehouse College in Atlanta, one of the most respected black colleges in the nation, when he was only fifteen. He became a popular student leader and a serious student.

When he was eighteen, not long before he graduated from Morehouse with a B.A. in sociology, King decided to stop resisting an inner calling to the Christian ministry. So his father proudly ordained the young man who had finally decided that he would not take the path of law or medicine, possibilities that had intrigued him for a while. At that point in his life young "M.L." was often torn between the image of ministry he saw in his father, a pietistic man with an engaging, emotionally charged approach, and the one he found in Benjamin Mays, Morehouse's president. Mays's combination of profound spirituality, intellect, and commitment to social justice left a deep mark on the lives of many of his "Morehouse Men."

Martin King, Jr., left Atlanta in 1948 to enroll at Crozer Theological Seminary in Chester, Pennsylvania (one of the few white theological schools that accepted more than one or two black men in each entering class). He carried with him a profound sense of identity with the black church, community, and extended family that had done so much to shape and nurture him. Although he knew that he did not want to be the kind of preacher that his father was, King was deeply appreciative of the older man's unwavering religious faith and his readiness to confront racism.

So although Crozer was King's first extended experience in an overwhelmingly white institution, he was spiritually and mentally prepared for it. By now the young Atlantan, whose eloquence was praised by his professors, was firmly grounded in the way of thinking that marked the lives of many young black people in those days. He knew that his life and career were not simply matters of personal success and advancement. Instead, he recognized and acknowledged an inextricable connection to the "cause" of black advancement, to the responsibility he bore for fighting for "the uplift of the race." King graduated from Crozer in 1951 as valedictorian of his class and received a coveted fellowship to pursue his doctorate at Boston University. The decision to do doctoral work reflected King's continuing exploration of the possibility that he might somehow combine his love for academic work with his passion for the Christian ministry.

In Boston, King was introduced to Coretta Scott, a bright, attractive young woman who had grown up not far from Selma, Alabama. Living in the rural South of the thirties and forties, Coretta saw many instances of violently enforced white domination, including the beating of her father. With these disturbing memories of the past and her own professional ambitions on her mind, Coretta King was strongly inclined to stay out of the South. And King was attracted by invitations to consider positions in the North. But, King later remembered, "The south, after all, was our home. Despite its shortcomings we loved it as home. . . ." At the same time,

Martin and Coretta King were part of the long black Southern tradition that called on its educated young people to work to change the South they had known.

So Coretta was neither very surprised nor very resistant when her husband finally declared that they were going to live in the South. By the spring of 1954 King had accepted an invitation to the pastorate of Dexter Avenue Baptist Church in Montgomery, Alabama, the city known as "The Cradle of the Confederacy." Montgomery was where Jefferson Davis had been sworn in as president of the pro-slavery states that seceded from the Union in 1861. By the time King began his official tenure as pastor of Dexter's middle-class congregation in September 1954, it was clear that the city's black population of close to fifty thousand was on the brink of a new time.

Like their counterparts throughout the South, many of the most activist-oriented members of Montgomery's black population had been prodded into new forms of organizing. For instance, the expanding, state-by-state defeat of the segregated white primary system inspired the creation of a number of voter registration organizations and campaigns in Montgomery. It also encouraged a variety of risky experiments to challenge the humiliating segregation of everyday life.

One of the most important of these experiments was the formation of the Women's Political Council (WPC), a well-organized group of black, middle-class women. They developed an important telephone communications link (called a "telephone tree" in those days) among their members, initially used for voter registration campaigns. But eventually the group expanded its concerns to other issues faced by a black community in a white-dominated segregated city. In the early fifties these issues ranged from black citizens' seeking access to the public parks that their taxes helped to maintain to the constantly vexing matter of the harsh treatment black people received on the local buses.

It was not long before King discovered that the creative and outspoken chairperson of the WPC, JoAnn Robinson, a faculty member at Alabama State College, the local black college, was a member of Dexter's congregation. He quickly recruited her to lead the church's Social and Political Action Committee, which he had organized. In turn, as Robinson and her conscientious group of women took their concerns into the chambers of the Montgomery City Council, she often called on her young pastor to go with them to add his sharp mind, eloquent voice, and passionate commitment to justice to their arguments for change.

In Montgomery, as elsewhere in the South, those black citizens demanding justice included many military veterans. The Reverend Ralph David Abernathy, pastor of First Baptist Church, was one of the best known of these veterans. He had served with the U.S. Army in Europe, then returned to study at Montgomery's Alabama State College and earn his master's degree in sociology at Atlanta University. As Abernathy later recalled of those days in Montgomery, "Many of the older clergy were in favor of sweeping social change, but they were willing for it to come about slowly, when white society was ready to accept it." He also remembered that "those of us in our twenties were less patient and less afraid of making trouble. . . . As we talked with one another, we began saying that we were willing to help tear down the old walls, even if it meant a genuine uprising."

Another highly regarded veteran freedom worker who was ready for change was E. D. Nixon, the gruff-voiced, outspoken Pullman car porter who had worked for years with the legendary A. Philip Randolph organizing the Brotherhood of Sleeping Car Porters. Now in his fifties, Nixon was probably best known for his role as president of the Alabama branch of the NAACP and as an unrelenting campaigner for black citizenship rights, especially the right to vote. In his NAACP role, Nixon was quietly and efficiently assisted by a highly respected woman in her early forties who served as secretary to the local NAACP branch and as adviser to the organization's youth council. A seamstress by profession, she was named Rosa Parks, and she turned out to be less patient than she sometimes seemed.

By 1955, it was not just Montgomery's black pastors, NAACP members, and community leaders who sensed with Martin and Coretta King that something remarkable was happening. Many of the city's ordinary black citizens recognized that they were entering a new time.

Of course, they (and the rest of the nation, even the world) also knew about the brutal lynching of fourteen-year-old Emmett Till, who was beaten and killed in Mississippi in 1955 by two white men after Till made the mistake of speaking familiarly to a white woman, the wife of one of the men. The black newspapers and journals spread the word (and the photos) of the murdered teenager whose Chicago upbringing had not prepared him for the proper approach to a white woman in rural Mississippi. The papers also reported that black Congressman Charles Diggs, Jr., of Michigan, and national NAACP officials went to Money, Mississippi, to attend the trial of Till's accused killers, along with Till's mother, Mamie Till, who helped to turn the tragedy of her son's death into a rallying point for the Civil Rights movement. Because she insisted on an open casket, and allowed photographs, people nationwide saw firsthand the horrors of Southern lynching.

In spite of the predictable not-guilty verdict in the Till murder case that summer, the black people of Montgomery realized they had seen signals of a new time: In the heart of Bilbo's Mississippi, keepers of the past had been forced to hold a trial and to face a black member of the U.S. House of Representatives; they had been pressed to recognize the rising power of an inflamed black community at home and to answer hard questions from people of color and of conscience from around the world.

For many ordinary black citizens, some of their most painful and consistently humiliating encounters with white power and injustice took place in public, especially on city buses. In the mid-fifties the automobile had not yet become the ubiquitous presence that it is now especially not for the thousands of black people in Montgomery who earned their living as maids, cooks, janitors, porters, and the like. High-school and college students were also part of the seventeen thousand or so black people who made up some seventy-five percent of the passengers on the segregated buses. During their daily rides, blacks were relegated to the often-crowded back area and were forbidden to take vacant seats in the forward white section, even if no white passengers were present. Beyond this were the all-too-common encounters with rude and hostile white bus drivers (there were no black ones) who often called their black passengers "apes," "niggers," "black cows," and other demeaning names. Often they demanded that blacks get up and surrender their seats to white passengers when the white section was full. Black passengers were also required to pay their fare in front and then get off to re-board through the rear door.

Such practices were common on the buses in cities all over the South, but that did not make them any more palatable. In the spring of 1955 a teenaged Montgomery high-school student named Claudette Colvin loudly resisted both the driver's orders to give up her seat and the police who were called to arrest her. Colvin's screams and curses were not quite what leaders like Robinson and Nixon had in mind as they searched for a case that could be used to challenge the constitutionality of Montgomery's segregated seating. Their aim was to rally the black community to experiment with a brief boycott of the buses that would focus not only on the segregated seating but on the humiliating treatment. Colvin was not the test case they needed, but Nixon and the waiting WPC forces knew that someone else would eventually be pressed beyond the limit and would resist. Evicted in the early forties for sitting too far forward, Rosa Parks, who had long served as a freedom worker, provided the opportunity that Nixon and the WPC needed.

On December 1, 1955, quiet, soft-spoken Rosa Parks did what she had to do. After all, she was a veteran freedom worker and in many ways one of the most prepared for this historic moment. During the previous decade, she had served as secretary of the Montgomery branch of the NAACP, worked on voter-registration campaigns, and had run the local NAACP Youth Council. Because of her earlier challenge to bus segregation ordinances, a few bus drivers refused to stop for her. Perhaps she remembered how right she had felt the previous summer at the Tennessee training center for social change called Highlander Folk School, as she talked with other black and white participants about Montgomery and what was needed there. They talked about their South and how they might contribute to the powerful transformation unfolding everywhere. Perhaps she remembered the young people of her NAACP Youth Council and the models they needed.

So when a bus driver told Parks and three other black people in her row to get up and relinquish their seats to a white man who was standing, she had to say no. There were no shouts, no curses, no accusations, just an inwardly powerful woman sensing the strength of her conviction and refusing to move. When, inevitably, policemen boarded the bus and one ordered her to get up, she still had to say no, realizing that arrest would be the next step. Rosa Parks, the magnificently proper and respectable church member, prepared to go to jail, in a time when such people

Rosa Parks, who refused to give up her bus seat to a white man in Montgomery, was accompanied by NAACP activist E. D. Nixon (second from left) as she appealed her conviction.

did not go to such places. But first she responded to the policeman who asked her why she did not obey the driver. She said, "I didn't think I should have to." Then she asked the officer, "Why do you push us around?" His response may have been the only one he could give: "I don't know." Yet he revealed his own entrapment in the system: "But the law is the law, and you are under arrest." And he took Rosa Parks to the police station.

At the station Parks called her friend and NAACP coworker, E. D. Nixon. For the veteran freedom worker, the shock of Parks's arrest was immediately mixed with the conviction that this was the test case that would challenge the city's bus segregation laws. After informing Parks's husband, Raymond, and her mother, Nixon immediately contacted two local whites he knew he could depend on, Clifford and Virginia Durr. Clifford Durr was a white lawyer in private practice, and he and Nixon went to the station to bail out Rosa Parks. Immediately they began discussing with her the possibility that her arrest could develop into the test case they all needed, and that she needed to recognize the physical and economic risks this might entail. After some hesitation on the part of her husband, Parks and her family were ready.

But history, JoAnn Robinson, and the black people of Montgomery soon overtook those original plans. For when Robinson heard the news of Parks's adventure she realized that the arrest of her friend was potentially more powerful than a legal case. She began to use the telephone tree that her WPC had developed for its voter-registration work, and soon dozens of black people knew that the highly respected Rosa Parks had been arrested for refusing to cooperate with the humiliating bus segregation practices that troubled them all. Working all that night and into the next morning, Robinson managed to compose, type the stencil, and run off more than thirty thousand mimeographed copies of a leaflet that said:

> Another Negro woman has been arrested and thrown in jail because she refused to get up out of her seat on the bus for a white person to sit down. It is the second time since the Claudette Colvin case that a Negro woman has been arrested for the same thing. This has to be stopped. Negroes have rights, too, for if Negroes did not ride the buses, they could not operate. Three-fourths of the riders are Negroes, yet we are arrested, or have to stand over empty seats. If we do not do something to stop these arrests, they will continue. The next time it may be you, or your daughter, or mother. This woman's case will come up on Monday. We are, therefore, asking every Negro to stay off the buses Monday in protest of the arrest and trial. Don't ride the bus to work, to town, to school, or anywhere on Monday. You can afford to stay out of school for one day if you have no other way to go except by bus. You can also afford to stay out of town for one day. If you work, take a cab, or walk. But please, children and grown-ups, don't ride the bus at all on Monday. Please stay off all buses Monday.

That morning, Friday, December 2, with the assistance of some of her students and WPC coworkers, Robinson blanketed the black community with the leaflets. By then, Nixon had begun to mobilize the traditional black community leaders, especially the ministers. It soon became clear that both his and Robinson's best instincts had been right: There was a powerful and positive reaction to the call for the leaders to meet and respond both to Parks's arrest and to Robinson's call for a boycott.

By that evening the local community leaders, including King, had decided to confirm Robinson's initiative and agreed that the next Monday, December 5, would be the day for a one-day experimental boycott. Since that was also the day for which Parks's trial was scheduled, it seemed logical to call for a mass community meeting that evening. In order to spread the word of Monday's boycott and mass meeting, the leadership group was depending upon another leaflet, many phone calls, and crucially, the dozens of black church services scheduled for Sunday, December 4. Then, when one of the leaflets got into the hands of a white employer and was passed on to the *Montgomery Advertiser,* the city's daily newspaper, a great gift of publicity was handed to the planners: a Sunday-morning front-page story on the planned boycott and mass meeting.

Of course, no one could be certain how the black community would respond to the call. There was significant fear among the leaders, including King, that a combination of apathy and fear might overwhelm the sense of righteous indignation that people felt. Nor could anyone predict how white people, especially the more rigid and violence-prone segregationists, would respond. All over the South, many white men and women had been eagerly rallying to the calls of the White Citizens Council to defend segregation by any means necessary. The local Ku Klux Klan was also very much alive and well, carrying on its periodic marches and car caravans through Montgomery's black community, knowing that their reputation for lynchings, beatings, and bombings was enough to drive most blacks off the streets and porches behind the relative safety of closed doors. It was clear to blacks that there was real physical danger involved in the simple act of not riding the buses. But for a lot of black riders there might also be economic danger if their employers objected to such black initiative and protest.

As a result, it was impossible to predict what the results of the boycott attempt would be. The leaders of the courageous experiment felt the action would be successful if sixty percent of the riders stayed off the buses. That cold and cloudy morning, as Martin and Coretta King looked out their front window toward a nearby bus stop, the uncertain victory now seemed clear. Most of the buses moving by were empty. Neither apathy nor fear had prevailed. Then, as King went out to drive along the black community bus routes, he saw an extraordinary scene: everywhere, black people were walking, thumbing rides, riding mules, resurrecting old horse and buggy contraptions, taking taxis. Some older men and women were walking more than five miles each way, at times saying, "I'm walking for my grandchildren." Meanwhile, all the buses from the black communities were at least ninety-five percent empty.

King recognized instinctively that more than bus seating, more than painful memories of humiliation, even more than solidarity with Rosa Parks was at stake here. As he said later, "A miracle had taken place. The once dormant and quiescent Negro community was now fully awake." At the same time, King's own personal awakening, inextricably tied to the rising of the people of Montgomery, was still in process. That Monday afternoon, he gathered with twenty or so other local leaders to assess and celebrate the overwhelming success of the almost spontaneous boycott and to plan for the evening's mass meeting. King was then surprised to find himself—one of the youngest and newest community leaders—nominated and elected president of the new organization that they had just brought into being at that session, the Montgomery Improvement Association (MIA).

The immediate task of the new MIA leaders was to build on the powerful momentum of the one-day boycott. They decided to move rather slowly, to focus first on the simple need for more courteous and humane treatment of black bus riders. They also called for what Coretta King and later others ruefully described as "a more humane form of segregation," which would allow white riders to fill the buses from the front to the middle, black riders from back to middle, with no need for anyone to have to give up a seat. They also pressed for the hiring of black drivers in black neighborhoods. The new MIA leadership decided to call for black people to continue the boycott until these changes were made.

That night at the first mass meeting at the large Holt Street Baptist Church, the leaders immediately recognized that an extraordinary spirit was taking hold. The crowd was so dense and animated that King and the other speakers had a hard time pushing their way to the pulpit. One of the few white reporters on hand, Joe Azbell of the *Advertiser,* was almost awestruck by the experience he witnessed, including the consideration shown to him as a white person. The next day he wrote, "The meeting was much like an old-fashioned revival with loud applause added. . . . It proved beyond any doubt that there was a discipline among Negroes that many whites had doubted. It was almost a military discipline combined with emotion."

As the new MIA president and featured speaker, King had to decide how to position himself in the midst of the dynamic power he had recognized among the people since early in the morning. The twenty-six-year-old pastor later described his struggle to figure out the correct approach:

> How could I make a speech that would be militant enough to keep my people aroused to positive action and yet moderate enough to keep this fervor within controllable and Christian bounds? I knew that many of the Negro people were victims of bitterness that could easily rise to flood proportions. What could I say to keep them courageous and prepared for positive action and yet devoid of hate and resentment? Could the militant and the moderate be combined in a single speech?

In what might be called a freedom sermon, combining the vivid preaching style found in the black churches with the content of the freedom movement, the young pastor set the people and their movement in their largest context that night. He identified them "first and foremost" as American citizens, citizens who had the right and the responsibility to protest injustice and to work for a better society. At every point he grounded himself in the concrete experience of Montgomery's black people and their experiences on the buses and elsewhere in their unjust, humiliating, and segregated city. So there was constant enthusiastic and empathetic verbal response all through his presentation, particularly when King uttered the words, "There comes a time when people get tired of being trampled over by the iron feet of oppression." He pushed even further, pressing on the audience a sense of identity beyond their status as victims of oppression, declaring, "I want to say that we're not here advocating violence. . . . We have never done that. . . . I want it to be known throughout Montgomery and throughout this nation that we are a Christian people. . . . We believe in the Christian religion. We believe in the teachings of Jesus. The only weapon that we have in our hands this evening is the weapon of protest." All through that statement of their central religious identity the people shouted and applauded, moved with King, pressed him forward even as he urged them toward their own best possibilities. He said, "We, the disinherited of this land, we who have been oppressed so long, are tired of going through the long night of captivity. And now we are reaching out for the daybreak of freedom and justice and equality."

So the issue was already far beyond the buses, encompassing freedom, justice, and equality. Calling upon the people to continue to work together for much more than a desegregated bus seat, King set an example for the freedom movement leadership. For he declared to his community:

> Right here in Montgomery, when the history books are written in the future
> . . . somebody will have to say, "There lived a race of people . . . who had the
> moral courage to stand up for their rights. . . . And thereby they injected a
> new meaning into the veins of history and of civilization." And we're going
> to do that. God grant that we will do it before it is too late.

The excited, inspired people hardly had time to consider this grand calling to be the bearers of new universal values when they were brought right back to the concrete realities of their new movement. Right there in the meeting they were called upon to vote their approval of the proposals the MIA leadership was using as a basis for their negotiating with the city administration and the bus company. They were also told that private automobiles and black-owned taxis had to be volunteered, along with drivers, for use in a car pool that would soon become the most highly organized element of the boycott movement. And, of course, money had to be collected, for gas, for maintenance, and for all the other expenses connected to the development of an essentially volunteer organization. So the marvelously ordinary black men and women who were just being called upon by King to inject "a new meaning into the veins of history and of civilization" were also being asked to drop their hard-earned quarters and dollars into the MIA collection baskets.

The sense that something new was being born in Montgomery's black churches had drawn black leaders from other parts of Alabama to the initial meeting that night. They came from such places as Birmingham, Mobile, Tuskegee, and Tuscaloosa, both to encourage the people of Montgomery and to gain new inspiration for their own struggles. Still, it is quite possible that the expansion of the boycott's inspiring potential might have simply been confined to Alabama if its white opponents had not made a series of mistakes, mistakes based on their stubborn refusal to realize that a new time and a new black community were emerging.

First, in the earliest attempts at negotiation, the representatives of the city and the bus company refused to make even the slightest accommodation to the relatively modest changes the MIA leadership was proposing. This stiff resistance on the part of the white leaders helped to steel the resolve of the aroused and walking people. Then the city commissioners inaugurated what they called a "get tough" policy with the boycotters and their leadership. Legal harassment of the crucial cabs and car pool, and an unjustified arrest of King for speeding were part of the strategy of intimidation. This was soon followed by a publicly announced decision by all three city commissioners to join the local White Citizens Council, a slightly more respectable version of the Klan.

Such actions only compelled black Montgomery to form a deeper resolve to stay off the buses. Then the most important of the early opposition mistakes took place on Monday night, January 30, 1956, almost two months into the boycott. That night, while King was at one of the mass meetings, his wife and young child were at home accompanied by a member of Dexter Church. The two women heard something hit the front porch. They ran to the back room where three-month-old Yolanda Denise was sleeping. What they had heard was a stick of dynamite landing on the front porch, and its explosion blew a hole in the porch floor, shattered four windows, and damaged a porch column. Running to the back had saved Coretta King and her friend from possible injury.

Called out of the mass meeting, King arrived at his house some fifteen minutes after the blast. There he found hundreds of angry black people, some of them armed, milling around his front porch. After determining that his family was safe, he came back out to address the crowd, some of whom were fiercely challenging the chief of police and the mayor to match them gun for gun, and defiantly refusing to obey police orders to disperse. "Getting tough" was obviously an approach that had epidemic possibilities, but when King appeared he maintained an extraordinary and crucial composure that transformed the situation. After assuring the crowd that his family had not been harmed, he said,

> We believe in law and order. Don't get panicky. . . . Don't get your weapons. He who lives by the sword will perish by the sword. Remember, that is what God said. We are not advocating violence. We want to love our enemies. Be good to them. Love them and let them know you love them.

After urging that stern and demanding post-dynamite discipline upon himself and the crowd, pressing them to apply the tenets of their religion to the crisis of that night, King went on to remind the quieting crowd, "I did not start this boycott. I was asked by you to serve as your spokesman." Then he added, "I want it to be known the length and breadth of this land that if I am stopped this movement will not stop. . . . What we are doing is just. And God is with us." The gathered people responded by spontaneously breaking into song, including hymns and "My country 'tis of thee, sweet land of liberty, of thee I sing."

It was the terrorist bombing and King's mature and challenging response to it that effectively began to push the Montgomery story beyond the confines of the African-American press and the local newspapers into the nation's mainstream mass media and into the consciousness (and consciences) of hundred of thousands of its citizens, irrespective of color.

Meanwhile, the white defenders of Montgomery continued to misread the times and the people with whom they were dealing. Shortly after the dynamite attack on

King's house, a bomb was thrown into the front yard of MIA treasurer and movement stalwart E. D. Nixon. Two weeks later eleven thousand white people gathered in Montgomery for a White Citizens Council rally, where they cheered the mayor and police chief for holding the line in the cause of bus segregation. Perhaps encouraged by their own mass meeting, the city officials decided to ask a grand jury to indict nearly one hundred leaders of the MIA on charges of conspiracy. That broadside approach and the refusal of the MIA leadership to be intimidated by it only intensified the national media interest in Montgomery and in King.

The first time that the Montgomery story appeared on the front page of the internationally respected *New York Times* and *New York Herald Tribune* was when these papers reported the mass meeting held the evening after the leaders were arrested, and immediately bailed out, on the conspiracy charge. Readers around the world were able to catch the spirit of determined, nonviolent resistance as thousands of boycotters gathered to hear the news from the courtroom and to stand in solidarity with their leaders. Thus the nation received King's message: "This is not a war between the white and the Negro but a conflict between justice and injustice." Expanding his vision to include the largest possible participation, King went on, "If our victory is won—and it will be won—it will be a victory for Negroes, a victory for justice, a victory for free people, and a victory for democracy." In a sense, there were hundreds of thousands of distant listeners as he proclaimed, "If we are arrested every day, if we are exploited every day, if we are trampled over every day, don't ever let anyone pull you so low as to hate them. We must use the weapon of love."

The nation began to respond in a variety of ways. The proprietor of Sadie's Beauty Shop in the black community of Gastonia, North Carolina, took up a collection in her shop for Montgomery's walkers. The first African-American winner of the Nobel Peace Prize, Ralph Bunche, who served as an official of the United Nations, wrote to praise and encourage King and the people of the movement: "Your patient determination, your wisdom and quiet courage are constituting an inspiring chapter in the history of human dignity." In hundreds of black churches across the country the combination of praying and organizing produced scenes like the one in Concord Baptist Church in Brooklyn, New York, where a collection of four thousand dollars was taken up for Montgomery in trash cans and cake boxes after the collection plates were filled.

This vital connection between King and Montgomery's church-based movement and the black churches throughout the country was crucial in transforming the nation after the Second World War. Supplementing the news that came from black newspapers and magazines like *Jet, Ebony,* and *Sepia,* as well as from the newly attentive white-owned media, black churches served as a massive network for information and mobilization regarding Montgomery. Other committed groups—the skycaps at Newark Airport and some longshoremen in San Francisco, for example—made their own contributions, sometimes just an hour's pay.

King and the movement attracted the attention of two of the most important religiously based pacifist groups in the country: The Fellowship of Reconciliation (FOR) and the American Friends Service Committee, better known as Quakers. Many of their members had hoped and worked for a long time to see Mahatma Gandhi's religiously inspired organizing combined with the courageous, nonviolent spirit of Jesus in the cause of racial justice and equality in the United States. Though predominantly white, they were often joined and even led by a number of African Americans, such as Howard and Sue Thurman, Benjamin Mays, Mordecai Johnson, and Bayard Rustin, the radical Quaker and peace activist. Indeed, when Montgomery broke into the mainstream news, the national chairman of the FOR was Charles Lawrence, a 1936 Morehouse College graduate who was then teaching sociology at Brooklyn College in New York. Lawrence, a firm, articulate, and jovial believer in the nonviolent struggle for justice, wrote to King as soon as he saw the newspaper reports on the post-indictment mass meeting and claimed that he found the stories "among the most thrilling documents I have ever read." He wrote, "Who knows? Providence may have given the Negroes of Montgomery the historic mission of demonstrating to the world the practical power of Christianity, the unmatched vitality of a nonviolent loving approach to social protest."

Inspired by such grand hopes, Lawrence and his FOR colleagues sent their national field secretary, Glenn Smiley, on an exploratory visit to Montgomery that winter. Smiley, a white Texan who was an ordained minister in the Southern Methodist Church, had been involved with the Fellowship since the early forties and had been a conscientious objector on religious grounds during the Second World War. According to Lawrence's instructions, Smiley's FOR mission in Montgomery would be "primarily that of finding out what those of you who are involved directly would have those of us who are 'on the outside' do."

Meanwhile, Rustin, one of the best-known activists in the pacifist movement, also went independently to offer his services to King and the Montgomery struggle. A personable, brilliant, nonviolent strategist and writer, Rustin did not, unfortunately, stay long in Montgomery. Ironically, in the eyes of some of the MIA officers, Rustin's past involvement with communist-related organizations and his prior arrest for a homosexual liaison made him more of a risk than Smiley. Nevertheless, both men helped King on what he later called his "pilgrimage to nonviolence," introducing him to leading religious pacifists, such as Howard Thurman and Harry Emerson Fosdick; introducing him to the classic published writings on nonviolence, such as Fosdick's *Hope of the World*; and assisting the MIA in developing its own training workshops in nonviolence. Rustin, in particular, helped King prepare important articles on the Montgomery struggle for a number of religious journals.

By the end of the winter of 1956, as the boycott moved into its fourth month, King's picture had appeared on the cover of a number of national magazines, and his name and message were familiar in many other parts of the world. He carried the message across the nation, his powerful baritone voice reverberating in scores of large churches, on college and university campuses, in municipal auditoriums, at conventions of the NAACP and the National Urban League, at fraternal and religious conventions, even at a black funeral directors' convention.

By the fall of 1956 Montgomery had become the unmistakable symbol of transformation in the nation, a symbol of its African-American citizens and its Southern-based traditions of legal segregation, white domination, and the subversion of democratic hope. That symbol belonged to all the licensed practical nurses, the maids and skycaps, the scholars and Nobel laureates, the prisoners, students, artists, and pastors who would eventually create their own versions of Montgomery across the nation.

By this time the Montgomery movement had also provided a crucial set of opportunities for King and his coworkers to experiment with Gandhian nonviolent action (or "passive resistance," as King sometimes described it) on behalf of freedom and justice. King could now announce with confidence, "We in Montgomery have discovered a method that can be used by the Negroes in their fight for political and economic equality.... We fight injustice with passive resistance.... Mohandas Gandhi ... used it to topple the British military machine.... Let's now use this method in the United States."

At the same time, while he increasingly referred to Gandhi, King kept returning to his fundamental grounding in the black church experience. "The spirit of passive resistance came to me from the Bible," he said, "from the teachings of Jesus. The techniques came from Gandhi." Summing up what the events in Montgomery meant for a religiously sensitive region and nation, King continued to affirm that "This is a spiritual movement, depending on moral and spiritual forces."

But such a spiritual vision did not exclude the use of practical methods. For instance, the white authorities' unwillingness to negotiate and the continued harassment and violence directed at the black community compelled the MIA leaders to take their struggle into the courts. In consultation with the local and national NAACP lawyers, the MIA initiated a legal suit to challenge the constitutionality of Montgomery's segregated bus system. They had moved far beyond the initial quest for "a more humane form of segregation." Now they were challenging the Jim Crow transportation system itself. The case was identified as *Gayle* v. *Browder* (1956). And when the U.S. Supreme Court ruled in favor of the black citizens of Montgomery, it was clear the South was about to change forever.

The Court's ruling in *Gayle* v. *Browder* was announced on November 13, 1956, but no one knew when the official papers of notification would reach Montgomery. The city commission refused to allow the bus company to make any changes in its practices until the court documents actually arrived in their offices. But the people of the movement prepared themselves for the next phase of the journey they had begun on December 5, 1955. On the night when the Supreme Court decision was announced, a caravan of forty cars of Klan members drove through the city's black neighborhoods. But no one ran into their houses. No one pulled down the shades. Instead, many "New Negroes" stood and watched calmly. Some even waved to the disconcerted white-robed visitors, and soon the visitors drove away.

The next night there were two mass meetings to accommodate all the people full of courage who had come to give thanks for the past and plan for the future. It was natural that the MIA executive committee called on King to address the meetings that night. Speaking at Holt Street Church, where they had begun together, King said, "These eleven months have not all been easy. . . . We have lived with this protest so long that we have learned the meaning of sacrifice and suffering. But somehow we feel that our suffering is redemptive." Forever the teacher, King felt that he had to encourage the people to consider what it would mean to "press on" to their next steps "in the spirit of the movement." For him, two elements were crucial. One was the need to avoid arrogance as they made their victorious return to the buses. Taking on a personal tone, he said to the people, "I would be terribly disappointed if anybody goes back to the buses bragging about, we, the Negroes, have won a victory over the white people." Instead, King called on them to remember the need to open both the struggle and the victory beyond racial lines. So he said that when the legal papers finally arrived, "it will be a victory for justice and a victory for goodwill and a victory for the forces of light. So let us not limit this decision to a victory for Negroes. Let us go back to the buses in all humility and with gratitude to the Almighty God for making this [court] decision possible."

Even at such a high point in their struggle, King knew that he was pressing his people toward a fiercely demanding discipline. He said, "I know it's hard" but keep pushing: "the strong man is the man . . . who can stand up for his rights and yet not hit back."

King knew they were on a dangerous path. They were poised at a crucial moment in history, a moment that required disciplined courage and disciplined love, especially in the light of the South's long history of violence against black attempts to gain justice. Finally, King faced his people with the ultimate encouragement—his willingness to sacrifice his own life. Normally not given to this kind of self-focus, it was a clear sign that he saw the moment as a moment of crisis, one similar to that January night on his bombed-out porch. So he said to the visibly moved assembly:

> I'm not telling you something that I don't live. [Someone yelled, "That's right!"] I'm aware of the fact that the Ku Klux Klan is riding in Montgomery. I'm aware of the fact that a week never passes that somebody's not telling me to get out of town, or that I'm going to be killed next place I move. But I don't have any guns in my pockets. I don't have any guards on my side.
>
> But I have the God of the Universe on my side. I'm serious about that. I can walk the streets of Montgomery without fear. I don't worry about a

thing. They can bomb my house. They can kill my body. But they can never kill the spirit of freedom that is in my people.

Finally, on December 20, the Supreme Court mandate made its way to Montgomery, affirming the people and their audacious struggle. The next morning a restrained but happy group, including King, Abernathy, and Smiley, boarded the first desegregated bus, beginning a new phase of the long journey toward freedom and justice for all.

## Old Order, New Order

By the time the victory was won in Montgomery, the struggle had lasted for more than a year. All along the way there were dramatic, compelling new events, bombings, indictments, rallies in other cities, and courtroom trials reminding people, especially black people, that the Montgomery movement was alive. Black folks had stuck together and grown together in the longest sustained campaign for justice that the nation had ever seen.

And, of course, the movement's prime symbol, Martin Luther King, Jr., seemed to be everywhere, proclaiming and exemplifying the emergence of a new people and a new time. By the time the legal victory was announced in Montgomery, it appeared that King was right: It was far more than a victory for the black walkers of Montgomery (although *that* victory certainly needed to be savored and celebrated), and wherever people claimed the fruits of the long ordeal, a powerful energy of hope and a sense of new possibilities appeared.

Sometimes the Montgomery connections to other places in the nation was obvious. In cities such as Mobile and Birmingham, Alabama, and nearby Tallahassee, Florida, ministers tried to repeat the Montgomery success with their own bus boycotts. In January 1957 King and the Fellowship of Reconciliation brought together some sixty representatives of these and other boycott movements to a conference in Atlanta. They discussed the possibility of forming a regional organization based on the Montgomery experience. Before the summer of 1957 was over, King and his fellow black ministers had established the Southern Christian Leadership Conference (SCLC).

The major early accomplishments of SCLC were the sponsorship of several conferences and organizing, with Bayard Rustin and A. Philip Randolph, a "prayer pilgrimage" of about twenty thousand people in Washington, D.C., who were calling for civil rights legislation. SCLC also hoped to undertake a "Crusade for Citizenship," projected as a massive Southwide voter-registration campaign based in the black churches. Due to lack of personnel, planning, and finances, this campaign never materialized.

Even with its provocative founding announcement that "we have come to redeem the soul of America" and the predictable choice of King as president, the mostly Baptist group was not, however, able to focus and mobilize the new energies in the ways that King, his Alabama comrades, and his Northern allies had hoped. This was partly because the approximately one hundred men (there were only men in mainstream black church leadership) who formed the core of the SCLC were only a small minority of the black ministers of the South. And, besides, SCLC's ministers had had no real experience in forming a regional organization that would be both flexible and open to new strategies yet also structured enough to mount a sustained challenge to the system of legal segregation.

So for a number of years after the Montgomery victory, the energies that were released there had to be channeled into less obvious places than the Southern black churches that had anchored the celebrated boycott. As a result, the expansion of the Southern freedom movement depended on unlikely groups of people, emerging from unexpected places.

For instance, there was the teenager John Lewis, a short, slightly built, slow-speaking country boy from Troy, Alabama, who had first heard King's pre-boycott preaching on a local black radio station. The unassuming but religiously rooted Lewis had been training himself for his own calling by preaching to the live-stock in his family's yard, and baptizing some of them too. Regardless of his unconventional training and practice congregation, Lewis knew that there was work for him to do, and King and the people of Montgomery were his models. Throughout the post–Montgomery decade, John Lewis took that work and those models into some of the most dangerous frontiers of the Southern-based struggle for freedom, accumulating many scars and much honor in the process. As a Freedom Rider in 1961, Lewis rode buses throughout the South, testing the law that made segregated buses and station facilities illegal. He became the first Freedom Rider to meet with violence when he was struck by some white men as he attempted to go through the white entrance to the Rock Hill, South Carolina, Greyhound bus station.

In the same way, few people would have predicted that a matronly, middle-aged black South Carolinian named Septima Poinsette Clark would be one of the most effective carriers of Montgomery's best spirit. In her fifties when the victory was won, the Charleston woman was not too old to be a "new Negro." A veteran teacher in the public school system of Charleston, she had led important struggles for the equalizing of salaries for black and white teachers.

Then, on April 19, 1956, a law was passed prohibiting state and city employees from having an affiliation with any civil rights group, including the NAACP. Clark refused to obey the law and lost her job. She now joined forces with the white Southerners who had founded the Highlander Folk School in the mountains of eastern Tennessee. Highlander was established in the thirties as a nontraditional educational center to encourage local citizens and others to build a more just and democratic society across racial lines.

At Highlander the soft-spoken but iron-willed Clark created a program based on work she had been doing for decades. She called it Citizenship Education, and it involved an informal but carefully crafted workshop combination of storytelling, political analysis, American and African-American history, religious education, autobiographical sharing, careful study of arcane voter-registration laws and forms, and much singing and mutual encouragement. With such deceptively simple methods, Clark and her expanding group of coworkers performed an almost unbelievable task. They helped thousands of marginally literate (and sometimes illiterate) black people not only learn to read and write their way to voter-registration skills, but also to teach others, and to become committed believers in the freedom movement.

By that time many people had discovered that the path blazed by Rosa Parks, Martin Luther King, Jr., and the Montgomery boycotters was not meant to be duplicated exactly. That was clear not only in efforts of people like John Lewis and Septima Clark. It could also be seen in the failed attempts to build Montgomery copycat boycotts in places like Mobile and Tallahassee, failures that inspired people to search for other methods. Indeed when King had declared near the close of the Montgomery boycott that "nothing can kill the spirit of my people," he probably understood that the spirit needed to take many different forms.

That spirit was seen, for instance, in the fiery determination of Fred Shuttlesworth, the Birmingham pastor who became a staunch comrade to Martin King in the next stages of the Southern freedom movement. A contrast to King in almost every conceivable way, Shuttlesworth was a native of Alabama's backwoods—a wiry, volatile, and gritty man. Before he answered the inner call to the Christian ministry, he had been a truck driver, cement worker, and operator of the family's whiskey still. Indeed, he was just the kind of utterly courageous, sharp-tongued, quick-tempered believer in nonviolence that the movement needed. Though profoundly inspired by King and Montgomery, Shuttlesworth was his own man. When white-led governments across the South responded to black assertiveness by banning established organizations such as the NAACP, Shuttlesworth's independence proved invaluable.

In Alabama the white authorities formally blamed the national organization and its local branches for organizing an illegal boycott by black residents of Montgomery and used that as their excuse for outlawing the organization in the state. The state demanded its membership lists (a demand that the NAACP managed successfully to resist for the eight years that it took to get the state action reversed in federal courts). Just a few days after the NAACP ban went into effect, Fred Shuttlesworth angered the local authorities when he formed a new, replacement organization from his Birmingham base, calling it the Alabama Christian Movement for Human Rights (ACMHR). Led essentially (and somewhat autocratically) by Shuttlesworth, the ACMHR became one of the most vital affiliates of the Southern Christian Leadership Conference, temporarily providing a mass movement-oriented substitute for the NAACP and eventually carrying the spirit of Montgomery to another level of confrontation. The ACMHR fought against bus segregation in December 1956 and October 1958, using direct-action tactics. It also tried to integrate Birmingham schools and train stations in 1957.

In other states, such as Mississippi and Florida, courageous NAACP officials and those who tried to stand with them were sometimes run out of the state or assassinated. On Christmas night 1951, Harry T. Moore, executive secretary of NAACP branches in Florida, and his wife were killed when their house was bombed in Mims, Florida. Shuttlesworth himself was subjected to everything from midday beatings by mobs of white segregationists to the nighttime bombing of his house and church. The attacks intensified after the intrepid pastor insisted on personally desegregating the Birmingham city buses and on trying to enroll his children in an all-white school in the stubbornly segregated city school system.

Indeed, public opinion polls revealed that eighty percent of white Southerners were opposed to school desegregation in the immediate post–*Brown* period. Although the terms of opposition were framed in various ways, so much finally came down to the basic truth that South Carolina Governor James Byrnes had expressed. If taken seriously, desegregation marked "the beginning of the end of civilization in the South" as white people, especially privileged white people, had known it. In the same way, there was no room for misinterpreting the so-called "Southern manifesto" that had been signed in March 1956 by ninety Southern members of the House of Representatives and by all of the senators except Estes Kefauver and Albert Gore of Tennessee and Senate majority leader Lyndon Johnson. In this document these respected senators and representatives denied that the Supreme Court had a right to rule on racial issues in the realm of public education, as it had in the *Brown* decision, and called upon their constituents to disobey the court's order, offering "massive resistance" to the ruling.

In addition, the person who might have been expected to provide some firm guidance to the nation in this crucial time of transition was offering a version of his own resistance. The widely admired military hero Dwight D. Eisenhower had been elected president in 1952 and again in 1956. He probably had more leverage to lead the nation down the path of peaceful change than any other public figure, but he never really came to the aid of African Americans. Rather, the president chose to condemn what he called "the extremists on both sides" of the school desegregation question, thereby equating courageous children and their communities who were working for democratic change with men and women who defied the Supreme Court, dynamited buildings, and assassinated leaders.

Though Eisenhower never made a clear public statement of opposition to the Court's action in *Brown,* neither did he ever publicly support it. He felt that "forcing" desegregation would raise white resistance. But as the nature of the battle for desegregation progressed, Eisenhower was forced to take action on behalf of the federal government.

Faced with such a range of opposition midnight bombers, an uncommitted president, members of Congress urging "massive resistance," and the Supreme

Court's own ambiguous 1955 call for school districts to move to implement the *Brown* decision not by any certain date but "with all deliberate speed," it would not have been surprising if Southern blacks had given up the quest for desegregated schools. But they were constantly reminding each other that "we've come too far to turn back."

Children, ranging in ages from six to seventeen, were on the front lines of this phase of the struggle. In hundreds of schools across the South, the children had to face hatred, ignorance, and fear. As they arrived at newly desegregated schools, they had to face screaming, cursing, threatening presences of white men, children, and women who had appointed themselves as protectors of the social and educational bastions of white supremacy.

Still, the black children went into the schools—sometimes to the accompaniment of white rioting in the streets, sometimes under the protection of federal marshals or troops.

Eventually, all the possibilities and complications of the post–Montgomery struggles for a desegregated nation seemed to gather around Little Rock's Central High. Little Rock was considered a city that was reasonably open to the powerful surges of change that were mounting in the South, and in 1954 it had been the first Southern city to respond positively to the *Brown* decision. Less than a week after the decision was announced, the Little Rock school board declared its intention to voluntarily desegregate its public schools, beginning with the two-thousand-student Central High, located in a working-class white neighborhood. However, it was not until 1957 that the board announced that it would actually begin the desegregation process on a rather timid level that fall. Then seventy-five students volunteered to lead the way. Of those, twenty-five were chosen. The all-white school board, worried about a brewing politically inspired white reaction, soon pared the number down to nine. Six young women and three young men were chosen to "carry the banner."

Unfortunately, the white community of Little Rock and the state of Arkansas once again lacked the kind of courageous moral leadership that would have helped guide them. Instead the confused and searching citizens were subjected to the mercurial and election-driven performance of Governor Orville Faubus. A racial "moderate" in pre-1954 Southern white terms, he had become convinced that in order to be reelected, he had to respond to the worst fears of the white parents and politicians who were busy galvanizing opposition to the school board's modest desegregation plan. This led to the spectacle of Faubus calling out the Arkansas National Guard that fall to block the way of the black students as they—with amazing poise—moved past a crowd of screaming adults and young people and tried to enter Central High.

Such a use of state troops to resist a U.S. Supreme Court order, carried out in front of national network television cameras, finally pushed Eisenhower to action. But his initial attempt to use his personal powers of persuasion on Faubus turned

Armed soldiers confront white students at Central High School in Little Rock. Because of the serious challenge to federal authority in Arkansas, President Eisenhower sent one thousand U.S. Army troops to protect the nine black students who had defied white protests and threats of violence to enroll at the school.

out to be too little too late and served only to help heighten the crisis. Ten days after the beginning of the Little Rock crisis, Eisenhower summoned Faubus to a private conference. The governor left his conversation with the president to return to Little Rock and pull away the Arkansas National Guard, leaving only the local police to deal with the constantly expanding crowd of white adult opponents at the school building. Their hysterical calls for resistance to integration finally erupted into violence against several black journalists. At the same time there were reckless threats from the mob to lynch one or more of the black students. The scenes of white crowds surging against the overwhelmed and under-committed local police moved across the nation's television screens. (The medium was new, and the black struggle for freedom in the South was its first major ongoing story.) Many people also saw the electrifying image of Elizabeth Eckford, one of the black students in Little Rock, accidentally cut off from the rest of the group of students, surrounded by the hostile mob, moving in silent, terrified dignity, finally joined by a tall white woman, Grace Lorch, who stood by her side and then helped her board a bus to safety.

Eisenhower finally did what he had pledged never to do: send federal troops to Little Rock "to aid in the execution of federal law," he said to the nation. But he also sent more than a thousand riot-trained troops from the 101st Airborne Division to protect the right of nine young citizens to make use of the opportunity that the Supreme Court had guaranteed to them.

The Little Rock pioneers stayed the course, managed to live through an academic year of hateful taunts and actual assaults, managed also to find a few friends. For a while each student was accompanied in the school by a soldier, but these military companions could not go into locker rooms, lavatories, classrooms, the cafeteria, and other spaces that had become danger spots. There came a time when one of the nine, Minnie Jean Brown, finally gave in to the deep frustration they were all feeling and one day poured her bowl of chili on the head of a persistent tormenter. Her unexpected action evoked a spontaneous round of applause from the black cafeteria workers, but it also led to a suspension from school, and Minnie Jean finished her academic year in New York City. Meanwhile the other students continued, making their way through Central High's school year, carrying the banner—and the pain—all the way. Crucial to their endurance was the community support that they found.

Many people in both the South and the North, however, were not convinced that a just and humane new nation could be born on this bloody ground. These reluctant unbelievers simply could not convince themselves that American democracy could ever become a reality for black people.

As a matter of fact, even as the Little Rock struggle was going on in the 1957–58 academic year, in Monroe, North Carolina, a rather different scenario was developing. Ex-Marine Robert Williams, who had been so ecstatic with hope at the time of the *Brown* decision, had returned to his hometown of Monroe after the Korean War. He soon became president of the local branch of the NAACP and also became convinced that his military training provided a better alternative for dealing with the terrorists of the Klan and other white groups than King's way of nonviolent resistance. With the help of the National Rifle Association, Williams created a rifle club within his NAACP branch and began talking of the need to "meet lynching with lynching." But by the middle of 1959 Williams found himself attacked and disowned by the national NAACP organization and hounded as a fugitive by local and national law enforcement agencies. Two years later, he was forced to flee the country altogether as a result of trumped-up kidnapping charges. Eventually he became an exile from the land that once inspired his hope, finding political asylum in Cuba, which had just undergone its own socialist revolution. He later went to China and then the East African nation of Tanzania before returning to America almost a decade later.

Nevertheless, Williams's demand for an alternative to nonviolent resistance did not end with his departure. His calls for armed self-defense and physical retaliation were familiar themes in the traditions of black American resistance. Indeed, even then an important variation on this theme was rising up in the northern cities of the nation.

When all eyes seemed to be on Montgomery, in the black communities of Detroit, New York, Chicago, Los Angeles, and elsewhere a growing number of young black men, impeccably dressed in suits and bow ties, and young women, wrapped in long, flowing white dresses, became a regular part of the urban landscape. These quiet, dignified, disciplined black folk were practicing Muslims, members of the Nation of Islam (NOI). The NOI was founded by an obscure self-styled prophet named W. D. Fard in the thirties. Fard and his handpicked successor, Elijah Poole (who would later take the name Elijah Muhammad), preached a modified version of Islam. It combined claims of black racial supremacy (such as the idea that black people were the original people and whites were "devils" invented by a mad scientist named Yacub) with elements of the orthodox Islamic tradition and borrowed heavily from the style and structure of black Christian churches. Despite their reputation for being a radical sect, the NOI promoted fairly conservative ideas and values. It sought to "uplift" the race by establishing black-owned businesses and "teaching" black ghetto dwellers the importance of discipline, self-help, and cleanliness. It imposed strict rules about personal behavior: Alcohol, drugs, tobacco, gambling, dancing, adultery, premarital sex, profanity, or watching movies with sex or "coarse speech," for example, were simply not allowed. The NOI even impressed black conservative George Schuyler, managing editor of the New York office of the black-owned *Pittsburgh Courier,* who praised them for their values and moral vision. "Mr. Muhammad may be a rogue and a charlatan," wrote Schuyler in 1959, "but when anybody can get tens of thousands of Negroes to practice economic solidarity, respect their women, alter their atrocious diet, give up liquor, stop crime, juvenile delinquency and adultery, he is doing more for the Negro's welfare than any current Negro leader I know." Although the NOI officially stayed out of politics, focusing its energies on the spiritual uplift of African Americans and offering an alternative to the "white man's religion," it did practice self-defense and did not shy away from violence. During the thirties in Detroit, for example, black Muslims, as members of the NOI were known, attracted attention

The Nation of Islam attracted thousands of urban blacks to the disciplined life of abstinence, prayer, and black self-determination.

during a bloody shootout with police. And under Fard's leadership, the NOI even established a paramilitary organization known as the Fruit of Islam. They kept order at big gatherings, served as bodyguards for "the Messenger" (Muhammad), and were trained to defend NOI institutions at any cost.

The NOI remained a fairly small religious sect until the Second World War. Its membership began to increase after Elijah Muhammad and about one hundred other Muslims were jailed for resisting the draft. As a result, the NOI not only garnered more national publicity but it began to recruit members from the ranks of black prisoners. One of those prisoners who discovered the Nation was Malcolm Little, whose name was changed to Malcolm X by Elijah Muhammad. He wrote in his autobiography that he received the X from the Nation of Islam as a symbol of his unknown African ancestry. More than any other figure, Malcolm X was responsible for turning the NOI into a national force to be reckoned with. And more than anyone else, he embodied the NOI's militant, uncompromising, and, when needed, violent image, one that would scare many white liberals and nurture a new generation of black radicals.

The son of Earl Little, a Baptist preacher, and his wife, Louisa, Malcolm and his siblings experienced dramatic confrontations with racism. According to his autobiography, hooded Klansmen burned their home in Lansing, Michigan. Earl Little was killed under mysterious circumstances, welfare agencies split up the children and eventually had Louisa Little committed to a mental institution, and Malcolm was forced to live in a detention home run by a racist white couple. By the eighth grade he had left school, moved to Boston to live with his half-sister Ella, and discovered the underground world of African-American hipsters and petty criminals. His downward spiral ended in 1946, when he was sentenced to ten years in jail for burglary.

After discovering Islam, Malcolm Little submitted to the discipline and guidance of the NOI and became a voracious reader of the Koran and the Bible. He also immersed himself in works of literature and history in the prison library. Upon his release in 1952, Malcolm X, a devoted follower of Elijah Muhammad, rose quickly within the NOI ranks, serving as minister of Harlem's Temple No. 7, where he went in 1954. He later ministered to temples in Detroit and Philadelphia. Through speaking engagements, television appearances, and by establishing *Muhammad Speaks*—the NOI's first nationally distributed newspaper—Malcolm X called America's attention to the Nation of Islam. His criticisms of civil rights leaders for advocating integration into white society instead of building black institutions and defending themselves from racist violence generated opposition from both conservatives and liberals.

But Malcolm showed signs of independence from the NOI line. During the mid–fifties, for example, he privately scoffed at Elijah Muhammad's interpretation of the genesis of the "white race" and seemed uncomfortable with the idea that all white people were literally devils. More significantly, Malcolm clearly disagreed with the NOI's policy of not participating in politics. He not only believed that political mobilization was indispensable but occasionally defied the rule by supporting boycotts and other forms of protest. He had begun developing a Third World political perspective during the fifties, when anticolonial wars and decolonization were pressing public issues. Indeed, Africa remained his primary political interest outside black America: In 1959 he toured Egypt, Sudan, Nigeria, and Ghana to develop ties between African Americans and the newly independent African states.

African Americans had long seen themselves as part of a larger world, as more than "minorities" within the confines of the United States. But there was never a time like this, when every corner of the earth seemed engaged in a struggle for freedom, and the black freedom movement in America seemed to be at the eye of the international storm.

## Freedom Now!: The Student Revolutionaries

On a Sunday morning late in November 1959, Martin Luther King, Jr., announced to his congregation at Dexter Avenue Baptist Church in Montgomery, Alabama, that he had decided to leave the city and return to his native Atlanta. The major reason was the need to connect himself more firmly to the Southern Christian Leadership Conference, which had been headquartered in Atlanta since its founding in 1957. In the years since its establishment, SCLC had been having a hard time getting organized. In the statement he made to the Dexter congregation that Sunday, King seemed to be trying to rally himself, his organization, and the larger developing freedom movement to a new state of activity. He said, "The time has come for a broad, bold advance of the Southern campaign for equality.... Not only will it include a stepped-up campaign of voter registration, but a full-scale assault will be made upon discrimination and segregation in all forms.... We must employ new methods of struggle involving the masses of our people."

In this "bold advance" King envisioned SCLC as a crucial force, and he was convinced that a great deal of the energy that was needed would come from black young people. Indeed, King said, "We must train our youth ... in the techniques of social change through nonviolent resistance." It is likely that King was envisioning a youth movement that would be firmly based in the SCLC organization. But by the time King moved to Atlanta in January 1960, SCLC had not yet done anything to organize a youth movement. Fortunately, the young people were not waiting. Beginning independently from several Southern bases, an ever-expanding nonviolent army of black young people and their white allies began to put an indelible mark on the sixties.

On January 31, 1960, at North Carolina Agricultural and Technical College (known as A&T), one of the South's many black colleges, four freshmen decided to move from words to deeds. Ezell Blair, Jr., Joseph McNeil, Franklin McClain, and David Richmond decided that they were going to confront one of the most demeaning symbols of segregation: the all-white lunch counter at the local Woolworth's department store. Like all the chain stores in the South, the Greensboro store accepted the money of its African-American customers at the various merchandise counters, but the lunch counter was a different story. Black people were not permitted to sit for a snack, a meal, or even a drink of water. Usually, such segregationist practices were enforced by local ordinances, state laws, and coercion by whites acting almost out of habit. Whites considered public space theirs to control and define, and they were especially sensitive about public eating places, where white employees might be perceived as serving blacks (as opposed to merely accepting their payments at other store counters).

The young men from A&T planned to go into Woolworth's on Monday morning, February 1, shop for some small items in other parts of the store, and then go to the lunch counter. They would sit there quietly, with dignity and with a firm insistence on their right to be served. For these students the central issue was not the hamburgers or Cokes. The issues were justice, human dignity, fairness, equality, and freedom. They were all driven by the desire to reach the fundamental goal: "Jim Crow Must Go."

The three young men who had grown up in Greensboro (McNeil came from Wilmington) were fully aware of a strong local tradition of challenging segregation. They and their parents had been active in the NAACP, and they had heard of blacks who fought to desegregate the local schools. They attended NAACP-sponsored public presentations by black student pioneers of the effort to desegregate Central High in Little Rock. And, of course, they all had as an example the noble actions of Rosa Parks and Martin Luther King, Jr., the best-known public heroes of the successful Montgomery bus boycott. When King spoke in Greensboro in 1959, Ezell Blair, Jr., remembered that his sermon was "so strong" that "I could feel my heart palpitating. It brought tears to my eyes." The young men knew that they could go to jail. Or there could be violence. So it was not surprising that David Richmond later recalled that "all of us were afraid" that Sunday night before their planned action; yet, he added, "We went ahead and did it."

Monday morning, February 1, 1960, was the day they "did it." When they sat down and asked clearly for coffee and snacks and were told that they could not be served, they refused to get up from their seats. Like Rosa Parks, they believed that holding their seats was essential to affirming their dignity and their place as citizens. So Blair, their chosen spokesman, responded to the refusal of service with a polite but probing inquiry: "I beg your pardon," he said, "but you just served us [at the other counters], why can't we be served here?"

By that time other customers were noticing the four neatly dressed, quietly determined young black men. The manager asked them to leave, but they refused, still quiet, still polite. As a matter of fact, not only did they say they would stay until the store closed, but they announced that they would return again the next day, and the days after that, until they were served, until all black people could be served and their humanity duly recognized—at least at that lunch counter.

When McClain recalled that first sit-in in an interview more than twenty years later, he reported, "If it's possible to know what it means to have your soul cleansed, I felt pretty clean at that time. I probably felt better on that day than I've ever felt in my life. . . . I felt as though I had gained my manhood, so to speak, and not only gained it, but had developed quite a lot of respect for it."

That afternoon's action concluded when the manager ordered the store closed. By the time the four freshmen returned to the campus, word of their action had streaked through the classrooms, dormitories, dining halls, and gymnasiums. Many of their fellow students soon pledged their determination to return to the lunch counter the next day.

The example set by the freshmen was so powerful that the new excitement could not be confined to one campus or one city. The students at Bennett College, a private, black women's school nearby, heard the news and joined the fight. Within a few days this powerful moral action had also become a challenge to local white undergraduates, starting with students at the elite Women's College of the University of North Carolina, located in Greensboro. Beginning on Thursday, February 4, small groups of them decided to join the demonstration and risk all the protection of their whiteness, to risk their social and family connections, and to reconsider the meaning of democracy, Christianity, and human dignity.

Before the week was over, the relatively low-key action of the four sit-in leaders

To occupy their time while they were waiting to be served, students participating in sit-ins did their home-work and wrote letters.

had escalated to unexpected levels. Nineteen students came to Woolworth's on the second day, and more than eighty were present on Wednesday. Now there were more students ready to sit in than there were seats at Woolworth's lunch counter. So, the nearby S. H. Kress store became the next target, and by Saturday of that first week hundreds of students from A&T were streaming into the downtown area to participate in what had become a kind of student crusade. Even members of the A&T football team—including a quarterback named Jesse Jackson—abandoned the apolitical, disengaged stance that marked so many college athletes. They were on the scene when gangs of young white men, waving Confederate flags, began to harass the black students, attempting to block their access to the lunch counters. On at least one occasion, members of the A&T football team, waving small U.S. flags, opened a path through the threatening white crowd for the sit-in squads.

By the next week the new, youth-led movement had spilled over into other North Carolina cities, as students in Durham, Winston-Salem, Charlotte, Chapel Hill, and elsewhere began their own sit-in campaigns. In Chapel Hill, as in other cities, there were demonstrators with picket signs on the streets as well as students sitting at the lunch counters. Several of the Chapel Hill demonstrators carried signs that expressed the message they wanted all Americans to hear: "We do not picket just because we want to eat. We can eat at home or walking down the street. We do picket to protest the lack of dignity and respect shown to us as human beings."

None of this activity had been pre-planned or coordinated. But, as one Charlotte student put it, the sit-ins provided a "means of expressing something that had been on our minds for a long time." Speaking for his generation of activists, Greensboro's Joseph McNeil said, "I guess everybody was pretty well fed up at the same time."

By the middle of February 1960, the nation had begun to discover that "everybody" really meant *everybody* and not just the North Carolina students. Within weeks the sit-ins had become a powerful social movement, ranging across the South and evoking imaginative responses of support from many places in the North. Students organized sit-ins at the New York affiliates of Woolworth's, for example. Longtime black social activist Bayard Rustin and singer and actor Harry Belafonte helped organize the Struggle for Freedom in the South, which raised funds to cover legal fees of arrested sit-in participants. Television helped to spread what people called "sit-in fever" across the South and demanded the nation's attention. But there were also human networks that carried the news. All over the South, adult veterans of the long struggle for justice and equality made phone calls, wrote letters, traveled by car to make sure that others knew what had begun in North Carolina and encouraged them to consider what needed to be done in their own communities.

The students themselves contacted friends, relatives, and members of their fraternities and sororities on other campuses in other states. Lunch counters were usually the focus of the action, but the students soon turned their attention to other forms of public accommodations as well. They created "wade-ins" at segregated public pools and beaches, "kneel-ins" at churches, "read-ins" at public libraries, and "bowl-ins" and "skate-ins" at segregated recreation centers. Usually, the students combined those nonviolent "direct action" challenges with marches and picketing at local city halls, seeking negotiations, demanding that the white elected officials take responsibility and take action to change the segregation statutes.

After the initial white surprise at these challenges to the laws and traditions of segregation, resistance to the student actions became very real. In some places it came in the form of arrests by the local police. In other situations the police stood by as white citizens took affairs in their own hands. Angry, frightened, and determined to maintain their historic positions of domination and control, white people frequently attacked the students. Sometimes sit-in participants were dragged from the lunch-counter stools and beaten. Ketchup was poured on their heads. Lighted cigarettes were pressed into their hair and on their exposed necks and shoulders. Women swung handbags at them, and men and boys used sticks and bats. Consistently, the students refused to allow themselves to be diverted from their central purpose or from their nonviolent stance, and they chose not to strike back at their attackers.

In Atlanta, one of the early targets of the demonstrating black students was the cafeteria in City Hall, where a sign announced, "Public Is Welcome." Julian Bond, a Morehouse College student leader and son of Dr. Horace Mann Bond, an internationally known scholar, led a student contingent into the cafeteria on March 15, 1960. There, they were greeted by the manager, who asked, "What do you want?" When Bond replied, "We want to eat," the manager's response was, "We can't serve you here." Bond then said, "The sign outside says the public is welcome and we're the public and we want to eat." They got their food, but the cashier refused to take their money. Bond and seventy-five of his companions did not get a meal in the public cafeteria that day but a cell in the nearby city jail. However, when they were bailed out of jail the next day, the group immediately organized themselves and other students in the Atlanta University complex (which included Spelman College, Clark College, Gammon Theological Seminary, Morehouse, and Morris Brown College) into what became known as the Committee on an Appeal for Human Rights. This turned out to be the first step toward its emergence as one of the most important student movement groups in the South. Its eloquent and thoughtful "Appeal for Human Rights" eventually appeared in the *Congressional Record*, the *New York Times*, and publications in many other parts of the world:

> We ... have joined our hearts, minds, and bodies in the cause of gaining those rights which are inherently ours as members of the human race and as citizens of the United States.
>
> We do not intend to wait placidly for those rights which are already legally and morally ours to be meted out to us one at a time.... We want to state clearly and unequivocally that we cannot tolerate, in a nation professing democracy and among people professing Christianity, the discriminatory conditions under which the Negro is living today in Atlanta, Georgia.

People who knew Southern black communities of that time would have expected Georgia's capital city to produce a significant student movement. Its six black institutions of higher education, the presence of Martin Luther King, Jr., and the SCLC, the tradition of a distinguished and relatively progressive African-American middle class, and the existence of a white leadership group that was concerned about maintaining its reputation for moderation (exemplified by Ralph McGill and his *Atlanta Constitution*, the best-known Southern newspaper)—all of these factors could have led contemporary observers to predict that Atlanta students would rise to the occasion of the new movement. They did, but it was actually the student sit-in leadership of Nashville, Tennessee, not Atlanta, that provided the focal point for the emerging student movement.

Nashville was home to one of the nation's oldest and best-known black schools,

Fisk University, alma mater of W. E. B. Du Bois. In the largely segregated city, black students were also enrolled at Meharry Medical School, the American Baptist Theological Seminary, and Tennessee Agricultural and Industrial College, a large, all-black state school. But it was one of the first black students at Vanderbilt University who played the central role. James Lawson, son of a Methodist minister and a strong and devout mother, had originally gone to Nashville from Ohio in 1958 as Southern field secretary for the Fellowship of Reconciliation. The FOR was a mostly white organization of religious pacifists that had long been involved in a quiet search for nonviolent methods of fighting for racial justice in America. Lawson first met Martin Luther King, Jr., when King was visiting Oberlin College in Ohio and Lawson was one of its older undergraduates. When King learned about the impressive personal history and Gandhian commitments of the articulate, self-assured, and spiritually grounded young man, he urged Lawson to come South and work with him in the expanding freedom movement.

Lawson, a year older than King, had already explored many aspects of the world of nonviolent action. In 1951, while active in organized Methodist youth work, Lawson had refused to register for the military draft that was then gathering young men for service in the Korean War. Basing his objection to participation in the war on the nonviolent teachings of Jesus, Gandhi, and his own mother, Lawson had been arrested for resisting the draft after he was denied conscientious objector status. He spent more than a year in jail. While in prison he met other black and white men who were refusing military service based on their religious and philosophical commitment to pacifism and nonviolence. Eventually, Lawson was released on parole in the care of the Methodist Board of Overseas Missions, and he spent three years as a Christian fraternal worker in India under the board's auspices. During this time, while teaching and coaching sports in Methodist schools, Lawson was able to explore more deeply his strong interest in Gandhian nonviolent action. He had already decided that he wanted to help create an American version of Gandhi's spiritually based liberation movement when he happened to see the first story about the Montgomery bus boycott in an Indian newspaper. As he read the article, Lawson literally jumped for joy and vowed to deepen his own commitment to work for racial justice and reconciliation in the United States. So King's later invitation was a powerful affirmation of what Jim Lawson had long been preparing for.

Responding to King's challenge, Lawson decided to explore an earlier invitation from the Fellowship of Reconciliation to become its Southern field secretary, possibly based in Nashville. Lawson also accepted an invitation to develop workshops on nonviolence from the Nashville Christian Leadership Conference (NCLC), an affiliate of King's SCLC that was led by the outspoken black Baptist pastor Kelly Miller Smith. Joined by his white FOR colleague and fellow Methodist minister Glenn Smiley, Lawson began his Nashville responsibilities by leading a workshop on nonviolent action for the NCLC in March 1958. By the fall of that year, he had decided to enroll as a student at the Divinity School of Nashville's all-white, Methodist-affiliated Vanderbilt University. He was soon offering extended versions of his initial workshop, focused now on ways in which Nashville's segregated world of public accommodations could be challenged and changed by well-trained, committed teams of nonviolent volunteers.

By the beginning of 1960 there were some seventy-five regular participants in Lawson's weekly workshops at First Baptist Church. Some of them had even experimented with sitting in at some of the downtown lunch counters and then leaving when refused service. They set up role-playing situations, anticipating what they would do and say when they encountered the expected violent opposition in words or deeds.

Then the word came from North Carolina. It appeared as if the action they were preparing for in Nashville had actually begun several hundred miles away. That Friday night at their usual meeting time, the regular Nashville participants were overwhelmed by some five hundred students and adults who wanted to join the fight. Because Lawson's corps of nonviolent trainees had been getting ready, they quickly decided to sit in at the segregated Nashville outlets of Woolworth's and Kress, and they wanted to begin the next morning, Saturday, February 6.

The students who became the heart of the Nashville movement included Marion Barry, a Mississippi native who was a graduate student in chemistry at Fisk University (and later became mayor of Washington, D.C.); Diane Nash and Angela Butler, two student leaders from the Fisk campus; and a trio of students from the all-black American Baptist Seminary, James Bevel, John Lewis, and Bernard Lafayette. After two weeks of almost daily sit-ins without arrests, attacks, or lunch-counter service, they began to hear that the police were ready to begin arresting them and that local white troublemakers were prepared to attack them physically. Undeterred, the Nashville students (joined by several white exchange students on their campuses) were determined to continue their campaign.

When the Nashville students went back downtown, at the start of the third week, the jailing, the ridicule, the spit, the fierce attacks were all waiting for them—and eventually the world saw it. Perhaps even more important, the black community began to experience a new level of solidarity. Adults rallied to the side of their children and students. Such solidarity became one of the hallmarks of the sit-in phase of the movement, providing an important source of strength for the ongoing freedom struggle. Thousands of black citizens showed their willingness to come forward with every needed kind of assistance, from bail money, to food for the imprisoned students, to the impassioned offering of long and deep prayers on behalf of their young freedom fighters.

At the same time, there were some black adults who thought the students were too brash, too uncompromising, too dangerously provocative, and these various points of view led to significant tensions. But the college students' spirit of bold, nonviolent defiance was infectious, and its effect on an even younger generation may have been at least as significant as its challenge to the elders. One of Nashville's high-school students from those days later recalled that when the sit-ins began, he paid relatively little attention to them, for he was very wrapped up in his private ambition of becoming a famous and wealthy rock star. So even when the college students started marching right past his high school, Cordell Reagon was still "unconscious," as he put it. Then, Reagon said, "One day they came by, and just on impulse I got some friends together and said, 'Let's go.' We weren't committed to the cause or anything. We just wanted to see what they were up to—it looked exciting."

That day the marching students had a stop to make on their way to the lunch counters, a stop that opened new possibilities for young Cordell Reagon's life. He said,

> They were marching to the jail, where Diane Nash, one of the main student leaders in the movement, was being kept. We go down to the jail, and we're all singing. There up in the jail cell we could see Diane. And everyone was shouting and waving. And I'm just looking. There is something amazing— a black woman only a couple of years older than me, up in this cell. There was some spirit, some power there, I had never seen before. Suddenly, I realized that everyone had marched down the street, and I was all alone staring at the cell. I ran down and caught up with the end of the march. But I figured then I better not let these people go. There is some power here that I never experienced before.

Responding to that power, holding on to those people, Reagon eventually moved toward the center of the movement, becoming one of the first full-time field secretaries for the Student Nonviolent Coordinating Committee (SNCC, pronounced "snick"). He was also a member of SNCC's Freedom Singers, carrying the music, the stories, and the action of the movement around the world. There were young people like Cordell Reagon all over the South. Not long after Reagon caught up with the end of the powerful line in Nashville, students in downtown Orangeburg, South Carolina, demonstrated. There, they faced tear gas, high-powered fire hoses, and police beatings. In Tallahassee, Florida, the students from Florida Agricultural and Mechanical College also encountered tear gas and violence, but they met up at the lunch counters with white students from neighboring Florida State University who had pledged to arrive before them and to share their food if the black students were refused service.

Everywhere in the South black students were meeting these mixed realities: harsh resistance, some overly cautious elders, new self-confidence and transformation, the emergence of new, sometimes unexpectedly courageous white allies, the beginning of some desegregation victories, and a fresh sense of themselves and the meaning of their movement. At the same time, in spite of the growing sense of solidarity, other black adults were troubled and frightened by the unprecedented boldness of the student action. Too familiar with the world of white violence and intimidation, these adults wondered what harsh reactions the student uprising would bring. What jobs would be lost, what homes and churches bombed, what bank loans canceled, what licenses revoked, which young careers aborted, which lives lost? Because of such understandably adult concerns, the students especially appreciated the consistent support and encouragement from Martin King's public statements.

Indeed, it seemed as if King clearly recognized that these students embodied some of his own best dreams for the future of a nonviolent, mass-based freedom movement. So he offered great encouragement to their activities whenever possible and tried to interpret them to the world. Speaking in Durham, North Carolina, King said, "What is fresh, what is new in your fight is the fact that it was initiated, led and sustained by students. What is new is that American students have come of age. You now take your honored places in the world-wide struggle for freedom."

Then he urged them to move ahead and "fill up the jails." Ever since the days of Gandhi in India, resistance leaders had issued the call to fill up the jails as both a personal and strategic challenge. On the personal level in America, it urged nonviolent warriors to overcome their justifiable fear of dangerous Southern jails as well as the sense of shame that respectable families experienced when their children ended up there. On the strategic level, it was a call to present so many challengers to the legal system that its machinery would be blocked, making it difficult to carry on business as usual.

By the end of the winter of 1960 the mostly black contingent of Southern students was taking King—and their own consciences—seriously; their sit-ins were reaching into every Southern state except Mississippi, which was too harsh in its resistance; they were filling up at least some of the jails of the region, and their sophisticated political consciousness and courageous action were catching the attention of the nation and the world. In March some of the leaders of the local movements got a much-needed opportunity to meet together for the first time to catch their breath. The occasion was what had originally been an annual conference of mostly white Southern college student activists. The 1960 session at Highlander Folk School in Tennessee reflected the rapidly changing nature of the Southern student leadership scene. Now, more than half of the eighty-five participants in the Annual Leadership Workshop for College Students were black student sit-in leaders.

Highlander Folk School, established in the thirties, was run by a white couple, Myles and Zilphia Horton. Highlander's adult education programs, sometimes conducted by an interracial staff, included interracial conferences and workshops to train citizens to work for social change. It was an extraordinary and risky set of activities in the South in those days.

As a result of its nonconformist agenda and its left-wing friends, the school had experienced much harassment and persecution from local and state government authorities. Nevertheless, the Hortons persisted in their work, making Highlander a well-known resource center for labor movement organizers and for Southern freedom movement workers such as Septima Clark of Charleston, E. D. Nixon, Rosa Parks, Martin Luther King, Jr., and Fred Shuttlesworth.

Since 1953 Highlander had held an annual workshop for college student leaders. For the 1960 workshop, the Hortons chose a new, post-Greensboro theme: "The New Generation Fights for Equality." In that retreatlike mountainside setting, leaders from the sit-in movements and their potential white allies shared experiences, exchanged strategies, and recognized fellow pioneers. They considered long-range goals, explored new meanings of nonviolence, and talked about not only surviving but prevailing while in jail.

And there was time for singing, singing, singing—the flooding soulful glue that held everything and everyone together. By now it was obvious that this was to be a singing movement, especially as it developed in Nashville, where James Bevel, Bernard Lafayette, and the young Cordell Reagon had taken their love for rhythm and blues street-corner singing and moved right into the hymns and spirituals of their home churches.

At Highlander, Zilphia Horton had discovered anew the power of song in social movements. In her work with union organizers, she had heard the old nineteenth-century African-American religious song "I'll Be Alright," which became "I Will Overcome." Then she heard the song transformed by black women labor organizers in the forties, who took it to the picket lines of the justice-seeking Food and Tobacco Workers Union in Charleston, South Carolina, as a great rallying call: "We shall overcome. . . . Oh yes, down in my heart I do believe, we shall overcome some day." Eventually, it became a kind of community anthem at Highlander. Spontaneously developing new verses out of their own sit-in experiences ("We are not afraid; We shall live in peace; Black and White together"), students sang it into the night, feeling the power of the expanding interracial band of sisters and brothers.

The gathering at Highlander was a valuable development in the necessary process of turning a set of semi-spontaneous, creative, youthful challenges into a powerful, sustained, insurgent mass movement that would eventually break the decades-old bondage of legal segregation in the South. Indeed, some adult veterans of the long black struggle for freedom had already begun to plan for a more formal meeting of the sit-in leaders.

Central among the movement veterans was Ella Baker, a native North Carolinian who in the twenties had dreamed of becoming a medical missionary. Unfortunately, the financial pressures of the Great Depresssion made her medical school dream unattainable. So after graduation from Shaw University, a black Baptist institution in Raleigh, North Carolina, she moved to Harlem. Soon, she became involved in a number of political and economic organizing activities. These included the development of a consumers' cooperative organization and attempts at organizing African-American domestic workers, who badly needed better wages and working conditions. By the beginning of the forties, Baker was on the national staff of the NAACP, serving an important and often dangerous role as a roving organizer of NAACP chapters in the hostile South.

Later, when the Montgomery movement began to catch the attention of the world, Baker became part of a small group of New York–based social activists who called themselves "In Friendship." They initially focused their attention on raising funds to assist black and white Southerners who had suffered economic losses because of their freedom movement activities or sympathies. As a result of her work with "In Friendship," Baker met King and was later encouraged by her New York colleagues—including Bayard Rustin—to return to the South and help SCLC as its temporary executive director, operating from its Atlanta office.

A brilliant grassroots organizer, Baker was also an articulate and outspoken woman with a feminist consciousness far ahead of her time. Baker therefore found it difficult to work effectively in a leadership role in an organization made up of black pastors who were too often accustomed to seeing women only as compliant subordinates. Nevertheless, as a result of her SCLC position, Baker was strategically located when the Southern student sit-in movement erupted. And as soon as she began to grasp what was happening among the young people, she decided to find a way to bring their leaders together.

Later Baker said that she wanted to encourage their interests "not in being leaders as much as in developing leadership among other people." So she convinced administrators at Shaw University that they should host a conference of the sit-in leaders. She convinced Martin Luther King, Jr., and other SCLC leaders that the organization should put up eight hundred dollars to cover the basic expenses for what was officially called a Southwide Youth Leadership Conference on Nonviolence, to be held April 15–17, 1960, the Easter weekend break.

Baker and King signed a letter of invitation and sent it out to student activists and their allies all over the nation. The letter called the sit-in movement and its accompanying nonviolent actions "tremendously significant developments in the drive for Freedom and Human Dignity in America." (Many of the more active leaders and grassroots participants in the Southern movement used "freedom" and "human dignity" to describe the goals of their struggle much more often than "civil rights.") Now, according to King and Baker, it was time to come together for an evaluation of the burgeoning movement, "in terms of where do we go from here."

The young student leaders were ready for such a gathering. Responding to letters, phone calls, and other personal contacts, more than two hundred students and adult observers made their way to Raleigh. Of these, about one hundred twenty came from more than fifty black colleges and high schools in twelve Southern states. They brought with them a rich treasury of experiences and stories about organizing, about marching, about opposition forces and their weapons, about nonviolent resistance, about jails, about the jokes that made it possible for them to laugh in some of the most perilous situations. And of course they brought their songs of defiance, of empowerment, of hope.

In an opening address to the conference on Friday night, April 15, the eloquent and insightful Baker spoke pointedly to the adults present when she said, "The younger generation is challenging you and me.... They are asking us to forget our laziness and doubt and fear, and follow our dedication to the truth to the bitter end." King, who was only thirty-one years old himself, picked up a similar theme in another address when he declared that the student movement "is also a revolt against the apathy and complacency of adults in the Negro community; against Negroes in the middle class who indulge in buying cars and homes instead of taking on the great cause that will really solve their problems; against those who have become so afraid they have yielded to the system." In the post–Raleigh years, this double-edged role of the young warriors would continue: inspiration *and* tough challenge to the adult community.

Because he was the freedom movement leader best known to the press, King was initially the focus of attention for the small press contingent at Shaw. But in the course of the first evening's speeches, they had to deal with the powerful presences of James Lawson and Ella Baker. Baker was acknowledged by the students as their prime mentor. Lawson, the official coordinator of the conference, and Baker both encouraged the students to think about forming an independent organization of their own. By the time the evening was over, the students had become the center of the weekend.

And they were eager to seize the opportunities presented to them. Well-attended workshops ranged from discussions of nonviolence to the political and economic implications of their crusade. They discussed and debated proposals for future organizational structure and spent much time and energy exploring the moral and strategic significance of refusing bail. One of the ten discussion groups that day focused on the role of "white supporters" in the rising movement. From the heart of that discussion a powerful insight emerged, one that would mark the student-led campaigns for several years. According to the notes kept by one of the participants, the workshop participants declared, "This movement should not be considered one for Negroes but one for people who consider this a movement against injustice. This would include members of all races."

By welcoming idealistic, non-black participants into their struggle, blacks confirmed one of the best self-definitions of the Southern-based freedom movement: Freedom for black Americans freed all Americans. This vision was a central reason why so many socially committed whites were attracted to the movement at large and particularly to the politically conscious and religiously motivated nonviolent student workers. It was not surprising to find among the "observers" at Shaw representatives from such groups as the ecumenical National Council of Churches; the

Northern-based Congress of Racial Equality (CORE), which fought for integration; the Fellowship of Reconciliation (FOR); and the overwhelmingly white National Students Association, which represented college students.

The conference concluded with the birth of the Student Nonviolent Coordinating Committee. Conferees elected Marion Barry as the new organization's first chairman. Barry held that post through the fall of 1961, when he returned to graduate school in Nashville. During his brief tenure, he established a tone that characterized the group well into the late sixties. He professed SNCC's intention of directly and forcefully confronting segregation and injustice, even vowing to go to jail to achieve results.

## The Arduous Task: Rooting Out Fear and Getting Out Votes

In one of his characteristically insightful essays on the American condition, Ralph Ellison wrote, "The business of being an American is an arduous task." In the context of the African-American struggles of the sixties, this was perhaps an understatement. For what emerged from the Southern freedom struggle by the beginning of the sixties was the clear recognition that the arduous task for black people would be redefining what it means to be an American. Nowhere was this work of recreation more evident than in the battles for justice that took place in Alabama, Georgia, and Mississippi in 1961.

In May of that year, CORE organized an interracial group of activists to challenge a Supreme Court order outlawing segregation in bus terminals. Calling themselves Freedom Riders, they set out across the South to see if they could integrate all bus terminal facilities, including lunch counters, waiting rooms, and rest rooms. They began their ride in Washington, D.C., and originally hoped to end it in New Orleans. Where they failed, they hoped to draw attention to the continued racism in the South and the need for federal intervention to protect black rights. All was relatively peaceful until they entered Alabama. But the riders met with violence in almost every city they stopped in throughout that state. In Anniston, for example, mobs actually threw a bomb on the bus and set it on fire.

As a result of international publicity, President John F. Kennedy and Attorney General Robert Kennedy tried to persuade the riders to stop their journey. When they refused, the Kennedys struck a deal with Mississippi officials, allowing them to maintain segregated facilities as long as the Freedom Riders were not harmed. Instead of being attacked, riders in Mississippi were simply arrested. Altogether, at least 328 Freedom Riders served time in Mississippi's jails. Realizing that the negative publicity would not die down and that CORE would continue to challenge segregation, Robert Kennedy asked the Interstate Commerce Commission (ICC) to issue an order banning segregation in terminals that catered to interstate transportation. That September, the ICC complied with the attorney general's request, issuing a statement that all interstate facilities must obey the Supreme Court ruling.

The next battle took place in Albany, Georgia, a city of approximately sixty thousand people that was intimately shaped by its agricultural setting and the racial attitudes of its Black Belt location. Bernice Johnson, who later married Cordell Reagon, was one of the most powerful participants in the Albany movement. She was a student at the segregated Albany State College in 1961 when the emerging Southern movement began to take hold in Albany.

As an officer of the Youth Council of the local NAACP, Johnson had been one of the students who marched in 1961 on the college president's house to protest the administration's failure to develop adequate security measures against white intruders from town. Such men regularly harassed students on the campus and more than once sneaked into women's dormitories in an attempt to intimidate and sexually threaten the students.

So Johnson, many of her fellow students, and some of their parents were already preparing to challenge the system when representatives of SNCC appeared in Albany that fall of 1961. Recognizing that it was really not able to coordinate a widely scattered Southern student movement that had already begun to change its character, the fledgling organization had decided to become essentially a committed group of antisegregation organizers. More than a dozen of the core group of SNCC people announced late that spring and summer that they were dropping out of school for a year in order to commit themselves to the struggle for justice, dignity, and hope. It was also during this summer of 1961 that the group decided that it would send out "field secretaries" to do grassroots organizing, especially educating and preparing potential voters across the South, working for SNCC at subsistence wages of twenty-five to forty dollars per week, depending on whether they were single or married. It was during that same period that the young freedom workers engaged in a series of very long and piercing debates with each other about whether the organization should continue to commit itself to nonviolent direct action or focus instead on voter registration in the Deep South.

SNCC's ongoing internal debates became so heated at times during that summer of 1961 that the new organization seemed in danger of breaking apart. One of the major forces pushing the organization to focus on voter registration was President John F. Kennedy and his brother, Robert, the U.S. attorney general. They were urging the Southern freedom movement organizations to take their primary action "out of the street" and focus on what the Kennedy brothers assumed would be a less volatile, and therefore less internationally embarrassing, action of registering black voters. As a part of their proposal, the Kennedys promised to round up foundation funds for the voter-registration campaigns and to ensure federal protection for its participants. Of course, not only were the Kennedys and their friends hoping to get the movement off the front pages of the world's newspapers, but they expected that the vast majority of any new black registered voters would be ready to cast their votes for the Democratic party, especially if that party appeared to be committed to securing their rights.

Many of SNCC's young people brought a high level of moral sensitivity and political savvy to their work. So it was not surprising that in the course of the long meetings, many of them thought they saw political and financial bribery at work in the Kennedys' offers. For some who had recently come out of the terror of the Freedom Rides and the resultant rigors of Mississippi's Parchman Penitentiary, any call to turn away from such direct action was a call to betray their history. So the internal battle was a hard one, and it was only the wisdom of their trusted mentor, Ella Baker, that finally led the students to the decision that avoided a split. The "band of brothers," as they had begun to call themselves, reflecting both the sexism of the time and the deep love and respect these young men and women shared for each other, decided to set up a "direct action" project and a "voter registration" project within the one organization.

That fall two SNCC voter-registration organizers headed into Southwest Georgia, considered by black people to be a region of the state most resistant to such activities. SNCC had already begun to develop its risky practice of choosing the most difficult and dangerous places to start its projects, working on the assumption that once the "hardest nuts" in a state were cracked, it would be possible to assure local people and their own members that they could take on anything else. But "Terrible" Terrell County, SNCC's chosen starting point, proved to be too much at first. It was a place too filled with the fear and the bloody memories of its black people and the brutality of its white citizens to be ready for the voter-registration action that Charles Sherrod and Cordell Reagon had in mind. Sherrod was a seminary student from Virginia who had left school to join SNCC's crusade. His eighteen-year-old companion was the same Cordell Reagon who had been drawn out of his Nashville classroom the previous year by the sheer power of that city's student movement.

So they turned toward Albany, the largest town in the area. Because an order of the Interstate Commerce Commission banning segregation in all interstate travel facilities (notably, bus terminals and train stations) was scheduled to take effect on November 1, 1961, Sherrod and Reagon decided that they should encourage the local black young people of Albany to test the ICC mandate. In this way they could take "direct action."

As the first SNCC people on the scene in Albany, Sherrod and Reagon had to improvise in organizing the black people there. The two men also had to figure out a way to reach the most receptive young people in the African-American community without seeming to compete with the local NAACP chapter and its own Youth Council. Reagon later remembered: "We would sit in the student union building on the college campus all day long, drinking soda, talking with the students, trying to convince them to test the public accommodations at the bus station." SNCC organizers like Reagon and Sherrod were key in bringing teenagers into the center of the freedom movement of the sixties.

The SNCC workers and their young student compatriots appeared at the Trailways

bus terminal in Albany on November 1, 1961, ready to test the new federal desegregation mandate. On that same day, other bus terminals in scores of Southern and border cities were tested in a CORE-inspired follow-up to the Freedom Rides. The Albany
action that day marked the beginning of a rising tide of student-led nonviolent confrontations with the city's police force as blacks met an incoming train carrying an
interracial group of Freedom Riders. Although the passengers disembarked without
incident, the confrontation inspired the formation of a coalition among SNCC, the
local NAACP, a local ministers group, and others, which became known as the Albany
Movement.

Albany's young people staged their challenge to the bus system on Wednesday,
November 22, the day before Thanksgiving. Normally, on that day, Albany State's
many out-of-town students would file dutifully into the "colored" side of the bus
and train terminals to travel home for the holiday break. This time, even before the
crowd of college students arrived, three high-school students from the SNCC-
revived NAACP Youth Council walked into the white side of the bus terminal.
When the police ordered them to move, they refused, and were arrested. Although
they were quickly bailed out by the head of the local NAACP branch, who was not
happy about the path on which Reagon and Sherrod were leading his youth, their
audacious action was like the first crack in a dam.

Before long the college students arrived at the terminal. They had heard about
the arrest of the high-school students, and their college dean was there to try to
make sure his students were not carried away by their new sense of duty. He directed them to the "colored" side. Nevertheless, two Albany State students from the
SNCC workshop, Bertha Gober and Blanton Hall, refused. A detective informed
them that their presence in the white ticket line was creating a disturbance, and
when Gober and Hall did not leave, they were arrested.

Their presence in Albany's dirty jail over the holiday became the magnet that
drew the larger black community of the city together. Not only did people bring
Gober and Hall a steady stream of Thanksgiving dinners, but the Albany Movement leaders took the arrests, along with those of the high-school students, as a
sign that they had to join their children in the challenge to the old ways. The city
and its youth-inspired movement caught the attention of the national press, and
the Albany Movement held its first Montgomery-like mass meeting on the
Saturday evening after Thanksgiving, November 25. By then Gober and Hall had
been bailed out of jail, but they had also been suspended from college by their easily intimidated administrators, a decision that only solidified black community
support for the students. At the Saturday-night mass meeting, all the religious fervor of Albany's black people was poured into the songs that the students had
brought out of their workshops and their jail cells and transformed for the occasion. The Albany Singers, including Bernice Johnson, were principally responsible
for defining the music of the Civil Rights movement. Later, Johnson founded the
women's singing group Sweet Honey in the Rock.

By now the people at the meeting were ready to do more than sing and listen to testimonies. They were prepared to march on City Hall to demand enforcement of federal law, the reinstatement of the Albany State students, and the end of segregation. Over the next two weeks, at least three groups marched, praying for and demanding change, and when they did, they were arrested in scores. The steady rising of their inspired people actually surprised the leaders of the Albany Movement, among them movement President Dr. William Anderson, a local osteopath, and Vice President Slater King, a local realtor. They were not prepared for a situation in which nearly a thousand people, including parents and breadwinners, were at one point stranded in jail with no bail money available and no significant response to their call for desegregation of public transportation facilities.

It was at this point that some of the leadership, especially Anderson, decided that they needed the help of Martin Luther King, Jr. Anderson was a college friend of Ralph Abernathy and a fraternity brother of King. He decided to use these connections to bring in the best-known hero of the Southern movement to see if his presence could bring greater national attention to their struggle, and thereby shake the resistance of the white establishment.

This determination to call in King and SCLC widened divisions that were already present in the Albany Movement leadership. For instance, additional SNCC forces had come in to help Sherrod and Reagon as the work expanded, and SNCC adamantly opposed calling in King and SCLC. Its leaders argued that the media attention King would attract might well suffocate the creative development of a local grassroots leadership and that they could become too dependent on the star of the freedom struggle.

Nevertheless, King, Abernathy, and some of their SCLC staff arrived in Albany for a December 16 mass meeting that they understood to be a one-night inspirational event. But at the meeting Anderson publicly maneuvered King into leading a march the next day. As a result, King and his organization became enmeshed in a very difficult situation.

Increasingly, Albany attracted black and white allies from across the nation. Religious communities were especially attracted to the strong church component of the movement's mass meetings, marches, and mass jailing. But Albany's black leaders, now joined by King and the SCLC, were working for something that had never been attempted in the South before. They had moved beyond the immediate confrontational settings of the bus and train terminals and were pressing for the desegregation of the entire city, beginning with its municipally owned public accommodations and its local bus lines. Such a development was a necessary and inevitable step in the burgeoning Southern struggle, but no one knew how to organize for it or to develop a citywide strategy.

The movement's task was complicated by the fact that Laurie Pritchett, the chief of police, was not a volatile loose cannon like some of his counterparts in other

Southern communities. Instead, Pritchett was very concerned about public relations and insisted that his officers rein in their tendencies toward violent treatment
of the black community, especially when they were under the scrutiny of the mass
media. This strategy was meant to deprive the movement of emotional rallying
points and to deprive an already recalcitrant federal government of any reasons for
entering the Albany situation. Partly because of Pritchett's strategy, partly because
of divisions within the Albany Movement, partly because of the unprecedented
demands that they were pressing on the segregated city, and partly because of their
own inexperience with such a setting, King, SNCC, and the Albany Movement
leaders were unable to reach their immediate goals of achieving the desegregation
of public facilities. Pritchett undermined the very basis of nonviolent passive resistance by refusing to respond with violence. There were no dramatic images of
activists being attacked or beaten by mobs. Instead, they were peacefully arrested
for breaking the law.

There was no victorious breakthrough in Albany for several reasons. The
Kennedy administration agreed not to intervene directly, either to enforce the ICC
ruling or to protect the civil rights activists, as long as the Albany authorities could
keep the peace. Pritchett succeeded not only in keeping the peace and reducing
publicity, but in defeating the movement there. By the end of 1962, a year after the
Albany campaign started, SCLC called the campaign off, although SNCC activists
remained in Albany for another six years. Segregation was still firmly in place, and
only a handful of African Americans could vote.

Nevertheless, even in failure, the movement gained a new vision, a new voice.
Partly by accident it had chosen to try to challenge the segregation patterns of an
entire Southern city. This was the first time in the post–Montgomery years of the
freedom movement that young people and their elders had marched and gone to
jail together, had together shaped an organization to challenge segregation. As
important, the movement had discovered its capacity to take on more than a boycott, or a sit-in, or a voter-registration project. It had learned something through
failure. These lessons would be important when King and the forces of SCLC eventually responded to the invitation from their fearless comrade, Fred Shuttlesworth,
and moved in the spring of 1963 toward Birmingham, perhaps the toughest, most
terrifying city in America in which to stage a fight for desegregation.

The road to Birmingham was not the only path that the Southern movement
took in those years following the sit-ins and the Freedom Rides. Even while the
Albany Movement was at its height, a small but steady stream of SNCC's voter-registration workers arrived in the counties that Sherrod and Reagon had originally
targeted. As the Albany campaign slowed down in 1962, Sherrod himself went back
into the nearby rural areas to lead the work on the voter-registration project in
Baker, Terrell, Lee, and Dougherty counties.

Although it rarely received the same kind of media attention as the dramatic public confrontation of marches, demonstrations, and sit-ins, this sort of tedious, demanding, unglamorous, and dangerous day-to-day work of voter registration was an essential step in providing blacks with the tools, and the power, to transform the nation.

The work of these voter-registration campaigners began simply: They made themselves known in the local black community—where they were often identified as "Freedom Riders." They visited homes, churches, schools, individuals, and families, and they sought out black community leaders. Central to their strategy was always the work of "canvassing." Moving on foot, on bicycles, in cars, on mules, the young men and women went from house to house, often at night, asking if people were registered or if they wanted to register, telling them about the benefits of voting, letting them know that classes were being set up to help people deal with the intentionally complicated registration process, and calming their fears.

The atmosphere of confrontation and overcoming fear became most evident in a meeting in Sasser, a country town in Terrell County. On Monday night, July 25, 1962, Sherrod, some of his interracial SNCC comrades, and several of the local black leaders and participants were carrying on their weekly voter-registration meeting at Mount Olive Baptist Church. There were some thirty or thirty-five people in the building. Attendance was lower than usual partly because of a threat from whites that the gathering would be broken up.

But the meeting went on, likely encouraged by the presence of three national newspaper reporters who had also heard about the threat. The session began, as usual, with a hymn, a prayer, and a Bible reading, the necessary ingredients for starting a meeting anywhere in the black South. Sherrod was in charge of this part of the meeting. The anxiety level was higher than usual that night, but the SNCC organizer kept his voice even and calm as he opened the session. They sang, "Pass me not/O gentle Savior," and then repeated the Lord's Prayer together. Sherrod led them in repeating the Twenty-third Psalm, slowing down on the words, "Yea, though I walk through the valley of the shadow of death, I will fear no evil." Just then they heard the sound of car doors slamming in the driveway.

Sherrod had begun to read one of his favorite passages from the New Testament. When he heard the car doors, he said quietly, firmly, "They are standing just outside now. If they come in I'm going to read this over again." He read from Romans 8:31, "If God be for us, then who can be against us?" At that point about fifteen white men from Sasser walked in, including one in a deputy sheriff's uniform, along with Sheriff Mathews, in plain clothes. They lined up against the wall in the back of the church while Sherrod completed the reading. Then, without missing a beat, the young freedom minister began to pray: "Into thy hand do we commend our minds and souls and our lives every day.... We've been abused so long.... We've been down so long." The "Amens" and "Uh-huhs" of the people had begun to roll into place between his phrases, and they came again when Sherrod went on.

"All we want," he said, "is for our white brothers to understand that Thou who made us, made us all. . . . And in Thy sight we are all one." Sheriff Mathews had bowed his head and closed his eyes.

Sherrod led the strangely mixed congregation in the Lord's Prayer, and then someone began singing, "We are climbing Jacob's ladder." Soon after the song began, the men in the back filed out. At the end of the song Sheriff Mathews, accompanied by two of his deputies and the sheriff of neighboring Sumter County, walked back in. One deputy now had a large revolver holstered on his belt, and the other one was brandishing a two-foot-long flashlight, a familiar weapon.

By this time, Lucius Holloway, the local chairman of the voter-registration drive, had begun to lead the meeting, and he called out to the lawmen, "Everybody is welcome. This is a voter-registration meeting." Sheriff Mathews responded:

> We are a little fed up with this registering business. Niggers down here have been happy for a hundred years, and now this has started. We want our colored people to live like they've been living. There never was any trouble before all this started. It's caused great dislike between colored and white.

Then the deputies began taking the names of everyone present, and they told the local black people that they did not need the outsiders from SNCC in order to register. They also issued ominous threats about what could happen to blacks after their outsider allies left the area. In the midst of the lawmen's performance, someone began humming "We Shall Overcome." Others picked up the song. The lawmen retreated to the back of the church and the people continued their meeting, giving reports of registration attempts, testimonies of beatings, and statements of hope.

At the end of the meeting, they gathered in a circle at the church door to sing "We are not afraid." That night there was no violence, except to the tires of one of the reporters' cars. But several nights later, the church was burned to the ground. Eventually, most of the SNCC workers and community leaders who were at the meeting found themselves thrown in jail, and beaten, as usual. Still, the organizing and overcoming continued in Terrell County and elsewhere in the Deep South.

In these settings it had usually been so long since black people had voted that many local black people did not even know that the nation's laws guaranteed them that right. Voting and politics generally were considered "white folks' business," and there were terrible memories that reminded them of what could happen to blacks who tried to participate in that business. In addition to the physical terror that stood between African Americans and the ballot box, everyone knew of the economic intimidation that was often used against them, sometimes forcing them off the land they were farming as sharecroppers, putting them out of the miserable shacks they lived in, making it impossible to get jobs with local employers, ultimately forcing them to leave the area. These were the settings that had produced black registered voting percentages of zero to five percent in many places where black people made up more than fifty percent of the population.

But in every such setting, there were always people willing to work for a new day. That was certainly what Bob Moses found when he went into Mississippi. Moses had been working in Atlanta as a volunteer in the SNCC office staff in the summer of 1960. He was sent to Alabama and Mississippi that summer to recruit participants for the next SNCC organizing conference, scheduled for the fall. In preparation for the trip, Ella Baker supplied Moses with the names of people she had worked with during her days as an NAACP organizer in the South.

One such person was Amzie Moore, president of the local, somewhat bedraggled NAACP chapter in Cleveland, Mississippi. When Moses met Moore, the forty-nine-year-old Mississippi movement veteran was farming part-time, working a few hours each day in the local post office, and running his own gas station. Because Moore had insisted on trying to develop a voter-registration campaign in Cleveland in the mid-fifties, and because he refused to put up the legally required "colored" and "white" signs in his station, he had almost lost his business and his life. But he was still there when Moses arrived, looking for recruits for SNCC.

Moore convinced Moses that what Mississippi needed more than a group of young SNCC-like recruits going off to Atlanta was a band of SNCC's arduous freedom workers coming to Mississippi to create a major voter-registration campaign, starting right there in Cleveland. Moses said he would take the message back to Atlanta. But Moses promised that regardless of what SNCC formally decided, he would personally return to Cleveland the following summer. When Moses returned South in the summer of 1961, much had changed throughout the nation. Most important among the changes was the influence of the Freedom Rides and the hope they inspired. And in Mississippi itself, Medgar Evers, the head of that state's NAACP organization, was openly calling for the city government of Jackson, the capital city, to desegregate public facilities.

But the time was still not quite right for a voter-registration campaign in Moore's Delta area. White reaction to black assertiveness was swift and violently brutal, federal protection could not be assured, and many blacks questioned the wisdom of "stirring up trouble." Instead, some local NAACP leaders in Southwest Mississippi had heard about the possibility of a SNCC team coming to the state to work on voter registration, and they asked their friend Moore to put them in touch with Moses. As a result, SNCC's voter education wing began its Mississippi development in a small town called McComb, near another town named Liberty. Courageous older NAACP veterans from the area, like C. C. Bryant, E. W. Steptoe, and Webb Owens helped to open the way for Moses, who was soon joined by two former Freedom Riders, John Hardy and Reginald Robinson.

The SNCC forces started in the usual way. With the help of the committed older men and women in the town, they began to introduce themselves to other local

Poll taxes, literacy tests, and citizenship exams—as well as other, more brutal methods—were routinely used to keep blacks away from the polls in the South.

leaders and soon sought out the young people as well. Many of the teenage group were fascinated by the fact that these activists had come to their town, and they were ready for any kind of exciting direct action. Their elders, however, knew that people in their area had been beaten, killed, or driven out of town for trying to register to vote. So when Moses and his team began to set up a "school" to help people prepare for the intimidating moment when they might face a hostile registrar, the response was slow. Moses made it a practice never to pressure local people to register, because he knew, and they also knew, that he was asking them to risk their lives, a decision that they had to make themselves.

But when the first group of three local volunteers, an older man and two middle-aged women, were finally ready, it was Moses whose life was most at risk. After helping his frightened candidates break their silence as they faced the registrar, Moses was attacked on the main street of McComb by a man who was the sheriff's cousin. He split Moses's scalp with the heavy handle of a hunting knife. About a week later Moses felt a different kind of pain when he had to identify the body of Herbert Lee, a black farmer who had risked his life to volunteer as a driver for the SNCC voter-registration team. Because of his movement association, Lee had been shot to death in daylight by a white segregationist—a Mississippi state legislator.

Meanwhile in McComb, the committed high-school students were too young to register and too impatient to wait. They wanted to enter the freedom struggle more directly than by teaching older people to read the registration materials. By now, SNCC people from the "direct action" contingent, like Marion Barry and Diane Nash, had also begun to gather in McComb, and they were leading workshops for the teenagers on nonviolent direct action. As soon as they could, the students put their training into action with a sit-in at a local lunch counter, the first in that part of Mississippi, an action for which SNCC had not planned. The sit-in squad was put in jail, and some of them were suspended from school. That led to a student-organized walkout from their school and a march to City Hall.

Sensing that the teenagers were moving into a dangerous action that they could not handle, Moses and some of his coworkers decided to march with them. The youngsters decided that they wanted to pray on the steps of City Hall. The police thought prayers belonged only in churches or homes, and they began to arrest the young people. The students were repeating the Lord's Prayer, and each time one was interrupted and arrested, another walked up the steps to continue the prayer. Finally, the police arrested more than one hundred young people and took them to jail. By then the spectacle had attracted a crowd of curious and angry white people.

Moses and his two SNCC companions offered a striking testimony to the spirit of SNCC. One of them was Charles "Chuck" McDew, an Ohio-born black college student who became a sit-in leader at South Carolina State College in Orangeburg. The other was Bob Zellner, the organization's first full-time field secretary assigned to recruiting white students. A native of Alabama, Zellner was the son of a white Southern Methodist minister, and he went to McComb instead of traveling to white campuses because he wanted to know what SNCC was actually doing in order to be an effective recruiter for the cause.

However, the white people of McComb wanted to know what *he* was doing there in the midst of the black troublemakers. Here, and in many future situations, Zellner was considered "a traitor to the white race." So as he came down the City Hall steps on his way to jail, several men rushed to attack him. There were many beatings and jailings in McComb that fall. At one point, all but one of the SNCC organizers were in jail. But it was the death of Herbert Lee that haunted people more than anything else. Despite the harsh white resistance that had forced the adults of McComb to temporarily slow down their attempts at voter registration, leading to SNCC's temporary withdrawal, still no one could miss the tremors of change throughout the state.

In 1962, the most spectacular tremor in Mississippi was the decision of black Air Force veteran James Meredith, with the support of the NAACP, to apply for admission to Ole Miss. Few institutions were considered more quintessentially white Mississippian, more worthy of defense against the black challenge than the University of Mississippi at Oxford. When Meredith first tried to enroll in the university, Governor Ross Barnett barred him from admission, a power that a federal court ruled Barnett did not possess. Barnett then encouraged white people in the state to believe that their active, armed resistance—even to a court-ordered change—could halt desegregation.

So by the end of September 1962, when it was time for Meredith to appear on campus to register for his first classes, thousands of white Mississippians—both students and others—believed that they could physically guard the university against the newly defined black presence that Meredith represented. Students and their segregationist allies rioted against the federal marshals who had slipped onto the Meredith campus the Sunday afternoon before registration. The rioters hurled rocks, bricks, lead pipes, and tear gas at the marshals, and finally even shot at them in a one-sided battle in which the marshals were ordered not to return the fire. In the course of the uproar, a foreign reporter and a local white worker were shot and killed, and some 350 others, mostly marshals, were wounded. The Kennedys had been trying to negotiate their way to a settlement with Barnett that would not require them to send in federal troops to protect Meredith's rights. However, in the end, the Kennedys decided they had to send in the troops. Though late, this federal intervention finally ended the white resistance.

The next day, James Meredith finally registered as the first black student at Ole Miss and became a powerful symbol to the black people of the nation.

As the SNCC workers reflected on their experiences in southwest Georgia and southwest Mississippi, they moved to the northwest area of Mississippi, known as the Delta. They stopped in Jackson to work out the details of a new coalition. Now they would coordinate their work with the activities of the NAACP, SCLC, and CORE, and together they formed the Council of Federated Organizations (COFO). This coalition was largely Bob Moses' idea, and it served as an important pipeline for the funds that supported registration work.

Ultimately, this united front was important for the morale of Mississippi's black people, providing them with a sense of the joint strength that was needed to break open the "closed society" of their state. Nevertheless, the essential energies and people power of the next stages of the COFO campaign came from SNCC, which was the heart of COFO. SNCC realized that the dangerous and essentially underground work of registering blacks had to become more visible to the world, not only to provide protection and build morale but also to prod the federal government into action.

From the spring of 1962 to the fall of 1963 the Mississippi voting-rights work was focused on the Delta region. It was known as one of the most terror-filled sections of a violence-prone state. Partly because of this reputation, partly because this was the area where Amzie Moore lived, Bob Moses, as the new COFO program director, took his voter-registration forces there, working to make Moore's old dream come true.

The reality of voter registration in the Delta was harsher than the dreams, however. Once again, the violence was persistent and nerve-wracking. As in every other voter-registration campaign in the Black Belt, however, SNCC and other groups were constantly meeting such men and women as Fannie Lou Hamer of Ruleville, a town not far from Greenwood. The forty-seven-year-old sharecropper with a sixth-grade education went to a mass meeting one night in 1962 and heard James Bevel, the charismatic leader who had emerged from the Nashville student movement, holding forth like an evangelist, calling people to a new life of struggle for freedom. Hamer later said, "Until then I'd never heard of no mass meeting and I didn't know that a Negro could register and vote." But when she found out, she was one of the first volunteers to go to the courthouse the next day.

Hamer knew she was volunteering for danger, and later she said, "I guess if I'd had any sense I'd a-been a little scared, but what was the point of being scared. The only thing they could do to me was kill me and it seemed like they'd been trying to do that a little bit at a time ever since I could remember." From that day on Hamer was at the heart of the movement.

While in Greenwood, Bob Moses wrote about how to face the long, hard, dangerous times when it was easy to give in to fear:

> You dig into yourself and the community and prepare to wage psychological warfare; you combat your own fears about beatings, shootings, and possible mob violence; you stymie by your own physical presence the anxious fear of the Negro community ... you organize, pound by pound, small bands of people who gradually focus in the eyes of Negroes and whites as people tied up in "that mess"; you create a small striking force capable of moving out when the time comes, which it must, whether we help it or not.

Of course no one could predict how and when the time would come, again and again, in these life-changing campaigns. But for people on the front lines, like Moses, the testing time was always nearby. This was the testimony of one of his coworkers, Marian Wright, a Spelman College graduate who was taking some time from her Yale Law School studies to join the forces of hope in Greenwood. She wrote,

> I had been with Bob Moses one evening and dogs kept following us down the street. Bob was saying that he wasn't used to dogs, that he wasn't brought up around dogs, and he was really afraid of them. Then came the march, and the dogs growling and the police pushing us back. And there was Bob, refusing to move back, walking, walking towards the dogs.

Neither Moses nor the dogs backed down, and one of the animals tore a piece out of his trousers before the dog's police handler finally pulled him away. Bob Moses kept walking.

In Greenwood, in 1962 and early 1963, no one knew how long they would have to walk and work, facing dogs, facing death, facing fear. But one thing began to be clear: They were not walking alone. For instance, in response to appeals from SNCC, communities in the North were donating truckloads of food and clothing for desperate Delta families. Dick Gregory, the socially concerned comedian, came to stand in solidarity and mordant humor with the people who continued to walk toward the courthouse and the registrar's office. Folksinger Bob Dylan arrived for his baptism in the work of the movement, sharing his songs and hope.

In the early spring of 1963, many of the full-time SNCC workers took time out from Greenwood's battleground to attend the annual SNCC staff meeting in Atlanta. The organization's full-time staff was now up to sixty people, and they came in from all over the South. Some 350 people attended the April gathering held at one of Atlanta's black theological schools, Gammon Seminary.

Reflecting later on the session, James Forman, who was the organization's indefatigable executive secretary during those crucial years, summed up the spirit and meaning of the experience: "The meeting was permeated by an intense comradeship, born of sacrifice and suffering and a commitment to the future, and out of a knowledge that our basic strength rested in the energy, love, and warmth of the group. The band of sisters and brothers, in a circle of trust, felt complete at last."

In the midst of a throbbing social movement nothing remained "complete" for long. Even as the SNCC meeting was going on, its companion and slightly elder organization, SCLC, was opening another front of the expanding Southern freedom movement. Responding to repeated invitations from Fred Shuttlesworth, leader of the Birmingham Civil Rights movement, and determined to learn crucial lessons from the many difficulties and experiments in Albany, in the spring of 1963 Martin Luther King, Jr., and his staff had gone to Birmingham, Alabama.

## Birmingham: The Days beyond "Forever"

When SCLC decided to challenge segregation in Birmingham, it was taking on a city with one of the worst records of anti–labor and anti–civil rights violence in the country. Because of its surrounding coal and steel industries, the city had always attracted labor-organizing activities. In 1931, the police force established the "Red Squad" to handle communist and other Left-Wing organizers with force, and from then on Birmingham's law-enforcement agencies—with much assistance from private citizens—were infamous for their brutal tactics. During the thirties, many black and white labor organizers were arrested, kidnapped, beaten, or even killed. And in 1941, Birmingham experienced a wave of police killings and beatings. The best-known incidents involved the deaths of two young black men, O'Dee Henderson and John Jackson. Henderson, who was arrested and jailed for merely arguing with a white man, was found handcuffed and shot the next morning in his jail cell. A few weeks later, Jackson, a metalworker in his early twenties, was shot to death as he lay in the backseat of a police car. He had made the fatal mistake of arguing with the arresting officers in front of a crowd of blacks lined up outside a movie theater.

After the Second World War, blacks often referred to the rigidly segregated city as "Bombingham." The name called attention to the frequent bombings of the homes and churches of those African Americans who dared to take even tentative steps toward the establishment of racial justice. This was the setting in which Birmingham minister Fred Shuttlesworth and his family had been beaten, bombed, attacked, and jailed. Many people agreed with Martin Luther King, Jr., when he said, "As Birmingham goes, so goes the South." Later, when he reflected on the Birmingham campaign, King wrote:

> We believed that while a campaign in Birmingham would surely be the toughest fight of our civil-rights careers, it could, if successful, break the back of segregation all over the nation. This city had been the country's chief symbol of racial intolerance. A victory there might well set forces in motion to change the entire course of the drive for freedom and justice.

After exploring the situation, SCLC moved into action in Birmingham during the first days of April 1963. This was a period of intense freedom movement activity all across the South, with thousands of demonstrators challenging segregation from Maryland to Louisiana. In Birmingham, SCLC and Shuttlesworth's Alabama Christian Movement for Human Rights (ACMHR) focused on breaking the hold of legalized segregation in all the public facilities, starting with its downtown stores and its municipal facilities, such as city-owned parks, pools, and drinking fountains. They also hoped to open up the police force to black officers. To work out details and to keep the process moving beyond the demonstrations, the black organizations pressed for the establishment of a city-sponsored biracial committee.

In light of Birmingham's history—and in the presence of Alabama's new governor, George Wallace, who had declared in his 1963 inaugural address, "Segregation now! Segregation tomorrow! Segregation forever!"—this relatively modest set of goals appeared to most white residents to be undesirable, and impossible. Complicating the situation was the fact that the white leadership of Birmingham was deeply divided. When SCLC came on the scene that spring, the city was awaiting a judicial decision concerning a recent, disputed municipal election. The decision would either establish Bull Connor, the police commissioner, as mayor or place in office a more moderate segregationist named Albert Boutwell. At the same time there was a white business community of expanding influence whose members were greatly concerned about their city's image, an image they were trying to refurbish "to look like Atlanta," the liberal showcase city of the region. But in the midst of all of this the Ku Klux Klan and its adherents were still dangerously active, rallying behind their new governor.

For most of April, SCLC's challenge to Birmingham seemed to have a hard time capturing the full energy and interest of local black people or the national press. Even when King and Abernathy were arrested and jailed for marching on Good Friday, April 12, the best of the nightly mass meetings could not produce more than fifty or sixty volunteers for the next morning's demonstrations, which were designed to demand an immediate end to racist employment practices and segregation in public accommodations.

It was important to note who did show up to march. At the outset of the campaign it was the older people who stepped forward. Eventually, the Birmingham grandchildren would respond to the elders.

While King sat in the isolation cell of Bull Connor's jail, one of his lawyers managed to smuggle in some newspapers. In one of the Birmingham papers King came across a statement signed by a group of local white clergymen who considered themselves friends of black people and open to "moderate" racial change. Expressing concern that the desegregation campaign could play into Bull Connor's hands, they urged King and SCLC to leave Birmingham's future in the hands of its moderate black and white leaders. King seized the opportunity to respond. After a yellow, legal-sized pad was passed on to him, King ended up with a lengthy handwritten document that attempted to lay out the justification for his presence in Birmingham, to express the meaning and purpose of nonviolent direct action, and to provide a statement concerning the role of the churches in the quest for racial justice. However, the single most powerful section of his long letter arose out of his determination to let the white clergymen—and any other readers— know something about what it meant to be a black person in the segregated South, and what it meant to be told by white "friends" and Christian brothers to wait for a more convenient time to protest and challenge the injustice and inhumanity of segregation.

King wrote, "I guess it is easy for those who have never felt the stinging darts of segregation to say, 'Wait.'" Then in the longest sentence he had ever written, or would ever write again, he poured out a statement that was more than a moan or a plea for understanding.

When you have seen vicious mobs lynch your mothers and fathers at will and drown your sisters and brothers at whim, when you have seen hate-filled policemen curse, kick, brutalize and even kill your black brothers and sisters with impunity, when you see the vast majority of your twenty million Negro brothers smothering in an air-tight cage of poverty in the midst of an affluent society; when you suddenly find your tongue twisted and your speech stammering as you seek to explain to your six-year-old daughter why she can't go to the public amusement park that has just been advertised on television, and see tears welling up in her little eyes when she is told that Funtown is closed to colored children, and see the depressing clouds of inferiority begin to form in her little mental sky, and see her begin to distort her little personality by unconsciously developing a bitterness toward white people; when you have to concoct an answer for a five-year-old son asking in agonizing pathos, 'Daddy, why do white people treat colored people so mean?'; when you take a cross-country drive and find it necessary to sleep night after night in the uncomfortable corners of your automobile because no motel will accept you; when you are humiliated day in and day out by nagging signs reading "white" and "colored"; when your first name becomes "nigger" and your middle name becomes "boy" (no matter how old you are) and your last name becomes "John," and when your wife and mother are never given the respected title "Mrs."; when you are harried by day and haunted by night by the fact that you are a Negro, living constantly at a tip-toe stance, never quite knowing what to expect next, and plagued with inner fears and outer resentments; when you are forever fighting a degenerating sense of "nobodiness"; then you will understand why we find it difficult to wait.

King's *Letter from Birmingham Jail,* one of the classic statements of the freedom movement, did not begin to reach the outside world until more than a month after it was written. It was published in a number of newspapers and magazines and in book form in 1964 as *Why We Can't Wait.*

As the Birmingham demonstrations grew larger and more public, young people were eager to join in. Soon, young people regularly attended the nightly mass meetings and begged their parents to let them join the marches. But the movement leaders debated about encouraging students to miss school for an almost certain rendezvous with prison, or worse. Marchers were attacked by police dogs, shot with high-power water hoses, and beaten with clubs. In that debate the views of SNCC leaders Diane Nash Bevel and her husband, SCLC staff member James Bevel, prevailed. James Bevel, who played a major role as a strategist for the Birmingham protests, argued that since the young people did not carry the burden of their family's economic responsibilities on them, they were free to meet the challenge of going to jail. But the situation soon became more complicated. For as soon as the announcement was made in mass meeting that Thursday, May 2, 1963, would be the day for high-school demonstrations, dozens of elementary schoolchildren declared their own readiness to march.

Now there was another debate among the leaders. What should be the minimum age for their freedom marchers? They decided that anyone who was old enough to volunteer to become a church member should be old enough to volunteer to become a member of the freedom corps. In that black Baptist-dominated setting, such a decision meant that children as young as six might be on the marching line when Thursday morning came.

That morning Sixteenth Street Baptist Church, the usual meeting place, was filled with hundreds of children. Shuttlesworth offered the morning send-off prayers, and the recently released King told the young people how important they were. Before the day was over, more than six hundred of the children discovered that the way to freedom led directly through Birmingham's jail.

The Birmingham fire hoses knocked protesters to the ground with enough force to take the bark off trees.

Bull Connor had been caught off-guard on Thursday by the surge of young marchers, moving around the police lines. He did not intend to be upstaged again by a flood of singing black children. So on Friday, May 3, when the young marchers came singing down the steps of Sixteenth Street Church, they saw fire trucks in the park facing the church. Andrew Young, who oversaw SCLC's fledgling voter-registration drive and was a chief negotiator in the Birmingham campaign, later described what happened:

> As groups of kids marched past the park headed for downtown, Connor issued the order to the firemen to uncoil their hoses. Police dogs had been seen before, and once again they were brought to the front of the barricades, straining at their leashes. But until now, the fire trucks had remained on the sidelines. Suddenly fire hoses didn't seem like fun anymore, and the kids watched with trepidation as the firehoses were unwound. They kept marching and their voices grew stronger with the comforting tunes of the freedom songs. It never ceased to amaze me, the strength that people drew from the singing of those old songs.... Suddenly, Connor ordered the firemen to open the hoses on both the marchers and the large crowd of onlookers who had gathered in the park. The water was so powerful it knocked people down and the line began to break as marchers ran screaming through the park to escape the water. Connor then ordered the police to

pursue the terrified kids with angry dogs, and to our horror actually unleashed some of them. The police ran through the park, swinging their billy clubs at marchers, onlookers, and newsmen—anyone in the way.

As the tension escalated, an international audience watched. By now it was clear that the nation's leaders could not continue to avoid direct engagement with the situation in Birmingham and still claim to be "leaders of the free world." The Kennedys, after some initial annoyance with SCLC's timing and methods, let it be known, first privately, then publicly, that they believed a negotiated way should be found through Birmingham's troubles. They sent personal emissaries to the city, especially to urge the business leaders to take responsibility for moving toward desegregation. Robert Kennedy himself made dozens of phone calls to corporate leaders nationwide whose Southern subsidiaries were located in the Birmingham area. He urged them to put pressure on their local people to cooperate with the movement's demands for desegregation.

With the rising pressure of the federal government, negotiations based on the movement's basic demands were finally begun. The negotiations were difficult, but they lasted less than a week. They led to an agreement that was announced on May 7, 1963, about a month after the demonstrations had begun. Under the agreement, an irreversible process of desegregation was begun in public accommodations and municipal facilities. SCLC won its demands for desegregated lunch counters, rest rooms, fitting rooms, and drinking fountains. Downtown store owners agreed to hire African-American clerks. Expanded hiring and promotion of black people had begun throughout the industrial community of Birmingham. All the imprisoned demonstrators were released on bail that was supplied from various local and national sources, and the cases against the released prisoners were soon dismissed. But there was a compromise: SCLC agreed to a timetable of planned stages rather than demanding that these changes take place immediately. It also agreed to the release of arrested demonstrators on bail rather than insist that the charges be dismissed outright.

But it would not be a simple matter to extricate Birmingham from its past. On the evening after the announcement, the Ku Klux Klan leadership bitterly condemned the arrangement at a rally on the edge of the city. Later that night a bomb badly damaged the home of A. D. King, Martin's younger brother, who was an activist pastor in the city and a participant in the movement. Soon, a second bomb exploded at the Gaston Motel, practically demolishing Room 30, the modest suite that King normally used as his headquarters. Fortunately, A. D. King's family was not hurt, Martin King had already left the city, and no one else was injured at the motel. But the bombings drew hundreds of outraged black people into the streets. Without waiting for a request from the new mayor, Albert Boutwell, Governor Wallace sent in state troopers to maintain order. However, the pushing, attacking, cursing troopers seemed intent on provoking the leaderless crowd into violence. In response, black people threw rocks and bottles and set some stores and cars on fire. For a moment it seemed as if a major explosion would blow apart the new agreement. Instead, some of the SCLC and local Birmingham leaders were able to work out a truce between the enraged black people and the brutally aggressive troopers.

The Birmingham campaign, saved from catastrophe, had not only energized the Civil Rights movement, but it had made the world aware of segregation's ugliness. Television was a critical factor. The new technology enabled millions of viewers to watch with rapt horror as the police attacked the youthful demonstrators. There was no mistaking the haunting scenes of Birmingham police dogs snapping at the legs of children. Nor could even the most casual viewer ignore the fire department's role in the daily confrontations.

It became clear to the White House that the civil rights activists would not abandon their cause without fundamental changes. An angry encounter between Attorney General Robert Kennedy and African Americans gathered by black writer James Baldwin highlighted the rawness of race relations in the country. Blacks bluntly told Kennedy that they expected more from him and his brother, the president. Robert Kennedy left the room angered by their demands, yet he later reflected that the encounter forever changed his views about race and the race problem in American life. Even the politically pragmatic John Kennedy would understand very soon that he could not shrink from the demands for full inclusion. To his credit, President Kennedy tried to get a new civil rights bill through the Congress. The new bill was stronger than all previous ones. It would end discrimination in all interstate transportation, at hotels, and in other public places; it ensured all who had a sixth-grade education the right to vote; and it gave the attorney general the power to cut off government funds to states and communities that continued to practice racial discrimination. It would be more than a year before Congress passed the Civil Rights Act of 1964. In the meantime, President Kennedy worried that any further demonstrations threatened his ability to secure sufficient bipartisan support for the legislation.

King and others sensed that it was time to bring the strategies of the Southern Civil Rights movement to the nation's capital. In a private conversation with friends Stanley Levison and Clarence Jones, recorded by an FBI wiretap, King broached the idea of a huge, one-hundred-thousand-person march on Washington. The FBI had begun to tap King's phone lines after FBI director J. Edgar Hoover convinced Robert Kennedy that Levison, who was white, was a member of the Communist party and had too much influence over King. Hoover, in fact, had a difficult time believing that blacks had initiated the movement and that it was led by blacks. Unaware that others were listening, King and his friends added other names to the list of possible organizers, including the venerable labor leader A. Philip Randolph, whose earlier threats to march on Washington had led President Franklin D. Roosevelt to issue Executive Order 8802, which banned hiring discrimination at military facilities and government agencies during the Second World War.

The planning committee brought together representatives from civil rights organizations and the labor movement, interested clergy, and entertainment figures. The logistics of putting together the August 28, 1963, event were an enormous challenge. Organizers had to plan, for example, for inclement weather, medical emergencies, transportation, sanitation, drinking water, and food. They also needed to coordinate speakers and to mobilize members of black communities nationwide who would attend. In the meantime, ever worried by the prospect of social disturbances, President Kennedy readied several thousand soldiers for riot control.

The response from Americans staggered the organizers. By the morning of the march, more than a quarter million people had descended on Washington from every state in the Union. They arrived in twenty-one chartered trains, in caravans of buses and cars, on bicycles, and on foot. One fellow rollerskated to the march from Chicago. Men and women, old and young, black and white, made their way to the summertime shadows of the Washington Monument. Although the occasion was sometimes festive, the mood was serious. Few knew of the behind-the-scenes crisis threatening to destroy the semblance of unity among sometimes rival civil rights groups.

But as folk singers such as Joan Baez, Odetta, Peter, Paul, and Mary, and Bob Dylan entertained the estimated quarter of a million people who assembled, march organizers worked to get SNCC leader John Lewis to temper his speech. Lewis's prepared text bristled with anger. In a shorthand fashion he recalled the painful lessons sandwiched between the Birmingham campaign and the Washington march. In that period bombs had exploded in Birmingham; civil rights workers June Johnson, Annell Ponder, and Fannie Lou Hamer endured a tortuous beating at the hands of Winona, Mississippi, police; Mississippi NAACP leader Medgar Evers was assassinated in his own driveway; and the Highlander Folk School in Tennessee was burned to the ground.

Lewis eventually agreed to the pleadings of Randolph, not because Washington area clergy threatened to boycott the affair, but because he respected and understood the power of the moment. Nonetheless Lewis advised those watching and listening that blacks would not go slow. He told the gathering, "We shall crack the South into a thousand pieces and put them back together in the image of democracy."

Though Lewis offered perhaps the most forceful message of the day, it was Martin Luther King, Jr.'s speech that became a sort of national motto. Fusing classical philosophy to the oral traditions of the black Baptist Church, King preached that day about an America that could be. He shared his dream of a day when race did not matter: "I have a dream that my four little children will one day live in a nation where they will not be judged by the color of their skin but by the content of their character. I have a dream today!"

King's speech—and the entire march—energized the black community with the hope of justice. Then on Sunday, September 15, 1963, little more than two weeks after the March on Washington, a package of dynamite ripped through the Sixteenth Street Baptist Church in Birmingham while worshipers were preparing for church services. When the smoke cleared, four young girls—ages eleven to fourteen—lay dead. Addie Mae Collins, Denise McNair, Carole Robertson, and Cynthia Wesley had not taken part in earlier demonstrations, but their young faces, appearing in newspapers worldwide, became instant symbols of both the tragedy of racism and the hope of the civil rights struggle.

Two months later, violence of another kind erupted in Dallas, and the victim this time was President Kennedy, who had gone to Texas to shore up his Southern base in the Democratic party. The 1964 election was a year away, and signs indicated that the Republicans might nominate the very conservative Barry Goldwater, a senator from Arizona. As his motorcade traveled the streets of Dallas on November 22, the sound of rifle fire rang out. The open limousine carrying Kennedy made him a ready target.

With Kennedy's death, Lyndon Baines Johnson, a Texan and former majority leader in the Senate, was sworn in as the country's new president. Among his first acts was to call for passage of the Civil Rights Act proposed by Kennedy. He told a joint session of Congress, "No memorial or eulogy could more eloquently honor President Kennedy's memory than the earliest possible passage of the civil rights bill for which he fought."

As Congress debated the merits of the legislation, blacks in Mississippi were continuing to demand their voting rights. In the fall of 1963, activists launched a Freedom Vote campaign to register voters statewide and to demonstrate the importance of black electoral participation. With help from sixty white students drawn from Northern colleges, canvassers went door-to-door, enduring beatings, intimidation, and the fear of physical injury, to get black Mississippians to vote in a mock election. Nearly one hundred thousand voted for a Freedom party slate, thereby indicating what they could do if they had the right to vote.

Following this campaign, longtime SNCC worker Bob Moses proposed an expansion of the earlier effort. He and others had in mind a Freedom Summer, during which white college students, in alliance with local black leadership and blacks active in SNCC, would canvass Mississippi, registering voters and teaching in Freedom Schools. Moses had in mind something other than another mock vote; this time he would register blacks for the coming presidential election in November 1964. Freedom Summer lasted three months, June, July, and August. About one thousand volunteers participated, three-quarters of whom were white and three hundred of whom were women. The students hailed from Western and Northern colleges and universities. After spending a week in a training session directed by SNCC Executive Director James Forman in Oxford, Ohio, the first two hundred volunteers embarked for Mississippi and the forty-three project sites scattered across the state.

Tragically, within the first two days of Freedom Summer, law-enforcement officials in Philadelphia, Mississippi, added three new names to the list of martyrs who made the supreme sacrifice on behalf of civil rights. Andrew Goodman was a college student at Queens College in New York and a Freedom Summer volunteer. Michael Schwerner had recently opened the CORE office in Meridian with his wife, Rita. CORE worker James Chaney was the only one who was black and a native Mississipian.

On June 21, 1964, the three had set out for Lawndale to investigate another church burning. Near Philadelphia they were arrested for speeding, but the police let them go. That was the last time anyone other than their murderers saw them alive. One hundred fifty FBI agents, aided by sailors, searched woods and rivers. Investigators did not locate the three men until August 4, after they received a tip from an informant motivated by a thirty-thousand-dollar reward. The three decomposed bodies were found buried under a manmade dam. Later testimony revealed that the bulldozer operator at the dam had been paid by Klan members to hide the bodies there. Each had been shot by a .38-caliber gun; and clearly Chaney had been severely beaten before being shot. The U.S. Justice Department indicted nineteen men, including police officers and Klansmen, for the murders; only seven were found guilty.

The horrifying events caused a few volunteers to drop out, but not many. Many would later recall that the summer of 1964 was a pivotal time in their lives. Many whites experienced the warm fellowship of local black Southerners, who freely adopted them into their lives and communities. Black and white participants struggled with the perceptions and realities of power. Some SNCC and CORE activists complained, for example, that white volunteers too quickly assumed they were experts and leaders. Each group had to be educated and reeducated about the other's abilities and sensibilities. But the politics of leadership was no small matter. The tension soon grew into calls for black control of civil rights groups.

More than anything, however, Freedom Summer highlighted the potential political empowerment of black Mississippians. And it turned the national spotlight on racial violence and voting injustices in the state, forcing the federal government to respond. As August came to a close, more than eighty thousand blacks joined the new Mississippi Freedom Democratic party (MFDP). They would use this new strength to wrest changes from the national Democratic party, forcing the national body to undo, reluctantly, the practice of locking blacks out of the Mississippi party.

## The Fire This Time

President Lyndon B. Johnson signed the Civil Rights Act into law on July 2, 1964. It not only outlawed segregation in public accommodations of every kind throughout the country, but it laid the foundation for federal affirmative action policy. Affirmative action programs were meant to ensure that victims of past discrimination would have greater opportunities to find jobs, earn promotions, and gain

The 1966 "March Against Fear" in Mississippi was initiated by James Meredith. After Meredith was shot, Martin Luther King, Jr., (front center) and others took over the march. Black militants denounced their tactics of nonviolence and urged blacks to defend themselves against attack.

admission to colleges and universities. In particular, Title VII of the Civil Rights Act outlawed employment discrimination by creating the Equal Employment Opportunity Commission (EEOC) to enforce the law. It not only applied to both governmental and nongovernmental employers but covered labor unions and employment agencies as well. Workers who believed they were discriminated against in the workplace because of their race, sex, creed, color, or religion could file a complaint with the federal government.

But the new law did not dismantle the obstacles to voting that blacks in the South still faced. In the summer of 1964, the Mississippi Freedom Democratic party (MFDP) filed a lawsuit against the Democratic party for discrimination and used the television cameras to take their story to the nation. Fannie Lou Hamer told the world how she had been beaten and tortured by white supremacists simply because "we want to register," and she pointed out that the white Democrats were not even loyal to President Lyndon B. Johnson. Those Democrats vehemently attacked Johnson's candidacy because of his commitment to civil rights and equal opportunity for all. Yet, while Johnson agreed with the MFDP's assessment, he and his party would not recognize its delegates as the legitimate representatives of the state of Mississippi at the Democratic National Convention.

Questioning both the horrors at home and the Democratic party's refusal to take their delegation seriously, Hamer asked, "Is this America? The land of the free and the home of the brave?" Johnson's response was to strike a deal: He signaled that he was prepared to select the liberal Minnesota Senator Hubert H. Humphrey as his running mate, if MFDP delegates and their surrogates cooperated by allowing the delegation to remain intact, with one modification. Two members of the MFDP would sit as members of the Mississippi delegation, while other MFDP delegates would attend the convention as observers. Although Martin Luther King, Roy Wilkins, executive secretary of the NAACP, and several mainstream black leaders urged the MFDP to accept the compromise, they refused. Most MFDP delegates felt the compromise minimized their claim of truly representing Democrats in Mississippi.

When election day arrived, all of Mississippi's electoral votes went to archconservative Republican Barry Goldwater. Indeed, the Republican party made history, not only winning the state of Mississippi for the first time but also declaring victories in Alabama, Georgia, South Carolina, and Louisiana. The Democratic party's failure to fully embrace Mississippi's black voters signaled the beginning of the end of the solid Democratic South.

Johnson won by a landslide, but the failure of the capital-D Democratic party to support small-d democratic forces in the South and the willingness of Martin Luther King and other national civil rights figures to go along with Johnson struck a blow to the movement. Increasingly, local activists in the rural South, SNCC activists, and urban activists associated compromise with weakness.

Less than a year later King supported another compromise that would further damage and divide the movement. It involved a struggle in Selma, Alabama, where SNCC activists had been locked in a battle with local forces and Governor George Wallace, who used brutal violence to suppress the movement there. After SNCC organizer Jimmie Lee Jackson was shot by a state trooper as he tried to shield his mother from officers' billy clubs during a civil rights demonstration, SNCC and SCLC decided to hold a march from Selma to Montgomery on March 7, 1965. After calling for the march, however, King reconsidered after a tortuous conversation with Attorney General Nicholas Katzenbach. It was clear that President Johnson did not want the march to happen, because the potential violence would generate bad publicity and, from his perspective, jeopardize his relations with Southern Democrats. Worried that his defiance of Johnson's wishes might undermine the goal of passing a voting rights bill, King decided to cancel the march at the very last minute. He and Ralph Abernathy left town, announcing that they had to minister to their congregations.

But the young people of SNCC were not about to postpone the march. They convinced SCLC leader Hosea Williams to go on with it, with or without King. (Many marchers, however, did not know what had happened and were surprised by King's absence.) But they never made it; the police and state troopers brutally attacked the racially mixed crowd as it reached the Edmund Pettus Bridge, forcing the marchers to turn back. Three days later, amidst criticism for his absence, King decided to lead another group of three thousand people, who had answered the call to go to Selma and complete the march, across the bridge. But unbeknownst to the crowd he had made a secret agreement with Attorney General Katzenbach to retreat as soon as they came up against the state troopers. So when King and the march leaders got within fifty feet of the troopers' blockade, they kneeled, prayed, and, as they rose, called on the marchers to retreat. Angry and confused, the marchers did what they were told. The march was eventually held a few weeks later, after much negotiation with the Johnson administration and Governor Wallace.

Despite its fits and starts, the Selma march contributed to the passage of an important piece of legislation by the federal government: the Voting Rights Act of 1965. Signed into law on August 6, 1965, the act prohibited states from imposing literacy requirements, poll taxes, and similar obstacles to the registration of black voters. Of course, the 15th Amendment to the Constitution, passed almost a century earlier, was supposed to guarantee this right to vote, but a federal system of "states' rights" had allowed Southern states to deny black people voting privileges through such measures as the poll tax, literacy tests, and grandfather clauses (until 1939).

With the Voting Rights Act, however, blacks could not be denied the vote any more. Federal examiners were now sent South to safeguard black citizens' right to register and vote. The impact of the act was dramatic: Between 1964 and 1969, the number of black adults registered to vote increased from 19.3 percent to 61.3 percent in Alabama, 27.4 percent to 60.4 percent in Georgia, and 6.7 percent to 66.5 percent in Mississippi. It took several more years before blacks turned the right to vote into electoral might.

The victory was bittersweet. King's role in the Selma march tarnished his reputation in the eyes of his followers. As respect for King's ideas and strategies began to wane among young people, groups such as SNCC began to envision new, more militant strategies. It became clear—from the failure of the MFDP at the 1964 Democratic National Convention to the Selma fiasco—that African Americans could not always rely on the federal government for support. A new generation of activists realized that black people needed more than friends in high places; they needed power.

Within SNCC, a recent Howard University graduate named Stokely Carmichael quickly emerged as a voice of uncompromising militancy and, later, black nationalism. Born in Trinidad and raised in New York City, Carmichael had been associated with interracial radical movements since high school. Like many of his contemporaries, he joined the Civil Rights movement but never fully embraced the philosophy of nonviolence. He and several other SNCC activists began carrying guns to protect themselves from violence. Carmichael led a militant voter-registration campaign, organizing open rallies and marches for black rights in the heart of the Black Belt—with its long history of white violence and terrorism against black sharecroppers. In Lowndes County, Alabama, in 1965, he founded the Lowndes County Freedom Organization (LCFO). An all-black group (mainly because whites would not join), the LCFO adopted the symbol of the black panther because, according to its chairman, John Hulett, the panther will come out fighting for its life when cornered.

The LCFO was only the beginning of the new black militancy. A few months later, a group of black SNCC activists in Atlanta circulated a position paper calling on white members to leave the organization and devote their attention to organizing white people in their own communities. Although most SNCC members, black and white, opposed this position, it became clear to many white activists that the character of the movement had changed profoundly. Several leading white figures resigned voluntarily or were forced to leave because, in their view at least, the political climate had become intolerable. Carmichael had successfully contested John Lewis for the chairmanship of SNCC and he, along with other SNCC militants such as veteran organizer Willie Ricks, began questioning the movement's integrationist agenda. Then, during the summer of 1966, the slogan Black Power emerged full-blown within SNCC as well as within the Congress of Racial Equality (CORE).

On June 5, James Meredith, the first black student admitted to the University of Mississippi, initiated a march from Memphis, Tennessee, to Jackson, Mississippi, in order to mobilize black Mississippians to register to vote. A few hours into the march, however, Meredith was shot and the march came to an abrupt end. Martin Luther King, Jr., Carmichael, and CORE leader Floyd McKissick decided to go to Memphis in order to finish the march to Jackson. From the very beginning, however, tensions between King and Carmichael created tensions within the ranks. Carmichael insisted that the Deacons for Defense, an armed black self-defense group based in Louisiana, provide cover for the marchers, a request to which King reluctantly agreed. At the same time, SNCC activist Willie Ricks began to promote the slogan Black Power among the membership, who seemed to embrace it enthusiastically. While King called it "an unfortunate choice of words," McKissick embraced it. As he explained, "Black Power is not Black supremacy; it is a united Black voice reflecting racial pride in the tradition of our heterogeneous nation. Black Power does not mean the exclusion of White Americans from the Negro Revolution; it means the inclusion of all men in a common moral and political struggle."

Not everyone agreed with this definition, of course, but it quickly became clear during the summer of 1966 that the issue of Black Power would transform the movement in multiple ways. Tired and impatient with the slow pace of the civil rights establishment, a new attitude overtook the movement: no more compromise, no more "deals" with white liberals, no more subordinating the movement to the needs of the Democratic party. Out of bitter disappointment rose this new slogan.

The Black Power of the sixties had roots in the Southern freedom movement, in the many compromises made by mainstream leaders, and in the recognition that ending Jim Crow was not enough to win full equality or political power. It also had roots in the increasingly black cities of the North and South, where poverty and police brutality were becoming increasingly visible. And it was nourished by the growing popularity of black nationalism—the idea that black people constitute a single community, if not a "nation," within the United States and therefore have a right to determine their destiny—as expressed by people such as former North Carolina NAACP leader Robert Williams, as well as SNCC leaders such as H. Rap Brown and Stokely Carmichael.

Perhaps *the* most important and controversial progenitor of the Black Power movement was Malcolm X. For many young people, particularly those in the Civil Rights movement, Malcolm's uncompromising stance toward white supremacy and his plainspoken oratory on black history, culture, and racism deeply affected a new generation of activists. Even efforts to portray Malcolm in a negative light, such as the special 1959 television documentary on the Nation of Islam called "The Hate That Hate Produced" revealed to many black viewers Malcolm's critique of nonviolence and of the strategy to ally with white liberals. He clearly saw the need for a movement in the urban North, one that would focus on the needs of the poor and deal with pressing issues such as police brutality, crumbling schools, and the lack of jobs. While preaching black self-reliance, he also attacked mainstream civil rights leaders for being sellouts. "The black masses," he argued, "are tired of following these hand-picked Negro 'leaders' who sound like professional beggars, as they cry year after year for white America to accept us as first-class citizens."

These civil rights leaders, Malcolm said, were leading a nonviolent Negro revolution, when what was needed was a black revolution. Whereas the Negro wants to desegregate, he said, the black demands land, power, and freedom. Whereas the Negro adopts a Christian philosophy of "love thy enemy," the black has no love or respect for the oppressor.

As long as Malcolm remained in the Nation of Islam, he was compelled to conceal his differences with Elijah Muhammad. But as Malcolm became more popular, the tensions between the two men became increasingly evident. The final blow came when Malcolm discovered that the NOI's moral and spiritual leader had fathered children by two former secretaries. The tensions became publicly visible when Muhammad silenced Malcolm for remarking after the assassination of President John F. Kennedy that it was a case of the "chickens coming home to roost." Malcolm's point was that the federal government's inaction toward racist violence in the South had come back to strike the president. When Malcolm learned that Muhammad had planned to have him assassinated, he decided to leave the NOI. On March 8, 1964, he announced his resignation and formed the Muslim Mosque, Inc., an Islamic movement devoted to working in the political sphere and cooperating with civil rights leaders. Despite his criticisms of black leadership,

Martin Luther King, Jr., and Malcolm X met accidentally and amicably in Washington, D.C., in 1964. Despite their differences in style and philosophy, they shared many of the concerns, goals, and risks involved in freedom-movement leadership.

Malcolm had always said that he should be actively involved in the struggles in the South and elsewhere, but Elijah Muhammad's rule that NOI members not participate in politics had hampered Malcolm. Free of the Nation of Islam, Malcolm sought alliances with those willing to work with him.

That same year he made his first pilgrimage to Mecca—the holy city of Islam, in Saudi Arabia. During his trip he changed his name to El-Hajj Malik El-Shabazz and embraced the multiracial Islam he found during his pilgrimage. He publicly acknowledged that whites were no longer devils, though he still remained a black nationalist and staunch believer in black self-determination and self-organization.

During the summer of 1964 Malcolm formed the Organization of Afro-American Unity (OAAU). Inspired by the Organization of African Unity, made up of the independent African states, the OAAU's program combined advocacy for independent black institutions (for example, schools and cultural centers) with support for black participation in mainstream politics, including electoral campaigns. Following the example of Paul Robeson and W. E. B. Du Bois, who had submitted a petition to the United Nations in 1948 claiming that black people in the United States were victims of genocide, Malcolm planned to submit a similar petition in 1965. The UN petition documented human rights violations and acts of genocide against African Americans. Unfortunately, Malcolm and members of the

OAAU never had a chance to submit the petition: On February 21, 1965, he was assassinated by gunmen affiliated with the NOI.

Malcolm had known he was in danger ever since he had left the NOI. He received regular death threats and was constantly followed by suspicious characters. One week before his murder, his home in Queens, New York, was firebombed. He had even begun to carry a gun for protection. But on Sunday, February 21, as he took the stage to speak to a small audience at the Audubon Ballroom in Harlem, two gunmen stood up and opened fire. One got away, but the crowd stopped the other, a Muslim named Talmadge Hayer. (One year later, Hayer was convicted of the murder of Malcolm.) The OAAU died with Malcolm X.

Although Malcolm left no permanent organizations (the Muslim Mosque, Inc., collapsed soon after his death), he did exert a notable impact on the Civil Rights movement in the last year of his life. Black activists in SNCC and CORE who had heard him speak to organizers in Selma just weeks before his death began to support some of his ideas, especially on armed self-defense, racial pride, and the creation of black-run institutions. Ironically, Malcolm's impact on black politics and culture was greater after his death than before it. In fact, not long thereafter, the Black Power movement and his ideas about community control, African liberation, and race pride became extremely influential. His autobiography, written with Alex Haley—the future author of *Roots*—become a movement standard. Malcolm's life story proved to movements such as the Black Panther party, founded in 1966, that ex-criminals and hustlers can be turned into revolutionaries. And arguments in favor of armed self-defense—certainly not a new idea in African-American communities—were renewed by the publication of Malcolm's autobiography and speeches.

One of the first radical organizations to be inspired by Malcolm's ideas was the Revolutionary Action Movement (RAM). It originated neither in the South nor in the Northeast. Rather, its founders were a group of black Ohio students at Case Western Reserve University in Cleveland, Central State College, and Wilberforce University. Active in SNCC, CORE, and local chapters of Students for a Democratic Society (SDS), a predominantly white national student group that emerged during the Vietnam War protests, this gathering began meeting in 1961 to discuss the significance of Robert Williams's armed self-defense campaign in North Carolina and his subsequent flight to Cuba. Led by Donald Freeman, a student at Case Western Reserve, the group agreed that armed self-defense was a necessary component of the black freedom movement and that activists had to link themselves to anticolonial movements around the world. Freeman was influenced by Malcolm X's speeches and the writings of an independent black Marxist intellectual named Harold Cruse, who argued that African Americans themselves lived under colonialism inside the United States. Freeman hoped to transform the group into a revolutionary movement akin to the Nation of Islam but one that would adopt the direct action tactics of SNCC. By the spring of 1962, they became the Revolutionary Action Movement (RAM).

Although RAM's leaders decided to organize it as an underground movement, it did attract activists across the nation. In the South, RAM built a small but significant following at Fisk University in Nashville, the training ground for many leading SNCC activists. In northern California, RAM grew primarily out of the Afro-American Association, a student group founded in 1962 based at Oakland's Merritt College and the University of California at Berkeley. Never a mass movement, RAM had a radical agenda that anticipated many of the goals of the left wing of the Black Power movement. Its twelve-point program called for the development of freedom schools, national black student organizations, rifle clubs, a guerrilla army made up of youth and the unemployed, and black farmer cooperatives not just for economic development but to keep "community and guerrilla forces going for a while." They also pledged support for national liberation movements in Africa, Asia, and Latin America as well as the adoption of socialism to replace capitalism across the globe.

After RAM spent years as an underground organization, a series of "exposés" that ran in *Life* magazine and *Esquire* in 1966 identified it as one of the leading extremist groups "Plotting a War on 'Whitey.'" RAM members were not only considered armed and dangerous but "impressively well read in revolutionary literature." Not surprisingly, these highly publicized articles were followed by a series of police raids on the homes of RAM members in Philadelphia and New York City. In June 1967, RAM members were rounded up and charged with conspiracy to instigate a riot, poison police officers with potassium cyanide, and assassinate NAACP leader Roy Wilkins and National Urban League Director Whitney Young. Though the charges did not stick, the FBI's surveillance of RAM intensified. By 1969, RAM had essentially dissolved itself, though its members opted to infiltrate existing black organizations, continue to push the twelve-point program, and develop study groups that focused on the "Science of Black Internationalism."

RAM's movement was, in part, based on the assumption that black people had the potential to launch a war against the U.S. government. Writing in exile from Cuba and later China, Robert Williams anticipated black urban uprisings in a spring 1964 edition of *The Crusader,* a publication RAM members regarded as an unofficial organ of their movement. Entitled "USA: The Potential of a Minority Revolution," Williams's article announced, "This year, 1964 is going to be a violent one, the storm will reach hurricane proportions by 1965 and the eye of the hurricane will hover over America by 1966. America is a house on fire—FREEDOM NOW!—or let it burn, let it burn. Praise the Lord and pass the ammunition!!"

Williams was not alone in this assessment. A year earlier, the writer James Baldwin had predicted that in the coming years race riots would "spread to every metropolitan center in the nation which has a significant Negro population." The next six years proved them right. With riots erupting in the black communities of Rochester, New York City, Jersey City, and Philadelphia, 1964 was indeed a "violent" year. By 1965, these revolts had indeed reached "hurricane proportions."

The hurricane also touched the West Coast in the black Los Angeles community of Watts. Sparked when a resident witnessed a black driver being harrassed by white police officers, a frequent occurrence on the streets of Los Angeles, the Watts rebellion turned out to be the worst urban disturbance in nearly twenty years. When the smoke cleared, thirty-four people had died, and more than $35 million in property had been destroyed or damaged. The remainder of the decade witnessed the spread of this hurricane across America: Violence erupted in some three hundred cities, including Chicago; Washington, D.C.; Cambridge, Maryland; Providence, Rhode Island; Hartford, Connecticut; San Francisco; and Phoenix. Altogether, the urban uprisings involved close to half a million African Americans, resulted in millions of dollars in property damage, and left two hundred fifty people (mostly African Americans) dead, ten thousand seriously injured, and countless black people homeless. Police and the National Guard turned black neighborhoods into war zones, arresting at least sixty thousand people and employing tanks, machine guns, and tear gas to pacify the community. In Detroit in 1967, for instance, forty-three people were killed, two thousand were wounded, and five thousand watched their homes destroyed by flames that engulfed fourteen square miles of the inner city.

Robert Williams was not too far off the mark: A real war erupted in America's inner cities. Elected officials, from the mayor's office to the Oval Office, must have seen these uprisings as a war of sorts because they responded to the crisis with military might at first. Later they turned to a battery of social science investigators, community programs, and short-lived economic development projects to pacify urban blacks. Just as the American military advisers in Southeast Asia could not understand why so many North Vietnamese supported the communists, liberal social scientists wanted to find out why African Americans rioted. Why burn buildings in "their own" communities? What did they want? Were these "disturbances" merely a series of violent orgies led by young hoodlums out for television sets and a good time, or were they protest movements? To the surprise of several research teams, those who rioted tended to be better educated and more politically aware than those who did not. One survey of Detroit black residents after the 1967 riot revealed that eighty-six percent of the respondents identified discrimination and deprivation as the main reasons behind the uprising. Hostility to police brutality was at the top of the list.

Although Robert Williams, James Baldwin, and many African Americans who survived each day in the crumbling ghettoes of North America knew the storm was on the horizon, government officials and policymakers were unprepared. After all, things seemed to be looking up for black folk: Between 1964 and 1969, the median black family income rose from $5,921 to $8,074; the percentage of black families below the poverty line declined from 48.1 percent in 1959 to 27.9 percent in 1969. However, these statistics also reveal a growing chasm between members of a black middle class who were beginning to benefit from integration, affirmative action policies, and a strong economy, and the black poor left behind in deteriorating urban centers. Dilapidated, rat-infested housing, poor and overcrowded schools, the lack of city services, and the disappearance of high-wage jobs in inner-city communities all contributed to the expansion of urban poverty and deprivation. But there is more to the story: The black freedom movement and the hope it engendered in black communities convinced many blacks that change was inevitable. Some historians have called it "rising expectations"; others simply identified it as "rights consciousness." Either way, an increasing number of African Americans, including the poor, adopted a new attitude for a new day. They demanded respect and basic human rights, expected decent housing and decent jobs as a matter of rights, and understood that social movements and protests were the way to achieve these things. This attitude manifested itself in the daily interactions between blacks and whites. For example, after buses had been desegregated in the South, white residents complained frequently of the growing impudence and discourtesy of black passengers. As one white Birmingham woman complained, "Can't get on the bus and ride to town because the colored have taken the buses."

But the same circumstances that unleashed such fervent opposition to segregation and emboldened ordinary black people to assert their rights also unleashed a more sustained effort on the part of the police to put things back in order. Police repression reached an all-time high between 1963 and the early seventies and black male youths from poor communities were involved in the majority of incidents.

There is a similar paradox evident in the growth in the number of welfare recipients during the sixties. In 1960, 745,000 families received assistance; by 1968 that figure had grown to 1.5 million. The most dramatic increase took place between 1968 and 1972, when the welfare rolls grew to three million. On the one hand, the surge in the welfare rolls reflects the expansion of poverty amidst plenty, the growing numbers of poor people (particularly among minority women and children) who needed assistance to survive. But the growth also reflects a "rights consciousness" among welfare recipients inspired by the Civil Rights and Black Power movements of the period. In 1966, the former associate director of CORE, George Wiley, created the Poverty Rights Action Center (PRAC) in order to help coordinate the activities of numerous local welfare rights organizations that had begun appearing during the early sixties. Out of discussions within PRAC, Wiley helped found the National Welfare Rights Organization (NWRO) a year later. Led primarily by black female welfare recipients, the NWRO educated the poor about eligibility for assistance under existing laws and pressured welfare agencies to provide benefits without stigmatizing applicants. They demanded adequate day-care facilities and criticized poorly planned job-training programs. They attacked degrading, low-wage employment and the practice of scrutinizing women's lives as a precondition for support (such as investigations to determine whether recipients were unwed mothers, had a man living with them, or spent their meager welfare check on things a social worker might find unnecessary, such as makeup). Moreover, they viewed welfare not merely as a gift from the government or a handout but as a right. By emphasizing that welfare was a right, the NWRO stripped welfare of its stigma in the eyes of many poor women and convinced them that they could receive assistance and retain their dignity.

The NWRO was not the only advocate for the increased demands of the black poor. Under President Lyndon Johnson, the federal government launched a "War on Poverty" as part of his overall vision of transforming America into a "Great Society." Most of the programs that fell under the broad title of the "War on Poverty" were created by the Economic Opportunity Act of 1964. Agencies such as the Job Corps, administered by the Department of Labor, sought to create employment opportunities for the poor. And through the newly created Office of Economic Opportunity (OEO), agencies such as the Legal Services Corporation, to provide civil legal assistance; the Community Action Program; Head Start, a preschool education program; and Volunteers in Service to America (VISTA) sought to provide services for the poor and incorporate them in the decision-making and policymaking process at the local level. The OEO's director, Sargent Shriver, called for the "maximum feasible participation" of the poor in these agencies and, more generally, in the process of solving the problems of poverty.

The only program that actively tried to implement "maximum feasible participation" was the Community Action Program (CAP). CAP's mission was to coordinate the work of more than a thousand federally funded, neighborhood-based antipoverty agencies and to make new services more accessible to the poor. Unlike other antipoverty agencies, CAP focused its efforts on rehabilitating the entire community rather than poor families or individuals who happened to fall below the poverty line. Although CAP quickly earned a reputation for "stirring up the poor," it mainly worked with prosperous local blacks and established black middle-class leadership. Indeed, despite directives from on high calling for maximum feasible participation, urban rebellions from below turned out to be what got the black activists and community people into the antipoverty agencies.

The bureaucrats and planners who implemented these poverty programs conceived of "maximum feasible participation" very differently from groups like the NWRO or leaders of the Civil Rights movement. After all, they were planned almost entirely by middle-class white men in the Johnson administration who set out to provide "a hand up" to the poorest segment of society, from the ghetto residents in America's sprawling cities, to the Mexican migrants on farms and in barrios in the Southwest, to the poor whites scratching out a living in Appalachia.

Overall, Johnson's Great Society programs did begin to reduce poverty ever so slightly. Ironically, the greatest successes were not products of the Equal Opportunity Act of 1964 but of other programs, notably the expansion of the food stamp program, free school meals and other nutrition projects, and the creation of Medicaid and Medicare programs (which provided the poor and elderly with free health care). But Johnson's War on Poverty fell short of the mark. First, agencies such as the Job Corps focused on job training rather than creating new, decent-paying jobs. Second, Johnson refused to raise taxes in order to pay for these programs, which proved disastrous because he had given the middle class a huge tax cut in 1964 and there was not enough money available. Besides, the cost of fighting the Vietnam War steadily drained federal resources away from the War on Poverty and contributed to rising inflation. Third, the War on Poverty operated from a very limited definition of poverty, one that included only families who fell below a fixed poverty line. The goal was not to change the structure of poverty, to reduce income inequality or help the working poor earn more money; rather, it was to change the behaviors that officials believed led to poverty by providing educational, legal, and job-training services to the very poor in order to give them the resources to rise up out of poverty. In other words, the Johnson administration believed the causes of poverty to be culture and behavior rather than political and economic forces. Rather than deal with issues such as low wages, a shortage of well-paying jobs, and blatant racism in employment and labor unions, the proponents of the War on Poverty sought to "correct" poor people's behavior or improve their social skills. The administrators and intellectuals working in these federal programs saw their task in terms of reversing "community pathology," breaking the "culture of poverty," or restoring the "broken family." The poor, especially the black poor, were considered "disadvantaged."

Most black activists did not believe liberal goodwill, as they viewed it, could eliminate poverty. They viewed the problem in terms of power and unequal distribution of wealth. As NWRO leader George Wiley put it: "I am not at all convinced that comfortable, affluent, middle-class Americans are going to move over and share their wealth and resources with the people who have none. But I do have faith that if the poor people who have the problems can organize, can exert their political muscle, they can have a chance to have their voices and their weight felt in the political process of this country, and there is hope."

Martin Luther King, Jr., concurred. In his book *Where Do We Go From Here?*, King wrote: "The plantation and the ghetto were created by those who had power both to confine those who had no power and to perpetuate their powerlessness. The problem of transforming the ghetto is, therefore, a problem of power."

So King and the Southern Christian Leadership Conference took the movement to the urban North, settling in Chicago in 1966. They initially tried to build a grass-roots union of poor black residents rather than opening their efforts with a direct-action campaign that would draw media attention, as King and his associates had done in Birmingham three years earlier. When the organizing drive failed to generate much support, King decided to lead a march through a white Chicago neighborhood to demand an end to racial discrimination in housing. King and the SCLC had gone there to appeal to the city, the state, and the nation for open housing for all, and to use the power of love to persuade white racists that segregation was immoral. Instead, King met an angry white crowd raining rocks and bottles on the protesters. In all of his years fighting racism and injustice in the South, he had never seen anything like this before.

The Chicago campaign marked another failure for King. To compound matters, his increasing opposition to the Vietnam War drew fire from nearly every major older mainstream black leader in the country, who feared alienating the volatile president, and further distanced him from the Johnson administration.

Given King's deep and abiding commitment to nonviolence, he was bound to come out openly against the war. And militants in CORE and SNCC had begun issuing antiwar statements as early as 1966. SNCC openly endorsed resistance to the draft. It declared: "Vietnamese are being murdered because the United States is pursuing an aggressive policy in violation of international law." King understood the link between the war abroad and the failure to wage a real war on poverty at home. He pointed out that the United States was spending close to five hundred thousand dollars to kill each enemy soldier but spent only a paltry thirty-five dollars a year to help a needy American in poverty. The more he criticized the war, the more isolated he became in mainstream civil rights circles. His longtime allies Bayard Rustin, Roy Wilkins, and Whitney Young denounced him publicly, and they were joined by a chorus of distinguished black spokesmen, including Ralph Bunche, Massachusetts Senator Edward Brooke, and former baseball star Jackie Robinson. And, of course, this diminished his standing with the White House. But King's national, and international, reputation after winning the 1964 Nobel Peace Prize meant he could not be ignored entirely.

As he endured criticism from white and black friends, King became more radical in key respects. He became more committed than ever to organizing the poor and he openly rejected liberal reform as the strategy for change. King and his aides at SCLC planned a massive Poor People's Campaign on Washington to take place in the spring of 1968. The march was to bring thousands of poor people from all ethnic and racial backgrounds to demand, among other things, a federally supported guaranteed income policy.

Despite plans for a new campaign, the movement and the criticisms had taken their toll on King. Many friends and associates described him as tired and depressed. He talked openly of death, his own death. As he fretted in the first months of 1968, behind the scenes King and his associates vigorously debated the wisdom of the Poor People's Campaign in Washington. A few encouraged King to support their call for a civil disobedience campaign that would close key streets in the nation's capital. Bayard Rustin, among others, considered such a strategy pure folly, given the outbreaks of violence that had marred the public landscape since 1965. King, moreover, worried that too little had been done to recruit those of all races who were very poor and chronically unemployed.

Meanwhile, in February 1968, in Memphis, another battle erupted, this one between municipal workers who sought union recognition and city officials who refused such recognition. Black garbage collectors in the city fumed when twenty-two of them were sent home without pay due to bad weather, while white workers were allowed to stay and were paid. The 1,300 members of AFSCME Local 1733, a nearly all-black local union representing the sanitation workers, refused to let the issue die; they demanded that the city acknowledge their union and refused to work otherwise. Memphis Mayor Henry Loeb refused to negotiate with the men or anyone else. Residents of the black community joined the men, boycotting downtown merchants and triggering a thirty-five percent loss of profit. Still the mayor refused to budge. And following an unsuccessful public meeting, a confrontation with police resulted in an ugly moment of violence, onlookers overturned police cars, and the police indiscriminately maced and clubbed everyone in their way.

Seeking to dramatize the plight of black workers and force the city to the bargaining table, longtime civil rights activist and minister of Centenary Methodist Church James Lawson placed a call to King for assistance. The fusing of race and economics had by now been a chief concern for King for several years. Still he put Lawson off at first, pleading fatigue and a tight schedule. King did go to Memphis and addressed more than fifteen thousand on the evening of March 18. He then promised to return the next week, a promise broken only by a rare foot of snow that forced a postponement of the march he was to have joined. In the interim, further negotiations with city officials produced little. On March 28 he did return, prepared to fight until victory was won.

Speaking before a black audience on April 3, King predicted that the Memphis sanitation workers' struggle would succeed. But in midstream, when the audience rose with his inspirational tone, King's speech changed rather abruptly. Sweat pouring down his face, he closed with these famous and fateful words:

> I don't know what will happen now. But it really doesn't matter to me now. Because I've been to the mountaintop. I won't mind. Like anybody, I would like to live a long life. Longevity has its place. But I'm not concerned about that now. I just want to do God's will. And He's allowed me to go up to the mountain. And I've looked over, and I've seen the promised land.... I may not get there with you but I want you to know tonight that we as a people will get to the promised land. So I'm happy tonight. I'm not worried about anything. I'm not fearing any man. "Mine eyes have seen the glory of the coming of the Lord."

The following evening, April 4, 1968, King was fatally shot by a white man named James Earl Ray. For some inexplicable reason, the police who had been guarding King's hotel happened to be absent at the time of his assassination. Although they caught the assailant, America lost a visionary.

The response to King's death was immediate and varied. Some white students at the University of Texas at Arlington screamed with glee, joyous that an assassin's bullet had taken out the "troublemaker" King. At the same time the *New York Times* editorialized, "Dr. King's murder is a national disaster." And that it was: Major riots engulfed Washington, D.C., Baltimore, and Chicago. All told, more than one hundred cities suffered from rioting after the assassination of King, leaving thirty-nine people dead and millions of dollars' worth of property destroyed. President Johnson declared April 7, 1968, a day of mourning, and in tribute to the man whose death brought condolences from leaders and citizens around the world, the country flew its flag at half mast. Between King's death and his funeral on April 9, Coretta Scott King and her children led a silent, peaceful march through the streets of Memphis.

On the hot, humid April day of the funeral, thousands of schoolchildren sat transfixed as black-and-white televisions were hauled into classrooms so that the nation could collectively mourn King's passing. What they witnessed that day was a unique assembly. In the Ebenezer Baptist Church in Atlanta sat Vice President Hubert Humphrey, presidential aspirants Democrat Robert Kennedy and Republican Richard Nixon, civil rights warriors young and old, Jacqueline Kennedy, who a few years earlier had suffered the loss of her own husband, as well as an assortment of friends, acquaintances, and loved ones. Ralph David Abernathy eulogized his old and dear friend. At Coretta King's insistence, Martin offered his own eulogy, too, as a tape recording of his "A Drum Major for Justice" sermon played for all to hear. That voice, deep and rich, so full of vitality, reminded all of the man who was made by the needs of his time.

A simple cart pulled by two mules hauled King's draped casket to its final resting place. His grave marker told the world what his life had come to symbolize:

FREE AT LAST, FREE AT LAST
THANK GOD ALMIGHTY
I'M FREE AT LAST.

## Where Do We Go from Here?

One year before his murder in 1968, Martin Luther King, Jr., published the book *Where Do We Go From Here: Chaos or Community?* More than the title itself, the subtitle captured what the year 1968 felt like to many Americans. With increasing regularity young men were fleeing the nation to escape the draft or returning from Vietnam in body bags.

Thousands of miles from that war, American support for a declining Portugal as it struggled to hang on to its African colonies in Mozambique, Angola, and Guinea-Bissau produced another kind of chaos. For those African Americans paying attention to liberation campaigns on the African continent, the support revealed the degree to which the United States would resort to violence to prop up an aging colonial power. The U.S. government supplied the Portuguese with military advisors and many weapons, including napalm bombs that were dropped on towns and villages where African nationalists had established bases.

Back in the United States, 1968 was a year of unprecedented chaos and considerable violence. Inner-city neighborhoods, such as Washington, D.C., Chicago, and Memphis, visited by race riots, continued to burn; incidents of police brutality rose steadily; dozens of black activists committed to protecting their communities from police violence were embroiled in several shoot-outs with law-enforcement officials; and political assassinations continued. Just weeks after the country watched the burial of Martin Luther King, Jr., a gunman named Sirhan Sirhan fatally shot Democratic party presidential candidate Robert F. Kennedy.

Liberals sought to turn this chaos into "community," to stem the country's division into two nations, one black and the other white. This was certainly the goal outlined in the report of the National Advisory Commission on Civil Disorders, a presidentially appointed committee whose study of the causes of urban uprisings was also published in 1968. Better known as the Kerner Commission (named after Ohio Governor Otto Kerner, the commission's head), its report acknowledged the urgent need for the government to bridge the widening gulf between blacks and whites. The report recommended massive job-training and employment programs, educational improvements, an overhaul of the welfare system, and a plan for integrating blacks into the nation's mainstream.

The authors of the report, a predominantly white group of liberal social scientists and policymakers committed to racial integration and ending poverty, made what seemed to many Americans a bold and startling claim: that racism was endemic to U.S. society. Racism was not merely the bad behavior of a few individuals but operated through institutions and forces of power. Thus in order to eliminate racism, massive changes in American institutions needed to take place. As the authors wrote, "The essential fact is that neither existing conditions nor the garrison state [referring to the massive numbers of police and National Guardsmen in riot-plagued communities] offered acceptable alternatives for the future of this country. Only a greatly enlarged commitment to national action, compassionate, massive, and sustained, backed by the will and resources of the most powerful and the richest nation on this earth, can shape a future that is compatible with the historic ideals of American society."

While the Kerner Commission proposed a plan to turn "chaos" into "community," African-American activists who embraced the politics of Black Power saw themselves already as community builders. They had previously viewed racism as institutionalized, and most had lost faith in the American creed of justice for all, the goal of integration, or the kindness of white liberals. Instead, they sought to build alternative institutions within black communities, to strengthen the black community itself, and to fight for political and economic power. Of course, precisely what Black Power meant was always open to debate. For some it was a movement for black political power with the hope of making American democracy more open and inclusive for all. For others it meant building black businesses. For many grassroots activists, Black Power meant creating separate, autonomous institutions within black communities.

The leadership of the Congress of Racial Equality (CORE), a leading force in the Civil Rights movement, had begun to embrace Black Power around the same time it shifted its focus from large, highly visible direct-action campaigns against segregation to less visible community organizing in poor African-American neighborhoods, especially in the urban North. CORE underwent a change in leadership when Floyd McKissick replaced James Farmer as executive director in January 1966. Farmer, who had been a charter member of the group and took over its leadership in 1961, had been a longtime proponent of integration and direct action, while McKissick had been among the early advocates of Black Power.

With the shift to a focus on building up black communities, CORE's black membership increased dramatically. Some of the increase can be attributed to McKissick. Among his many symbolic and substantive actions, he moved the national office from downtown New York City to Harlem. There, he combined an interest in economic development and an appreciation of cultural training, especially the teaching of African languages. Though he never advocated complete racial separation, CORE's new leader did preach a message of black autonomy and self-determination.

It was Roy Innis, who took over CORE in 1968, who linked black self-determination and black capitalism, that is, getting a fair share of the economic pie, especially control of businesses in urban ghettos. In some ways he saw the black community as a colony within the United States that could become independent only if it had a strong economic base. Innis therefore called for federal funds to establish black businesses. He envisioned a federal system in which black communities would be linked together in a federation, constituting a black "nation within a nation." The U.S. Constitution made no allowances for such a possibility, however. Innis eventually lost faith in black nationalism as a strategy of liberation. By 1972, he had thrown his support behind conservative Republican Richard Nixon and promoted a limited strategy of black enterprise and assimilation.

Others embraced a more conventional, if not conservative, form of economic black nationalism. A small but dominant group came from the rising black middle class. Many college-educated blacks who were nonetheless concerned about affairs within black communities interpreted Black Power to mean black capitalism. In fact, in an age when Black Power evoked fears of bomb-throwing militants and radicals with Afro hairstyles, it is interesting to note that the first Black Power conference was organized by conservative Republican Nathan Wright, and the second was cosponsored by Clairol, a manufacturer of hair-care products. Even Republican Richard Nixon, who won the 1968 presidential election, praised Black Power, since he, like the conservative business daily the *Wall Street Journal*, connected Black Power to black economic self-sufficiency.

Nixon was not the only symbol of the white mainstream who embraced black capitalism. A number of corporations promoted a black managerial class and supported black capitalism: Xerox sponsored the TV series "Of Black America"; Chrysler put a little money in a black-owned bank; and the lumber and paper products giant Crown Zellerbach set up subsidiaries run by black management.

Companies that to date had viewed blacks as no more than consumers even modified their lending policies in the years between 1968 and 1970. Prudential, the large life insurance conglomerate, made more than $85 million in loans to blacks in urban communities, after much of the property it owned and insured in Newark, New Jersey, was destroyed after the 1967 rebellion. Throughout 1968 and 1969, Nixon and other white conservatives supported black economic advancement as an alternative to rebellion or revolution. They believed if people had a real stake in society they would be less inclined to seek its overthrow.

In 1968 and 1969 the federal government and many average citizens openly worried about the overthrow of the government. Many saw chaos and feared true anarchy. College campuses, especially, were sites of antiwar demonstrations, calls for changes in curriculum, attempts to ban the Reserve Officers Training Corps (ROTC, a military training program), and other actions. Campuses became a cauldron of black protest, too. In the years 1968–69, fifty-seven percent of all campus protests involved black students. This level reflects both the growing numbers of black students on campuses and the increasing numbers who ended up at predominantly white colleges. Between 1964 and 1970, the number of black college students nearly doubled, from 234,000 to half a million, while the percentage attending black colleges dropped from fifty-one to thirty-four percent.

Black students often faced attacks from some white students who were uncomfortable with their increasing numbers on previously nearly all-white campuses; they found the campus environment hostile, given their small numbers, isolation from other students, discrimination by various student groups, and lack of African-American faculty and administrators; and they judged their classes as lacking relevance to their own lives.

Out of this atmosphere emerged the black studies movement. On campuses nationwide, Black Student Unions (BSUs) were formed to advocate further social and curricular changes, especially the introduction of black studies programs. Of course, scholars at many of these institutions and at historically black colleges have taught some aspects of African-American history or studies, but no department committed to developing a broad curriculum based on the lives of African peoples had ever been established. Students took the initiative, first forming political and cultural organizations such as the Afro-American Students Association at Berkeley and Merritt College in Oakland, California, and the Black Student Congress at Columbia University in New York. As early as 1967 students at Howard University called for the creation of a concentrated program in the study of African Americans.

Black students at Cornell University in 1969 launched their own effort to force substantial curricular changes. Since 1967, scores of colleges and universities, both black- and white-dominated, had to address the demands of blacks. In fact, between 1960 and 1969, the scene of the sit-in shifted from the lunch counter to the university president's office. Protests visited campuses as varied as the University of Massachusetts, Duke, Harvard, Columbia, Yale, Simmons College, and Antioch.

At Cornell, a particularly dramatic episode transfixed the nation. Through the mid-sixties Cornell had had a dismal record of attracting and graduating African-American students. But beginning around mid-decade the school began in earnest to recruit blacks. Once there, however, the black students complained of overtly racist acts and general alienation. They also sought to institute a black studies department. After a series of incidents, including the tossing of a burning cross into a dormitory, tensions reached a critical phase, and black students took over part of the student union during Parents Week in April. Fearing more violence, especially given their small numbers (only two hundred and fifty of the more than ten thousand students on campus were black), a few black students managed to smuggle guns into the union. After long negotiations, which ultimately led to Cornell's first black studies program, the students filed out peacefully and ended the standoff. When the incident ended without loss of life, the country recalled only the image of gun-toting black students. What many outside commentators failed to realize was that students wanted more than freedom by 1969; they wanted liberation, and they were willing to fight for their demands, educational or otherwise.

The link between liberation and education was not confined to the university. By 1968 the struggle for Black Power in education had reached down to public schools in many locales. More and more community activists began demanding control over local schools. Black parents and teachers objected to a curriculum that excluded Third World cultural perspectives. They objected, too, to the tracking of their children into remedial and special education classrooms, which they considered just another form of segregation; and they objected to the failure to funnel blacks and Latinos into college preparatory classes. More than anything, they objected to the fact that they had so little control over what their children learned.

For some blacks, the fight to transform education was merely a small part of a larger revolutionary movement. Organizations sprang up during this period that sought to transform the whole country, to eliminate all forms of inequality and racial discrimination. Perhaps the best-known of the radical black organizations was the Black Panther party (BPP). Although it is often identified as a proponent of Black Power, the BPP was essentially a Marxist organization. Embracing the ideology of the nineteenth-century German political philosopher Karl Marx, BPP members believed that the poor and oppressed peoples of the world would eventually mount a revolution to overthrow capitalism.

Calling itself the Black Panther Party for Self-Defense, it was founded in October 1966 in Oakland, California. The group was led by Huey P. Newton and Bobby Seale, former student activists at Merritt College in Oakland. At its founding, the party issued a ten-point program calling for, among other things, full employment, decent housing, relevant education, black exemption from military service, an end to police brutality, freedom for all black prisoners, and trials with juries of their peers. Seeing themselves as part of a global liberation movement, the Panthers also spoke of the black community as a colony inside the United States.

A 1968 Black Panther rally in New York. Carrying guns and wearing their trademark berets, the Panthers believed blacks should arm themselves against police brutality. Over the next few years, shoot-outs with police officers and FBI agents were frequent.

Yet, unlike many other black or interracial radical groups of their day, they never advocated secession or the creation of a separate state. Instead, they preferred interracial coalitions when possible. They joined forces with the predominantly white Peace and Freedom party (a third party of socialists and peace activists) and developed strong ties with Students for a Democratic Society (SDS).

In alliance with the Peace and Freedom party, the Black Panther party put up candidates in both the national and California state elections of 1968. The coalition's presidential candidate was Eldridge Cleaver, an ex-prisoner who wrote the best-selling book *Soul on Ice* (1968). He had joined the party in February 1967. As a writer and speaker, Cleaver emerged as the main spokesperson for the Panthers after Bobby Seale was arrested for armed invasion of the State Assembly chamber in Sacramento and Newton was jailed for allegedly shooting an Oakland police officer. The charges against Newton were eventually dropped, but only after a long national campaign to free him.

The Black Panthers felt that armed struggle was the only way to defend the black community from police repression. By carrying loaded firearms in public (which was legal in California at the time), the Panthers drew a great deal of attention from the media and wrath from the police and FBI. Perhaps because of their notoriety, their ranks grew; by 1970 Panther chapters had taken root in nineteen states and in more than thirty cities, and eventually in England, Israel, and France.

A deft combination of style and substance accounted for the party's popularity. Early BPP members looked sharp in their all-black outfits of jeans, shirt, beret, and sunglasses. They affected a politics of style, making themselves look daring, mysterious, dangerous, and powerful. But style alone would fail, they quickly realized. As a result, the Panthers sponsored several community-based initiatives in most cities in the country, including clothing drives, a community day-care center, a Panther school, and a free breakfast program. Their free breakfast program provided meals to two hundred thousand children daily. Most amazingly, they proved that grassroots movements could make a difference, even when the U.S. government vowed to eliminate the organization by any means necessary.

Federal law enforcement officers, especially the FBI, targeted a growing list of black-run organizations in the late sixties. Since the mid-sixties the agency had spied on Martin Luther King, Jr., Malcolm X, and other notable black leaders. By 1968 spying had come to include an active policy of group infiltration, in which FBI informants posed as members of radical or militant organizations. Local and federal police began a crackdown. In 1969, for example, police arrested 348 Panthers for a range of offenses, among them murder, rape, robbery, and assault.

The FBI and local police declared war on the Panthers. In 1968 alone, at least eight Black Panthers were killed by police in Los Angeles, Oakland, and Seattle. And the during the following year, two Chicago Panther leaders, Mark Clark and Fred Hampton, were killed in their sleep during an early morning police raid. The violence and constant surveillance by the FBI reflected the position of FBI Director J. Edgar Hoover: The only good Panther was a dead Panther. Without question, the FBI helped destroy the Black Panther party.

Yet it was much more difficult to snuff out all who were swayed by the appeal of Black Power. In Detroit, for example, radical Black Power ideology influenced one of the most militant labor movements in the country. Eventually calling themselves the League of Revolutionary Black Workers (LRBW), the group was founded by several young black auto workers, many of whom worked at Detroit's Dodge Main Plant. Led by activists such as Luke Tripp, General Baker, John Watson, Mike Hamlin, and Ken Cockrel, they were a unique bunch. All had been students at Wayne State University and had worked together in a black nationalist organization called Uhuru (Swahili for "Freedom"). Uhuru had been loosely associated with RAM—the same organization from which several founding members of the Black Panther party came.

Two events spurred the creation of the league. The first was the Detroit riots of 1967, which revealed the degree of unrest, poverty, and police brutality in the "Motor City." The Detroit chapter of the NAACP was flooded with complaints about police treatment of African Americans. Even black police officers were subjected to brutality.

The second event was more immediate: On May 2, 1968, General Baker and several other black militants in the Dodge Main Plant led a walkout of four thousand workers, the first in that factory in fourteen years and the first organized and led entirely by black workers. The strike was over a speedup of the assembly line, which in the previous week had increased from forty-nine to fifty-eight cars per hour. Out of this strike emerged the Dodge Revolutionary Union Movement (DRUM). It was the first of several Revolutionary Union Movements (RUMs) that popped up at auto plants in and around Detroit, and which subsequently led to the formation of the League of Revolutionary Black Workers.

DRUM's specific demands—safer workplaces, lower production demands, an end to racist hiring practices—echoed past grievances. Of course they wanted to win better working conditions and wages for black workers, but their ultimate goal was freedom for all workers, and that meant, in their view, the end of capitalism. DRUM members knew that racism limited the ability of workers to unite, and that white workers, as well as black workers, were hurt by this. But they also argued that white workers benefited from racism in the form of higher wages, cleaner and safer jobs, and greater union representation.

Not everyone in the league agreed as to the best way to achieve Black Power and workers' power. One group, led by General Baker, believed the movement should focus on shop-floor struggles, while Watson, Hamlin, and Cockrel felt that the league needed to organize black communities beyond the factories. Thus, the latter got together and organized the Black Economic Development Conference (BEDC) in the spring of 1969. At the urging of former SNCC leader James Forman, who had recently arrived in Detroit, the league became heavily involved in the planning and running of the conference.

Out of BEDC came Forman's proposal for a Black Manifesto, which demanded, among other things, $500 million in reparations from white churches and synagogues to be used to purchase land in the South, fund black publishing companies, a research skills center, a black Southern university, and a national black labor strike fund. The work in BEDC took the league leadership, of which Forman was now a part, away from its local emphasis. Their efforts led to the founding of the Black Workers Congress (BWC) in 1970. The BWC called for workers' control over the economy and the state to be brought about through cooperatives, neighborhood centers, student organizations, and ultimately a revolutionary party. And they demanded better wages and working conditions for all workers.

Meanwhile, the league's local base began to disintegrate. Dodge had fired several league activists, including General Baker. The General Policy Statement of the league, which based everything on the need for vibrant DRUM-type organizations, seemed to have fallen by the wayside. Divisions between the leadership groups were so entrenched that no one could cooperate any more.

Influenced by events on the factory floor and in the universities, writers laid claim to their own interpretations of Black Power. Starting with John Oliver Killen's 1954 novel *Youngblood,* and increasing in frequency by the mid-sixties, black writers debated whether there was something distinctive about black culture, something that made it different from "white" or European-American culture. The debate had less to do with whether black writers would write about black life—

they had been doing so since the days of the first slave narratives in the United States—and more to do with a universal definition of a black aesthetic. In the midst of the debates and disagreements that ensued, some sense of a general consensus did emerge. Black was not only powerful, it was beautiful. And it was up to black people to express and celebrate both the power and the beauty.

Thus, the political revolution in black America was accompanied by a profound cultural revolution. A new generation of artists created literature, art, and music that celebrated black people and promoted rebellion against racism and poverty throughout the world. They encouraged African Americans to celebrate their African heritage and to embrace their blackness not as a mark of shame but as a symbol of beauty.

To understand this revolution, however, we need to go back to the fifties, when Africans declared war on European colonialism and began to win their independence. Inspired by Africa's example, jazz pianist Randy Weston recorded the album *Uhuru Afrika* (1960); drummer Max Roach brought together African and African-American musicians to produce *We Insist: Freedom Now Suite* (1960); and the brilliant saxophonist John Coltrane recorded songs such as "Dahomey Dance" (1961), "Africa" (1961), and "Liberia" (1964). African Americans even began to emulate African styles or create new styles that, in their mind, represented African culture. During the early sixties a number of black women artists, most notably the folk singer Odetta, the jazz vocalist Abbey Lincoln, and the exiled South African singer Miriam Makeba, styled their hair in medium to short Afros. They refused to straighten their hair and instead allowed it to grow naturally.

All of these independent cultural developments emerging out of the late fifties and early sixties began to coalesce into a full-blown movement just when America's cities began to explode. In 1965, following the assassination of Malcolm X, the poet and playwright Leroi Jones and several other black writers, namely Larry Neal, Clarence Reed, and Askia Muhammad Toure, founded the Black Arts Repertory Theater School (BART) in an old brownstone building on 130th Street in Harlem. With meager support from federal War on Poverty programs, they held classes for Harlem residents and launched a summer arts and culture program that brought music, drama, and the visual arts to the community virtually every day of the week.

Like many artists of his generation, Leroi Jones could not ignore the black freedom movement in his midst. Before founding BART, he was the senior member of the downtown New York literary scene. Born to a working-class family in Newark, New Jersey, Jones attended Howard University (a historically black college), served briefly in the Air Force, and ended up a struggling writer in New York's Greenwich Village. After the success of his first book of poetry, *Preface to a Twenty Volume Suicide Note* (1961), his first book of prose, *Blues People: Negro Music in White America* (1963), and his first play, *Dutchman* (1964), he no longer had to struggle. Indeed *Dutchman*, a surreal encounter between an educated black man and a white woman who, as a symbolic representative of the racist state, taunts the man and eventually kills him, earned him many awards and accolades. After *Dutchman,* Jones could have pursued a lucrative career as a writer but chose instead to use his artistic insights to build a political movement.

In 1966, a year after founding BART, Jones moved back to his hometown of Newark, started a similar institution called Spirit House, and changed his name to Imamu Amiri Baraka. Although Spirit House also sponsored community arts programs, it developed a more explicit political orientation after Newark's ghettos exploded in 1967. In the aftermath of the riots, Spirit House held a Black Power conference that attracted several national black leaders, including Stokely Carmichael, H. Rap Brown, Huey P. Newton of the Black Panther party, and Imari Obadele of the newly formed Republic of New Africa (a black nationalist organization that demanded land on which African Americans could settle and form an independent nation, and was partly an outgrowth of RAM). Shortly thereafter, Spirit House became the base for the Committee for a Unified Newark (CFUN). In addition to attracting black nationalists, Black Muslims, and even a few Marxists, CFUN bore the mark of Maulana Karenga's US Organization.

Karenga, originally a West Coast leader of RAM, insisted that the crisis facing black America was first and foremost a cultural crisis. He envisioned "US" as a movement of cultural reconstruction, creating a new synthesis between traditional African culture and African-American culture. Drawing on African religions, philosophies, and ideas about family and kin relations, US attempted to create a political movement rooted in communal ties between people of African descent rather than competition or individualism. Although tensions arose between Karenga and some of the Newark activists over his treatment of women and the overly centralized leadership structure CFUN had imported from the US Organization, the movement continued to grow.

In this setting, the search for artistic expression became known as the Black Arts Movement. In addition to Baraka, other leading lights included poets Nikki Giovanni, Don L. Lee (Haki Madhubuti), Jayne Cortez, and Sonia Sanchez; playwrights Ed Bullins, Ben Caldwell, and Jimmy Garrett, to name a few. Although openly critical of whites and brutally critical of blacks who seemed to go along with a system of white supremacy, the members of the Black Arts Movement were important for the innovations they introduced in literary form. Determined to bring poetry and prose to the people, they experimented with freer forms and drew heavily on jazz rhythms and the everyday vernacular language of black folk. They often turned the hip, cool phrases of black youth into hot, angry declarations of war against American racism and exploitation.

While literary artists made an appeal for the hearts and souls of the black majority, it was musicians who achieved mass appeal in the late sixties, a time of intense experimentation and political expression. Some of them, such as James

Brown (known as the "godfather of soul") and poet/singer Gil Scott-Heron, adopted a Black Power stance more clearly than others. Within jazz circles, artists such as saxo phonists Ornette Coleman, John Coltrane, Albert Ayler, and Archie Shepp, pianists Cecil Taylor and Sun Ra, and many others, lauded a new sound, variously known as "free jazz," "the new thing," the "jazz avant-garde," or the "new black music." Detractors, on the other hand, called the music "anti-jazz" or "nihilism." Essentially, the new jazz musicians began playing free form, breaking out of traditional harmonies, rhythms, and song structures. Inspired by music from Africa and Asia, they often improvised freely over a single musical phrase. Furthermore, many of these musicians identified with the black arts movement; Ayler, Shepp, Sun Ra, and others performed frequently at BART, and the jazz avant-garde even had its own publications calling for the creation of revolutionary music. The key journal at the time was called the *Gracle: Improvised Music in Transition.* In the *Gracle,* black musicians debated the music's relationship to the movement, thought about ways to fuse music and literature, and discussed the importance of political education for black artists.

Although the jazz avant-garde sought to establish direct ties to black communities, its music never achieved the popularity of "soul" music. The creators of soul consciously searched for black roots; their products reflected gospel's major influence. Aretha Franklin's early music, for example, was characterized by gospel-style piano playing.

A product of mid- to late-sixties transformations, soul was also much more political than rock and roll. Its themes have to do with more than equality; they deal with conditions in the urban North such as poverty, the powerlessness of black folk, and drug use. The titles tell the story: James Carr's "Freedom Train," the Chi-Lites' "Give More Power to the People," and Tony Clarke's "Ghetto Man."

Still, there was no single ideology of Black Power in soul music. Singers Curtis Mayfield and James Brown simultaneously promoted reform of the system and acceptance into it. While recording songs promoting black pride like "Say it Loud, I'm Black and I'm Proud," and "Soul Brother No. 1," Brown also came out with the patriotic assimilationist tune "America is My Home." After King was assassinated and riots began erupting, Brown went on national television to urge blacks to go back home. He even came out in support of the conservative and sometimes openly racist President Richard Nixon, mainly because of Nixon's advocacy of black capitalism as a way of achieving racial equality.

The Temptations and Marvin Gaye were also politically conscious, but unlike Mayfield, whose songs were of hope and possibility, theirs were songs of pessimism: Gaye's "Inner City Blues" and "What's Goin' On?" and the Temptations' "Message from a Black Man," "Cloud Nine," and "Ball of Confusion." In the last, before the chorus, "Ball of Confusion, that's what the world is today," we hear a baritone voice sing-ing "And the band plays on," signaling business-as-usual politics, indifference, and apathy. The "band" is symbolically drowning out the noise of poverty and resistance. The irony of this world as described by the Temptations is captured in the line "The only safe place to live is on an Indian reservation."

As millions of black Americans tuned in to the sounds of soul and jazz, they also tuned in to the dramatic television broadcast from the 1968 Mexico City Olympics. What happened there represented the most international expression of Black Power. To call attention to racism in sports here and abroad, former San Jose State basketball and track and field star Harry Edwards formed the Olympic Project for Human Rights. Its intent was to organize an international boycott of the 1968 games.

Edwards hoped to draw attention both to the treatment of black athletes as well as to the general condition of black people throughout the world. As he put it, "What value is it to a black man to win a medal if he returns to the hell of Harlem?" Specifically, he and others sought to ban athletes from South Africa and Southern Rhodesia (both at the time were white-dominated African countries that segregated and exploited the African population) from the Olympics, the appointment of a black member to the U.S. Olympic Committee, appointment of an additional black coach on the U.S. team, the desegregation of the New York Athletic Club, and the removal of the International Olympic Committee's president, Avery Brundage. Among other things, Brundage was quoted as saying he would sell his exclusive Santa Barbara, California, country club membership before admitting "niggers and kikes" as members.

Instead of boycotting the Olympics, however, black athletes decided to use the event as a way to draw attention to racism and the black struggle. They agreed to wear black armbands and developed strategies to protest during the victory ceremonies. The most famous demonstration involved track stars Tommie Smith and John Carlos, who mounted the awards platform wearing knee-length black socks, no shoes, and a black glove on one hand (Smith also wore a black scarf around his neck). When the band played the U.S. national anthem, they bowed their heads and raised their gloved fists toward the sky in the Black Power salute. In an interview with sportscaster Howard Cosell, the pair explained that the closed-fisted salute symbolized black power and unity; the socks with no shoes represented the poverty most black people must endure; and Smith's scarf symbolized black pride. They bowed their heads in memory of fallen warriors in the black liberation movement, notably Malcolm X and Martin Luther King, Jr.

Although their actions did not harm anyone or incite violence, the U.S. Olympic Committee decided to suspend Smith and Carlos from the games and strip them of their medals for being overtly political. Angered by the decision, many of their fellow black athletes continued to protest. The three U.S. medalists who swept the 400-meter dash wore black berets on the victory stand, as did the 1600-meter relay team (which also broke the world record). Bob Beamon and Ralph Boston, medal winners in the long jump, wore black socks without shoes to protest both the condition of black people and the treatment of their teammates. And Wyomia Tyus, anchor in the women's four-hundred-meter relay team, dedicated her gold medal to Carlos and Smith.

The political stance of black athletes in Mexico City combined with other examples of forceful advocacy of Black Power to provoke fear and a backlash. By 1969, after passage of the Civil Rights Act of 1964, the Voting Rights Act of 1965, and the Fair Housing Act of 1968, many white Americans began to ask: What more does the Negro want? Dissatisfied with the responses they heard to that question, more and more whites found their own answers in the politics of rage endorsed first by George Wallace and then by Richard Nixon.

George Wallace had surfaced as a national political force in the early sixties, after he made a highly publicized effort to block the desegregation of the University of Alabama. He had been active in Alabama politics since before the start of the Second World War. Steeped in the traditions of Alabama and the South, he held views on race that were neither enlightened nor particularly regressive. Each race had its own genius and place in the life of country, he asserted at the time. To him this was less a disputable fact than merely an obvious truth.

He held fast to that view through the Alabama gubernatorial campaign of his mentor "Big Jim" Folsom in the mid-fifties. With the *Brown* v. *Board of Education* decision fresh in people's minds, with Montgomery roiling from the effects of the bus boycott and news of similar boycotts forming across the region, Wallace staked out a new political image. It was an image that distanced him from his mentor, ensured his own selection as governor of Alabama in 1962, and forever solidified his reputation as the embodiment of Southern obstruction of black rights.

But it was Wallace the presidential candidate rather than Wallace the governor who attracted more attention. George Wallace's ascendancy as a legitimate third-party candidate in 1968 signaled a clear backlash. He openly courted whites who felt disenfranchised by governmental policy. For his efforts he won five Southern states in 1968 and between eight and fifteen percent of the vote in more than a dozen Northern and Western states. Before an assassin's bullet nearly killed him in 1972, Wallace had received nearly as many popular votes in the Democratic presidential primaries as George McGovern, the Democratic party's eventual candidate. Wallace's most important influence, however, may have been inspiring the Republican party to adopt a strategy that catered to white fears of social equality for blacks.

Richard Nixon quickly moved into the political space Wallace had created. Aided by the conservative push in his own party, the electoral appeal of law and order themes in 1968, and his own realization that Republicans could use race as an issue to drive Southern whites into their party, he outlined a plan for what became the Republican party's Southern strategy. Heading into the spring of 1968, polls showed Nixon tying either Robert F. Kennedy or Hubert H. Humphrey, the two leading contenders for the Democratic nomination. Kennedy's assassination left Humphrey, the old liberal now too closely aligned with Lyndon Johnson's failed social and military policies. Nixon won the election in part due to his ability to channel a racial backlash. This backlash came just as black Americans intensified their demands for social, economic, and political action.

Despite backlash politics and the rising tide of racism, this was also the moment Black Power in some ways entered the realm of electoral politics. Nearly a generation after a new wave of black migrants moved into urban areas, during what became known as the Second Great Migration, their numbers had grown sufficiently—and whites had fled city centers in large enough numbers—to give blacks electoral majorities, or at the very least working margins. This change in the racial makeup of cities improved the likelihood that African Americans could gain a stronger political foothold in major urban centers. In some cases, they were successful. The mayoral victories of Carl Stokes in Cleveland and Richard Hatcher in Gary, Indiana, in 1967 raised black hopes that electoral politics might offer real opportunities, at least at the municipal level. However, despite a growing black electorate in the nation's cities, African Americans held few really important political offices.

During the early seventies, for example, black elected officials tended to hold low-level city and county jobs, especially in law enforcement, on school boards, and on some city councils. Most of these black elected officials were in the South. The lack of more significant black political representation in big Northern cities where African Americans made up forty to fifty percent of the population was particularly striking. To pave the way for participation at higher levels of city government, black political leaders worked hard on devising strategies to win local elections.

When the clock ticked off the last minute of 1969 and African Americans took stock of the last few years, they thought not only about the changes they had witnessed but also about the ones they still hoped to see. They knew they were the caretakers of King's dream of living in a nation where character was more important than color. And they knew they had to take charge of their community. After all, the civil rights and Black Power eras had forged change through community action. Although many blacks may have sensed that all progress was tempered by the social, economic, and political realities of a government and a white public often resistant to change, they could not ignore the power of their own past actions. America in 1969 was not the America of 1960 or 1965. At the end of the decade, a chorus could be heard rising from the black community proclaiming, "We changed the world."

## CHAPTER 5

# Into the Fire

## 1970 to the Present

*Robin D. G. Kelley*

Anyone strolling through the black ghettos of Chicago, Newark, or Los Angeles in 1973 probably noticed posters advertising Oscar Williams's new film, *Five on the Black Hand Side,* pasted along the sides of temporary plywood walls or on abandoned buildings. You could tell by the poster's cartoon illustrations that this was a comedy. In the center is a conservatively dressed black businessman surrounded by dozens of crazy-looking people: Some are protesting, some are fighting, some are simply enjoying each other's company. Even though the characters in the poster are decked out in bell bottoms, platform shoes, and serious Afro puffs, this film is not another action-packed ghetto drama about pimps, hipsters, and black crime-fighters, like the ever-popular *Superfly* or *Shaft.* Instead it is a comedy about the trials and tribulations of the black middle class. Challenging the more common films about hustlers and ghetto violence, the text of the poster summons us all to the theater: "You've been coffy-tized, blacula-rized and super-flied—but now you're gonna be glorified, unified and filled-with-pride ... when you see *Five On the Black Hand Side.*"

The poster, like the film itself, marked a transition taking place in black political attitudes. During the early to mid-seventies, there was a little less talk of revolution and more emphasis on winning local elections. The push for black pride and black unity we often associate with the "sixties generation" did not die, however. On the contrary, the ideas of the Black Power movement reached its apex in the seventies. Black was in. Afros and African garments were not only in style but had become even more popular among ordinary African Americans. The slogan "Black is Beautiful" lingered well after the decline of Black Power. Militant black nationalist organizations, such as the Black Panther party, the Republic of New Afrika, and the Black Liberation Front, continued to gain local support in urban neighborhoods for their advocacy of armed self-defense, black control over political and economic institutions, and efforts to build black pride and self-esteem. Yet, with legal segregation finally gone, thanks to the Civil Rights movement, upward-

One of the goals of Oscar Williams's *Five on the Black Hand Side* was to explore the trials and tribulations of the black middle-class—a subject most black action films, such as *Shaft* and *Superfly*, avoided.

ly mobile black families headed for the suburbs, and many working-class parents believed their children would enjoy a better life than they had.

The vast majority of African Americans who could not afford the luxury of sub-urban life were left behind in America's overcrowded ghettoes. But if leaving was not an option, fighting back certainly was. The first year of the new decade, 1970, was marked by violence, militant campaigns, racial tensions, and new movements demanding social justice. Urban rebellions and police-community violence continued to be a source of tension in several cities, including Philadelphia; New Orleans; New Bedford, Massachusetts; and Hartford, Connecticut. The issue of school desegregation was hardly settled, particularly after court-ordered busing was proposed as a solution to integrate public schools. Throughout the country, white opponents of school integration frequently turned to violence to defend all-white schools. In September 1970, the Black Panther party and activists from the women's and gay liberation movements organized the Revolutionary People's Constitutional Convention, which attracted some six thousand people to the city of Philadelphia with the goal of rewriting the U.S. Constitution.

In spite of these events, few black activists and perhaps fewer inner-city residents believed change was inevitable or that the government was on their side. The person African Americans overwhelmingly voted *against* in the 1968 presidential election, the conservative Republican Richard M. Nixon, was now in the White House. Nixon attacked welfare mothers, blamed the black poor for their own poverty, and tried to link the social movements of the sixties to criminals and drug addicts. Nixon's conservative agenda was a far cry from the Civil Rights movement's vision of a country without poverty or race hatred, a view noticed and articulated by the man whom Nixon replaced in the White House, Lyndon Baines Johnson.

Yet Nixon was surprised when he failed to attract black votes during his reelection campaign in 1972. After all, he had appointed a handful of African Americans to mid-level federal posts, and he even called himself a supporter of Black Power when he proposed reducing welfare in favor of grants and tax cuts for black-owned businesses. Despite these measures, very few African Americans trusted Nixon. His cabinet was openly less concerned about racism than the Johnson administration had been. Indeed his domestic advisor, Daniel P. Moynihan, passed on a confidential memo proposing "the time may have come when the issue of race could benefit from a period of 'benign neglect.'" Moynihan felt that enough progress had been made and there was no need to actively combat racial inequities. More important, Nixon and his advisers understood that the Republicans' success came in part because of their attacks on radical social movements, such as the Black Panthers, and on liberal policies, such as Johnson's War on Poverty.

A large segment of the white middle class believed that African Americans, especially the poor, received too many government handouts, and they were tired of "paying the bill." They believed that African Americans had nothing to complain about because, in their view at least, racism no longer existed. They were tired of the Vietnam War and felt besieged by the constant protests by hippies, ghetto residents, feminists, and welfare rights activists. Fearing that ghetto rebellions would spill into their suburbs and that too much of their taxes was going to support welfare, the overwhelming white vote for Nixon partly reflected an anti-black backlash.

One of Nixon's campaign promises was to get rid of "troublemakers," especially militant black nationalist organizations like the Republic of New Afrika, the National Committee to Combat Fascism, the Black Liberation Front, and the Black Panther party—whom FBI director J. Edgar Hoover once called "the greatest threat to the internal security of this country." During the Nixon years, the FBI and local police forces intensified their efforts to squelch dissent of any kind. And it did not matter if their tactics were legal or not. In Chicago, for example, local police not only raided the headquarters and homes of black activists frequently but they also kept files on prominent outspoken African Americans, including future presidential candidate the Reverend Jesse Jackson. At the time, Jackson led Operation PUSH (People United to Save Humanity), a fairly mainstream grassroots organization that sought to help African Americans get off welfare, find jobs, and motivate poor children to stay in school.

Jailings, beatings, and constant surveillance conducted by local police and the FBI were part and parcel of what most political movements during this era had to contend with.

One very important case centered around the Reverend Benjamin Chavis, a young black minister of the United Church of Christ who would eventually serve a brief stint as executive director of the National Association for the Advancement of Colored People. It all began when Chavis tried to organize a nonviolent campaign in Wilmington, North Carolina, to improve education for African-American children. The campaign was still in its early stages when, in February 1971, a white-owned store was burned in the midst of the campaign. Chavis, along with eight black student leaders and one white woman activist, was charged and convicted of arson and conspiracy. Altogether, their combined sentences totaled 282 years; the twenty-four-year-old Chavis received 34 of those years. Human rights activists from around the world questioned the convictions from the very beginning. Not only was there no solid evidence against them, but it was revealed that at least one jurist was a member of the Ku Klux Klan. Even Amnesty International, a worldwide organization dedicated to monitoring human rights abuses, called Benjamin Chavis and his fellow inmates "political prisoners." They quickly became known as the Wilmington Ten.

Despite many appeals, the Wilmington Ten remained in prison throughout most of the decade. Then, in 1977, one of the key witnesses for the state admitted that he had been pressured into lying on the stand. Another witness said he was given a job at a local service station and a minibike in exchange for testimony that would lead to a conviction. Yet, in spite of these new developments in the case, the judge would not reverse the decision. He insisted that the defendants' constitutional rights had not been violated. Yet because of increasingly negative publicity surrounding the case, the governor of North Carolina persuaded prison administrators to parole Chavis in 1979. A year later, the U.S. Court of Appeals overturned the original decision, ruling that the Wilmington Ten had been denied a fair trial.

Many African Americans and movement sympathizers believed that federal, state, and local governments arrested activists on false charges in order to stop them from protesting and organizing. While this may seem to contradict American ideals of freedom, the release of secret files of the FBI's Counter Intelligence Program (COINTELPRO) and the voluminous files local police departments kept on suspected dissidents revealed that some activists were indeed jailed and harassed because of their politics. The FBI devoted much of its energies to collecting information on "radical" organizations. Under COINTELPRO, FBI agents also used fake press releases to spread false rumors about social activists; hired undercover agents to commit crimes in the name of the more militant Black Power movements; violently attacked competing organizations; and created an atmosphere of tension, confusion, and division within the organizations under surveillance. COINTELPRO was finally disbanded in 1972 after the death of J. Edgar Hoover. A congressional investigation of the program not only revealed that Hoover had kept tabs on many prominent African Americans—including political leaders Martin Luther King, Jr., Roy Wilkins, and Whitney Young; athletes Muhammad Ali, Joe Louis, Jesse Owens, and Jackie Robinson; and cultural figures such as Lena Horne, Paul Robeson, and James Baldwin—but that President Nixon himself used the FBI to attack his enemies and wage war against alleged dissidents.

Clearly the most celebrated "political prisoner" of the early seventies was Angela Davis. "Free Angela" posters, buttons, and T-shirts became as much a part of the changing urban landscape as liquor stores and "soul food" restaurants. Tall, lean, with a raised fist and an Afro, a flashing smile, and an aura of confidence, Angela Davis offered the African-American community a striking image to rally around. To her many supporters—young and old, male and female—she was a young, beautiful, militant intellectual boldly challenging "the system."

Born and raised in Birmingham, Alabama, Angela Davis was the daughter of schoolteacher and early civil rights activist Sallye Davis. The oldest of three children, Angela Davis lived a fairly comfortable life in some respects, but segregation and racial tensions also made for a very dangerous environment. Two of her friends were killed in a church bombing in September 1963. The bombing was orchestrated by white supremacists retaliating for the civil rights demonstrations in Birmingham. And as a very young child, she lived in a neighborhood where black-owned homes were firebombed so frequently that it was nicknamed "dynamite hill." The bombings were the work of white residents attempting to keep black families out of that section of Birmingham.

Anxious to leave Birmingham (or "Bombingham" as black residents began calling it), Davis moved to New York City when she was fifteen to attend Elisabeth Irwin High School, a renowned experimental private school in Greenwich Village. She went on to Brandeis University, the Sorbonne in Paris, and Goethe University in Frankfurt; in 1967 she moved to California to work toward a Ph.D. in philosophy. Always concerned about the plight of African Americans, she soon became active in the Student Nonviolent Coordinating Committee.

As a SNCC activist, Davis saw both the possibilities and limitations of the organization. She not only encountered sexist attitudes on the part of several male leaders, but she realized that SNCC and other Black Power organizations did not have an adequate explanation for why people remained poor. Insisting that the "free market" exploits workers by paying them poorly and making them dependent on the marketplace and wages to survive, she regarded the capitalist economy as the source of many social ills. Many of her ideas were based on the writings of Karl Marx and Frederick Engels, two nineteenth-century German radical thinkers whom Davis was introduced to in high school. Reading Marx and Engels'

*Communist Manifesto* (1848) as a teenager changed her life. "Like an expert surgeon," she wrote in her autobiography,

> this document cut away cataracts from my eyes.... What had seemed a personal hatred of me, an inexplicable refusal of Southern whites to confront their own emotions, and a stubborn willingness of Blacks to acquiesce, became the inevitable consequence of a ruthless system which kept itself alive and well by encouraging spite, competition and the oppression of one group by another. Profit was the word: the cold and constant motive for the behavior, the contempt and the despair I had seen.

Although there are different varieties of Marxism, adherents generally argue that all wealth is created by labor. Capitalists, or the owners of businesses, are able to exploit labor by denying workers access to other sources of income through the private ownership of land and factories. Thus workers have no choice but to work for wages to survive, a condition which breeds conflict and resentment between those who own wealth and those who do not. Marxists believe that this conflict between workers and owners is a fundamental aspect of capitalist society. To resolve it, they advocate replacing capitalism with "socialism"—a system whereby working people, in theory, share the fruits of their labor. The land and factories would not be owned by private individuals but by the people who work them. The goal of labor would not be to enrich the few but to improve the quality of life for all. Quality education and health care would not be things one would pay for individually but would be paid for by and available to all members of society. Of course, there have been attempts to create such a system in places like China and the former Soviet Union, but in these countries it never worked in practice the way it was imagined to work in theory. Nevertheless, in the minds of many Marxists and liberals who sympathized with the Marxist point of view, the failure of socialism in other countries did not diminish the fact that capitalism made some people's lives miserable while making a handful of people very wealthy.

As a Marxist, Davis was convinced that the building of a new socialist society would go a long way toward creating the kind of equality many labor, student, and civil rights activists dreamed of. Thus in 1969 she made the fateful decision to join the Communist party of the United States (CPUSA), longtime advocates of socialism whose origins go back to 1919. That same year the University of California at Los Angeles hired her to teach philosophy. However, once her party membership became public knowledge, the California Board of Regents and Governor Ronald Reagan fired her, citing a state law that banned communists from teaching at state universities.

Davis and the many who rallied to her defense were undoubtedly upset over her dismissal. She challenged the decision in court, arguing on the basis of the First Amendment that she had the right to freedom of expression. The jury and judge agreed; the law was overturned and the regents were forced to reinstate her.

Nevertheless, they eventually succeeded in forcing her out of the University of California system by censuring Davis for her political activism and closely monitoring her classes. Losing her job did not keep her from organizing. She became actively involved with the Black Panther party and worked with radical black prisoners—most notably George Jackson.

George Jackson had been an inmate at Soledad prison in California for nearly a decade when he first came into contact with Davis. After spending the first fourteen years of his life in a Chicago ghetto, in 1957 he moved with his family to South Central Los Angeles, where he fell in with neighborhood gangs. He was constantly in trouble with the law; he was arrested several times as a juvenile for theft, burglary, and robbery. At age fifteen he was sentenced to eight months at a California Youth Authority camp—a state-run juvenile detention center. He escaped twice from the camp, once fleeing to Illinois, where he was involved in a knifing and subsequently returned to California in chains. Paroled after sixteen months, Jackson continued to pursue a life of crime. In February 1961 he was arrested for being an accessory to armed robbery of a gas station in Bakersfield, California. Because no one was hurt and only seventy dollars was taken, the public defender persuaded Jackson to plead guilty in exchange for a light sentence. To his surprise, the judge sentenced him to "one year to life." He was nineteen years old.

Jackson was initially sentenced to San Quentin, where he gained a reputation as one of the meanest, toughest inmates in the prison yard. He participated in prison gangs, received disciplinary action at least forty-seven times for assaulting guards, and was feared by most of his fellow inmates. But by the fifth or sixth year of his sentence, Jackson began to undergo a dramatic change. He began reading books he had never read in school, and he eventually linked up with the Black Panther party. In his quest to understand why so many of his fellow inmates were black men, why so many were driven to steal, Jackson studied the writings of revolutionary leaders from across the globe and read broadly in the fields of history, sociology, and politics. He came to the conclusion that racism, the economy, and the government's covert efforts to put a lid on black rebellion were the main reasons for the rise in African-American prisoners. In one sense, he argued, virtually all of the inmates were "political prisoners":

> There are still some blacks here who consider themselves criminals—but not many. Believe me, my friend, with the time and incentive that these brothers have to read, study, and think, you will find no class or category more aware, more embittered, desperate, or dedicated to the ultimate remedy—revolution. . . . They live like there was no tomorrow.

By the late sixties, Jackson emerged as one of Soledad's most outspoken radicals. He introduced fellow prisoners to a variety of radical ideas, including Marxism and black nationalism. Influenced by the various protest movements erupting outside prison walls, Jackson and a few of his fellow convicts set out to "transform the black criminal mentality into a black revolutionary mentality." Quickly, prison authorities identified him as a serious threat when he attempted to organize the inmates to fight for better conditions.

In 1969, the activities and plight of George Jackson became nationally known after he and two fellow inmates, Fleeta Drumgo and John Clutchette, were accused of murdering a prison guard. Since the state had very little evidence against the three men, most of their supporters believed they were being framed for political reasons. Jackson, Drumgo, and Clutchette were well known in Soledad for their political activism. Once the case went public, they became known as the Soledad Brothers. Throughout the country, student activists, black militants, and people concerned about prisoners' rights organized demonstrations demanding the release of the Soledad Brothers. Donations for their legal defense came from all over the country. Leading publications, including the *New York Times Magazine,* carried articles about Jackson and the others. Within a few months, they were celebrities. Their most vocal defenders included actress Jane Fonda, child psychiatrist Benjamin Spock, and poet Allen Ginsberg.

The Soledad Brothers' most dedicated advocate turned out to be George Jackson's younger brother Jonathan, also a close acquaintance of Angela Davis's. On August 7, 1970, the younger Jackson, barely seventeen years old, somehow smuggled several guns into the Marin County (California) Courthouse during the trial of James McClain, another black Soledad prisoner accused of stabbing a guard. After watching the proceedings from the audience for a while, Jonathan Jackson rose to his feet, drew a sawed-off shotgun from under his coat and announced, "All right, gentlemen. I'm taking over now." He then passed the other guns he had concealed to McClain and Ruchell Magee, a Soledad inmate who had been brought to trial as a witness to the stabbing. They took the judge, the deputy district attorney, and three jurors hostage in a van parked outside. As they left the courthouse, according to one witness, McClain shouted, "Free or Release the Soledad Brothers by twelve thirty or they all die!" The police and San Quentin guards in the area responded promptly. Remaining true to their "no hostage" policy, the guards opened fire on the van as it pulled off. When the smoke cleared Jonathan, along with two prisoners and the judge, lay dead. (Soon after the Soledad Brothers were acquitted of murder, prison guards killed George Jackson during an alleged escape attempt. The guards claimed Jackson had hidden a gun in his Afro.)

Young Jonathan Jackson's actions directly affected Angela Davis. The guns he used were hers—firearms he had taken without permission. Because Davis owned the guns and because she was a noted radical activist in California, the FBI issued a warrant for her arrest and placed her on its "Ten Most Wanted" list. Following her capture, an international campaign demanding her release was born. Even the celebrated soul singer Aretha Franklin offered to pay her bail: "I'm going to set Angela free . . . not because I believe in communism but because she's a Black woman who wants freedom for all Black people." After spending eighteen months in jail, she was finally released in February 1972 on $102,000 bail. She was eventually acquitted of all charges.

The decade of the seventies, therefore, was hardly the end of a militant era. The violent repression and jailings of black radicals no doubt transformed the movements they led, sometimes making leaders ineffective, other times turning them into martyrs. New debates and new circumstances compelled African-American activists to think about politics in new ways. African-American women activists began to chart their own course, creating a dynamic black feminist movement that challenged male-dominated black nationalism and white-dominated women's rights organizations. Moreover, black elected officials joined community activists and artists to develop a new approach to the ballot.

## "It's Nation Time!": From Black Feminism to Black Caucus

Black community activist Margaret Wright was tired of being told by male leaders in the Black Power movement that black women oppressed black men, that black women were domineering, that successful black women stripped black men of their manhood. "Black women aren't oppressing them," she announced in a 1970 interview. "We're helping them get their liberation. It's the white man who's oppressing, not us. All we ever did was scrub floors so they could get their little selves together!" The very idea that black women kept black men down made her even more angry when she thought about the role most black women had to play in the Civil Rights and black liberation movements. "We run errands, lick stamps, mail letters, and do the door-to-door. But when it comes to the speaker's platform, it's all men up there blowing their souls, you dig."

Margaret Wright knew the truth. Black women, in general, were not only more exploited and oppressed than black men but they were often oppressed *by* black men. As an activist in the Los Angeles–based group Women Against Repression, she confronted issues ranging from wife battering to inequities in household chores. Most black women not only worked for wages but were responsible for child care, cooking, and cleaning. And when it came to participating in political movements, black women were often shunted aside or told that the struggle for liberation is "a man's job." While she acknowledged that black men and white women were also oppressed, she wanted both groups to understand how they unintentionally contributed to the exploitation of black women:

> Black women have been doubly oppressed. On the job, we're low women on the totem pole. White women have their problems. They're interviewed for secretarial instead of the executive thing. But we're interviewed for mopping floors and stuff like that. Sometimes we have to take what's left over in Miss

Ann's refrigerator. This is all exploitation. And when we get home from work, the old man is wondering why his greens aren't cooked on time.

Margaret Wright voiced the opinions of a growing number of African-American women, some of whom joined forces with the feminist movement that had reemerged in the sixties. While there was no single definition of feminism, most feminists agreed that male domination—in the family and the government—pushed women into an inferior status in society. They argued that women were paid less for the same job, underrepresented in positions of power and authority, and expected to take responsibility for housework and other domestic duties, not because they were less able than men, but because they were discriminated against.

Even the culture women lived in contributed to their subordination. Women were portrayed as passive and weak or as sex objects for male pleasure. Feminists did not merely want to take men's places in positions of power, to substitute male dominance with female dominance; they fought to replace male domination with a more just, equitable society.

Ironically, this new wave of black feminism was partly a response to male chauvinism within the Civil Rights, Black Power, and student movements of the period. Many cultural nationalists—activists who believed that black people in the United States should adopt traditional African cultures—emphasized that women ought to remain in "their place." One pamphlet distributed by a nationalist organization in Newark laid out, in no uncertain terms, what men and women's roles should be: "It is only reasonable that the man be the head of the house because he is able to defend and protect the development of his home.... Women cannot do the same things as men—they are made by nature to function differently. Equality of men and women is something that cannot happen even in the abstract world." Of course, not all male advocates of black nationalism were hopelessly sexist; on the contrary, some opposed statements such as these. Moreover, not all black women active in nationalist movements agreed with this sort of logic. Women frequently challenged such remarks. Nevertheless, the overall tenor of the Black Power movement emphasized the struggle for power, equality, and rights as a struggle for "manhood."

Concerned about the rising tide of black male sexism and chauvinism, many African-American women active in political and social movements spoke out. Toni Cade Bambara, a writer and activist who edited an important anthology in 1970 titled *The Black Woman,* wrote: "We rap about being correct but ignore the danger of having one of our population regard the other with such condescension and perhaps fear that that half finds it necessary to 'reclaim his manhood' by denying her her peoplehood." Some African-American women were drawn to mainstream feminist organizations, such as the National Organization for Women (NOW), or small radical feminist groups such as the Redstockings and WITCH. However, during the early to mid-seventies, most black feminists avoided the predominantly white women's movement. Several leading white feminists, including Susan Brownmiller, Jo Freeman, and Kathie Sarachild, had cut their political teeth in the civil rights struggles of the early to mid-sixties and compared the oppression of women with the oppression of African Americans. But many black feminists found their white counterparts unaware of the importance of race and racism, and some resented the way white women equated their plight with black people. When white women appealed to sisterhood, African-American women were quick to point out that historically their relations with one another had been as domestic servants (or other employees) to employers. More important, most black women activists did not separate their fight for women's rights from issues affecting the entire black community. The majority of black feminists did not believe, as many of their white counterparts did, that all men were the enemy.

In 1973 several African-American women's groups were founded, the most important of which was the National Black Feminist Organization (NBFO). The first NBFO conference was held in New York City and was attended by approximately four hundred African-American women. The atmosphere was electric; no one attending the conference had ever witnessed such a large gathering of black women speaking about issues that directly affected them. It became clear from the speeches that the NBFO's emphasis would be on combating sexist and racist discrimination against black women and struggling for greater involvement in the political process. Many journalists and activists took special note of the diversity of participants—black women from all walks of life, from domestic workers to lawyers, welfare rights organizers to polished elected officials. Although the different backgrounds of these women enriched the discussion from the floor, it also created tensions. After its first year, black women active in the welfare rights movements began to feel that the NBFO sidestepped the problems of poor women, and many African-American lesbians criticized the NBFO for ignoring homophobia and for speaking only to issues affecting heterosexual women. Partly in response to the NBFO's shortcomings, new black women's groups were formed to address issues that the NBFO did not choose to address, such as homophobia and the replacement of capitalism with socialism.

Despite such differences, black politics in the seventies—as in the sixties—emphasized unity above all else. With unity came strength, black political leaders argued, and with strength came real power. Nowhere was the potential for real power more evident than in electoral politics. After the Voting Rights Act of 1965 was passed, and organizations like SNCC waged massive voter-registration campaigns, the ballot seemed to be an increasingly powerful weapon. Changes in the racial makeup of cities, in particular, improved chances for African Americans to gain a stronger political foothold in major urban centers.

With the formation of the Congressional Black Caucus (CBC) in 1971, a group of black members of Congress committed themselves to working jointly in the interests of African Americans. The origins of the CBC go back to 1969, when

Congressman Charles Diggs of Detroit led a committee of nine black representatives to oppose President Nixon's policies. The CBC initially worked for reforms in job training, health care, welfare and social services, and other areas of social policy that directly affected African-American communities. It also tried to fashion a national strategy to increase black political representation. The formation of the CBC attracted a wide range of political activists, including cultural nationalists such as Imamu Amiri Baraka, the popular playwright and poet whose Newark, New Jersey–based movement, New Ark, had just played a key role in electing that city's first black mayor in 1970. Like many other progressives, Baraka believed that the CBC and black voters could pressure the Democratic party into becoming more accountable to black people. For Baraka and other radical supporters of the CBC, however, the ultimate goal was not to have more influence over the Democratic party. Rather, they wanted to build an independent black political movement.

The idea of a national black political campaign generated a lot of excitement among black artists as well as among elected officials and community activists. Although black writers, musicians, and visual artists had a long tradition of linking politics and art, the generation of black artists that emerged in the sixties and seventies set a new standard for their direct political involvement and community activism. Poets such as Baraka, Don L. Lee (Haki Madhubuti), Mari Evans, Kalamu ya Salaam, and Sonia Sanchez were among the leading voices calling for a coordinated black political movement. Thus, prompted by Baraka and Richard Hatcher, mayor of Gary, Indiana, several African-American political leaders organized a national convention to create a black agenda and to discuss possible strategies for gaining greater black political power. The idea proved enormously popular, and throughout the fall and winter of 1971, grassroots political movements elected delegates, people raised money for transportation, and political activists passed out leaflets informing local communities about the event.

In March 1972, some eight thousand African Americans (three thousand of whom were official delegates) arrived in Gary, Indiana, to attend the first convention of the National Black Political Assembly, which was more commonly known as the "Gary Convention." The roll call, the tall floor signs identifying each state's delegates, the constant calls to order were much like the Democratic or Republican conventions we see on television. But the comparison stopped there; at Gary all the faces were black and many were working class. And this sea of eight thousand black faces was chanting, "It's Nation Time! It's Nation Time!" No one in that room had ever seen anything like this before.

The feeling among the delegates that it was, indeed, "Nation Time" captures the political sensibilities dominating the convention. The radical black nationalists clearly won the day; moderates who supported integration and backed the Democratic party were in the minority. Most of the delegates—at least the most vocal ones—agreed that African-American communities faced a social and economic crisis, and that nothing short of fundamental changes in the political and economic system could bring an end to this crisis. As the famous Gary Declaration put it:

> A Black political convention, indeed all truly Black politics, must begin from this truth: *The American system does not work for the masses of our people, and it cannot be made to work without radical, fundamental changes.* (Indeed, this system does not really work in favor of the humanity of anyone in America.) . . .
>
> The challenge is thrown to us here in Gary. *It is the challenge to consolidate and organize our own Black role as the vanguard in the struggle for a new society.* To accept that challenge is to move to independent Black politics. There can be no equivocation on that issue. History leaves us no other choice. White politics has not and cannot bring the changes we need.

The convention's agenda included a bill that would expand voter registration and provisions to ensure community control over such institutions as police, government, and city services.

To arrive at such a radical document was not easy. From the very outset local issues clashed with efforts to create a national agenda, and delegates representing different outlooks had trouble compromising. Indeed, part of the Michigan delegation walked out of the convention to protest the separatist tone of the resolutions. Most elected officials also believed the delegates had gone too far: Resolutions were passed calling for the creation of independent black schools and opposing court-ordered busing. And, as politicians active in the Democratic party, they strongly rejected the pledge to create an independent black political party.

Gary was an amazing example of democracy at work. Most mainstream political leaders and elected officials did not expect such a radical agenda to come out of this convention. But the three thousand official delegates and the additional five thousand in the audience believed they had a voice, a right to express their thoughts on black liberation.

Unfortunately, the vision created in Gary was soon abandoned. First, grassroots activists committed to the Gary Declaration did not have national visibility. Black elected officials and leaders who did have that visibility were concerned with being reelected or losing white allies. Therefore, most black elected officials did not dare echo Gary's call for revolutionary changes in American society. Besides, many black politicians felt betrayed by the convention. They dismissed the delegates for being insensitive to and ignorant of the kind of "hard-nosed" negotiations black elected officials must participate in. Real politics, they argued, involved compromising and coalition building, not demands for revolutionary change.

By the time the 1972 presidential election campaign was well under way, the historic Gary Convention seemed to be but a faint echo in the world of electoral politics. Most black politicians scrambled to endorse white Democrats, either Hubert

Shirley Chisholm thanks her supporters after her failed bid for the Presidency during the 1972 Democratic National Convention in Miami.

Humphrey or George McGovern, for the presidential nomination. Others, like Floyd McKissick, a Black Power proponent and head of the Congress of Racial Equality, joined fellow CORE leaders and endorsed Republican Richard Nixon. In particular, Nixon's support for black business and his advocacy of self-help appealed to CORE leaders, whose politics had grown increasingly conservative. Meanwhile, amid the backroom negotiating and political deals being made between white men and black men, an African-American congresswoman from New York stepped to the fore and sought the Democratic party's nomination for president. Shirley Chisholm's bid for president surprised everyone. She certainly did not develop a reputation as a radical outside the political process. Indeed, she joined those who abandoned the original goals of the National Black Political Assembly, and in fact felt betrayed by parts of the Gary Declaration. And yet, she was not your typical politician. Born Shirley St. Hill in Brooklyn in 1924 and raised by working-class Barbadian parents, Chisholm earned a bachelor's degree from Brooklyn College and an M.A. in early childhood education from Columbia University. After several frustrating years as an active member of the Democratic party in the Bedford-Stuyvesant section of Brooklyn, in 1968 she ran against former CORE leader James Farmer (who by then had joined the Republican party) for a newly created congressional seat representing Brooklyn. She soundly beat Farmer, becoming the first black woman elected to the House of Representatives. Her active support for equal rights, affirmative action policies, and women's liberation attracted the attention of both women's organizations and civil rights advocates. She turned out to be among the most outspoken feminists in Congress, serving as an active member of the National Organization for Women, a founder of the National Women's Political Caucus, and member of the National Abortion Rights Action League. In a memorable speech delivered at the Conference on Women's

Employment organized by the Congressional Committee on Education and Labor, Chisholm called on women to "rebel."

> Women in this country must become revolutionaries. We must refuse to accept the old, the traditional roles and stereotypes. . . . We must replace the old, negative thoughts about our femininity with positive thoughts and positive action affirming it, and more. But we must also remember that we will be breaking with tradition, and so we must prepare ourselves educationally, economically, and psychologically in order that we will be able to accept and bear with the sanctions that society will immediately impose upon us.

When Chisholm made her bid for the presidency in 1972, she was poised, experienced, and knowledgeable about issues affecting African Americans and women. And she earned supporters. On the first ballot she garnered over 150 votes at the Democratic National Convention. But, to her surprise and disappointment, very few white women's organizations, black male politicians, or black organizations led by men came out in support of her candidacy. Chisholm was disillusioned by black male politicians who refused to take her campaign seriously precisely because she was a woman. The only major black political organization to endorse her candidacy was the Black Panther party, which by then had a substantial number of women in leadership positions.

Chisholm lost the nomination to George McGovern, who was then summarily crushed in the 1972 election. Nixon's popularity had soared, especially among white working- and middle-class voters. After all, he promised to be tough on crime and extra hard on dissidents. Ironically, Nixon's own administration harbored a number of crooks, and the president himself seemed to be the ringleader. Less than a year after his reelection a Senate investigation revealed that Nixon directed or had knowledge about a whole litany of crimes against political rivals, including the June 1972 break-in at the campaign headquarters of the Democratic National Committee. On August 9, 1974, just before the House of Representatives was to vote on impeachment, Nixon resigned. The Watergate affair ended in the first resignation of a president in U.S. history, the imprisonment of twenty-five Nixon aides, and a crisis in American politics.

Watergate was a serious blow to the rising hopes that many African Americans had placed in electoral politics. For others it confirmed what they already believed: The white-dominated political system was corrupt and completely bankrupt. A few activists tried to resurrect the political spirit of the Gary Convention by continuing to support a path independent of the Democrats and Republicans. But the very idea of an independent black political party, which had inspired the Gary Convention in the first place, was no longer a goal. Indeed, it would be another four years before a national black independent political party was formed. The National Black Political Assembly drew only one thousand delegates to its third national convention in 1976. One year later, its membership had shrunk to a paltry three hundred. Political apathy and cynicism was also evident in the declining number of African Americans willing to vote. The percentage of voting-age blacks who actually went to the polls dropped from 52.1 percent in 1972 to 49 percent in 1976.

By the time the United States geared up for its bicentennial celebration in 1976, African Americans had reason to look upon the democratic process with mixed feelings. They had certainly made progress in the electoral sphere. In 1969, 994 black men and 131 black women held public office nationwide; by 1975 the number of black elected officials grew to 2,973 men and 530 women. Black politicians won mayoral races in several major cities, including Los Angeles, Atlanta, New Orleans, Philadelphia, and Washington, D.C. By 1974, more than two hundred African Americans served as state legislators, and seventeen sat in Congress— including four women: Shirley Chisholm, Cardiss Collins of Illinois, Barbara Jordan of Texas, and Yvonne Brathwaite Burke of California. For all the pessimism surrounding presidential races, municipal victories were greeted with optimism.

These were victories for black politics, for sure, but bittersweet ones. Once the victory parties were over, many residents still had a difficult time obtaining city services, affordable housing, or improved schools. In some cases, local politicians consciously tied their fate to big business. Some black citizens began to question whether having an African American in city hall even made a difference. But most black mayors really wanted to help the communities that put them into office. What they had not counted on was a reduction in federal spending on cities, white and black middle-class flight to the suburbs, a rapid growth in urban poverty and unemployment, and one of the most severe economic recessions in U.S. history.

## Inner-City Blues: Urban Poverty in the Seventies

North Lawndale was once a thriving Chicago community made up of European immigrants and U.S.-born whites and blacks. A community of working-class neighborhoods, North Lawndale before 1970 was home to people who worked for International Harvester, Western Electric, Sears Roebuck, Zenith, Sunbeam, or any one of several other factories and retail outlets in the area. By 1980, most of these firms had closed up shop, leaving empty lots and burned-out buildings in their wake. The dominant retail outlets by the early eighties were bars and liquor stores. In less than a generation, North Lawndale's economy had evaporated, leaving fifty-eight percent of its able-bodied workers unemployed and half of its population on welfare. As jobs disappeared, so did most of the white and black middle-class residents. Once a thriving industrial hub, North Lawndale became one of the poorest black ghettos in Chicago.

The story of North Lawndale was repeated in almost every major city in the United States after 1970. What are the reasons for such economic devastation? Why has the collapse of the urban economy had such a profound impact on African Americans? To answer these questions, we need to first acknowledge that the economies under the free enterprise system have always had their ups and downs. Sometimes manufacturers produce more than the market can absorb, which not only results in lower prices but leads many companies to fire excess workers. Other times new technology intended to make production faster and more efficient leads to layoffs or reduced wages because new machinery often requires workers with less skill. These and other worldwide economic conditions have caused the U.S. economy to swing between economic surges and periods of economic recessions or outright depressions. And in virtually every case of recession, African-American workers were the "last hired and first fired."

But by the mid-seventies, parts of the U.S. economy appeared to be in a permanent crisis. Ironically, just as programs were being implemented to correct racial imbalances in the workplace, and laws barring discrimination in hiring were being enforced a little more vigorously than before, much of the manufacturing part of the economy began a downward cycle from which it never seemed to recover. Even if protection for black workers improved slightly, changes in the global economy created massive unemployment and led to an expansion of poverty among African Americans not seen since the Great Depression of the thirties.

A series of events and policies during the early seventies contributed to the decline of the U.S. economy, especially its heavy industry—steelmaking and the manufacture of automobiles, tires, textiles, and machines of various kinds. In 1973, the Organization of Petroleum Exporting Countries (OPEC), an alliance of mostly Arab oil-producing countries that joined together in 1960 to reduce competition and set higher oil prices, declared an embargo on oil shipments to the United States and Western Europe to protest Israel's war with its Arab neighbors. Because the United States had become dependent on foreign oil supplies, the embargo had a devastating impact on the economy, making it difficult for individual consumers and big business to obtain inexpensive fuels. Plants shut down in large numbers. In 1974 alone, sales and manufacturing of American automobiles declined drastically, unemployment nearly doubled, and inflation more than doubled. Over the next ten years the economy never really recovered; the value of imported manufactured goods from places like Japan and Western Europe grew from less than fourteen percent of the U.S. domestic economy in 1970 to almost forty percent in 1979, while at the same time inflation sharply increased. With increased inflation came a steady loss in the standard of living for all Americans.

President Nixon tried to control inflation, but his policies actually made matters worse, especially for the poor. First, in August 1971 he temporarily froze wages, prices, and rents. But because prices and rents were already high, those earning low wages found themselves in the same situation as before. Second, Nixon placed a tariff on Japanese-made cars. This was intended to reduce competition between Japanese auto manufacturers and American manufacturers, but all it did was increase the price of otherwise affordable Japanese economy cars. American-made cars, for the most part, were still rather expensive and tended to use more gas than foreign cars. And in an economy in which oil prices were rising faster than just about any other item, cars that required less gas continued to be popular in the United States.

In spite of Nixon's measures, inflation continued to rise rapidly and low wages and growing unemployment made it impossible for large numbers of consumers to buy American products, no matter how much the government tried to protect the market with tariffs. Moreover, massive military spending exacerbated the country's economic woes. It dramatically increased the national debt and redirected much-needed investment away from roads, schools, and industries unrelated to the military buildup. Just months before President Nixon signed a peace agreement withdrawing U.S. troops from Vietnam, the national deficit had grown to $40 billion.

President Gerald Ford continued Nixon's economic policies, and when Democrat Jimmy Carter took over the presidency in 1976, the situation for African Americans improved only slightly. He appointed Patricia Harris, an African-American woman, as Secretary of Housing and Urban Development, and Andrew Young, a black veteran of the Civil Rights movement, as ambassador to the United Nations. The Carter administration did little to lessen unemployment, and the jobless rate for African Americans increased during his first two years in office. Like the Republican presidents before him, Carter gave corporations a big tax cut, reduced financial aid to black colleges and universities, provided minuscule support for the nation's declining cities, and slashed federal spending for social programs—notably welfare, free lunch programs for children, and health services. He even backpedaled on his promise to reduce defense spending: The military budget for 1978 reached $111.8 billion, the highest level in U.S. history up to that point.

The creation of multinational corporations in the post–Second World War era was the most important change in the new global economy. These multinational corporations no longer had a stake in staying in a particular country or region. Instead, they moved their firms wherever labor and taxes were cheaper, pollution laws were less stringent, and labor unions were either weak or nonexistent. Some manufacturers moved from the Midwest and Northeast to the Southern United States in search of cheaper labor with weaker unions, although the South hardly experienced an economic boom during the seventies. The more common trend was for big companies to set up shop in countries like Mexico, Brazil, and South Africa, leaving in their wake empty American factories and huge numbers of unemployed workers. By 1979, for example, ninety-four percent of the profits of the Ford Motor Company and sixty-three percent of the profits from Coca-Cola came from overseas operations. Between 1973 and 1980, at least four million U.S. jobs were lost when firms moved their operations to foreign countries. And during the decade of the seventies, at least thirty-two million jobs were lost as a result of shutdowns, relocations, and scaling-back operations.

The decline of manufacturing jobs in steel, rubber, auto, and other heavy industries had a devastating impact on black workers. Although black joblessness had been about twice that of whites since the end of the Second World War, black unemployment rates increased even more rapidly, especially after 1971. During these economic downturns, white unemployment tended to be temporary, with a

A city employee on strike outside a San Francisco cable car barn in 1970. During the 1970s, many blacks looked to labor unions to protect their rights and advance their interests.

higher percentage of white workers returning to work. For blacks, layoffs were often permanent. While the number of unemployed white workers declined by 562,000 between 1975 and 1980, the number of black unemployed *increased* by 200,000 during this period—the widest unemployment gap between blacks and whites since the government started keeping such statistics.

The loss of well-paying industrial jobs affected not only African Americans but the entire working class. Some workers looked to labor unions affiliated with the AFL-CIO to battle factory closures and wage reductions. At the height of the recession in the seventies, however, most labor unions were on the defensive, fighting desperately to hold on to the gains they had made a decade earlier. To make matters worse, many black industrial workers felt that white labor leaders were not very responsive to their needs. These leaders did not actively promote African Americans to leadership positions within the unions. In 1982, for example, the AFL-CIO's thirty-five member Executive Council had only two black members, a figure that fell far short of representing actual black membership. Indeed, African Americans tended to have higher rates of participation than whites in union activities: By 1983, more than twenty-seven percent of black workers were union members, compared to about nineteen percent of white workers.

Politically, the AFL-CIO leadership took stands that openly went against the interests of the majority of black workers. In 1972 George Meany supported

Nixon's bid for the presidency, which was interpreted by black rank-and-file members as a clear sign that the AFL-CIO was deserting African Americans. In response, a group of black trade union activists formed the Coalition of Black Trade Unionists (CBTU) in 1972. Under the leadership of veteran labor organizer William Lucy, secretary-treasurer of the American Federation of State, County, and Municipal Employees (AFSCME), the CBTU not only condemned the Nixon administration for what it felt were racist policies but also attacked AFL-CIO President George Meany for endorsing Nixon. The CBTU also issued a statement critical of union leaders who did not actively oppose discrimination and support minority and rank-and-file efforts to have a greater voice in the affairs of the union.

The loss of manufacturing positions was accompanied by an expansion of low-wage service jobs. The more common service jobs included retail clerks, janitors, maids, data processors, security guards, waitresses, and cooks—jobs with little or no union representation. Not everyone who was laid off in the seventies and eighties got these kinds of jobs, and those who did experienced substantial reductions in their income. Many of these new service jobs paid much less than manufacturing jobs. They tended to be part-time and offered very little in the way of health or retirement benefits.

Black men and women who were laid off from auto plants and steel mills in the Midwest and South suddenly found themselves working at fast-food and sanitation jobs to make ends meet. Young people entering the job market for the first time quickly discovered that the opportunities their parents once had were fading quickly. Many African-American youths without the option to go to college chose the military as an alternative to low-wage service work. As the United States pulled out of Vietnam, the military became one of the biggest employers of African Americans: The percentage of blacks in the armed forces rose from eighteen percent in 1972 to thirty-three percent in 1979.

These dramatic changes in the economy meant greater poverty for African Americans. One of the most striking features of the seventies was the widening income gap between blacks and whites. At the beginning of the decade, African Americans in the northeastern United States made about seventy-one cents for every dollar whites made; by 1979 that ratio dropped to fifty-eight cents. In 1978, 30.6 percent of black families earned income below the official poverty line, compared with 8.7 percent of white families.

Black women and children were the hardest hit by the economic crisis. Hemmed in by limited job opportunities, more and more working-class black women found themselves having to raise children without the benefit of a spouse to help pay the bills or participate in child care. The number of black homes without male wage earners rose from twenty-two percent in 1960 to thirty-five percent in 1975. Since black women, especially those in their teens and twenties, were the lowest paid and had the highest unemployment rate, it is not an accident that black single-mother households headed the list of families below the poverty line. In 1969, fifty-four percent of all black families below the poverty line were headed by women; in 1974 this figure rose to sixty-seven percent.

Several politicians and academics blame the rising number of "female-headed households" for the decline of inner cities and the rise of black crime and violence. This crisis of the black family, they argue, is new and unprecedented. They insist that the inability of single mothers to control and discipline their children, combined with the lack of male role models, has led to a whole generation of out-of-control youth. But a lot of these claims are based on misinformation. First of all, single-mother families are not a uniquely "black" crisis; between 1970 and 1987 the birth rate for white unwed mothers rose by seventy-seven percent. Second, out-of-wedlock births are not entirely new to African-American communities. Studies have shown that at least since the days of slavery black women are more likely than white women to bear children outside of marriage and to marry at later ages, after becoming mothers. Part of the reason has to do with the fact that black families have tended not to ostracize women for out-of-wedlock births.

Why have the number of female-headed households grown, and what impact has it had on the social and economic fabric of black communities? First, the declining number of employed black men has contributed to the growth of single-parent households. Aside from a rapid increase in permanently unemployed black men who suddenly cannot support their families as they had in the past, black men have a higher chance of dying young than any other male population in the United States. They are more often victims of occupational accidents, fatal diseases, and homicides than other men. And throughout the seventies and eighties, the black male prison population increased threefold; by 1989, twenty-three percent of black males ages twenty to twenty-nine, or almost one out of every four, were either behind bars or on legal probation or parole. Another important factor is that African Americans have a higher divorce and separation rate than whites. High unemployment for black males certainly contributes to marital instability among poor families, but welfare policies also play a major role. In at least twenty-five states, two-parent families are ineligible for Aid to Families with Dependent Children (AFDC), and in many cases black men have to leave the household in order for the women and children to have access to welfare and Medicaid.

Although single-parent families (including those run by males) tended to suffer more than two-parent families because they lacked a second wage earner, the structure of the family was not the *cause* of poverty. Most of these households were poor not because the women were unmarried but because of the lack of employment opportunities for women, lower levels of education, and the gross inequality in wages as a result of race and sex discrimination. One study shows, for example, that while seventy-five percent of unemployed black women heading families were poor in 1977, only twenty-seven percent of employed black women heading families were poor. Besides, the vast majority of women who ended up as single parents were poor *before* they had children or experienced divorce, separation, or the death of their husband.

Finally, single-parent families are not always the product of economic deprivation. Oftentimes they reflect the efforts of black women to escape abusive situations and to raise their children in a more supportive environment. As Barbara Omolade, an African-American scholar and activist, explained it: "My children and other children of black single mothers are better people because they do not have to live in families where violence, sexual abuse, and emotional estrangement are the daily, hidden reality.... In a society where men are taught to dominate and women to follow, we all have a lot to overcome in learning to build relationships, with each other and with our children, based on love and justice. For many black single mothers, this is what the struggle is about."

Because many families headed by single women are poor, they frequently must turn to welfare to survive. The amount of financial support available to welfare recipients in most states barely allows families to make ends meet. In a recent study of welfare in the eighties, for example, one researcher met a divorced mother of two whose combined cash aid and food stamps amounted to a mere twelve dollars per day. "This is probably about the lowest point in my life," she admitted, "and I hope I never reach it again. Because this is where you're just up against a wall. You can't make a move. You can't buy anything that you want for your home. You can't go on vacation. You can't take a weekend off and go see things because it costs too much." The stigma attached to welfare made matters worse. Using food stamps often brought stares and whispers of disgust from clerks and consumers standing by.

The majority of single black mothers who received welfare during the eighties, however, did so for an average of only six months, and most had to supplement aid with odd jobs in order to make ends meet. Besides, not all poor African Americans received public assistance, nor were they the primary beneficiaries of welfare. In 1991, sixty-one percent of all people on welfare were white. Blacks, by comparison, made up only thirty-three percent of welfare recipients. And many who did qualify for some form of public assistance did not always receive it. A 1979 study revealed that seventy percent of all unemployed blacks never received any unemployment benefits; more than half of all poor black households received no AFDC or General Assistance; half of all black welfare households received no Medicaid coverage; and fifty-eight percent of all poor black households received benefits from only one or two of the seven income programs available to assist the poor. There are many reasons why a substantial number of poor people did not receive full benefits. In some cases, the lengthy application process discouraged applicants; in other instances, computer errors, misplaced files, or unsympathetic or ill-informed case workers were to blame. But in many cases, black men and women living below the poverty line were simply too proud to accept welfare.

## Living the Dream? The Black Middle Class

To the residents of Philadelphia, July 1976 must have felt like the hottest month in that city's history. Throngs of people from all over the country and throughout the world invaded the "City of Brotherly Love" to celebrate the 200th birthday of the Declaration of Independence. Waving overpriced flags and wearing red, white, and blue outfits, they came to examine the famous crack in the Liberty Bell and see firsthand the document that announced the beginning of this country's democratic journey.

In the neighborhoods just north, west, and south of the celebrations, a growing number of jobless and working-poor African Americans were fighting to survive. While the patriotic celebrations of the moment cast a shadow over Philadelphia's dark ghettos, hiding much of the recent devastation that would characterize the next two decades, a group of African-American leaders was trying to get the bicentennial committee to acknowledge the black presence in the past two hundred years of history. The fact that the majority of Africans in America were still slaves when the Declaration of Independence was signed made many bicentennial organizers uncomfortable. Instead, they tried to integrate the celebrations by highlighting black achievement in business, politics, the arts and entertainment, sciences, and education.

By emphasizing black achievement and paying less attention to the crumbling ghettos in earshot of the Liberty Bell, the organizers of the bicentennial were not being entirely dishonest. Just as the majority of African Americans experienced immense poverty, segregation, violence, and rising racism, some black professionals and entrepreneurs were reaping the fruits of integration. Of course, there had always been middle- and upper-class blacks, but in the past they succeeded in a segregated economy, lived in segregated neighborhoods, and had to operate in an atmosphere of outright racial discrimination. Although discrimination did not disappear entirely, the civil rights struggles of the previous two decades helped usher in affirmative action programs that gave minorities and women preference in hiring and college admission to compensate for past and present discrimination.

"We were all . . . children of the civil rights movement: the nation had changed its laws and, in some respects, its ways during our childhoods and adolescences. We were living the opportunities for which generations of black folk had fought and died. Walking paths wet with the blood of our martyrs, we felt an uneasy fear that taking advantage of those opportunities was changing us."

These words were written in 1991 by Yale law professor and best-selling author Stephen L. Carter. Carter exemplifies what it meant for a generation of young people to live the American Dream. A graduate of Yale Law School, Carter turned out to be a gifted legal scholar and talented writer. In another era, a black person of his considerable talents might not have had the chance to attend Yale or to accept a major professorship at his alma mater. But affirmative action policies and an aggressive recruitment effort to attract African Americans to the school opened doors for him that had been closed to previous generations. He is clearly one of those who "made it." Between his salaries, royalties on his book sales, and fees for speaking engagements, Professor Carter makes more than enough money to live a comfortable middle- or upper-middle-class existence.

And yet, Carter is somewhat ambivalent about how his success and the particular road he had to take to achieve it has changed him and other black professionals. Everywhere he turned, his white colleagues hinted that he did not make it on his own merit; that every college and every law firm opened doors to him because he was black, not because he was good. Some days he believed this argument. Other days he felt enraged that so many of his colleagues viewed him as the representative of a race rather than as an individual. Occasionally he convinced himself that his success was entirely the result of his own initiative and hard work. Indeed, there were moments when Carter believed that the old racial barriers of the past had been completely destroyed. But just when life seemed good, the handsomely attired and articulate scholar would be reminded of his race. "When in New York, for example, if I am traveling with a white person, I frequently swallow my pride and allow my companion to summon the taxi as I hang back—for to stand up for my rights and raise the arm myself would buy only a tired arm and no ride. For a black male, blue jeans in New York are a guarantee of ill-treatment. There are the jewelry-store buzzers that will not ring, the counter clerks who will not say 'Sir,' the men's departments with no staff to be found."

Carter's mixed feelings about his success are characteristic of a rapidly expanding class of black urban and suburban professionals who came of age during the fifties and sixties. Their numbers increased substantially during the seventies. In 1970, 15.7 percent of black families had incomes over thirty-five thousand dollars; by 1986 the percentage had grown to 21.2 percent. Likewise, black families earning more than fifty thousand dollars almost doubled, increasing from 4.7 percent in 1970 to 8.8 percent in 1986. And like Carter, their rapid success can be partially attributed to antidiscrimination laws and affirmative action programs first established in the sixties and expanded under President Jimmy Carter during the mid- to late seventies.

The roots of recent affirmative action policies can be traced to the Civil Rights Act of 1964 and the establishment of the Equal Employment Opportunity Commission (EEOC) and the Office of Federal Contract Compliance (OFCC). Both of these agencies were created to monitor employment discrimination and enforce the law. Unfortunately, the staff at the EEOC and the OFCC was small relative to the number of cases it received each year.

While lack of personnel within these institutions has led to a huge backlog of cases and limited their effectiveness, the EEOC, especially, has put pressure on firms to hire more women and minorities. For example, in 1973 the EEOC successfully sued the U.S. Steel Corporation for failing to promote black workers at its Fairfield, Alabama, plant. The court ordered U.S. Steel to expand job opportunities for its African-American workers. The EEOC discovered blatant incidents of white workers with less seniority being promoted to better jobs—mainly skilled machinist, clerical, technical, and managerial occupations. The court ruling required equal hiring of black and white apprentices and black and white clerical and technical employees until African Americans held about a quarter of these jobs.

Soon thereafter, the Detroit Edison Company was fined $4 million in punitive damages for discriminating against African-American employees, and a Detroit union local of the Utility Workers of America (UWA) was slapped with a $250,000 fine. The suit was initiated by a group of black Detroit Edison workers after the UWA and the International Brotherhood of Electrical Workers refused to file their grievance for them. Their primary complaint was that Detroit Edison employed very few black workers, turned down a large number of qualified black applicants, and kept blacks in the lowest-paid jobs. The judge in the case ordered the company to increase the proportion of black employees from eight percent to thirty percent and to set hiring guidelines that would ultimately place more black workers in higher-paying jobs with more authority.

Affirmative action policies were also responsible for briefly increasing black enrollment at major colleges and universities starting in the late sixties. Black enrollment rates rose from twenty-seven percent in 1972 to thirty-four percent in 1976, before dropping steadily during the next decade. Many leading black scholars and corporate leaders who came of age in the fifties and sixties benefited from affirmative action initiatives. Because such policies were more strongly enforced at the federal, state, and municipal levels, African Americans employed in the public sector gained the most. By 1970, twenty-eight percent of all employed African Americans held government jobs, and approximately sixty percent of all black professional workers were employed by governmental bodies. This is particularly striking when we consider that in 1970 African Americans held only one percent of the managerial and administrative jobs in manufacturing. Thus, the expansion of public sector jobs for minorities has been largely responsible for the growth of the black middle class.

However, the inclusion of African Americans in public sector jobs and managerial positions did not always translate into big salary increases. Many black families reporting middle-class incomes were often the result of two parents working full-time for fairly low or moderate wages. Besides, in 1979, eighteen percent of all black female managers and thirteen percent of all black male managers actually earned wages below the poverty line. Many middle-class black families who had purchased suburban homes during the seventies lived from paycheck to paycheck; one layoff could mean the loss of their home. In fact, all economic indicators show that middle-class blacks, on average, possess substantially less "wealth" (savings, money invested in buying a home, stocks, bonds, retirement accounts, et cetera, minus debts) than middle-class whites who earn the same income.

Much of African-American wealth is concentrated in the hands of independent entrepreneurs, some of whom also benefited from affirmative action initiatives to provide more minority firms with government contracts and loans. The purpose of such programs was not to provide a handout to struggling businesses. Rather, they sought to rectify policies that had kept minority firms from obtaining government contracts in the first place and to improve the economic status of all African Americans by establishing a strong foundation for "black capitalism." The Nixon administration, for example, created several subsidy programs to assist black businesses, including the Office of Minority Business Enterprise, the Manpower Development and Training Program, and the Minority Enterprise Small Business Investment Company. Although these programs might have been effective if properly funded, they were never given much of a chance: After Ronald Reagan was elected president in 1980, virtually all of these programs were cut back.

Between 1972 and 1977, the number of black-owned firms and their proportion of total industry revenue declined for the most part. The number of black-owned auto dealerships fell by twenty-four percent; black-owned hotel and lodging facilities dropped by twenty-one percent; and the number of food and eating establishments declined by ten percent. In 1977, black-owned firms made up only three percent of all businesses in the country. By 1980, more than eighty percent of all black-owned firms did not have a single paid employee aside from the owner, and at least one-third of these firms failed within twelve months of opening.

Competition with other businesses only partly explains the failure of certain black-owned ventures. Black entrepreneurs have had more difficulty securing loans for their businesses than their white counterparts. A recent survey of five hundred black entrepreneurs with an annual revenue of one hundred thousand dollars or more revealed that ninety percent had been turned down by banks when they applied for business loans. Of those surveyed, seventy percent had to rely on personal savings to finance their business. Often, black business people have to turn to black-owned community banks for help.

Not all black business suffered during the seventies recessions and Reagan-era cutbacks. On the contrary, the last decades of the twentieth century are filled with remarkable stories of black entrepreneurship. One rising corporate star during the seventies was Naomi Sims, a high-fashion model originally from Oxford, Mississippi. After earning a degree in psychology from New York University and studying at the Fashion Institute of Technology, Sims quickly emerged as one of the most popular black women models in the country, making several magazine-cover and television appearances. In 1973, she helped develop a new fiber for a line of wigs and founded the Naomi Sims Collection, selling cosmetics and hair-care products nationwide. By 1977, her firm reported annual revenues of about four million dollars.

Reginald F. Lewis's road to success was a bit more traditional. Born in Baltimore, Maryland, Lewis was helped by affirmative action policies that enabled him to earn a law degree from Harvard in 1968. After working for one of New

York's most prestigious corporate law firms, Lewis, with fellow attorney Charles Clarkson, started his own law firm on Wall Street in 1970. His firm helped minority-owned businesses obtain financing and structure deals. In 1983, Lewis launched the TLC Group, an aggressive investment firm with the specific purpose of acquiring companies. And acquire he did: In 1984 TLC bought McCall's Pattern Company (a manufacturer of sewing patterns) for $25 million—and sold it for $90 million three years later. Then in 1987, the TLC Group made history by purchasing BCI Holdings, the former international division of the Chicago-based Beatrice Foods. Comprised of sixty-four companies operating in thirty-one countries, BCI Holdings manufactured and distributed a wide range of food products, including ice cream, meats, chocolates, and soft drinks. Lewis's firm paid $985 million for BCI Holdings, making it the largest leveraged buyout of an overseas operation in the history of American business up to that time.

The year before Lewis's death in 1993, TLC Beatrice had revenues of $1.54 billion and Lewis himself had amassed assets of more than $300 million, making him the wealthiest African American in U.S. history.

Perhaps the best-known black millionaire is publishing magnate John H. Johnson, founder of *Ebony* and *Jet* magazines. Born in Arkansas in 1918, he migrated to Chicago with his mother at age fifteen. While working for the black-owned Supreme Liberty Life Insurance Company in 1942, twenty-four-year-old Johnson decided to launch *Negro Digest,* a small magazine summarizing longer articles for and about African Americans. Raising the money was hard. "Most people had seen *Reader's Digest* and *Time,*" he recalled, "but nobody had seen a successful black commercial magazine. And nobody was willing to risk a penny on a twenty-four-year-old insurance worker." That is, except for the Citizens Loan Corporation of Chicago, one of the few financial institutions willing to loan money to African Americans. They loaned him five hundred dollars, but only after Johnson's mother offered to put up all of her new furniture as collateral. It was a good investment, for within eight months of its founding *Negro Digest* was selling fifty thousand copies a month nationally. Three years later, Johnson launched *Ebony* magazine, a photo magazine modeled after *Life.* By 1991, the Johnson

John H. Johnson, the founder of *Ebony* and *Jet* magazines, headed a publishing empire that recorded total gross sales of $252 million in 1991.

companies reported total gross sales of $252 million. According to *Forbes* magazine, Johnson headed one of the four hundred richest families in the United States.

The combination of higher incomes and the dismantling of legal segregation enabled many rising middle-class black families to flee collapsing ghettos and move out to the suburbs or to lavish townhouses and brownstones in wealthy urban communities. The trend is reflected in the rapid suburbanization of the African-American population during the seventies and eighties: Between 1970 and 1986, the black suburban population grew from 3.6 million to 7.1 million. Although they often left behind deteriorating neighborhoods, a growing drug economy, and a rapidly expanding army of unemployed men and women, most blacks could not escape bigotry. To their surprise, some middle-class black families who moved into predominantly white suburbs discovered burning crosses on their lawns, hate mail, and letters from property owners' associations concerned that their presence would lower property values.

Potential black home buyers also had to deal with real estate agents who deliberately steered them to poorer, predominantly black neighborhoods, and with financial institutions that blatantly discriminated against African Americans. The evidence of discrimination against African Americans in housing is overwhelming. Numerous studies conducted in major metropolitan areas since the sixties demonstrated that real estate agents frequently showed black home buyers different properties, withheld information, or simply lied about the status of the property in question. This practice of steering black home buyers toward nonwhite neighborhoods is a form of discrimination known as "redlining." Similarly, a massive study of ten million applications to savings and loan associations between 1983 and 1988 revealed that the rejection rate for blacks applying for home mortgages was more than twice that of whites, and that high-income African Americans were rejected more than low-income whites.

What is clear from such stories of discrimination is that the dismantling of legal barriers to segregation has not been completely effective. Indeed, by some measures racial segregation has increased in the urban North during the last three decades. Despite evidence that middle- and upper-income African Americans were the greatest beneficiaries of integration, it is interesting to note that in some major cities African Americans earning more than fifty thousand dollars were as segregated as those making less than twenty-five hundred dollars annually. Of course, in a few cases middle-class blacks have chosen predominantly black suburban enclaves in well-to-do communities such as Prince George's County, Maryland (just outside of Washington, D.C.), or sections of Westchester County, a community north of New York City. Their decision is understandable given the history of violence and discrimination directed at African Americans who try to integrate all-white suburban communities. But fear of racist attacks and the desire for respectful neighbors indicate the narrowness of choices that are offered to blacks compared to whites.

School integration, another component of African Americans' desire to reach for the American Dream, quickly became one of the most contested racial battle-fields during the post–civil rights era. A quarter of a century after the landmark case of *Brown* v. *Board of Education of Topeka, Kansas* (1954), the nation's public schools looked as segregated as they had ever been. Although black children made up about one-fifth of the total public school enrollment, almost two-thirds went to schools with at least fifty percent minority enrollment. This pattern is even more striking in major cities, where African-American children attended underfunded public schools while many white students, often the children of urban profession-als, have deserted the public school system for private institutions. By 1980, for example, whites made up only four percent of public school enrollment in Wash-ington, D.C., eight percent in Atlanta, nine percent in Newark, and twelve percent in Detroit.

Drastic measures were needed to remedy this situation, especially since middle-class families who had migrated to the suburbs took precious tax dollars needed to run city schools. With fewer well-paid, property-owning families living in urban areas, the property taxes so essential to funding education and other city services declined considerably. Under pressure from black families who wanted to send their children to better-funded schools in the suburbs and civil rights groups that believed the nation should live up to the *Brown* decision, school boards across the country tried to achieve racial balance by busing students to schools in different neighborhoods.

The nation was sharply divided over the issue of busing. President Nixon vehe-mently opposed court-ordered busing, officials in the Department of Health, Education and Welfare thought it was a good idea, and the Supreme Court re-mained unsure whether it was constitutional or not. The clearest expression of resistance to mandatory busing came from white parents who believed the addi-tion of black children from the inner city would bring down the quality of educa-tion. Indeed, in some cities busing programs were met with militant protests that frequently led to violence. Throughout the early to mid-seventies, organized resis-tance erupted in cities throughout the country, including Pontiac, Michigan; Louisville, Kentucky; Pasadena, California; and Kansas City, Missouri. The best-known clashes were in Boston, where most public schools had been racially segre-gated until an NAACP-led campaign won a court order in 1975 to bus children from predominantly black and poor Roxbury to Charlestown, a largely working-class Irish community. Over the course of the next three years, Boston police were called in to protect black children from white mobs screaming racial epithets and occasionally throwing bricks and fists.

The Boston busing controversy died down by the early eighties, partly be-cause liberal black and white politicians created a coalition that elected more sup-porters of integration to the city council and to the Board of Education. Besides, proponents of school integration could hardly claim a victory. By 1980, white flight to the suburbs and a decrease in the use of busing by conservative judges caused a resegregation of most big city school systems.

In the area of higher education, the backlash against affirmative action policies and financial aid for minorities took on many forms. During the late seventies and through the eighties, the number of reported racial assaults and acts of intimidation against blacks on college campuses showed a marked increase. The specific cases are chilling.

At Wesleyan University in 1981, black students found racist graffiti and flyers riddled with epithets and threats, including a leaflet advertising a fraternity "dedicated to wiping all goddamned niggers off the face of the earth." Ten years later, a white sorority at the University of Alabama hosted a party at which pledges painted their faces black and dressed as pregnant welfare mothers. Usually white backlash is much more subtle. One black college administrator vividly described the attitudes of white freshmen toward African Americans at his university: "Somebody will have the idea that the dorm is exclusively theirs, so therefore we can't have these 'germy, diseasey, dirty, filthy,' black kids live in their dormitory. . . . Black kids are seen as a gang now. They must be on drugs or crazy or something."

By far the most devastating form of white backlash in higher education was the partial dismantling of affirmative action initiatives. In the case of *Regents of the University of California* v. *Bakke* (1978), Allan Bakke, an unsuccessful white applicant, claimed that he was discriminated against because the University of California, Davis, admitted African Americans with lower test scores than his in order to meet their quota of minority students. The Supreme Court ruled that Bakke had been unfairly denied admission to the medical school. The court did not overturn all forms of affirmative action, but it did argue that quotas—setting aside a specific number of slots for designated groups—were unconstitutional. The medical school's denial of admission to Bakke in order to increase the number of minority students was regarded by the court's majority opinion as "reverse discrimination."

Although Bakke won the case, the unspoken facts behind U.C. Davis's admissions policy call into question the court's opinion that he was a victim of reverse discrimination. First, the sons and daughters of influential white families—potential donors or friends of the dean of the medical school—were also admitted over Bakke despite lower test scores. As had been the case historically, the dean controlled a handful of slots to admit special cases. Second, most minority applicants had higher scores than Bakke. This is an important fact, for the Bakke case left many observers with the incorrect impression that U.C. Davis admitted unqualified minorities. Most importantly, the decision was a major setback for efforts to achieve racial equality through social policy. Justice Thurgood Marshall, the first African American to serve on the Supreme Court, dissented from the majority opinion. Marshall, who viewed the Bakke decision as a tragedy, did not believe that America was even close to becoming a color-blind society. "The dream of America as a great melting pot," he wrote in his dissenting opinion in the Bakke case, "has not been realized for the Negro; because of his skin color he never even made it into the pot."

Most African Americans who stood at the threshold of the Reagan era knew they had entered the worst of times. *Equal opportunity, welfare, civil rights,* and *Black Power* became bad words in the national vocabulary. Most white Americans believed they had given all they could give, and that any form of government support would be nothing more than a handout. A small but growing contingent of black conservatives agreed. And if this was not enough, the crumbling cities that African Americans and other minorities had inherited turned out not to be the utopia for which they had hoped. They were dangerous, difficult places where racist police officers still roamed and well-paying jobs fled the city limits. Despite the rising number of black mayors, it became clear by the eighties that a new freedom movement was needed.

## "How We Gonna Make a Black Nation Rise?": The Struggle for Political Power

In December 1979, Arthur McDuffie, a thirty-three-year-old black insurance executive, was beaten to death by police officers in Dade County, Florida. The police said he was driving recklessly and had resisted arrest, but eyewitnesses believed it was a clear-cut case of brutality. African Americans who had followed the case closely knew who the real criminals were, and McDuffie was not one of them. To everyone's shock and dismay, however, in May 1980 an all-white jury returned a not-guilty verdict for all of the officers involved. That night black Miami exploded. Many inhabitants of the predominantly black and poor communities of Liberty City, Brownsville, Overton, and Coconut Grove took to the streets—turning over cars, setting fire to buildings, looting, throwing rocks and bottles at police and National Guardsmen. When the smoke cleared, Miami's losses exceeded $250 million; at least 400 people were injured and several were killed; more than 1,250 were arrested; and a 52-square-mile area of Dade County was placed under curfew from 8:00 P.M. to 6:00 A.M.

On closer inspection, it is clear that the Miami rebellion was not just a spontaneous response to an unfair verdict. It was a product of black frustrations caused by joblessness, economic deprivation, and immigration policies that clearly favored white Cubans over black Haitians, added to a string of incidents of police brutality and racial harassment that had gone unchecked during the seventies prior to McDuffie's death. It also marked the most dramatic example of the growing feeling of political powerlessness among poor and working-class African Americans. In an age when the number of black elected officials had increased dramatically and civil rights leaders achieved tremendous influence in national policy making, Miami's black rebels displayed distrust toward their "leaders." When Andrew Young, former U.N. ambassador under President Carter and veteran civil rights

In May 1980, riots erupted in Miami after a jury found four policemen not guilty in the beating death of a prominent black businessman. After the riots members of the Florida National Guard stood watch outside a looted store.

leader, attempted to talk to black youths, he was shunned. As historian and social activist Manning Marable put it, "History and black people had pushed their so-called leaders aside."

The Miami uprising and the failure of black leadership was just a foreshadow-ing of the dark days yet to come. Throughout the country, African Americans had become the most likely victims of police violence. According to one study, African Americans constituted forty-six percent of people killed by police in 1975. By the end of the seventies, police killings and nonlethal acts of brutality emerged as a central political issue among African Americans.

Racist violence was clearly on the rise in the eighties. The number of racially motivated assaults rose dramatically, many of them on college campuses. Between 1982 and 1989, the number of hate crimes reported annually in the United States grew threefold.

Other signs pointing to a resurgence of racism in the eighties include the pro-liferation of white supremacist organizations such as the Ku Klux Klan. By the late seventies the Klan had tripled its membership and waged a nationwide campaign of intimidation against African Americans. In 1978–79, Klansmen initiated a reign of terror against black people, which included the firebombing of homes, churches, and schools in more than one hundred towns and rural areas, and drive-by shootings into the homes of NAACP leaders. Very few of these incidents led to convictions. The Klan and other white supremacist organizations also gained influence in electoral politics. In 1980 Tom Metzger, the "Grand Dragon" of the Ku Klux Klan, garnered enough votes to win the Democratic primary in southern California's 43rd congressional district. Similarly, David Duke, former Klansman and founder of the National Association for the Advancement of White People, was elected to the Louisiana House of Representatives.

Although racists like Duke and Metzger were in the minority, their electoral wins signaled a changed mood in the eighties in the United States toward African Americans and other racial minorities. A new conservative movement emerged that strongly opposed affirmative action, immigration, and welfare. Even if this so-called "New Right" did not condone the resurgence of racism in the United States, its policies ultimately had a negative impact on African Americans. In particular, the election of former California Governor Ronald Reagan to the White House in 1980 had disastrous consequences for black Americans, especially the poor. Reagan was a staunch believer in the "trickle down" economic theory—the idea that building big business would benefit everyone because its profits would somehow "trickle down" to the poor and middle class. With this philosophy as justification, the Reagan administration cut back social programs in favor of corporate investments and tax breaks to the wealthy. During his two terms in office, military spending increased by forty-six percent while funding for housing was slashed by seventy-seven percent and education by seventy percent. Money for Aid to Families with Dependent Children and the Food Stamp program were also cut back substantially.

By the time Reagan began his second term in 1985, the living conditions of poor and working-class blacks were worse than they had been at the height of the 1973–75 recession. In 1985, about one out of every three African Americans, most of whom were women and children, lived below the poverty line, and the official black unemployment rates hovered around fifteen percent nationwide. In Midwestern cities such as Chicago, Detroit, and Milwaukee, the percentage of blacks without jobs ranged from twenty-five to thirty percent.

Reagan-era spending cuts were especially hard on cities, where the vast majority of African Americans lived. In addition to closing down the Neighborhood Self-Help and Planning Assistance program, which allotted $55 million to assist inner cities in 1981, aid to cities was reduced to a fraction of what it had been under President Nixon a decade earlier. City governments were forced to cut their budgets as well, leading to massive layoffs of low- and mid-level city workers. Because blacks held many of these government jobs, they were hardest hit by these cutbacks.

Most of the black mayors elected since the late sixties inherited this new urban crisis. With shrinking tax revenues caused by tax revolts and the flight of the middle class to the suburbs and almost no support from the federal government, most big city black mayors sought out whoever had money—which often turned out to be real estate developers and investors interested in building downtown financial centers. Coleman Young in Detroit, Maynard Jackson and Andrew Young in Atlanta, Ernest Morial in New Orleans, Carl Stokes in Cleveland, W. Wilson Goode in Philadelphia, to name a few, all faced this dilemma.

Perhaps the most telling example of this problem occurred in Los Angeles under Mayor Tom Bradley, a former Los Angeles police officer who was elected to the city council in 1963 and mayor in 1973. During his twenty-year tenure as mayor, from 1973 to 1993, Bradley promoted policies that favored the development of the downtown business district at the expense of poor communities in South Central Los Angeles that put him in office.

Because of the shutdown during the late seventies and eighties of numerous steel and rubber plants that had employed many African Americans in these neighborhoods, in some ways the decline of South Central was beyond Bradley's control. Economic conditions in South Central deteriorated faster than in any other L.A. community. A 1982 report from the California legislature revealed that South Central neighborhoods experienced a fifty percent rise in unemployment while purchasing power dropped by one-third. The 1982 median income for South Central L.A.'s residents was a paltry fifty-nine hundred dollars—that is, twenty-five hundred dollars below the median income for the black population *in the late seventies.* Youths were the hardest hit. For all of Los Angeles County, the unemployment rate of black youth remained at about forty-five percent.

Just when no one thought life in South Central Los Angeles could get any worse, crack cocaine entered the illegal drug scene in the mid-eighties. Crack, or "rock," was a cheap, highly addictive version of powdered cocaine that is smoked rather than inhaled through the nose. When this new drug hit the streets, it had an immediate and devastating impact on South Central Los Angeles as well as on other inner-city communities across the country. During 1984–85, emergency room admissions for cocaine trauma doubled and the number of juvenile arrests for drug dealing and related crimes increased fivefold. Violence also intensified as old gangs and new groups of peddlers battled for control of the crack market.

In spite of the violence, the constant threat of arrest, and the devastating health crisis generated by the drug, for many black youngsters selling crack was the only way to make a good income. Although the crack market might have put money into some people's pockets, for the majority it turned their neighborhoods into small war zones. Police helicopters, complex electronic surveillance, even small tanks armed with battering rams became increasingly familiar additions to the landscape of black Los Angeles. Housing projects were renovated along the lines of minimum security prisons and equipped with fortified fencing and mini-police stations. Some housing project residents were required to carry identity cards and visitors were routinely searched.

The intensive "law-and-order" policies of the Los Angeles Police Department were duplicated in most U.S. cities, with mixed results. Some black citizens complained that their communities were turning into police states. In Philadelphia, for example, tensions between police and civilians escalated into one of the most brutal episodes of violence in at least a decade. After Wilson Goode was elected the first black mayor in Philadelphia's history in 1983, he immediately found himself caught between a white constituency who wanted a law-and-order mayor and a police force with a legacy of corruption and brutality. In fact, in 1986 a federal grand jury indicted seven Philadelphia police officers who had worked in the narcotics division for racketeering and extorting at least four hundred thousand dollars plus quantities of cocaine from drug dealers.

But the key event was Goode's decision to allow the police to bomb the headquarters of a black nationalist organization called MOVE in May of 1985. Located in a Philadelphia neighborhood called Powelton Village, MOVE was mostly a militant black back-to-nature movement that had attempted to create a rural, communal environment in the middle of the city. As a result of complaints from neighbors and MOVE members' hostile attitude toward police, Mayor Frank Rizzo tried to root them out in 1978, culminating in a shoot-out that left one officer dead and several injured on both sides. In a similar standoff seven years later, Goode authorized the dropping of an aerial bomb which killed eleven people, including five children, destroyed sixty-one homes, and left two hundred and fifty people homeless. The MOVE bombing marred Goode's administration and his relations with Philadelphia's black community until he left office in 1991. Perhaps the biggest blow to Goode's administration was that the commission appointed to investigate the bombing concluded that racism strongly influenced the actions of the Philadelphia police force. This was crystal clear from the first words spoken by Philadelphia Police Commissioner Gregore J. Sambor, who announced over the bullhorn at the beginning of the assault: "Attention MOVE! This is America!"

Increasingly, African Americans began to realize that putting a black person in the mayor's office was not enough to solve the problems facing black America. Unlike the days of the Civil Rights movement, when politics appeared to be clearly etched in black and white, the political landscape of the eighties became more complicated. The appearance of a strong, vocal contingent of black pro-Reagan conservatives added to the confusion. Black conservatism was not new. The legacy of black conservatives advocating self-help and free-market economics goes back at least to the mid-nineteenth century. But during the Reagan years, black conservatives gained greater visibility in national politics and federal policy, distinguishing themselves for their advocacy of Reagan's "trickle down" theory and staunch opposition to affirmative action policies. (Ironically, most of these intellectuals had benefited from affirmative action in education and hiring.)

The most important spokesperson for this group, economist Thomas Sowell of the Hoover Institution at Stanford University, insisted that the problem of poor African Americans was one of values and the lack of a work ethic. He believed welfare and affirmative action policies undermined middle-class values of hard work and thrift and forced African Americans to become too dependent on government assistance. Black Harvard economist Glen Loury made similar arguments, insisting that racial preferences and equal opportunity legislation are worthless since the problems of the black poor are largely products of weak cultural values, broken families, and irresponsible parenting.

While many African Americans agreed with aspects of what the black Right had to say, particularly its insistence on self-sufficiency and its critique of welfare, most rejected neo-conservatism as a strategy to solve the black community's problems. A 1982 public opinion survey revealed that eighty-five percent of African Americans opposed Reagan-era policies of cutting back social welfare programs. On the other hand, while most polls conducted in the eighties indicated that African Americans supported increased government spending on the disadvantaged and endorsed affirmative action programs, they also revealed strong conservative views toward issues such as abortion and crime. Some African Americans, therefore, looked to political organizations and social movements that combined conservative social policy with racial militancy. The most potent example of this trend was the Nation of Islam, which grew dramatically during the eighties.

The NOI had undergone a dramatic change after the death of Elijah Muhammad in 1975. As soon as Wallace D. Muhammad, Elijah's son, took over the leadership of the NOI, he denounced his father's earlier teachings that the white man was the devil and that white people were created by an evil black scientist. Wallace, a respected Muslim scholar who had studied Arabic in Egypt, adopted an orthodox approach to Islam, changing the name of the organization to the World Community of al-Islam in the West. He even invited whites to join the group. In 1978, Louis Farrakhan, a devoted follower of Elijah Muhammad, broke from the World Community and reestablished the old NOI under Elijah's original beliefs. Under Farrakhan's leadership, the reconstituted Nation of Islam attracted a huge following among young people, many of whom were in search of solutions to joblessness, drug addiction, and the inability of poor African Americans to effect change in the political structure. Ironically, the Nation for the most part continued to distance itself from direct political participation and supported a fairly conservative agenda. Its policies centered on self-help, the creation of black business, and the maintenance of traditional relations between men and women.

The popularity of the NOI stems in part from its efforts to root out drug dealers from inner-city communities and its emphasis on community economic development. Through its economic wing, People Organized and Working for Economic Rebirth (POWER), the NOI has tried to create a nationwide cooperative of black businesses so that consumers and entrepreneurs can coordinate a massive "buy black" campaign. POWER has also introduced its own products, from soaps and shampoos to food items, which it markets through black stores or street-corner vendors. By encouraging young, jobless African Americans to sell POWER products, they sought to create alternatives to crime and drug dealing and instill in them a sense of entrepreneurship.

Despite its conservative social policies and its tendency to stay out of electoral politics (an important exception being its support for Jesse Jackson's 1984 bid for the presidency), the NOI is still regarded by many as an extremist organization. The Central Intelligence Agency and the Reagan administration remained convinced that the NOI maintained ties to Arab terrorist organizations, especially after Libyan President Muammar Qaddafi extended a five-million-dollar interest-free loan to the Nation to help start POWER. Furthermore, the NOI developed a reputation as a proponent of anti-Semitism because of several remarks made by Farrakhan and other NOI leaders. In 1983, for example, Farrakhan caused a national controversy when he described Nazi leader Adolf Hitler as "wickedly great." Although his point was to show how greatness could be used in the service of evil, the press reports interpreted Farrakhan's remark as praise for Hitler.

Although more radical black political activists rejected the NOI's conservatism, they agreed that African Americans needed to develop a road to political power independent of either the Democrats or the Republicans. Indeed, they had tried to build such a movement back in 1972, when the National Black Political Assembly first met in Gary, Indiana. But as more and more black elected officials became integrated into the Democratic party machine (and to a lesser extent, the Republican party), the idea of an independent road lost its appeal during the late seventies. However, the failure of the Carter administration to respond to black needs, followed by the election of Reagan, compelled black political activists to reopen the discussion of an independent movement.

Thus in 1980, the National Black Independent Political Party (NBIPP) was formed to meet the challenge. Conceived as a democratic, mass-based political movement capable of embracing a range of organizations and ideas without suppressing differences, NBIPP attracted between fifteen hundred and two thousand delegates to its founding convention in November 1980. NBIPP's constitution called for strategies to work within the electoral arena and the development of community institutions that would involve ordinary people in local decision-making and ultimately shape public policy. Perhaps NBIPP's most revolutionary proposal was to put in place mechanisms that would ensure gender equality throughout the organization. Among other things, its charter and constitution called for equal gender representation in all leadership positions.

Unfortunately, NBIPP could not compete with the Democratic party, which continued to attract the vast majority of black voters. Nevertheless, it did set the stage for two historic political campaigns: Harold Washington's 1983 mayoral race in Chicago and Jesse Jackson's bid for president in 1984. Although both of these

Chicago mayor Harold Washington at a press conference announcing funding for a community center in 1986. As Chicago's first black mayor, Washington struggled against the entrenched power structure that had long denied access to blacks.

campaigns took place within the Democratic party, they can be characterized as "independent" since they drew more on grassroots organizing than mainstream party support.

No one believed Harold Washington could win when he announced his candidacy for mayor in 1983. Chicago had never had a black mayor, and given its long history of racial animosity and its well-entrenched Democratic political machine in city hall as well as in Congress, a black challenger was viewed as a long shot. Chicago did not have a black majority, and the percentage of African Americans who went to the polls had not been very high. To win such an election, Washington would have to appeal to a significant proportion of white and Latino voters and convince hundreds of thousands of complacent, frustrated black adults to register and come out to the polls.

A veteran of Chicago politics and a native of the city, Harold Washington understood what he had to do. After earning a B.A. from Roosevelt University in 1949 and a J.D. from Northwestern University Law School in 1952, Washington worked as assistant city prosecutor in Chicago until he was able to establish his own private law practice. As a Democrat, Washington became a rising star in state politics, serving in the state House of Representatives from 1965 to 1976 and the

Illinois State Senate from 1977 to 1980. In 1980, campaigning on a progressive agenda of racial equality and justice for working people and the poor, Washington was elected to the U.S. House of Representatives.

By 1983, Washington felt the time had come to make a bid for mayor of Chicago. African Americans, in particular, were frustrated with the incumbent, Jane Byrne, whose policies did little to help the poor, provide jobs, or place blacks in appointed positions within city hall. In opposition to the Byrne administration, local black and Latino activists began to mobilize support for Washington's campaign. The movement not only waged successful voter-registration campaigns, increasing the number of black voters by eighteen hundred thousand in 1982, but enjoyed substantial support from liberal whites.

In a hotly contested primary election in which the white vote was split between Byrne and Richard M. Daley, the son of former Mayor Richard Daley, Washington scored a narrow victory. Last-minute Byrne campaign propaganda played on the racial fears of Chicago's white voters, subtly warning that a black mayor would undermine white privilege. Such fears were made even more explicit in the general election, especially after Byrne briefly announced her intention to run as a write-in candidate in order to save a "fragile" city that, in her words, was "slipping." When Byrne realized this tactic would not work, however, she withdrew. Despite heightened racial tensions and a very nasty campaign, Washington also beat his Republican challenger, Robert Epton, in yet another close election.

Once in office, however, Washington soon discovered that he was a long way from "victory." Members of the city council tied to the old Chicago machine opposed virtually everything the Washington administration tried to do. Yet, in spite of this opposition, he created the Commission on Women's Affairs, successfully pushed for a state law giving public employees the right to form labor unions, and implemented affirmative action policies to increase the number of women and minorities in government.

Yet, like all big-city mayors, Washington faced problems beyond his control. The Chicago Police Department still had a reputation for brutality and terrorism against minorities. Big business was reluctant to increase investment in Chicago since Washington was labeled a radical and his ability to govern in opposition to the machine was constantly being questioned. Moreover, he spent much of his time trying to clean up generations of mismanagement, corruption, graft, and budget deficits. He was reelected in 1987, but his reform efforts came to a halt when he died of a heart attack soon after returning to work.

Meanwhile, as Harold Washington launched his historic campaign for mayor, a group of black activists—mainly independents, Democrats, and labor organizers—began debating the pros and cons of running an African American in the 1984 presidential elections. Most agreed on the futility of running an independent, especially in light of NBIP's inability to become a powerful force in politics. Instead, they wanted to run someone within the Democratic party who could pressure mainstream white candidates to be more responsive to black needs. Black elected officials and other party supporters were afraid that the Democrats were promoting more conservative policies in order to attract white working-class voters who had voted for Reagan in 1980. A black candidate, it was argued, could not only show how valuable blacks were to the party but could run on a more liberal and even radical agenda. Such a candidate would not merely espouse racial justice and civil rights; rather, he or she would focus on workers' rights, the environment, nuclear disarmament, and issues affecting women, Latinos, Asian Americans, and gays and lesbians.

Few established black politicians in the early eighties believed such a campaign could be anything but symbolic, and few were in the mood for symbolism. Even before a candidate was named, several African-American leaders opposed the plan.

However, one of the strongest supporters of a black presidential candidate was Jesse Jackson. Because Jackson was so outspoken about the need to run a black candidate, he quickly emerged as the movement's spokesman. In no time, the media dubbed him the next presidential candidate, a label Jackson himself did little to dispel. By the spring of 1983, opinion polls revealed that Jackson ranked third among the potential slate of Democratic candidates.

Jesse Jackson turned out to be an ideal choice. Born in Greenville, South Carolina, in 1941, he left South Carolina to attend the University of Illinois in 1959, hoping that life in the North would prove less humiliating than life in the segregated South. It wasn't true. Following several bouts with racism, he returned to the South to attend North Carolina Agricultural and Technical College, where he starred on the football team and quickly emerged as a leader in the civil rights sit-ins in Greensboro, North Carolina. After earning a bachelor's degree in sociology, Jackson entered Chicago Theological Seminary, where he was ordained as a Baptist minister in 1968. An activist in the Southern Christian Leadership Conference since 1965, Jackson founded Operation PUSH (People United to Save Humanity) in 1971 in order to further the cause of human rights around the globe and to help the poor develop strategies to rise out of poverty.

Although Jackson was consistently described by the media as representing a "black agenda," his campaign and platform reflected the interests of many different groups. His staff included environmentalists, feminists, and labor organizers as well as black and Latino grassroots community activists. The campaign encompassed so many different issues and different ethnic groups that Jackson dubbed it the "Rainbow Coalition." Most importantly, Jackson brought to the presidential race a vision for a new America that challenged politics as usual. In a speech before the Democratic National Convention in 1984, he issued the following challenge to a new generation of Americans:

> Young people, dream of a new value system. Dream of teachers, but teachers who will teach for life, not just for a living. Dream of doctors, but doc-

tors who are more concerned with public health than personal wealth. Dream of lawyers, but lawyers who are more concerned with justice than a judgeship ... of authentic leaders who will mold public opinion against a headwind, not just ride the tailwinds of opinion polls.

In spite of Jackson's vision, support from mainstream black politicians within the Democratic party was slow in coming because many believed a vote for Jackson would undermine efforts to beat the incumbent, Ronald Reagan. Jackson also maintained strained relations with the Jewish community, partly because he supported the right of Palestinians in Israel to have a homeland and because he would not repudiate his relationship with the Nation of Islam, especially NOI leader Louis Farrakhan. But the most damaging incident occurred with the publication of an anti-Semitic remark Jackson made in private, which virtually destroyed whatever Jewish support he had in 1984.

Despite these and other problems, Jackson ran a respectable campaign, winning several state primaries and caucuses and garnering 3.5 million popular votes. He lost the nomination to Walter Mondale (who was subsequently crushed by Ronald Reagan in a landslide election), but Jackson's Rainbow Coalition made some very important strides. Its massive voter-registration drive brought hundreds of thousands of new voters—notably African Americans and Latinos—into the Democratic party. He also gave the struggle against apartheid in South Africa far more visibility than it had had before and sharply criticized U.S. military intervention in Central America and the Caribbean.

By the time the 1988 election rolled around, more and more Democrats had come to realize that Jackson was a serious candidate. In spite of several impressive showings in a number of states, he again lost the nomination—this time to Michael Dukakis, the governor of Massachusetts. Dukakis was in turn defeated by George Bush, Ronald Reagan's vice president. In one of the most viciously race-tainted campaigns in U.S. history, Bush attacked Dukakis as "soft on crime" because under Dukakis's administration in Massachusetts a black man named Willie Horton had been paroled from prison and subsequently committed a rape. The image of black men as criminal rapists out to violate white women was an old theme that tapped into the already heightened racial fears of white Americans. The infamous Willie Horton ads not only helped secure Bush's victory but proved once again the power of race to shape American politics.

## "One Nation under a Groove": African-American Culture since 1970

As the seventies opened, the cultural revolution born in the sixties had reached its height then slowly sputtered out. Afros and dashikis—loose shirts made of bright African fabrics—were the style of the day. The music was soul, and James Brown was still the Godfather—even if his record sales had declined a bit from his peak

Afrika Bambaataa (front), pictured here with his group, the Soul Sonic Force, was an early pioneer of rap music, integrating European electronic dance music with South Bronx hip-hop. He also founded the Zulu Nation in the 1970s—a politically conscious organization of rappers, break dancers, graffiti artists, and others associated with hip-hop culture.

years in the late sixties. Even the "ghetto" was a place to be proud of, a place where pure soul could be found. By the end of the decade, however, things got to be a lot more complicated. As the language of soul and Black Power began to fade, black music crossed over to white listeners and more black faces appeared on television shows about family life.

As in virtually every previous era, African-American culture stood at the center of American life. But more than ever, this culture was extremely diverse, reflecting generational and class differences within black communities. In the late twentieth century, there seemed to be less agreement about "how to be black" than at any other period since the first generation of African captives—with their many different cultural and linguistic backgrounds—arrived on these shores.

Black popular music in the seventies is often described as "crossover" because it either adopted elements of other nonblack musical styles or was deliberately produced in a way that would attract white audiences. In a period when the sounds and scenes of urban rebellion slowly faded from the evening news, and when at least some sections of American society were becoming more and more racially integrated, the very idea of "crossover" seemed to be a fitting label. Of course, black popular music has always "crossed over"—from the popularity of jazz among urban whites in the twenties to the irreverent sounds of Chuck Berry and Little Richard in the fifties.

From 1968 to the early seventies, one of the most revolutionary "crossover" bands was Sly and the Family Stone. The first major pop band to be integrated by race and sex, it combined the heavy-bass line associated with James Brown (also known as funk music) with rock to create a new sound that appealed to black and white audiences. The lyrics explored political themes, particularly in songs such as "Everyday People," "Thank You for Talkin' to Me Africa," and "Stand!"

An even more poignant example of a crossover musician is Jimi Hendrix, the Seattle-born master of the electric guitar. Although he died quite young in 1970, Hendrix paved the way for greater black involvement in heavy metal. A major figure in the heavy metal and psychedelic rock movements, Hendrix did not shy away from political themes; his instrumental version of "The Star Spangled Banner," which evoked powerful images of war, suffering, and anger within the United States, is still a classic example of late-sixties protest music.

As the militant mood of the late sixties died down, and as black radio stations attracted more and more white listeners, black artists developed styles that reflected the changing times. The Philadelphia-based songwriting team of Kenny Gamble and Leon Huff gave birth to a new musical format known as "soft soul." Utilizing orchestral arrangements, lots of ballads, and a very smooth rhythmic pulse, they created a pop sound that quickly became popular in discotheques—dance clubs where records replaced live bands—across the country. Some of the more famous examples of the Gamble and Huff sound include Harold Melvin and the Blue Notes' "If You Don't Know Me By Now," and the O'Jays' "Love Train."

Disco had its roots in black and Latino dance music, and its strongest links were to the gay community. Indeed, the rise of disco coincided with the gay liberation movement and the push for open expressions of homosexuality. One of the most important places for "coming out" happened to be the multiracial underground dance clubs and ballroom dance halls. These were places where performers such as Sylvester, a black gay disco singer, adopted feminine or "camp" stage presences much like Little Richard had done two decades before. The Village People, a multiracial group of gay men, made a big splash parodying macho culture and attitudes. While these performers made it big well beyond the gay community, lesser-known artists who were even more explicit about their sexuality rarely got contracts with big record companies. In fact, the first major record label to release a disco song with an explicitly gay theme was Motown; in 1978 it recorded Carl Bean's "I Was Born This Way."

Initially, early disco artists did not get much airtime on the radio, although their music was popular in the clubs. The first groups to cross over into radio include the Hues Corporation with "Rock the Boat" (1974) and the extremely popular Donna Summer tune, "Love to Love you Baby" (1975). As disco became more popular among whites, it also became "upscale" and trendier. New York disco clubs moved to expensive downtown locations that often refused to admit poor black and Puerto Rican youths. By the late seventies, however, disco had become so much a part of the white mainstream that the media ultimately dubbed the Bee Gees, a British group, the kings of disco.

The irony for black artists and audiences was that, while black musicians were losing precious radio airplay to disco music performed by whites, all dance music began declining in popularity. As more and more radio stations specializing in heavy metal adopted anti-disco slogans, the fortunes of black performers declined considerably in the larger world of popular music. A telling case in point is Music Television, better known as MTV. Launched in 1981, when the disco craze was beginning to wane, MTV started out playing only rock music videos, which targeted MTV's main audience of suburban white youth. In 1983, only sixteen of the eight hundred videos in rotation were by black artists—mainly performers like Prince, who had a large rock-fan following. MTV executives began to rethink their strategy after Michael Jackson released *Thriller*, which sold thirty-three million albums worldwide, and Prince released a succession of big-selling albums. It was the massive popularity of rap music, however, that compelled MTV to place more black artists in rotation. In the process, the corporate executives and marketing experts finally realized that their "target audience" was more diverse in both background and tastes than they had realized.

Meanwhile, as disco moved up from the underground and artists like Prince moved "crossover" music to still another level of sophistication, the African-American underground scene took on new dimensions. George Clinton revolutionized black music despite the fact that he had virtually no big sellers or Top 40 hits. Leading groups like Parliament and Funkadelic, Clinton expanded Sly Stone's fusion of rock and soul and built on James Brown's funk style to create music whose impact was still being felt two decades later. With albums such as *Maggot Brain, Chocolate City, America Eats Its Young,* and *One Nation Under a Groove,* the

Parliament/Funkadelic family not only introduced a complex, improvisational style to pop music but retained a black nationalist edge that had all but disappeared in the mid-seventies.

Some of George Clinton's biggest followers could be found in the parks and school yards of New York, among poor African-American, West Indian, and Puerto Rican kids who were themselves at the forefront of a cultural revolution. Known to the world at large as hip-hop, this predominantly black and Latino youth culture included rap music, graffiti art, and break dancing, as well as the language and dress styles that have come to be associated with the hip-hop generation.

The oldest component of hip-hop culture is graffiti. Of course, wall writing goes back centuries, from political slogans and gang markings to romantic declarations. But the aerosol art movement was quite different. Calling themselves writers, graffiti artists, aerosol artists, and subterranean guerrilla artists, the kids who started this art form in the early seventies came from a variety of different ethnic groups and neighborhoods throughout the city of New York. Subway trains provided the most popular canvases. Writers often "bombed" the interiors of trains with "tags"—quickly executed and highly stylized signatures, often made with fat markers rather than spray cans. Outside the trains they created "masterpieces," elaborate works of art carefully conceived and designed ahead of time. Incorporating logos and images borrowed from TV and comic books, stylistic signatures, and inventive lettering techniques—bubble letters, angular machine letters, and the very complex "wild style"—the best aerosol artists produced complicated compositions using a vast array of colors.

By the late seventies, the Metropolitan Transit Authority in New York City was spending $400,000 per year cleaning the trains and added 24 million dollars worth of ribbon wire fencing designed to ensnare and shred the body or object attempting to cross it. Ironically, while the MTA largely succeeded in keeping the trains graffiti-free, aerosol art exploded throughout other parts of the city and spread across the world during the eighties and 1990s. Tags became commonplace in most cities and masterpieces continued to pop up on the sides of housing projects, school yards, abandoned buildings and plants, under bridges, and inside tunnels that service commuter trains.

Rap music is clearly the most enduring and profitable component of hip-hop culture. Although rap music as we know it originated in New York during the seventies, it has a long prehistory in African-American culture that can be traced back to preaching, singing the blues, the rhyming styles of black radio DJs, and toasting (oral stories performed in rhyme that are usually humorous but often filled with explicit sex and violence). But what made hip-hop music unique was the technology: DJs and producers transformed oral traditions by adding electronic drum machines, turntables, mixers, and, later, digital samplers. (Sampling is the practice of incorporating portions of other records, or different sounds, into a new recording.)

Soon the parks, school yards, and underground clubs throughout New York were overrun with DJs. One important figure was Grandmaster Flash, who is credited with inventing "scratching" or back-cueing records on the turntable to create a new percussive sound. The DJs were followed by MCs (meaning "masters of ceremony," though they were much more than that) whose job was to keep the crowd moving and the parties "jumping." The early MCs often relied on call and response from the audience. A common phrase might be, "Just throw ya hands in the air / and wave 'em like ya just don't care / if your man has on clean underwear / somebody say 'oh yea.'" These simple party phrases became more complicated rhymes, and by the late seventies MCs, or rappers, were as much a part of hip-hop music as the DJs themselves. By 1977, Harlem and the Bronx claimed several pioneering rap groups: Double Trouble, The Treacherous Three, The Funky Four Plus One, Grandmaster Flash and the Furious Five, and Afrika Bambaata and his various groups. However, the first commercial rap hit, "Rapper's Delight" by the Sugar Hill Gang, was not recorded until 1979.

Women had been part of the hip-hop underground from its origins. Some of the pioneering New York women rappers include Lady B, Sweet T, Lisa Lee, Sha Rock, the Mercedes Ladies, Sula, and Sequence. But popular women artists such as Sequence or Roxanne Shante were often treated as novelty groups instead of legitimate rappers, despite the fact that the first wave of women rappers displayed skills equal to the best of the male rappers. Because rap was portrayed as "the voice of the ghetto," the tough street culture associated with men, women were discriminated against by promoters who believed they could not sell many records. It was not until the appearance of Salt N' Pepa, and later MC Lyte and Queen Latifah, that women rappers gained legitimacy and respect. Like female MCs who came after and before them, they challenged the notion that boasting and profanity were distinctly "men's talk."

Although early rap artists were known for their humorous or boasting lyrics, groups such as Grandmaster Flash also recorded songs such as "White Lines" and "The Message" that critiqued contemporary racism, poverty, police brutality, and drug use. Out of that tradition emerged dozens of rap groups devoted to radical political themes, including Public Enemy, KRS-1, Brand Nubians, and the X-Clan. Other groups, such as the so-called "gangsta rappers" dominant on the West Coast, produced chilling stories of modern "bad men," tales of street life, police brutality, crime, and domination over women.

Though not all rappers were driven by political and social themes, the use of profanity and sexually explicit lyrics pushed several rap groups into the center of controversy. In 1990, for instance, 2-Live Crew became a symbol for those who wanted to protect freedom of speech under the First Amendment after obscenity laws were vigorously enforced in several states to ban sale of their recordings as well as live performances. In 1993, several black community groups, led by the Reverend Calvin Butts of the Abyssinian Baptist Church in New York and representatives of various African-American women's organizations, denounced "gangs-ta rap" for its offensive, violent, and sexist lyrics. The backlash against rap music, in fact, spurred congressional hearings to investigate the matter.

Despite these attacks, hip-hop was clearly a dominant force in American popular music by the millennium's end. It had grown in several different directions and developed its own subgroups, incorporating elements of Jamaican reggae, jazz, punk rock, and heavy metal. Hip-hop even sparked a literary revival among young people, causing an explosion in "spoken word" performances all over the world. Black and Latino poets such as Tracie Morris, Saul Williams, Carl Hancock Rux, and Jessica Care Moore rose directly out of hip-hop culture to publish, perform, and record works that have earned international acclaim.

By 2004, innovative artists such as "The Roots" and "Outkast," who had radically transformed the genre by their use of live instruments, diversity of musical choices, and inventive lyrics, had achieved a level of commercial success that was unheard of for experimental groups in the 1990s. Indeed, a few years into the new millennium, rap artists such as Jay-Z, Kanye West, Missy Elliot, Fifty-Cent, Nelly, and Eminem, topped the pop charts, outselling all other genres of popular music. A quarter century after it's birth, hip-hop had become a worldwide, multi-billion dollar industry. From France to Australia, Kosovo to Cape Town, Tokyo to Tanzania, young rap artists from every part of the globe perform and record in their own language, and incorporate local rhythms into their songs. Like rappers everywhere, their lyrics speak to the daily social and political realities they confront in their home countries. Many European rap groups, such as France's "Saian Supra Crew" or Denmark's "Outlandish" descend from immigrants from Africa, Asia, the Middle East, and Latin America, and their lyrics speak to issues of race, poverty, and citizenship.

Hip-hop might be the newest addition to the world of black music, but it is successful precisely because it draws on what came before. Jazz continued to be a mainstay in African-American culture, and its popularity seemed to have skyrocketed in the eighties and nineties. Modern jazz experienced a kind of renaissance with the overnight success of trumpeter Wynton Marsalis and his brother, saxophonist Branford Marsalis, and the return of trumpeter and jazz pioneer Miles Davis (who had retired in 1975). Despite its renewed success, by the early nineties the jazz world was sharply divided. On one side stood the "purists," strong advocates of more traditional jazz forms, or what is often called "repertory jazz." The strongest voice for the maintenance of tradition has been the Jazz at Lincoln Center Orchestra and the Smithsonian Jazz Masterpiece Ensemble. These ensembles highlight the music of major jazz composers, notably Louis Armstrong, Duke Ellington, and Thelonious Monk.

On the other side stood musicians who experiment with "free jazz" or incorporate rock, funk, and hip-hop in their music. Artists as varied as saxaphonists Steve Coleman, Ravi Coltrane, and David Murray, pianists Geri Allen and Jason Moran, trombonist Craig Harris, clarinetist Don Byron, cornetist Graham Haynes, and vocalist Cassandra Wilson continued to work in the jazz tradition but were not afraid to mix musical genres. Composers such as Anthony Davis, T. J. Anderson, and Olly Wilson ushered in a revolution by bringing together jazz, blues, and other black musical forms with opera and symphonic music. Working with librettist/poet/novelist Thulani Davis, Anthony Davis won international acclaim for operas such as *X: The Life and Times of Malcolm X*(1985) and *Amistad* (1998). Greg Osby and Joshua Redman were among the more prominent young artists to fuse jazz and hip-hop, although some veterans, including vibist Roy Ayers, trumpeter Donald Byrd, and drummer Max Roach, had also moved in this direction.

Musicians such as Graham Haynes, Don Byron, and Geri Allen represented a new generation of black artists who resisted categories, who embraced all kinds of music from classical to rock. They joined other like-minded artists in the Black Rock Coalition (BRC). Founded in 1985 by guitarist Vernon Reid (formerly of Living Colour), writer Greg Tate, and artist/manager Konda Mason, the BRC attracted a wide range of musicians, writers, and artists committed to working collectively, improving conditions for black performers in the music industry, and breaking down barriers that limit black musicians to certain genres (jazz, soul, hip-hop, for example). BRC members were activists, as well. According to their founding manifesto, they vowed to oppose "those racist and reactionary forces within the American music industry which deny Black artists the expressive freedom and economic rewards that our Caucasian counterparts enjoy as a matter of course."

Film and television has had a profound impact on race relations in the United States. In an age when segregation was becoming more entrenched, most Americans confronted black people through the big screen or their home television sets. The images of African Americans as violent, oversexed, lazy, and ignorant are as much a product of modern media as of old-fashioned racism. And yet, the same media can take credit for breaking down old stereotypes, for changing our ideas about history and creating a more complex image of what it means—or meant—to be black in the United States.

In the early seventies films about black ghetto life became extremely popular among black and white audiences alike. Often called "blaxploitation cinema," these films were less a response to black political radicalism of the era than the film industry's realization that African-American consumers were a potentially profitable market, particularly in urban areas where white flight to the suburbs left inner-city theaters empty unless they catered to local audiences.

The signature film of that era was clearly Melvin Van Peebles's *Sweet Sweetback's Badasss Song* (1971). Shot on a shoestring budget in nineteen days, *Sweetback* quickly became the largest-grossing independent production up to that point—an amazing accomplishment when we consider the fact that it was rated X. In this film, Van Peebles plays a regular hustler whose bout with the police forces him to flee Los Angeles, always staying one step ahead of the cops, vigilantes, and attack dogs. His flight, assisted by ordinary community people, ultimately turns him into

Gordon Parks, Sr., a noted photographer and writer, was the first African American to direct full-length feature films for a major Hollywood studio. His best known films are *Shaft* (1971), about a suave black detective, and *The Learning Tree* (1969), which Parks also wrote as a novel.

a rebel. Despite the mass appeal in the black community, *Sweetback* was attacked by black and white critics alike, who called it degrading, self-hating, and invidious.

What made *Sweetback* and films like it so popular to poor and working-class black audiences? Van Peebles and such black filmmakers as Gordon Parks, Sr., Gordon Parks, Jr., and Ivan Dixon generally focused on the lives of ghetto residents and emphasized racial pride, community solidarity, and Black Power. No matter how stereotyped the characters were, the people in "the streets" were constantly fighting back and winning. The police and government were the source of corruption, and even pimps, dope dealers, and petty criminals showed more morals than white authority.

Not all dramatic films about African Americans were set in the ghetto or emphasized violent revenge. *Sounder* (1972) was a "coming of age" film set in the rural South. Starring Cicely Tyson, Paul Winfield, and Kevin Hooks, it tells the story of a poor sharecropping family during the thirties struggling to make ends meet. Also noteworthy was the highly acclaimed *Lady Sings the Blues* (1972), the moving story of jazz singer Billie Holiday's descent from being one of the most brilliant vocal stylists of the century to a heroin addict. And black cinema had its share of deeply sensitive love stories, such as *Claudine* (1974) and *Sparkle* (1976). Taken together, these films at least challenged the one-dimensional portrayal of African Americans created by the overload of blaxploitation cinema.

By the eighties, as the number of black-oriented films declined, the possible range of roles actually widened. Now black characters—mainly men—had more supporting roles in films where their race was incidental. Roles written with white actors in mind, such as Lou Gossett, Jr.'s part as a Marine drill sergeant in *An Officer and a Gentleman,* created new opportunities for black actors to reach a wider audience. Actors such as Billy Dee Williams, Richard Pryor, Morgan Freeman, Eddie Murphy, Denzel Washington, Alfre Woodard, and Whoopi Goldberg achieved superstardom in this new era. *A Soldier's Story* (1984), an intricate tale centering on the murder of an unpopular black army sergeant on a Louisiana military base during the Second World War, and *The Color Purple* (1985), a film about domestic violence, black male exploitation of black women, and lesbian encounters among black women, were two notable films of this era.

By the late eighties Hollywood's relationship with black films shifted yet again. One cause of this change was the appearance in 1986 of Spike Lee, a young black independent filmmaker just out of New York University's film school whose first feature film turned out to be a box-office smash. *She's Gotta Have It* was a comedy about a young black woman's search for romance and sexual freedom in the eighties and the three very different men to whom she was attracted.

The success of *She's Gotta Have It* and Lee's subsequent films did not suddenly compel Hollywood to take chances on young black filmmakers. What *did* make a difference was the rapid popularity of hip-hop in American culture, which convinced advertisers and the film industry alike that there was big money to be made in the music and styles of black urban youth. Rap producers were called in to make soundtracks and the ghetto, once again, became the favored backdrop for a new wave of films. But unlike the blaxploitation films of the seventies, the cult status of Spike Lee placed a greater premium on having young, black, and especially male directors.

Called by some critics the major example of the "new ghetto aesthetic," the film that opened up this new era was made by none other than Mario Van Peebles, the son of Melvin Van Peebles. *New Jack City* was not young Van Peebles' first film, but up to that point it was clearly his most successful, grossing over $40 million at the box office. In *New Jack City,* the story of the rise of a Harlem drug cartel and the crack cocaine industry it created, Van Peebles literally reverses his father's message of two decades before: In this story the black community is the problem and the police are the solution. The only black woman filmmaker to merit entrance into what otherwise is a boys' club of new directors was Leslie Harris, whose funny and gritty *Just Another Girl on the IRT* was underdistributed and largely ignored by the critics.

By the mid- to late nineties, the "new ghetto aesthetic" began to slowly give way to more complicated, epic films drawing on African-American history. Spike Lee's *Malcolm X* (1994), starring Denzel Washington, gave viewers a spectacular visual history of postwar urban America and the Nation of Islam. Steven Spielberg explored the depths of the transatlantic slave trade and the heroic traditions of American abolitionism in *Amistad* (1997), and the following year Jonathan Demme put Toni Morrison's magical and terrifying Pulitzer Prize–winning novel *Beloved* on the big screen. All of these films generated debates over questions of historical accuracy, historical and contemporary representations of black people, the ability of white filmmakers to make "black films," and the willingness of nonblack audiences to see films about black subjects. Although the subject of slavery has been a central theme in American history—a theme that has affected all Americans—many viewers insisted that these films were primarily intended for black audiences.

The blaxploitation film craze did not translate to television so easily. Attempts to turn blaxploitation films into TV serials, notably "Get Christie Love" (1974–75), "Shaft" (1973–74), and "Tenafly" (1973–74), were flops. "The Flip Wilson Show" (1970–74), the first popular black show of the decade, was created with white audiences in mind. Using a comedy/variety show format, Wilson often played characters that relied on common stereotypes of African Americans. Sitcoms popular during the seventies, such as "Good Times," "What's Happenin'," "That's My Mama," and "Sanford and Son" focused on black working-class life, offering a slightly more sympathetic account of humor and perseverance in an age of rising unemployment, poverty, and violence.

The successful dramatic shows rarely appeared as serials. Rather, TV specials such as "The Autobiography of Miss Jane Pittman" (1974), the personal saga of an elderly black woman who lived most of her life under segregation, and the miniseries "Roots" (1977) based on Alex Haley's historical novel tracing his family from slavery to freedom, captured the attention of broad television audiences.

However one TV series, "The Cosby Show," which premiered in 1984, dramatically changed black television. Against TV executives' assumptions, Bill Cosby created a black middle-class family free of old stereotypes, yet capable of entertaining millions of Americans of all ethnic and racial backgrounds. The show centered around Cosby, who played a congenial doctor named Cliff Huxtable, his five children, and his wife Claire, a successful attorney played by Phylicia Rashad. Though "The Cosby Show" was often criticized for ignoring race or painting too rosy a picture of black life, it subtly introduced issues such as the Civil Rights movement and apartheid in South Africa without making them central to the story. Moreover, given the then-dominant images of African Americans as an "underclass" with broken families, it is no accident that the show emphasized black middle-class success, a stable and unified black family, and high morals. And by dealing with universal issues, notably the problems of parenting, it invited audiences from different backgrounds to identify with the Huxtables.

For black writers and artists, "What is black?" has been a never-ending question. The post-1970 generation of fiction writers continued to turn to African-American history for ideas, inspiration, and insights into contemporary issues they wished to explore in their art. But many more began recovering the dark side of black life—domestic violence, psychological trauma, the internal conflicts that rarely show up in heroic stories of black achievement. Others turned to satire, laughing at aspects of black culture and the absurdity of race.

Though this sort of self-criticism is hardly new to black literature, it became more visible in the post–civil rights era. Like most African Americans, black artists were products of a rapidly changing world in which defining one's culture or identity seemed more complicated than ever. An increasing number of middle-class African Americans raised their children in integrated settings. West Indians and Latinos of African descent, many of whom migrated to the United States after 1965, reminded other African Americans that all black people do not share the same ethnic heritage. Black gays and lesbians began to come out publicly, insisting on basic civil rights, respect and recognition for their sexual orientation, and a place in African-American history and culture. Black feminists grew increasingly vocal in African-American political, cultural, and intellectual life.

Partly an outgrowth of the resurgence of black feminism, black women writers such as Toni Cade Bambara, Rita Dove, Audre Lorde, Toni Morrison, Gloria Naylor, Ntozake Shange, Alice Walker, and Sherley Anne Williams brilliantly approached the subjects of sexism, domestic violence, and other forms of women's oppression. Through fiction, poetry, and political essays, these writers gave voice to the concerns and experiences of women, literally writing them into history. They challenged the trend among the previous generation of black nationalist writers to focus on men. And they revealed a complicated history of gender and family conflict that rarely found its way into history books, let alone African-American fiction.

In the process, these women writers set new standards for creative writing. Gloria Naylor won the American Book Award for her first novel, *Women of Brewster Place* (1983); Ntozake Shange's highly acclaimed play, *For Colored Girls Who Have Considered Suicide/When the Rainbow is Enuf* (1976), received several awards, including the coveted Obie Award; Alice Walker's *The Color Purple* (1982) won both the American Book Award and the Pulitzer Prize.

Out of this generation of black women writers emerged one of the late twentieth century's most celebrated novelists, Pulitzer Prize winner and Nobel Laureate

Toni Morrison. Born Chloe Anthony Wofford in 1931, Morrison grew up in Lorain, Ohio. After earning a B.A. from Howard University and a master's degree in literature from Cornell University, she taught briefly at Texas Southern University in Houston and then returned to Howard University in 1957. In 1966 she left academia to become an editor at Random House, spending whatever free time she had on her fiction writing. *Beloved* (1987), her fifth novel, was a masterpiece— one of the most important literary achievements of the century. This beautifully written and very complicated novel about slavery, family life, and memory won the Pulitzer Prize for fiction. Throughout her writing, Morrison has turned to black culture and history as a way to explore the diversity of the human experience in the context of both love and hate, degradation and defiance, community and individualism. In 1993 she received the Nobel Prize for Literature.

Since the seventies and eighties, several black writers have finally been recognized in genres in which African Americans have tended to be overlooked. By the early nineties, for example, one of the country's most popular crime-detective novelists was black, Los Angeles author Walter Mosley. Each of the books in his trilogy, *White Butterfly, A Red Death,* and *Devil in a Blue Dress,* were instant successes. In the field of science fiction, Samuel Delany and Octavia Butler won major literary prizes for their work. They turned to the future rather than the past to explore issues of race, gender, and sexuality in contemporary society. Delany, a prolific author of sixteen novels and novellas and at least five nonfiction books, twice won the coveted Nebula Award from the Science Fiction Writers of America. Octavia Butler published nine novels between 1976 and 1989, and her novella, *Bloodchild,* won both the Hugo Award and the Nebula Award in 1985. Her first series of novels actually linked the ancient African past to the future; its central characters include African healers, a four-thousand-year-old Nubian "psychic vampire," and a variety of powerful, independent black women.

In the world of visual arts, earlier generations of artists—collagist Romare Bearden, painters Jacob Lawrence, Elizabeth Catlett, Robert Colescott, and sculptor Martin Puryear—continued to have a huge influence on the American art scene throughout the seventies and eighties. More recently, black artists have deliberately broken with traditional conventions like painting and sculpture. Acclaimed sculptor David Hammons playfully used objects such as human hair, chicken parts, watermelon, and elephant dung to comment on racial stereotypes and African-American culture. Faith Ringgold, a Harlem-born painter and political activist, turned to the older "folk" tradition of quilting as her primary medium in the early eighties. Adrian Piper has used photography, as well as drawings, texts, collage, and video technology, to bring out and thoroughly challenge her audience's racial fears and attitudes. A fair-skinned African-American woman who can sometimes "pass" as white, Piper made use of her own body to question people's assumptions about who is black and who is not.

The nineties witnessed the emergence of a younger generation of artists who turned to photography, painting, collage, sculpture, video, and performance to explore controversial aspects of race, gender, and sexuality. By revisiting stereotypes, exploring diversity within black communities, and turning to the interior, often hidden dimensions of black life, artists such as Dawoud Bey, Michael Ray Charles, Ellen Gallagher, Lyle Ashton Harris, Kerry James Marshall, Alison Saar, Gary Simmons, Lorna Simpson, Kara Walker, and Carrie Mae Weems have expanded what it means to be black in America.

Called by one critic "the post-soul era," black culture since the seventies seems limitless in range and depth. Never before have there been so many different ways to be black, so much so that even those who mimic African-American culture have had a difficult time trying to decide what to copy. The history of black culture in the late twentieth century is living proof that "blackness" has been—and will continue to be—multicultural.

## "Ain't No Stopping Us Now": Black Politics at the End of the Century

For African Americans, the end of the twentieth century looks very much like the end of the nineteenth century. The '60s and '70s, like the 1860s and 1870s, were decades of immense struggle and high expectations. Emancipation of sorts had been achieved and black communities looked to each other, and occasionally to the federal government, to help them secure their freedom. Most black people were optimistic. And they had a right to be, especially as they approached the nineties. The successful mayoral bids by Michael White in Cleveland, Sharon Pratt Dixon in Washington, D.C., and David Dinkins in New York City were not only indicative of the growing political strength of African Americans in major metropolitan areas but proved that black politicians were capable of winning over large numbers of white voters. This was certainly the case with Douglas Wilder's historic election as governor of Virginia in 1989; he became the first African American elected governor of any state. The same can be said of the successful mayoral campaigns of Norman Rice in Seattle, the Reverend Emmanuel Cleaver in Kansas City, and Wellington Webb in Denver. In all three cities, the majority of voters were white.

Yet despite these impressive gains, in 1988 blacks comprised only 1.5 percent of all elected officials, more than half of whom served on local school boards or city or town councils. Moreover, in many other respects the situation for African Americans actually worsened. Aside from the economic disaster caused by the loss of decent-paying jobs, reductions in social spending, and the decline in government subsidies to cities, racism and racist violence against African Americans actually intensified.

Since 1990, black customers and employees have filed suits against several nationally known restaurants for discrimination. In December 1991, for example, a group of black college students successfully sued an International House of Pancakes in Milwaukee, Wisconsin, for refusing to seat them. They were told that the restaurant was closed, though white customers were allowed in. The most notorious case involved Denny's restaurants. After the U.S. Department of Justice discovered a pattern of discrimination in the Denny's chain in 1993, Denny's corporate executives agreed to provide its employees with special training in non-discriminatory behavior and to include more minorities in its advertising. Yet, in spite of these attempts to change its corporate behavior, Denny's continued to discriminate against black customers. In one striking case that led to a separate lawsuit, six black Secret Service agents patronizing a Denny's in Annapolis, Maryland, waited an hour for service while the white customers, including their fellow white agents, were served promptly. Other instances of discrimination frequently encountered by African Americans occur when shop owners refuse to open their doors to black customers.

Some of the Denny's employees who testified suggested that this kind of treatment of black customers was part of the company's rational efforts to reduce robberies and disruptive behavior. The fear of crime and the presumption that black people are more likely than whites to commit crime, regardless of their age or class background, has led retail outlets to adopt blatantly discriminatory measures. For example, in several cities, one must ring a buzzer in order to be admitted to certain stores during business hours. If the customer looks legitimate, the salesperson, manager, or security guard admits him or her. Not surprisingly, African-American patrons are frequently left outside to window shop.

Such incidents, compounded by the impoverishment of a large segment of the black population, compelled African Americans to question the costs and benefits of integration. This never-ending battle with white racism convinced some former advocates of integration to turn inward, to build separate black institutions. Others believed integration has failed precisely because the new generation of black youth did not have a sense of history and pride in their cultural heritage. They insisted that the perspectives and experiences of African Americans be represented in classrooms, boardrooms, and political arenas. They saw no contradiction in celebrating their African heritage and participating as equals in the white world.

Not surprisingly, black nationalism has made a comeback among the nineties generation—the sons and daughters of the sixties generation. The militant nationalist and Muslim leader Malcolm X emerged as the decade's central black hero. Kinte cloth (a colorful and intricately woven West African fabric), beads, and leather medallions with outlines of Africa became popular consumer items. On many college campuses more and more young people could be seen wearing dreadlocks (twists of hair worn long and uncombed) and sporting T-shirts bearing such slogans as "Black by Popular Demand" or "Black to the Future." Membership in the Nation of Islam and other black Muslim groups rose dramatically during the late eighties and nineties.

In fact, during much of the 1990s, Minister Louis Farrakhan of the Nation of Islam enjoyed an upsurge of national and international popularity. He not only became a political force to be reckoned with among black leaders, but on October 16, 1995, he did what many said could not be done: He drew nearly one million African-American men to the nation's capital to pray, be in fellowship with one another, atone for their sins, and pledge to take responsibility for leadership in their communities and families. As Minister Farrakhan explained, the main purpose of the march was to "declare to the Government of America and the world that we are ready to take our place as the head of our families and our communities and that we, as black men, are ready to take responsibility for being the maintainers of our women and children and the builders of our communities." While it would be inaccurate to call the Million Man March a "protest," some of the speeches did criticize racism in the United States and lamented the erosion of the welfare system, and Farrakhan himself explained that the increase in the black prison population is related to the fact that prisons have become big business.

Even if the march did not produce a clear and concise political agenda, its powerful spiritual and emotional impact was undeniable. At the very least, the march spurred many men to become active in political organizations, trade unions, and community groups, and prompted a dialogue throughout African-American communities about the state of gender relations. It also inspired a Million Woman March in Philadelphia (October 25, 1997), and a Million Youth March in Atlanta and Harlem (September 5 and 25, 1998). Neither one of these gatherings attracted as many participants as the Million Man March, but they each articulated a more explicity political agenda. The women's gathering provided a forum to discuss, among other things, federal policies that adversely affect poor women, human rights abuses, and the need to establish more independent black schools. The youth march, led in New York by controversial ex-NOI minister Khalid Muhammad, was conceived both as an act of atonement as well as a political mobilization to protest racism, the deterioration of neighborhoods and schools, the decline in job opportunities, and police brutality. This otherwise peaceful event ended in violence when New York Mayor Rudolf Giuliani ordered the police to attack the crowd. Khalid Muhammad, who had exacerbated tensions between the crowd and police by inciting black youth to "take their guns" and then rushing from the scene of the protest, lost some respect among many of his young followers. When he attempted to organize another march one year later, it turned out to be a dismal failure. Nevertheless, taken together these marches proved that African Americans were prepared to come together for the sake of the entire community; it demonstrated the capacity for a renewed black grassroots social movement.

One important outgrowth of the upsurge in black nationalist sentiment has been the popularity of "Afrocentrism." Although there are many varieties of Afrocentric thought, the concept might best be described as a way of thinking and a type of scholarship that looks at the world from an African/African-American perspective. A good deal of Afrocentric scholarship argues that black people have a distinctive way of doing things, a set of cultural values and practices that are unique to their African heritage. Some scholars, such as Temple University Professor Molefi Asante, locate the origins of this distinctive African culture in the ancient African civilization of Egypt, and offer prescriptions for maintaining this Afrocentric way of life. Some black educators and parents have called for the incorporation of an Afrocentric curriculum in public schools. Others have turned to independent schools emphasizing Afrocentrism. The number of such schools has grown dramatically during the eighties and nineties, particularly in major cities such as Detroit, Washington, D.C., Los Angeles, and Oakland.

Though Afrocentrism and varieties of black nationalism are associated with radicalism, these philosophies share much in common with those of conservatives. Molefi Asante, for example, has been sharply criticized for arguing that an Afrocentric lifestyle includes distinct roles for men and women and that homosexuality is a form of deviance. Black Christian conservatives agree. Organizations such as Project 21, Concerned Citizens for Traditional Family Values, and the Traditional Values Coalition, and publications such as the *Black Chronicle* have mobilized conservative African Americans to protest legislation that would protect gay and lesbian rights and to attack the NAACP and the National Urban League for defending the rights of homosexuals.

Black feminists too have been attacked by Afrocentrists, black nationalists, and black conservatives who have called for a return to traditional male-female roles and placed a good deal of blame for the behavior of young black males squarely on the shoulders of single mothers, whom they characterize as irresponsible and incapable of disciplining their sons. One of the most controversial and best-known books to attack African-American feminists was *The Blackman's Guide to Understanding the Blackwoman* (1989). Written by a woman, Shahrazad Ali, a formerly unknown black street vendor of Afrocentric products, this vastly popular book caricatured black women as selfish, power hungry, aggressive, manipulating, and even dirty. Ali argued that true liberation required that black women return to their traditional African roles as child-care givers and supporters of black men.

The backlash against poor black women has had an even greater impact on social policies. The image of poor black women as promiscuous, highly irresponsible single mothers who spend years and years receiving welfare became increasingly popular in the late eighties and nineties. Although studies show that most women receive assistance for very short periods of time as a transitional stage between jobs, and many who do receive aid must nevertheless work part-time to make ends meet, the image of welfare cheats and overweight, indulgent, lazy black mothers was far more common among white voters. It was so pervasive that many liberal Democrats joined forces with Republicans to call for dramatic changes in public assistance. In fact, some of the most far-reaching changes in social welfare were initiated after George Bush was defeated by Democrat Bill Clinton in the 1992 presidential race.

In 1996 Clinton signed into law the Personal Responsibility and Work Opportunity Reconciliation Act, which replaced Aid to Families with Dependent Children (AFDC) with state block grants, denied benefits to legal immigrants, and cut funding for low-income programs, such as food stamps and Supplemental Security Income (SSI)—a program targeted to the elderly and disabled poor. The law was intended to force welfare recipients into the labor market, but it did not take into account the needs of children. Under the new law, for example, recipients whose youngest child is more than a year old must do some form of paid or unpaid work after twenty-four months of receiving benefits or lose their benefits altogether. And those who fail to find jobs within two months of receiving assistance are required to enroll in a mandatory workfare program. The Personal Resposibility Act does not include higher education in its definition of work or "training programs"; rather, welfare recipients are limited to vocational programs approved by the state. Furthermore, anyone convicted of a drug felony cannot receive direct aid or welfare for life.

The simmering backlash against African-American women and the efforts on the part of black feminists to reverse the trend were powerfully dramatized by a single event: the confirmation of Supreme Court Justice Clarence Thomas. A story of race, sex, and political intrigue, it was perhaps the biggest media spectacle of 1991. What began as a fairly routine and friendly hearing suddenly became a national scandal when the Senate Judiciary Committee called University of Oklahoma law professor Anita Hill to testify. Hill had worked for Thomas when he was with the Department of Education and later when he headed the Equal Employment Opportunities Commission. During the questioning, she revealed that Thomas had sexually harassed her—pestering her to go out on dates, bragging about his sexual prowess, and making explicit references to pornography.

Thomas's description of himself as a God-fearing, hard-working, self-made black man contrasted sharply with Hill's characterization of him as an avid consumer of pornography. Born in the little rural town of Pin Point, Georgia, he was raised by grandparents and attended Catholic schools most of his life. After earning a bachelor's degree from Holy Cross and a law degree from Yale University, he was hired as assistant attorney general for the state of Missouri in 1974, and in 1981 was appointed assistant secretary in the Office of Civil Rights in the Department of Education. In 1982 he accepted the chairmanship of the EEOC, which he held until 1990. The Reagan administration chose Thomas for these two important posts precisely because he opposed affirmative action and had criticized established civil rights leadership. His leadership of the EEOC effectively weakened the commission's role in combating discrimination on the basis of race, age, and sex.

Thomas's appointment to the Supreme Court was especially important for African Americans because he was to replace retiring Justice Thurgood Marshall—the first African American to serve on the Court. The Congressional Black Caucus and several other black leaders outside of the government came out strongly against Thomas because of his lack of judicial and intellectual qualifications and his staunch conservatism. Though himself a beneficiary of Yale University's affirmative action initiative to recruit more minority law students, Thomas opposed affirmative action, supported cutbacks in social programs geared to help the poor, and consistently attacked civil rights leadership.

When the confirmation hearings began, most black voters knew very little about Thomas or his views. Many African Americans who backed the confirmation of Thomas, for example, did not know that his actions within the EEOC eroded black civil rights substantially. Thomas's initial testimony and the White House press releases focused on his personal biography, emphasizing how he worked his way up from rural poverty to a successful career as an attorney and a judge. But lack of information is only part of the story. Many African Americans sided with Thomas simply because he was a black man about to hold one of the most powerful positions in the country. By emphasizing his impoverished rural upbringing he gained a sympathetic hearing from blacks eager to see a black man succeed. More importantly, he gained a sympathetic hearing from Democratic senators who were afraid to ask critical questions about his views on affirmative action and civil rights. Whenever these issues came up, Thomas would insist that he had an especially sensitive understanding of them because of his life as a black man from segregated Georgia.

While Anita Hill's allegations could have disgraced Thomas and cost him the nomination, they actually worked in his favor. Many African Americans dismissed Professor Hill as a spurned lover or a black woman out to destroy a black man's career—a characterization not unlike Shahrazad Ali's bizarre assertion in *The Blackman's Guide to Understanding the Blackwoman* that black women sabotaged the upward mobility of black men. Tragically, the alleged victim of sexual harassment was turned into the villain. On the other hand, several polls and interviews reveal that a majority of African Americans believed both Thomas and Hill were victims of white racism. They believed that Hill was being used by the Senate committee to keep a black man from occupying one of the most powerful positions in the federal government. Thomas manipulated these underlying feelings by testifying before the Senate Judiciary Committee that the hearings were a "high tech lynching for uppity blacks who in any way deign to think for themselves." On October 16, 1991, the Senate voted 52–48 to confirm Clarence Thomas as an associate justice of the Supreme Court.

In spite of a high black approval rating for Thomas as measured by polls, many black people—especially women—were outraged by Thomas's confirmation. Several black feminist organizations and activist groups publicly criticized the appointment and used the hearings to draw attention to the issue of sexual harassment and the general backlash against women in the United States. Sixteen hundred black women signed a three-quarter page advertisement in *The New York Times* denouncing the appointment and explaining the significance of the hearings for black women. The ad highlighted the long history of racial and sexual abuse black women have had to endure, the lack of protection against such violations, and the perpetuation of stereotypes that continue to represent black women as sexually promiscuous and immoral.

Throughout the country, the Senate Judiciary Committee's behavior during the Hill-Thomas hearings sparked women's organizations to promote more women to run for public office. In 1992, more women ran for office than ever before, and the percentage of women who went to the polls rose markedly, representing fifty-four percent of the American electorate.

One woman inspired by the Hill-Thomas hearings to run for the U.S. Senate from the state of Illinois was Carol Moseley-Braun. Born in Chicago in 1947, Braun earned a bachelor's degree from the University of Illinois and a law degree from the University of Chicago in 1972. Upon graduation she worked as assistant U.S. attorney for the Northern District of Illinois, and later she won a seat in the Illinois state legislature and was elected Cook County recorder of deeds. Although she had very little money and an understaffed campaign team, Moseley-Braun beat incumbent Alan Dixon (who voted for Thomas's confirmation) in her 1992 U.S. Senate race, thereby becoming the first black woman to be elected to the U.S. Senate.

Though Moseley-Braun's election certainly benefited from women's response to the Hill-Thomas hearings, black women had already begun to have a greater presence in national politics in the late eighties. Perhaps the most dynamic and uncompromising black elected official to emerge on the national scene in this period was California Congresswoman Maxine Waters. Born one of thirteen siblings in a housing project in St. Louis, Missouri, in 1938, she graduated from high school, got married, and took a number of low-paying jobs in order to make ends meet. She and her husband eventually moved to Los Angeles, where she worked in a garment factory and then for the telephone company. In the late sixties, Waters enrolled at California State University in Los Angeles, where she studied sociology, and then went on to teach in the Head Start program—a federally funded preschool program geared especially for poor and minority children.

Largely through her community work, Waters became involved in politics, winning a seat representing South Central Los Angeles in the state assembly in 1976. Her constant battles on the assembly floor produced some important pieces of legislation, including withdrawing investments of the California state pension fund from companies with ties to South Africa. Waters also established a vocational and education center in her district and increased access to social services for housing project residents in the Watts district. During this same period, she became active in national Democratic politics, serving as a key advisor to Jesse Jackson's 1984 presidential campaign.

In 1990 Waters was elected to the U.S. Congress from the 29th district of California, becoming one of the most vocal African Americans in the House of

Representatives. In 1991 she fought attempts to weaken laws requiring banks and savings and loans to service minority and low-income communities. In the aftermath of the riots that tore through Los Angeles in 1992, she emerged as the key spokeswoman for aggrieved residents of South Central Los Angeles. She and her staff organized residents of housing projects into carpools in order to get needed food, water, and other supplies that were unavailable during the uprising. Although she lamented the loss of life and destruction of property, she kept the issues surrounding the rebellion focused on the deteriorating social and economic conditions of African Americans and Latinos.

Not all significant political battles fought by African-American women took place in the sphere of electoral politics. Nor were they national in scope. Throughout the country poor, working-class, and some middle-class black women built and sustained community organizations that registered voters, patrolled the streets, challenged neighborhood drug dealers, and fought vigorously for improvements in housing, city services, health care, and public assistance. There was nothing new about black women taking the lead in community-based organizing. A century earlier, black women's clubs not only helped the less fortunate but played a key role in the political life of the African-American community. Even a generation earlier, when militant, predominantly male organizations like the Black Panther party and the Black Liberation Army received a great deal of press, black women carried on the tradition of community-based organizing. If one looked only at South Central Los Angeles in the mid-sixties, one would find well over a dozen such organizations, including the Watts Women's Association, the Avalon-Carver Community Center, the Mothers of Watts Community Action Council, Mothers Anonymous, the Welfare Recipients Union, the Welfare Rights Organization, the Central City Community Mental Health Center, the Neighborhood Organizations of Watts, and the South Central Volunteer Bureau of Los Angeles.

Black women activists continued the tradition of community organizing, but in the eighties and nineties they confronted new problems. Of the new battlegrounds, one of the most important has been the fight against toxic dumping in poor black communities. Calling themselves the movement against environmental racism or, alternately, the movement for environmental justice, local African-American, Latino, and Native-American groups, led largely by women, have fought against companies and government institutions responsible for placing landfills, hazardous waste sites, and chemical manufacturers dangerously close to low-income minority communities.

The evidence that poor African-American and other minority communities are singled out for toxic waste sites is overwhelming. One study released in 1987 estimated that three out of five African Americans live perilously close to abandoned toxic waste sites and hazardous commercial waste landfills. The study also revealed that the largest hazardous waste landfill in the country is located in Emelle, Alabama, whose population is 78.9 percent black, and that the greatest concentration of hazardous waste sites is in the mostly black and Latino South Side of Chicago. A 1992 study concluded that polluters based in minority areas are treated less severely by government agencies than those in largely white communities. Also, according to the report, federally sponsored toxic cleanup programs take longer and are less thorough in minority neighborhoods.

The effects of these policies have been devastating. Cases of asthma and other respiratory diseases as well as cancer have been traced to toxic waste. Accidents involving the mishandling of hazardous chemicals have ravaged some poor black communities, often with little or no publicity.

The roots of the environmental justice movement go back to 1982, when black and Native-American residents tried to block state authorities from building a chemical disposal site in Warren County, North Carolina. Since then, dozens of local movements have followed suit, including the Concerned Citizens of South Central (Los Angeles), and the North Richmond West County Toxics Coalition (near Oakland, California). By demonstrating, holding hearings and public workshops, conducting research, and filing suits against local and state governments, these groups have tried to draw attention to the racial and class biases that determine how hazardous waste sites are selected.

In the political arena, the nineties for African Americans have truly been the best of times and the worst of times. Black gains in the electoral sphere accompanied growing incidents of racism in public places; successful grassroots organizing followed discoveries of more toxic waste dumps; the spectacular rise of black women in national politics coincided with a vicious backlash against women in the society as a whole. And if this was not enough to complicate matters, the old order of black versus white was fast becoming obsolete. With the recent wave of immigration from nonwhite countries, African Americans found themselves surrounded by new neighbors, new cultures, and new issues with which they had to contend.

## Black to the Future: Immigration and the New Realities of Race

While the decade of the nineties was a period of resurgent black nationalism, it also was a period when what it meant to be "black" no longer was a simple matter. By the eighties, the increase in black *immigrants* to the United States, most of whom came from the Caribbean, profoundly changed the cultural makeup of black communities.

Black immigration from the Caribbean did not begin in the eighties; there had been vibrant West Indian communities, especially in New York City, at least as early as the twenties. However, several factors contributed to the massive influx of West Indians to the United States in the late twentieth century. First, the easing of restrictions on immigration to the United States after 1965 enabled greater numbers of West Indians to enter the country. Second, Britain imposed severe restrictions on immigrants from its own former colonies in 1962. Third, rising unemployment and poverty in the Caribbean during the seventies and eighties forced many West Indians to search for work in the United States. Thus, by the early eighties approximately fifty thousand legal immigrants from the English-speaking Caribbean and some six thousand to eight thousand Haitians were entering the United States annually, about half of whom settled in New York City.

Despite myths of West Indian affluence and financial success as a result of thrift and hard work, the majority of immigrants were very poor and worked mainly in service sector jobs, such as janitors, cooks, secretaries, and clerical work. Some established independent businesses—small groceries, taxi services, restaurants—but most of these are small, family-run enterprises. Haitians have faced the most difficulties because many are extremely poor refugees fleeing desperate poverty and political violence. To make matters worse, during the administrations of Presidents Reagan and Bush many Haitian refugees were detained by the Immigration and Naturalization Service and either deported or held in camps or prisons until they received a hearing.

There have been tensions between these new black immigrants and native-born African Americans, especially because they competed against each other in a shrinking labor market. Even during the first wave of immigration after the First World War, most West Indians have been fiercely independent in terms of maintaining their unique cultural heritage and not identifying more generally with "black Americans." As their communities grew, West Indians became even more distinctive, creating cultural institutions and political organizations that encouraged loyalty to their home island, and carving out a separate niche for themselves in black America.

On the whole, however, relations between West Indians and native-born African Americans have been good. Caribbean music, cuisine, and even dialects have been an integral part of African-American culture, especially on the East Coast. Caribbean youth were key contributors to the development of rap music.

The growth of Rastafarianism in the United States illustrates the impact black West Indian immigrants have had on African-American culture as a whole. Rastas, or members of the Rastafarian religious faith, regard the late Ethiopian emperor Haile Selassie as God. While preaching peace and love between the races, they also warn that some kind of race war is imminent. What made Rastafarianism appealing, aside from its highly spiritual form of black nationalism, was the culture surrounding it. Rastas tend to be vegetarians, do not drink alcohol, and wear their hair in dreadlocks. Their locks are never cut because hair is considered part of the spirit. The popularity of reggae music, in particular, was responsible for introducing Rastafarianism to American audiences. By 1990, there were about one million Rastas in the United States, at least eighty thousand of whom resided in New York City.

In the realm of politics, native-born African-American and Caribbean communities have worked collectively to fight racism in New York City, and some West Indians have even risen to important leadership roles in traditional civil rights organizations. (The Congress on Racial Equality has been headed by Virgin Islands native Roy Innis, although his Republican party affiliation has limited his political base among both West Indians and African Americans.) Similarly, African-American political leaders have maintained a long-standing interest in Caribbean politics. They have tended to support democratic political movements in the Caribbean and pushed for a more progressive U.S. policy toward that region. Some actively backed the struggle for independence from colonial rule back in the fifties and sixties.

As the number of Caribbean-born immigrants to the United States grows, what happens in the Caribbean takes on even greater importance in black politics. When President Reagan called for the invasion of the tiny island of Grenada in 1983, African Americans organized massive protests. Similarly, African-American political leaders have been among the most vocal supporters of Haitian refugees. After the democratically elected president of Haiti, Jean-Bertrand Aristide, was overthrown by the military and exiled in 1992, African Americans and West Indians consistently called for his return to power. Black political leaders have protested the Bush administration's harsh immigration policies toward Haiti, which often resulted in refusing entry to refugees fleeing political violence and starvation. Protests were also directed at the Clinton administration to develop a more active policy toward Haiti that would help restore democratic rule. As a result of demonstrations by several black members of Congress and a dramatic hunger strike waged by Randall Robinson, the president of a lobbying group called TransAfrica, President Clinton appointed former Congressman Bill Gray as special envoy to Haiti. In October 1994, Clinton went even further, pressuring the Haitian military to relinquish power and dispatching U.S. troops to restore Aristide to the presidency.

America's changing cultural and ethnic landscape not only calls into question the long-standing (and always false) presumption that the country was divided into two races—black and white. It transformed the meaning of race relations in America's inner cities. Before 1965, Jews were probably the most visible ethnic group with whom urban blacks had contact who did not simply fall into the category of "white." Relations between blacks and Jews in the past had always been mixed, running the gamut from allies in radical organizations to economic competitors. Because some Jews owned small retail outlets in African-American communities—largely because anti-Semitism kept them from establishing businesses elsewhere—blacks and Jews sometimes dealt with each other on the basis of a consumer/proprietor relationship. In the aftermath of the urban riots of the late sixties, however, most Jewish merchants sold off their businesses and the few still residing in the ghetto moved out. Except for places like Brooklyn's Crown Heights community, where tensions between blacks (mostly West Indians) and Hasidic Jews erupted in a major riot in 1991, few-inner city blacks live in close proximity to Jews.

But as the Jews moved out of the inner-city, new groups of immigrants moved in. The most prominent of the post-1965 wave of immigrants settling in or near

African-American communities were Asians from Korea, Vietnam, Cambodia, the Philippines, and Samoa, and Latinos from Central America, Cuba, Mexico, and the Dominican Republic.

The combination of economic competition, declining opportunities, scarce public resources, and racist attitudes led to a marked increase in interethnic conflict. In South Central Los Angeles, once an all-black community, Latinos made up about one-fourth of the population in 1992. Job and housing competition between Latinos (most of whom are Central American and Mexican immigrants) and African Americans created enormous tensions between these two groups. Black residents, who in the past had been indifferent to immigration, began supporting measures to limit the entry of Latinos into the United States.

On the other hand, Koreans have been singled out by both blacks and Latinos because a handful own retail establishments and rental property in the poorer sections of South Central Los Angeles. African-American and Latino residents believed the federal government favored Korean immigrants by offering them low interest loans and grants. The fact is, however, that few Korean merchants received federal aid. The majority in Los Angeles and elsewhere ran small family businesses—mainly liquor stores, groceries, discount markets, and specialized shops such as hair-care and manicure supply outlets. Often investing what little capital they brought with them from their home country, Koreans relied on family labor and maintained businesses with very low profit margins. Moreover, the idea that Koreans were denying blacks the opportunity to "own their own" businesses ignores the fact that most Korean establishments (particularly liquor stores) were purchased at enormously high prices from African Americans, who in turn had bought these businesses at high prices from Jews fleeing South Central in the late sixties and early seventies.

Last, and perhaps most important, the vast majority of Koreans were neither merchants nor landlords; they were low-wage workers. Nevertheless, blacks and Latinos perceived Koreans as thriving newcomers, backed by a white racist government, taking money and opportunities away from the residents. These perceptions were intensified by the myth that all Asian immigrants were "model minorities," hard-working and successful entrepreneurs who settled comfortably in the United States, and by a general anti-Asian sentiment that had swept the country after the recessions of the seventies and eighties.

But these interethnic tensions were not based entirely on myths. The daily interactions between blacks and Latinos and Korean merchants generated enormous hostility. A common complaint in Los Angeles and elsewhere (most notably, New York) was that Korean merchants treated black and Latino consumers disrespectfully. Fearful of crime, some Korean store owners have been known to follow customers down the aisles, ask to inspect customers' handbags, and refuse entry to young black males who they think looked "suspicious."

By the early nineties, tensions between African Americans and Korean merchants

After her 1990 election to the U.S. House of Representatives, Maxine Waters became one of the most vocal African Americans in Congress. Here, with Jesse Jackson, she speaks to reporters after meeting with the U.S. attorney general to discuss the Rodney King case.

escalated to the point of violence. In one six-month period in 1991, at least three African Americans and two Koreans were killed as a result of customer/proprietor disputes. The most dramatic encounter was the fatal shooting of fifteen-year-old Latasha Harlins in Los Angeles by Korean grocer Soon Ja Du, which was captured on videotape and played on network news programs throughout the country. The incident began when Du accused Harlins of stealing a $1.79 bottle of orange juice in spite of the fact that she held the bottle in clear view and had not attempted to leave the store. Angered by the accusation, Harlins exchanged harsh words with Du, and they engaged in some mutual shoving. As soon as Harlins struck a final blow and began to walk out of the store, Soon Ja Du pulled out a pistol from behind the counter and shot her in the back of the head.

African Americans were shocked and saddened by the shooting. Harlins's family pointed out that Latasha was an honor student at Compton High School and had no history of trouble. Local organizations called for boycotts of Korean-owned businesses, and tensions between merchants and community residents escalated even further. But black anger over the shooting turned to outrage when Judge Joyce Karlin sentenced Du to five years probation, a five-hundred-dollar fine, and community service, prompting a long-uttered lament among African Americans that a black person's life was of minimal value in the United States. Insult was added to injury when, five days after Du's sentencing, a black man from nearby Glendale, California, was sentenced to thirty days in jail for beating his dog.

The combination of interethnic tensions, white racism, and immense poverty exploded on April 29, 1992, when Los Angeles experienced the most widespread and devastating urban uprising in the history of the United States. The spark for the rebellion was a police brutality trial that ended in the acquittal of four officers who had savagely beaten a black motorist named Rodney King thirteen months earlier. Unlike most incidents of police brutality, this one was captured on videotape by George Holliday, a white plumbing company manager. Holliday tried to report the incident to Los Angeles Police Department officials, but he was rebuffed. Instead, he sold the videotape to a local television station and it soon became national news. The entire nation watched King writhe in pain as he absorbed fifty-six blows in a span of eighty-one seconds. In addition to punching, kicking, and whacking King with a wooden baton, police shocked him twice with a high voltage stun gun. When it was all over, King was left with a broken cheekbone, nine skull fractures, a shattered eye socket, and a broken ankle and needed twenty stitches in his face.

For most viewers, regardless of race, the videotape proved beyond a shadow of a doubt that the officers involved in the beating used excessive force. Thus, when the all-white jury handed down a not-guilty verdict on April 29, 1992, African Americans were shocked, saddened, and then very angry. Throughout Los Angeles, from South Central to downtown, groups of black people began to vent their rage. They were soon joined by Latinos and whites who were also shocked by the verdict. But as the violence unfolded, it became very clear that these riots were not just about the injustice meted out to Rodney King. As one black L.A. resident explained, "It wasn't just the Rodney King verdict. It's the whole thing, the shooting of Latasha Harlins and the lack of jail time for that Korean woman." In some neighborhoods, therefore, blacks and Latinos attacked Korean-owned businesses, white motorists, and each other rather than the police. Among the biggest targets were liquor stores, long seen as the cause of many of the black community's woes. And in the midst of chaos, virtually everyone went after property, seizing furniture, appliances, clothes, and most of all, food.

Unlike previous "race riots," the events in Los Angeles were multiethnic and not limited to the predominantly black ghettoes. Buildings burned from West Los Angeles and Watts to Koreatown, Long Beach, and Santa Monica. Of the first five thousand people arrested, fifty-two percent were Latino and only thirty-nine percent were African American. When the smoke finally began to clear on May 2, at least fifty-eight people were killed (twenty-six African Americans, eighteen Latinos, ten whites, two Asians, two unknown) and thousands were injured. The fires left more than five thousand buildings destroyed or badly damaged. The estimated property damage totaled a staggering $785 million.

More than any other event, the L.A. uprising dramatized to the rest of the country the tragic plight of urban America. And because it occurred during a Presidential election year, there was enormous pressure on President George Bush to offer a prompt response. He proposed Operation Weed and Seed, an urban policy that would provide big tax breaks to entrepreneurs willing to invest in inner cities, some limited programs for disadvantaged children, and a massive buildup of the police and criminal justice system. Indeed, the real emphasis was on the "weed" rather than the "seed" component; nearly eighty percent of the proposed $500 million allocation was earmarked for policing. Bush's proposals were severely criticized by liberal black political leaders and scholars. They felt that the "law-and-order"

A few days after the riots of late April 1992 ended in Los Angeles, members of several rival gangs called a press conference to announce a truce.

emphasis was misplaced and that giving tax breaks to companies was not enough to attract capital to South Central L.A. Attempts to do the same thing in the past have failed. On the other hand, black elected officials responded to the rebellion by holding meetings and conferences, and by visiting communities damaged by the riots. Established black leaders criticized the Bush administration's proposals but few proposed policies of their own. One exception was Representative Maxine Waters, who tried desperately but failed to get Congress to pass a sweeping and much-needed urban aid bill.

Ironically, one of the clearest and most comprehensive proposals came from leaders of the two largest black street gangs in Los Angeles. After a long and violent rivalry, leaders of the Bloods and the Crips called a truce and drafted a document called "Give Us the Hammer and the Nails and We Will Rebuild the City." The proposal asked for $2 billion to rebuild deteriorating and damaged neighborhoods; $1 billion to establish hospitals and health-care clinics to South Central Los Angeles; $700 million to improve public education and refurbish schools; $20 million in low-interest loans for minority businesses; $6 million to fund a new law-enforcement program that would allow ex-gang members, with the proper training, to accompany the LAPD patrols of the community. If these demands were met, the authors promised to rid Los Angeles of drug dealers and provide matching funds for an AIDS research and awareness center. Of course, some of these same gangs were involved in the drug trade themselves, suggesting that their proposal would eliminate an important source of their own revenue. Besides, it is doubtful that the Bloods and the Crips could raise matching funds. In any event, their efforts were to no avail; the mayor and the city council completely ignored the gang members' proposal.

Despite a deluge of plans and proposals, black Los Angeles remained pretty much unchanged in 1994. Two years after the riots, unemployment was still sky high, job opportunities were scarce, and the historic truce between the Crips and the Bloods had begun to unravel locally. Nevertheless, what happened in Los Angeles represented a kind of crossroads for the United States. It vividly called into question the idea that race relations in this country can be viewed as "black and white." It also underscored the extent of desperation in cities generated by the new global economy. The days when jobs were plentiful, even if they were low-wage jobs, are gone. Now America's inner city has an army of permanently unemployed men and women who have little or no hope of living the American Dream. Most keep pushing on. A handful turn to the underground, the illegal economy of bartering stolen goods and drugs. In some neighborhoods, that is all that is left. Meanwhile, the police deal with this tragedy by placing virtually every black person under siege.

Indeed, by the end of the century police harassment and brutality became the leading source of protest for African Americans, irrespective of class. The problem of police use of excessive force was dramatized by a series of high-profile beatings and shootings, including the 1997 assault on Haitian immigrant Abner Louima. New York police officers arrested, handcuffed, beat, and sexually assaulted Louima in the bathroom of a Brooklyn precinct house. After shoving a broken broomstick into Louima's rectum, officer Justin Volpe threatened to kill him if he told anyone about the assault. Louima did press charges, however, which resulted in Volpe's conviction and more investigations into other cases of racism and excessive force in the New York Police Department.

Less than two years later, members of the same NYPD Street Crimes Unit summarily shot to death another black immigrant, twenty-two-year-old street vendor Amadou Diallo. Despite the fact that he was unarmed, had no criminal record, and looked nothing like the alleged suspect in a Bronx rape case, four officers discharged forty-one bullets on him—nineteen of which entered his body. The Diallo killing prompted the largest police brutality protest in New York's history. Tens of thousands of protestors representing the entire spectrum of race, ethnicity, and age blocked the streets around city hall and engaged in civil disobedience that resulted in hundreds of arrests. Unfortunately, the Diallo killing and Louima beating were just the tip of the iceberg. During the first six months of 1999, for example, literally dozens of others in New York and across the nation were killed or badly beaten by police under dubious circumstances.

The most notable case highlighting racism in the criminal justice system centers around jailed journalist and activist Mumia Abu-Jamal. A former Black Panther party member whose exposés on police misconduct and racial discrimination in Philadelphia won awards and national acclaim, Mumia had been convicted of first-degree murder and sentenced to death for the alleged shooting of a white police officer on December 9, 1981. He had no prior criminal record, despite being subject to FBI surveillance since he was sixteen years old, and the evidence against Mumia was questionable, to say the least. An international movement, endorsed by many leading celebrities, lawyers, and social justice activists, arose demanding that he receive a new trial. A documentary film entitled *A Case for Reasonable Doubt* revealed a pattern of illegal behavior on the part of the Philadelphia police department, including suppressing evidence, intimidating witnesses, and paying off and threatening individuals to give false testimony, among other things. Even the secretary-general of Amnesty International expressed concern in a 1997 statement that "Mumia Abu-Jamal's original trial may have been contaminated by the deep-rooted racism that appears to taint the application of the death penalty in Pennsylvania." In late 1999, under a stay of execution, Mumia remained in prison fighting for a new trial.

Many black citizens were moved by these dramatic cases of police abuse, and some took to the streets in protest. But unequal police practices also affected ordinary African Americans directly in the form of "racial profiling," or what has been called "Driving While Black" (DWB). These are routine traffic stops by police used as a pretext to search for evidence. This practice is used ostensibly to target drug dealers and is based on the premise that most drug offenses are committed by people of color (mainly blacks and Latinos). Although the premise is factually untrue, the vast majority of motorists routinely stopped as alleged drug carriers are African Americans and Latinos. Between January 1995 and September 1996, the Maryland State Police stopped and searched 823 motorists on Interstate 95, of which 600 were black. Only 19.7 percent of those searched in this corridor were white. Some cases were highly publicized. In 1997 San Diego Chargers football player Shawn Lee and his girlfriend were pulled over, handcuffed, and detained by police for half an hour. The officer claimed that Lee's Jeep Cherokee fit the description of a vehicle stolen earlier that day. Records later revealed that the stolen vehicle was a Honda sedan. In 1998, a Liberian student named Nelson Walker was driving along I-95 in Maryland when he was pulled over by state police for not wearing a seatbelt. The officers proceeded to search his car for illegal drugs, weapons, or other contraband, to the point of dismantling a door panel, a seat panel, and part of the sunroof, but they found nothing. The overwhelming number of incidents like these became evident when victims began to sue and concerned politicians began promoting legislation to outlaw racial profiling. The state of New Jersey alone paid out over eight hundred thousand dollars in out-of-court settlements to victims of racial profiling.

The fact that the state of New Jersey could be compelled to make restitution payments to victims of racism is significant. The end of the 1990s marked a resurgence of a very old campaign to demand restitution or reparations to compensate African

Americans for the long history of discrimination, racist violence, and enslavement. The demand for reparations goes back at least to the nineteenth century. Abolitionist leader Sojourner Truth made the case for reparations through land distribution to ex-slaves, insisting that "America owes to my people some of the dividends. . . . I shall make them understand that there is a debt to the Negro people which they can never repay. At least, then, they must make amends." In 1890, a black woman named Callie House filed several suits and petitioned Congress for reparations. But by the year 2000, the dream of reparations has spawned a full-blown movement. Pointing to recent precedents in the form of reparations paid out to interned Japanese-Americans, Holocaust victims, Native land claims settlements, and isolated black victims of racial violence (e.g., in Rosewood, Florida), organizations such as the National Coalition of Blacks for Reparations in America (N'COBRA) and the African Reparations Movement (ARM) have argued strongly that government and private companies return the dividends made from centuries of slavery and institutionalized racism. And they have begun to win support. Michigan Representative John Conyers's decade-long efforts to get Congress to study the question of reparations began receiving nationwide support in 2000, especially after Democratic presidential-candidate Al Gore agreed that it was an issue worth investigating.

Reparations advocates also turned to the courts in an effort to sue firms that directly benefited from the slave trade. Deadria Farmer-Paellmann, the lead plaintiff in a high-profile suit against several U.S. companies, accused FleetBoston Financial, the railroad firm CSX, and the Aetna insurance company of benefiting directly from their corporate precedessors' roles in the Atlantic slave trade, which generated substantial profits that added to the capitalization of these modern firms. The suit, filed on behalf of thirty-five million African Americans, seeks reparations for stolen labor and "unjust enrichment," although no dollar amount is attached to the claim. Nevertheless, the legal team estimates that the current value of unpaid labor could amount to $1.4 trillion.

The reparations movement has received very little support outside of the black community, in large part because whites believe slavery is behind us and that African Americans have already received "handouts" from the government in the form of welfare. The general hostility toward reparations, however, reflects the last two decades of backlash against affirmative action. Supporters of reparations argue that what are now being called "special privileges" (welfare, anti-discrimination laws, state protection of equal opportunity) are not only "rights" but *payback* for two and a half centuries of exploitation and discrimination. Rather than blame the victim for their poverty, the reparations movement insists that the impoverished created much of America's wealth, that unpaid labor and discriminatory legislation— such as federal housing policies that consistently devalued black neighborhoods and subsidized middle-class white suburbs—explains racial disparities in wealth. Moreover, most reparations activists rarely call for individual payments but instead demand restitution in the form of massive investments in improving housing, schools, and infrastructure in predominantly black poor neighborhoods.

There have been some successful campaigns, though their victories proved bittersweet. In 1997 the Black Farmers and Agriculturists Association (BFAA) and the National Black Farmers Association (NBFA) filed a class action suit against the U.S. Department of Agriculture for a history of outright discrimination against farmers. The plaintiffs provided ample documentation of USDA officials denying black loan applications, altering applications in increase their likelihood of being rejected, and delaying the application process for black farmers until it was too late in the crop season to plant. A century of discrimination partly explains why the number of black farmers declined three times faster than whites. (In 1920, African Americans owned 14 percent of all U.S. farms. Eighty years later, blacks own only one percent of all farms.) After independent investigations corroborated the black farmers' allegations, the USDA agreed to settle the case in January of 1999. According to the consent decree, the USDA was expected to pay out about $400 million or more in total damages for violating black farmers' civil rights over the past sixteen years. The majority of black farmers covered by the suit were eligible to receive $50,000 and the cancellation of any USDA debt, if they could prove that they had been discriminated against. A small number with well-documented cases were eligible for higher awards but they had to agree to have their cases settled by a court-appointed arbitrator.

Neither the NBFA nor the BFAA were entirely happy with the settlement, especially since $50,000 is a paltry sum compared to the historic loss of property and the huge debt most black farmers accumulated from private loans after being consistently denied by the USDA. Nevertheless, they agreed and worked to help farmers file individual claims. The USDA worked, too, directing its energy to denying black farmers' claims, eventually turning down 90 percent of the growers who sought restitution. According to a report by the Environmental Working Group, about 96,000 black farmers made claims under the settlement; 72,438 of those claims were rejected in arbitration, and 7,800 for failing to meet filing deadlines. The report also revealed that the Justice Department spent 56,000 hours of attorney and paralegal time challenging 129 claims, which ended up costing the USDA $12 million. In the fall of 2004, black farmers retaliated with another class action suit against the USDA, this one seeking $20.5 billion on behalf of 25,000 growers who had been discriminated against since 1997 despite the settlement. The lawsuit alleges that the USDA not only continued its old practices, but also had singled out farmers who collected payments from the 1999 settlement.

## Another Nadir? African Americans in the New Millennium

Given all the individual success stories of African Americans in business, entertainment, and politics, it is easy to believe that black people swept into the new millennium triumphant. In fact, we can point to a few critical victories for Civil Rights and affirmative action during the first few years of the twenty-first century. In August of 1999, the NAACP declared a national boycott of resorts in South Carolina in an effort to compel the state government to remove the Confederate flag hoisted over the statehouse. The NAACP and many African Americans had come to see the Confederate flag as a symbol of slavery and white supremacy, and the campaign was part of an effort to get the nation to understand why the flag is so offensive. In January of 2000, the NAACP mobilized over 46,000 protesters to march on the state capitol. The boycott and the marches worked: South Carolina Governor Jim Hodges signed a bill that removed the flag on July 1, 2003.

Just days before "Old Glory" flew for the last time over the statehouse dome, the U.S. Supreme Court decided on two of the most important affirmative action cases since the Bakke decision of 1978. In *Grutter v. Bollinger*, in which a white law school applicant Barbara Grutter sued the University of Michigan Law School because she was rejected over minority applicants with lower overall test scores, the court voted 5-4 to uphold the law school's affirmative action policy of using race as one of many factors in order to maintain diversity. The majority opinion argued that race can be one of many factors considered by colleges when selecting their students because it furthers "a compelling interest in obtaining the educational benefits that flow from a diverse student body." In a similar case against the University of Michigan's undergraduate admissions policy, however, the court decided 6-3 to strike down its affirmative action program. The majority opinion, authored by Chief Justice William Rehnquist, argued that in this case the use of race as a factor violated the equal protection provisions of the Constitution and was not "narrowly tailored" to achieve the university's goal of diversity.

These victories aside, the dawn of the new millennium was characterized less by triumph and more by the continuing legacy of police violence, riots, discrimination, and poverty. In April of 2001, Cincinnati became the next Los Angeles after police officers fatally shot Timothy Thomas, a nineteen-year-old African American, in the predominantly black neighborhood of Over-the-Rhine. Police pursued the unarmed youth because they had a warrant out for his arrest for unpaid parking tickets. His murder sparked a massive insurrection in Over-the-Rhine and in other parts of Cincinnati that forced the Mayor to impose a state of emergency and compelled the governor to send in National Guard troops. Thomas's death was just the tip of the iceberg. He was the fifteenth black man killed by police since 1995, and the fourth to die since November of 2000.

When looked at from the vantage point of most poor and working-class African Americans, the state of race in the new millennium bears striking similarities with the turn of the last century—a period one historian characterized as "the nadir" or low point in African-American history. Just as the age of segregation and disfranchisement of black voters in the late 1890s and early 1900s followed in the wake of Reconstruction's promise of new democratic order, our Second Reconstruction—the black freedom movement of the 1950s, '60s and '70s—gave way to declining job opportunities, greater urban segregation caused by white flight, a reversal of many civil rights gains, a sharp increase in racist violence, and by some measures, a real threat to black voting rights.

Events in Florida during the closely contested 2000 presidential race between Republican George W. Bush and Democrat Al Gore taught black voters that, despite the 15th Amendment and the Voting Rights Act of 1965, their voting rights are not completely protected. Employing an 1868 statute denying convicted felons the right to vote, Florida's Secretary of State Katherine Harris issued a "purge" list of some 57,700 alleged felons to registrars containing many egregious errors, including the names of black citizens who had never committed a crime, received clemency, or had their record expunged. In Woodville, Florida, a police roadblock randomly stopped and searched black voters on their way to the polls. All in all, due to an array of technical problems, the state ended up discarding nearly 200,000 votes, most of which were from counties with large black populations. Florida was the key to the election; whoever won there would go to the White House. George W. Bush won by 537 votes. African Americans were not the only ones complaining about the election, but the NAACP filed suit against the Florida Secretary of State for violating the 14th Amendment and the Voting Rights Act of 1965, and the U.S. Civil Rights Commission launched an investigation and found evidence of "prohibited discrimination." The Congressional Black Caucus tried to file a formal complaint against the election, but without the signature of a single Senator, they could not make their case on the floor of Congress. No Senator was willing to sign; at the time of the 2000 election, there were no black Senators in office.

The suppression of the black vote—deliberate and unintended—was not limited to Florida. In the 2000 presidential elections, approximately 1.9 million ballots cast were deemed "spoiled" by election officials, and thus were never counted. According to research from the U.S. Civil Rights Commission and the Harvard University Law School Civil Rights Project, about half of these ballots were cast by African Americans. These ballots were thrown out because of machine malfunction, stray marks on the ballot, or in a few cases, voters writing in Al Gore instead of checking the box. The startlingly high percentage of spoiled ballots from black voters is partly the result of that fact that old and malfunctioning voting booths are more likely to found in low-income communities of color.

Of course, incidents of black voter suppression and intimidation predate the 2000 elections. In 1989 in North Carolina, the state Republican party and the Jessie Helms campaign sent postcards to one hundred twenty-five thousand voters, ninty-seven percent of whom were African American, giving them false information about voter eligibility and warning of criminal penalties for voter fraud. Indeed, there were enough violations of Southern black voting rights in the 1980s to warrant hearings, which contributed to the passage of the National Voter Registration Act (1993) intended "to remove the vestiges of discrimination which have historically resulted in lower voter registration rates of minorities and persons with disabilities."

Despite the legislation, incidents of discrimination and voter intimidation continued unabated. In Louisiana in 2002, African Americans were given flyers telling voters that they could go to the polls on Tuesday, December 10, three days after the date set for the Senate runoff election. More recently, the Civil Rights Commission and independent investigators reported several incidents of black voter suppression and intimidation. In 2004, armed, plainclothes police officers representing the Florida Department of Law Enforcement (FDLE) entered the homes of many elderly voters in Orlando, Florida, claiming to be investigating voting irregularities in the city's mayoral election. Although the FDLE had already closed its investigation, finding no evidence of wrongdoing, the officers questioned elderly black citizens, often with their guns in plain sight. Six members of Congress called on the Justice Department to investigate. In Kentucky, the state Republican party's plans to station "vote challengers" in black precincts during the 2004 elections was met with opposition from African Americans in their own party. "Vote challengers" were not limited to the South, however. In 2003, black voters in Philadelphia were approached by men holding clipboards with signs designed to look like law enforcement insignia. They tried to discourage voters with veiled accusations that they might be in violation of the law. These men, who drove around in black sedans, worked for no official agency; rather, they turned out to be operatives for the Republican party.

But unlike America a century ago, the party divisions were not so black and white. The Republican party had a small but influential following among African Americans, and George W. Bush made history when he appointed General Colin Powell to position of secretary of state and Condoleezza Rice to national security advisor. These were the first African Americans to hold such powerful positions, and Rice was the first woman ever to become national security advisor. Obviously, they were both quite loyal to the administration and ended up playing key roles in the development of President Bush's foreign policy—a policy that, at its heart, was committed to strengthening and expanding America's imperial power.

Here again, the comparison with the end of the nineteenth century is revealing, for both eras witnessed the expansion of American imperialism through war. With the closing of the frontier in the 1890s, several U.S. business and political leaders were looking for ways to expand the nation's empire beyond Hawaii and Alaska. When the Spanish sank the Maine, one of the U.S. fleet's prized battleships, in January of 1898, it sparked a war with Spain that enabled the United States to seize Puerto Rico, Cuba, and the Philippines. And it launched a new era for the United States as a preeminent political and economic force in the world.

A century later, the Bush administration had an even more grandiose vision of empire. Certainly, before Bush's election in 2000, the United States had been involved in many invasions and peace-keeping operations throughout the last two decades of the twentieth century (e.g., Grenada, Panama, Kosovo, and Somalia) and in 1991, waged an all-out war against Iraq. On September 11, 2001, the United States experienced its version of the Maine, but this attack was far more ghastly and devastating. On that fateful morning, four commercial airliners had been hijacked by Saudi terrorists and turned into weapons of mass destruction. One crashed into the Pentagon, two rammed into the two towers that once made up the World Trade Center in lower Manhattan, and the fourth plane crashed before reaching it's intended destination (possibly the White House). Altogether, over three thousand peopled died in these attacks, the vast majority in the World Trade Center. The hijackers were all linked to Al Qaeda, a terrorist organization led by Osama bin Laden. A member of the oil-rich bin Laden family of Saudi Arabia, Osama had once been a U.S. ally when he and his men fought to drive the Russian military out of Afghanistan.

President Bush immediately dispatched troops to Afghanistan to hunt for Osama bin Laden and to destroy Al Qaeda once and for all. Although the United States failed to capture bin Laden, they succeeded in overthrowing the Taliban government and installing a regime friendly to the United States. And then President Bush turned his sights on Iraq. Secretary of State Colin Powell made a case to the United Nations that Iraq, under president Saddam Hussein, was building and hiding illegal weapons of mass destruction that they planned to use to back terrorist attacks in the United States and elsewhere. He also claimed that Hussein had developed an alliance with bin Laden, despite their longstanding mutual dislike of each other. Powell would later recant his testimony, citing false and misleading intelligence. Indeed, his admission that there were neither weapons of mass destruction or a link between bin Laden and Hussein consequently put him at odds with the White House and other members of Bush's administration. Lacking in evidence, the Bush administration nevertheless made a case to invade Iraq and practically all of Congress voted to authorize the president to declare war—all, except one: an African-American congresswoman named Barbara Lee (D-Calif.). Lee not only cast the lone congressional vote against the war, but she authored a resolution calling on Congress to prohibit the nation from acting against world opinion. And world opinion was strong and unambiguous when it came to the war. Not only had the United Nations refuse to sanction the invasion, withholding it's own troops as a consequence, but on February 15, 2003, some six million people in cities all over the world took to the streets to protest the impending invasion. By most accounts, it was the biggest antiwar rally in history. But it did not stop the invasion: The first troops entered Iraq a little more than a month later.

Just as many African Americans opposed the U. S. occupation of the Philippines and Puerto Rico during the Spanish-American War, the majority of African Americans opposed the U. S. war in Iraq. A poll conducted by the Joint Center for Political Studies about a year after the invasion found only 19.2 percent of African Americans support a war with Iraq. Yet, not unlike a century earlier when black men fought heroically in Cuba and the Philippines, African Americans also figured prominently in the Iraq war. In 2000, about 30 percent of army enlistees were African American, while almost half of the army's enlisted women were black. Consequently, although African Americans made up about 12.5 percent of the nation's population, by April of 2004 they constituted about a fifth (20 percent) of all casualties in the Iraq war. So once again, the descendants of slaves figure centrally in key historical events. It is not clear what will happen in Iraq or how long the U.S. military will be there, but whatever the outcome African Americans will play a critical role in deciding the fate of the war and the nation.

The generation that came of age in the '70s, '80s, and '90s were called a lot of things: the post-soul generation, the post–civil rights generation, the postindustrial generation. But few standing "at the edge of history," to use the language of the Gary Declaration, thought in terms of being "post" anything. Rather, they entered a new period with tremendous efforts toward racial integration. For others it was the hope for greater political and social control of their lives. For most African Americans it was a combination of both with a little fun and pleasure thrown in for good measure.

Few anticipated the economic, social, and political crises poor urban blacks would have to face, and fewer still imagined the plush black suburbs of Prince Georges County, Maryland, or that several black-owned companies might one day dwarf Motown Records. Although each difficult day questioned their faith in this country, young mothers and fathers hoped that racism would diminish a little and life for their children would be much easier. In some cases their lives *were* much easier; in other cases a racist police officer's bullet or the fists, sticks, and stones of skinheads or random gang violence cut their young lives short.

But this story is not finished yet, and it need not have a tragic ending. The chapters to come will be written by all of us still living, including you who hold this book in your hands. What we add to this story depends, to a large degree, on us . . . all of us: black and white, Latino and Asian, Native American and Arab American, Jew and Gentile, women and men, rich and poor. If there is one thing we have learned from this book, it is that the problems facing African Americans are not simply outgrowths of a crisis in *black* America. They are products of America's crisis. We must constantly remind ourselves that America's future is bound up with the descendants of slaves and the circumstances they must endure. As police brutality victim Rodney King put it in his memorable press conference following the Los Angeles uprising, "We're all stuck here for a while."

# Chronology

### 1879–1881

First major migration of African Americans from the South to Kansas and Western territories occurs.

### July 4, 1881

Booker T. Washington opens Tuskegee Institute in Tuskegee, Alabama.

### October 15, 1883

In *Civil Rights Cases*, the U.S. Supreme Court reverses the 1875 Civil Rights Act.

### May 1884

Schoolteacher Ida B. Wells is removed from the Chesapeake, Ohio, and Southwestern Railroad and begins her lawsuit against the racial segregation of railway transportation.

### 1886

The Knights of Labor reaches its peak membership at seven hundred thousand, including between sixty thousand and ninety thousand African Americans.

### March 1888

The Colored Farmers' National Alliance and Cooperative Union is founded in Lovejoy, Texas.

### 1889

The federal government opens Oklahoma Territory to settlement, and some seven thousand African Americans participate in the land rush.

### 1890

The National Afro-American League is founded by T. Thomas Fortune.

The all-black town of Langston, Oklahoma Territory, is founded.

### 1892

Anna Julia Cooper publishes a set of theoretical essays, *A Voice from the South*, and Frances Ellen Watkins Harper publishes her novel *Iola Leroy*.

The Populist, or People's, party emerges as an independent political party with the support of black and white farmers and laborers.

### October 1892

Ida B. Wells gives landmark speech about lynching at New York City's Lyric Hall and publishes *Southern Horrors: Lynch Law in All Its Phases*.

### 1893

Black women leaders address the Women's Congress at the World's Columbian Exposition in Chicago.

Ida B. Wells makes anti-lynching lecture tour of Great Britain.

**June 1895**

W. E. B. Du Bois receives his Ph.D. from Harvard University, the first African American to do so.

**September 18, 1895**

Booker T. Washington delivers "Atlanta Compromise" speech at the Cotton States and International Exposition in Atlanta, Georgia.

**May 18, 1896**

In *Plessy* v. *Ferguson*, U.S. Supreme Court establishes principle that racial segregation is constitutional as long as "separate but equal" facilities are provided

**July 21, 1896**

The National Association of Colored Women is organized in Washington, D.C.

**July 1898**

Black troops participate in the Spanish-American War.

**August 23–24, 1900**

The National Negro Business League is formed in Boston.

**September 1900**

Nannie Helen Burroughs leads the founding of the Women's Convention of the National Baptist Convention in Richmond, Virginia.

**1901**

Publication of *Up from Slavery* by Booker T. Washington.

William Monroe Trotter establishes the *Boston Guardian.*

**1903**

Publication of *The Souls of Black Folk* by W. E. B. Du Bois.

**1905**

Robert S. Abbott establishes the *Chicago Defender.*

**July 1905**

Niagara movement founded to demand full citizenship for blacks and the abolition of all racial distinctions.

**September 1906**

Race riot in Atlanta.

**1910**

Founding of the National Association for the Advancement of Colored People.

**1914**

The First World War begins.

The Universal Negro Improvement Association is founded in Jamaica.

**1916**

Great Migration of blacks from the South to the North begins.

**April 1917**

United States enters the First World War.

**November 1918**

The First World War ends.

**1919**

Race riots break out in twenty-six cities across the United States.

**1920**

20th Amendment to the Constitution ratified, providing women the right to vote. Black women in the South, like black men, remain largely disfranchised.

Negro National League in baseball is founded.

## 1921–22

*Shuffle Along,* a musical written, produced by, and starring African Americans, is the most popular show on Broadway.

## 1923

Marcus Garvey is imprisoned for mail fraud.

## 1925

The Brotherhood of Sleeping Car Porters and Maids is founded.

Publication of *The New Negro,* edited by Alain Locke.

## 1928

Oscar DePriest (Republican, Chicago) becomes the first African American elected to Congress from a district north of the Mason-Dixon line.

## October 24, 1929

Stock market crashes; Great Depression begins.

## 1931

Communist party assists in the formation of the Alabama Sharecroppers Union.

## March 1931

Eight of the nine Scottsboro Boys are tried and convicted of rape in an Alabama court.

## 1932

U.S. Supreme Court overturns conviction of Scottsboro Boys in *Powell* v. *Alabama.*

## November 1932

Franklin D. Roosevelt elected president.

## 1933

The National Association for the Advancement of Colored People, the National Urban League, and other civil rights organizations organize the Joint Committee on National Recovery.

*Negro History Bulletin* begins publication under Carter G. Woodson.

## 1934

Socialist party organizes the Southern Tenant Farmers Union.

## 1935

In *Pearson* v. *Murray,* the Maryland Court of Appeals orders the University of Maryland to admit African Americans to the state's all-white law school or to set up a separate law school for blacks; the University of Maryland chooses to admit its first African-American students.

Brotherhood of Sleeping Car Porters and Maids receives an international charter from the American Federation of Labor.

Race riot breaks out in Harlem.

National Labor Relations Act (Wagner Act) is passed by Congress; National Labor Relations Board established.

U.S. Supreme Court again overturns convictions of Scottsboro Boys, in *Norris* v. *Alabama.*

## 1936

Nearly six hundred black organizations form the National Negro Congress; A. Philip Randolph is elected its first president.

## 1937

Brotherhood of Sleeping Car Porters and Maids signs its first contract with the Pullman Company.

**1938**

Joe Louis defeats German boxer Max Schmeling.

**1940**

Righard Wright's novel *Native Son* is published.

**June 1941**

A. Philip Randolph organizes March on Washington.

**June 24, 1941**

Franklin Roosevelt issues Executive Order 8802, establishing the Fair Employment Practices Committee.

**December 7, 1941**

Japan attacks Pearl Harbor; United States enters the Second World War the next day.

**1943**

Race riots break out in Harlem and Detroit.

**1944**

Swedish economist Gunnar Myrdal publishes *An American Dilemma: The Negro Problem and Modern Democracy.*

**August 14, 1945**

The Second World War ends; nearly one million African Americans served in the U.S. Armed Forces during the war.

**June 3, 1946**

U.S. Supreme Court bans segregation in interstate bus travel in *Morgan* v. *Virginia.*

**April 9, 1947**

Civil rights groups organize the first Freedom Rides to test compliance with bus integration law.

**April 10, 1947**

Jackie Robinson of the Brooklyn Dodgers becomes the first African American to play major league baseball.

**July 26, 1948**

President Harry S. Truman signs an executive order ending segregation of the armed forces.

**May 17, 1954**

U.S. Supreme Court rules in *Brown* v. *Board of Education* that school segregation is illegal.

**December 1, 1955**

In Montgomery, Alabama, a bus boycott begins after Rosa Parks is arrested for refusing to give up her seat on a bus to a white man.

**November 13, 1956**

U.S. Supreme Court rules in *Gayle* v. *Browder* that segregation in Montgomery's buses is illegal.

**September 1957**

President Dwight D. Eisenhower orders federal troops to enforce school desegregation in Little Rock, Arkansas.

**February 1960**

Students stage a sit-in to protest segregated lunch counters in Greensboro, North Carolina.

**September 30, 1962**

Riots erupt after James Meredith becomes the first black student to enroll at the University of Mississippi.

**May 3, 1963**

Police in Birmingham, Alabama, use dogs and fire hoses to attack civil rights marchers.

**June 11, 1963**

Governor George Wallace stands in the door of the University of Alabama to prevent a black student from enrolling.

**June 12, 1963**

Civil rights leader Medgar Evers is slain in Jackson, Mississippi.

**August 28, 1963**

Martin Luther King, Jr., leads twenty-five hundred thousand Americans in the March on Washington, D.C.

**September 15, 1963**

Four schoolgirls are killed when a bomb explodes at the Sixteenth Street Baptist Church in Birmingham.

**November 22, 1963**

President John F. Kennedy is assassinated in Dallas, Texas.

**June 20, 1964**

During Freedom Summer, one thousand civil rights volunteers go to Mississippi.

**July 2, 1964**

President Lyndon Johnson signs Civil Rights Act.

**August 20, 1964**

President Lyndon Johnson signs the Economic Opportunity Act.

**December 10, 1964**

Martin Luther King, Jr., receives the Nobel Peace Prize.

**February 1965**

Malcolm X is shot and killed in New York City.

**March 7, 1965**

Civil rights marchers in Selma, Alabama, are clubbed and gassed by police.

**March 9, 1965**

Under the protection of federal troops, civil rights marchers complete the trek from Selma to Montgomery.

**August 11, 1965**

Rebellion in the Watts section of Los Angeles results in thirty-four people dead and $35 million in property damage.

**June 26, 1966**

At a civil rights rally in Mississippi, Stokely Carmichael launches the Black Power movement.

**July 1967**

Riots in urban areas leave scores dead and many neighborhoods in ruins.

**October 2, 1967**

Thurgood Marshall is sworn in as the first African-American justice of the U.S. Supreme Court.

**February 29, 1968**

The Kerner Commission warns that America is becoming "two societies—one black, one white—separate and unequal."

**April 4, 1968**

Martin Luther King, Jr., is assassinated in Memphis, Tennessee.

**June 19, 1968**

The Poor People's Campaign brings fifty thousand demonstrators to Washington.

**1970**

Race riots erupt in several cities, including Philadelphia; New Orleans; New Bedford, Massachusetts; and Hartford, Connecticut.

**September 1970**

Black Panther party, along with women's and gay liberation activists, holds the Revolutionary People's Constitutional Convention in Philadelphia.

**October 13, 1970**

Angela Davis arrested and charged with murder, kidnapping, and conspiracy; case prompts an international campaign to free her. Two years later, she is found not guilty.

**1971**

Congressional Black Caucus is founded.

**1972**

Shirley Chisholm becomes first African American in history to seek the Democratic party's presidential nomination.

Coalition of Black Trade Unionists is founded.

**March 1972**

National Black Political Assembly holds its founding convention in Gary, Indiana.

**1973**

National Black Feminist Organization is founded.

Tom Bradley is elected first black mayor of Los Angeles.

**1973–75**

United States experiences worst economic recession in decades.

**1975**

NAACP wins court order to integrate Boston schools by busing black children from Roxbury to predominantly white schools in Charlestown; the transition is marred by violence.

Wallace D. Muhammad takes over Nation of Islam after death of his father, Elijah Muhammad. He denounces his father's teachings, adopts orthodox Islam, and changes the name of the organization to the World Community of al-Islam in the West.

**February 1977**

Television miniseries "Roots," based on Alex Haley's best-selling novel, is watched by a record 130 million viewers, sparking a national debate about race and African-American history.

**1978**

Black unemployment rate is nearly 2.5 times higher than white; this is the largest gap since the federal government began keeping such statistics.

Allan Bakke's charge of "reverse discrimination" against the University of California, Davis, Medical School weakens affirmative action policies when the Supreme Court rules in *Regents of the University of California* v. *Bakke* that he had been denied "equal protection of the laws" as required by the 14th Amendment.

Louis Farrakhan breaks with Wallace D. Muhammad and reestablishes the Nation of Islam under Elijah Muhammad's original beliefs.

**1979**

The Sugar Hill Gang releases the first commercially successful rap single.

**May 1980**

African Americans in Liberty City, Florida, riot after police officers are acquitted for killing an unarmed black man.

**November 1980**

National Black Independent Political party is founded.

**1982**

Alice Walker publishes *The Color Purple,* which received the American Book Award and the Pulitzer Prize.

The struggle to block a toxic waste dump in Warren County, North Carolina, launches a national movement against environmental racism.

**1983**

Harold Washington is elected first black mayor of Chicago.

**1984**

Jesse Jackson makes first bid for the Democratic party's presidential nomination, receiving about 3.5 million popular votes in the primaries.

"The Cosby Show" makes its debut, becoming the most popular regular program on television.

**May 1985**

Black Philadelphia Mayor Wilson Goode directs the police to bomb the headquarters of MOVE, a local black nationalist organization. The bombing leaves eleven people dead and two hundred and fifty people homeless.

**September 1985**

U.S. Census Bureau reports that one out of three African Americans is living below the poverty line.

**1986**

Spike Lee releases his first feature film, *She's Gotta Have It,* igniting Hollywood's interest in young black male filmmakers.

**1988**

Jesse Jackson seeks Democratic presidential nomination for a second time; he receives seven million votes and is Michael Dukakis's strongest challenger for the nomination.

The Black Women Mayor's Caucus is founded.

**1989**

Douglas L. Wilder is elected governor of Virginia and becomes the first African American elected governor of any state.

**1990**

Sharon Pratt Kelly (formerly Dixon) is elected mayor of Washington, D.C. She is the first African American and first native of the district to hold that post.

**1991**

Julie Dash releases *Daughters of the Dust,* the first feature film by an African-American woman.

**October 1991**

Anita Hill's testimony during the confirmation hearings of Supreme Court Justice Clarence Thomas launches a nationwide discussion of sexual harassment.

**1992**

Carol Moseley-Braun becomes first African-American woman elected to the U.S. Senate.

**April 29–May 1, 1992**

Acquittal of four Los Angeles police officers accused of using excessive force on black motorist Rodney King sparks the largest, most costly urban rebellion in U.S. history.

**1993**

Novelist Toni Morrison wins Nobel Prize for literature.

**May 1994**

Class-action suit forces Denny's restaurant chain to pay $54 million in damages for systematically discriminating against African-American customers.

## 1996

President Bill Clinton signs into law the Personal Responsibility and Work Opportunity Reconciliation Act, which replaced Aid to Families with Dependent Children (AFDC) with state block grants and cut funding for programs to help the poor.

## 1997

New York police officers beat and sexually assault Haitian immigrant Abner Louima; high-profile case calls attention to the problem of police brutality.

## January 4, 1999

Judge Paul Friedman signs a consent decree settling a class-action lawsuit against the U.S. Department of Agriculture for discrimination against black farmers. The settlement promises approximately $400 million in restitution to be paid out to thousands of claimants.

## February 4, 1999

New York police officers discharge forty-one bullets at black immigrant Amadou Diallo; the killing prompts the largest police brutality protest in New York's history.

## August 1999

The NAACP calls for a national boycott of vacation spots in South Carolina in an attempt to force the state government to remove the Confederate flag from the dome of its statehouse.

## January 17, 2000

More than forty-six thousand protesters march on the state capitol at Columbia, South Carolina, to protest the Confederate battle flag flying atop the statehouse dome.

## February 22, 2000

Florida bans race as factor in college admissions. Florida legislature approves education component of Govenor Jeb Bush's "One Florida" initiative, aimed at ending affirmative action in the state.

## December 2000

Condoleezza Rice is appointed by President-elect George W. Bush to serve as national security advisor. She becomes first African American and first women to serve in this position.

## January 20, 2001

General Colin L. Powell is sworn in by President George W. Bush as secretary of state. He becomes the first African American appointed secretary of state.

## April 2001

Cincinnati police fatally shoot unarmed black youth, Timothy Thomas—the fourth African American male killed by Cincinnati police in five months. The killing sparks a week of rioting, forcing the governor to call in the National Guard.

## September 11, 2001

Terrorists attack New York's World Trade Center and the Pentagon using hijacked commercial airliners; over three thousand die in these attacks.

## October 2001

U.S. and British forces invade Afghanistan.

## January 29, 2002

President George Bush identifies Iraq as part of the "axis of evil," and vows that the United States "will not permit the world's most dangerous regimes to threaten us with the world's most destructive weapons."

**October 11, 2002**

Congress authorizes an attack on Iraq. Representative Barbara Lee (Democrat, California) casts the lone vote against authorizing the president to wage war.

**March 20, 2003**

The war against Iraq begins.

**June 23, 2003**

In *Grutter* v. *Bollinger*, the Supreme Court upholds(5–4) the University of Michigan Law School's policy of using race as one of many factors in making admissions decisions. In a separate but related ruling, the court votes 6–3 to strike down University of Michigan's undergraduate affirmative action policy.

# Further Reading

## General African-American History

Anderson, James D. *The Education of Blacks in the South, 1860–1935.* Chapel Hill: University of North Carolina Press, 1988.

Aptheker, Herbert, ed. *A Documentary History of the Negro People in the United States.* Vols. 1–2. New York: Citadel Press, 1951.

Aptheker, Herbert, ed. *A Documentary History of the Negro People in the United States.* Vols. 5–7. Secaucus, N.J.: Carol Publishing, 1994.

Bennett, Lerone, Jr. *Before the Mayflower: A History of Black America.* 6th rev. ed. New York: Viking Penguin, 1988.

———. *The Shaping of Black America.* New York: Viking Penguin, 1993.

Berry, Mary Frances, and John W. Blassingame. *Long Memory: The Black Experience in America.* New York: Oxford University Press, 1982.

Blackburn, Robin. *The Overthrow of Colonial Slavery, 1776–1848.* New York: Verso, 1988.

Boles, John B. *Black Southerners, 1619–1869.* Lexington: University Press of Kentucky, 1983.

Conniff, Michael, and Thomas J. Davis. *Africans in the Americas: A History of the Black Diaspora.* New York: St. Martin's Press, 1993.

Cooper, Anna Julia. *A Voice from the South.* 1892. Reprint, New York: Oxford University Press, 1988.

Foner, Philip S. *History of Black Americans: From Africa to the Emergence of the Cotton Kingdom.* Westport, Conn.: Greenwood, 1975.

Franklin, John Hope, and August Meier, eds. *Black Leaders of the Twentieth Century.* Urbana: University of Illinois Press, 1982.

Franklin, John H., and Alfred A. Moss, Jr. *From Slavery to Freedom: A History of African Americans.* 8th ed. Boston: McGraw-Hill, 1999.

Garwood, Alfred N., comp. *Black Americans: A Statistical Sourcebook 1992.* Boulder, Colo.: Numbers and Concepts, 1993.

Gates, Henry L., Jr. *A Chronology of African-American History from 1445–1980.* New York: Amistad, 1980.

Genovese, Eugene. *From Rebellion to Revolution: Afro-American Slave Revolts in the Making of the Atlantic World.* Baton Rouge: Louisiana State University Press, 1979.

Giddings, Paula. *When and Where I Enter: The Impact of Black Women on Race and Sex in America*. New York: Bantam, 1984.

Gutman, Herbert G. *The Black Family in Slavery and Freedom, 1750–1925*. New York: Vintage, 1977.

Harding, Vincent. *There Is a River: The Black Struggle for Freedom in America*. San Diego: Harcourt Brace, 1981.

Harris, William H. *The Harder We Run: Black Workers Since the Civil War*. New York: Oxford University Press, 1982.

Hine, Darlene C., et al., eds. *Black Women in America*. New York: Carlson, 1993.

Hornsby, Alton, Jr. *Chronology of African-American History: Significant Events and People from 1619 to the Present*. Detroit: Gale Research, 1991.

Jaynes, Gerald David, and Robin M. Williams, Jr., *A Common Destiny: Blacks and American Society*. Washington, D.C.: National Academy Press, 1989.

Jones, Jacqueline. *Labor of Love, Labor of Sorrow: Black Women, Work, and the Family from Slavery to the Present*. New York: Basic Books, 1985.

Levine, Lawrence. *Black Culture and Black Consciousness: Afro-American Folk Thought from Slavery to Freedom*. New York: Oxford University Press, 1977.

Litwack, Leon, and August Meier. *Black Leaders of the 19th Century*. Urbana: University of Illinois Press, 1988.

Mintz, Sidney W., and Richard Price. *The Birth of African- American Culture: An Anthropological Perspective*. Boston: Beacon, 1992.

Nash, Gary B. *Red, White, and Black: The Peoples of Early America*. Englewood Cliffs, N.J.: Prentice-Hall, 1992.

Quarles, Benjamin. *The Negro in the Making of America*. 3rd ed. New York: Macmillan, 1987.

Rice, C. Duncan. *The Rise and Fall of Black Slavery*. Baton Rouge: Louisiana State University Press, 1975.

Salzman, Jack, David Lionel Smith, and Cornel West, eds. *Encyclopedia of African-American Culture and History*. 5 vols. New York: Simon & Schuster Macmillan, 1996.

Savage, William Sherman. *Blacks in the West*. Westport, Conn.: Greenwood Press, 1976.

## Chapter 1
### *Black Migration, Land Use, Labor, and Black Towns*

Arnesen, Eric. *Waterfront Workers of New Orleans: Race, Class, and Politics, 1863–1923*. New York: Oxford University Press, 1991.

Foner, Philip S., and Ronald L. Lewis, eds. *Black Workers: A Documentary History from Colonial Times to the Present*. Philadelphia: Temple University Press, 1989.

Fortune, T. Thomas. *Black and White: Land, Labor, and Politics in the South*. 1884. Reprint, New York: Arno, 1968.

Gutman, Herbert G. "The Negro and the United Mine Workers of America: The Career and Letters of Richard L. Davis and Something of their Meaning, 1890–1900" in *The Negro and the American Labor Movement*. Edited by Julius Jacobson. Garden City, N.J.: Anchor/Doubleday, 1968, 42–127.

Hamilton, Kenneth Marvin. *Black Towns and Profit: Promotion and Development in the Trans-Appalacian West, 1877–1915*. Urbana: University of Illinois Press, 1991.

Harris, William H. *The Harder We Run: Black Workers since the Civil War.* New York: Oxford University Press, 1982.

Hunter, Tera W. *To 'Joy My Freedom: Southern Black Women's Lives and Labors after the Civil War.* Cambridge: Harvard University Press, 1997.

Lewis, Ronald L. *Black Coal Miners in America: Race, Class, and Community Conflict 1780–1980.* Lexington: University Press of Kentucky, 1987.

Painter, Nell Irvin. *Exodusters: Black Migration to Kansas after Reconstruction.* New York: Knopf, 1976.

Rachleff, Peter. *Black Labor in Richmond, 1865–1890.* Urbana: University of Illinois Press, 1989.

Stokes, Melvyn, and Rick Halpern, eds. *Race and Class in the American South since 1890.* Providence, R.I.: Berg Press, 1994.

### Social and Political Histories

Ayers, Edward L. *Vengeance and Justice: Crime and Publishment in the 19th-Century American South.* New York: Oxford University Press, 1984.

Bederman, Gail. *Manliness and Civilization: A Cultural History of Gender and Race in the United States, 1880–1917.* Chicago: University of Chicago Press, 1995.

Foner, Jack. *Blacks and the Military in American History.* New York: Praeger, 1974.

Gatewood, Willard B., Jr. *"Smoked Yankees" and the Struggle for Empire: Letters from Negro Soldiers, 1898-1902.* Urbana: University of Illinois Press, 1971.

Gunning, Sandra. *Race, Rape, and Lynching: The Red Record of American Literature, 1890–1912.* New York: Oxford University Press, 1996.

Hahn, Stephen. *A Nation Under Our Feet: Black Political Struggles in the Rural South from Slavery to the Great Migration.* Cambridge: Harvard University Press, 2003.

Harris, Trudier. *Exorcising Blackness: Historical and Literary Lynching and Burning Rituals.* Bloomington: Indiana University Press, 1984.

Jaynes, Gerald David. *Branches without Roots: Genesis of the Black Working Class in the American South, 1862–1882.* New York: Oxford University Press, 1986.

Katz, William Loren. *The Black West.* Garden City, N.Y.: Doubleday, 1971.

Lofgren, Charles. *The Plessy Case: A Legal Historical Interpretation.* New York: Oxford University Press, 1987.

Mitchell, Michele. *Righteous Propagation: African Americans and the Politics of Radical Destiny after Reconstruction.* Chapel Hill: University of North Carolina Press, 2004.

Moss, Alfred, Jr. *The American Negro Academy: Voice of the Talented Tenth.* Baton Rouge: Louisiana State University Press, 1981.

Ortiz, Paul. *Emancipation Betrayed: The Hidden History of Black Organizing and White Violence in Florida from Reconstruction to the Blood Election of 1920.* Berkeley: University of California Press, 2005.

Painter, Nell Irvin. *Standing at Armageddon: The United States, 1877–1919.* New York: Norton, 1977.

Rabinowitz, Howard N. *Race Relations in the Urban South, 1865–1890.* New York: Oxford University Press, 1978.

Redkey, Edwin S. *Black Exodus: Black Nationalist and Back-to-Africa Movements, 1890–1910.* New Haven: Yale University Press, 1969.

Shapiro, Herbert. *White Violence and Black Response: From Reconstruction to Montgomery.* Amherst: University of Massachusetts Press, 1988.

Taylor, Quintard. *In Search of the Racial Frontier: African Americans in the American West, 1528–1990.* New York: Norton, 1998.

Thomas, Brook, ed. *Plessy* v. *Ferguson: A Brief History with Documents.* Boston: Bedford Books, 1997.

### Urban Histories

Borchert, James. *Alley Life in Washington.* Urbana: University of Illinois Press, 1980.

Brown, Elsa Barkley. "Mapping the Terrain of Black Richmond." *Journal of Urban History,* vol. 21, no. 3 (March 1995): 296–347.

Du Bois, W. E. B. *The Philadelphia Negro.* 1899. Reprint. New York: Schocken, 1967.

Lane, Roger. *Roots of Violence in Black Philadelphia, 1869–1900.* Cambridge: Harvard University Press, 1986.

———. *William Dorsey's Philadelphia and Ours.* New York: Oxford University Press, 1991.

Pleck, Elizabeth. *Black Migration and Poverty: Boston 1865–1900.* New York: Academic Press, 1979.

### Biographies and Autobiographies

Ashbaugh, Carolyn. *Lucy Parsons: American Revolutionary.* Chicago: Charles H. Kerr, 1976.

Boyd, Melba Joyce. *Discarded Legacy: Politics and Poetics in the Life of Frances E. W. Harper, 1825–1911.* Detroit: Wayne State University Press, 1994.

Chall, Malca, interviewer. "Frances Mary Albrier: Determined Advocate for Racial Equality." University of California, Berkeley, Bancroft Library, and the Schlesinger Library, Radcliffe College, Cambridge, Mass., 1977–78.

DeCosta-Willis, Miriam. *The Memphis Diary of Ida B. Wells.* Boston: Beacon Press, 1995.

Duster, Alfreda, ed. *Crusade for Justice: The Autobiography of Ida B. Wells.* Chicago: University of Chicago Press, 1970.

Foner, Philip, ed. *Life and Writings of Frederick Douglass.* New York: International Publishers, 1955.

Harlan, Louis. *Booker T. Washington, the Making of a Black Leader, 1856–1901.* New York: Oxford University Press, 1975.

Harlan, Louis, Stuart B. Kaufman, et al., eds. *The Booker T. Washington Papers,* vols. 2, 3, 4. Urbana: University of Illinois Press, 1972, 1974, 1975.

Harris, Trudier. *The Selected Works of Ida B. Wells-Barnett.* New York: Oxford University Press, 1991.

Jones, Beverly Washington. *Quest for Equality: The Life and Writings of Mary Eliza Church Terrell, 1863–1954.* New York: Carlson, 1990.

Lewis, David Levering. *W. E. B. Du Bois: Biography of a Race, 1868–1919.* New York: Holt, 1993.

McMurry, Linda D. *To Keep the Waters Troubled: The Life of Ida B. Wells.* New York: Oxford University Press, 1998.

Sterling, Dorothy. *Black Foremothers: Three Lives.* Old Westbury, N.Y.: Feminist Press, 1979.

Thompson, Mildred. *Ida B. Wells-Barnett: An Exploratory Study of an American Black Woman, 1893–1930.* New York: Carlson, 1990.

Thornbrough, Emma Lou. *Booker T. Washington.* Englewood Cliffs, N.J.: Prentice-Hall, 1969.

———. *Working with the Hands: Being a Sequel to Up From Slavery Covering the Author's Experiences in Industrial Training at Tuskegee.* 1904. Reprint, Salem, N.H.: Ayer, 1970.

———. *T. Thomas Fortune: Militant Journalist.* Chicago: University of Chicago Press, 1972.

Washington, Booker T. *Up from Slavery: An Autobiography.* 1900. Reprint, New York: Oxford University Press, 1995.

### African-American Women's History

Aptheker, Bettina. *Woman's Legacy: Essays on Race, Sex, and Class in American History.* Amherst: University of Massachusetts Press, 1982.

Brody, Jennefer DeVere. *Impossible Purities: Blackness, Femininity, and Victorian Culture.* Durham, N.C.: Duke University Press, 1998.

Cooper, Anna Julia. *A Voice from the South.* 1892. Reprint, New York: Oxford University Press, 1988.

Davis, Angela. *Women, Race and Class.* New York: Vintage, 1983.

Giddings, Paula. *When and Where I Enter: The Impact of Black Women on Race and Sex in America.* New York: William Morrow, 1984.

Guy-Sheftall, Beverly. *Daughters of Sorrow: Attitudes toward Black Women, 1880–1920.* New York: Carlson, 1990.

Higginbotham, Evelyn Brooks. *Righteous Discontent: The Women's Movement in the Black Baptist Church, 1880–1920.* Cambridge: Harvard University Press, 1993.

Hine, Darlene Clark. *Black Women in White: Racial Conflict and Cooperation in the Nursing Profession, 1890–1950.* Bloomington: Indiana University Press, 1989.

Lerner, Gerda, ed. *Black Women in White America: A Documentary History.* New York: Vintage, 1973.

Shaw, Stephanie J. *What A Woman Ought to Be and Do: Black Professional Women Workers During the Jim Crow Era.* Chicago: University of Chicago Press, 1996.

White, Deborah Gray. *Too Heavy A Load: Black Women in Defense of Themselves, 1894–1994.* New York: Norton, 1999.

### Literary Sources

Carby, Hazel. *Reconstructing Womanhood: The Emergence of the Afro-American Woman Novelist.* New York: Oxford University Press, 1987.

Chesnutt, Charles W. *The Conjure Woman.* 1899. Reprint, Ann Arbor: University of Michigan Press, 1969.

Dunbar, Paul Laurence. *The Complete Poems of Paul Laurence Dunbar.* 1913. Reprint, New York: Dodd, Mead, 1970.

Goss, Linda, and Marian E. Barnes, eds. *Talk that Talk: An Anthology of African-American Storytelling.* New York: Simon and Schuster, 1989.

Harper, Frances Ellen Watkins. *Iola Leroy.* 1892. Reprint, Boston: Beacon Press, 1987.

———. *Complete Poems of Frances E. W. Harper.* Compiled by Maryemma Graham. New York: Oxford University Press, 1988.

McHenry, Elizabeth. *Forgotten Readers: Recovering the Lost History of African American Literary Societies.* Durham: Duke University Press, 2002.

Salem, Dorothy. *To Better Our World: Black Women in Organized Reform, 1890–1920.* New York: Carlson, 1990.

## Chapter 2
### Leadership and Institutional Development

Anderson, James. *The Education of Blacks in the South, 1880–1935.* Chapel Hill: University of North Carolina Press, 1988.

Brown, Elsa Barkley. "Womanist Consciousness: Maggie Lena Walker and the Independent Order of Saint Luke," *Signs,* vol. 14, no. 3 (1989): 610–633.

Du Bois, William Edward Burkhardt. *The Souls of Black Folk.* 1903. Reprint, New York: Vintage, 1990.

Garvey, Amy Jacques. *The Philosophy and Opinions of Marcus Garvey, with an Introduction by Robert A. Hill.* New York: 1992.

Harlan, Lewis R. *Booker T. Washington: The Wizard of Tuskegee, 1901–1915.* New York: Oxford University Press, 1983.

Higginbotham, Evelyn Brooks. *Righteous Discontent: The Women's Movement in the Black Baptist Church, 1880–1920.* Cambridge: Harvard University Press, 1993.

Ottley, Roi. *The Lonely Warrior: The Life and Times of Robert S. Abbott.* Chicago: Henry Regnery, 1955.

Salem, Dorothy. *To Better Our World: Black Women in Organized Reform, 1890–1920.* New York: Carlson, 1990.

Shaw, Stephanie. *What a Woman Ought to Be and to Do: Black Professional Women Workers during the Jim Crow Era.* Chicago: University of Chicago Press, 1996.

### Biographies and Autobiographies

Johnson, James Weldon. *Along This Way: The Autobiography of James Weldon Johnson.* New York: Viking Press, 1933.

Johnson, Lyman T. *The Rest of the Dream: The Black Odyssey of Lyman Johnson.* Edited by Wade Hall. Lexington: University of Kentucky Press, 1988.

Pickens, William. *Bursting Bonds: The Heir of Slaves.* Boston: Jordan & More, 1923.

Rosengarten, Theodore. *All God's Dangers: The Life of Nate Shaw.* New York: Knopf, 1975.

Tarry, Ellen. *The Third Door: The Autobiography of an American Negro Woman.* Expanded ed. New York: Guild Press, 1966.

Washington, Booker T. *Up from Slavery: An Autobiography.* 1900. Reprint, New York: Oxford University Press, 1995.

Wright, Richard. *Black Boy: A Record of Childhood and Youth.* New York: Harper & Row, 1937.

### African-American Culture

Cripps, Thomas. *Slow Fade to Black: The Negro in American Film, 1900–1942.* New York: Oxford University Press, 1977.

Huggins, Nathan I. *Harlem Renaissance.* New York: Oxford University Press, 1971.

———. *Voices from the Harlem Renaissance.* New York: Oxford University Press, 1976.

Johnson-Feelings, Dianne, ed. *The Best of* The Brownies' Book. New York: Oxford University Press, 1996.

Levine, Lawrence L. *Black Culture and Black Consciousness: Afro-American Folk Thought from Slavery to Freedom.* New York: Oxford University Press, 1977.

Lewis, David Levering. *When Harlem Was in Vogue.* New York: Knopf, 1981.

Locke, Alain. *The New Negro: An Interpretation.* 1925. Reprint, New York: Arno, 1968.

The Studio Museum in Harlem. *Harlem Renaissance: Art of Black America.* New York: Abrams, 1987.

Watson, Steven. *The Harlem Renaissance: Hub of African-American Culture, 1920–1930.* New York: Pantheon, 1995.

### Community Studies

Daniels, Douglas Henry. *Black Pioneers: A Social and Cultural History of Black San Francisco.* Philadelphia: Temple University Press, 1980.

Du Bois, William Edward Burkhardt. *The Philadelphia Negro: A Social Study.* 1899. Reprint, New York: Benjamin Blom, 1967.

Kusmer, Kenneth L. *A Ghetto Takes Shape: Black Cleveland, 1870–1930.* Urbana: University of Illinois Press, 1976.

Lewis, Earl. *In Their Own Interests: Race, Class, and Power in Twentieth-Century Norfolk, Virginia.* Berkeley: University of California Press, 1991.

Spear, Allan H. *Black Chicago: The Making of a Negro Ghetto, 1890–1920.* Chicago: University of Chicago Press, 1967.

Taylor, Quintard. *The Forging of a Black Community: Seattle's Central District from 1870 through the Civil Rights Era.* Seattle: University of Washington Press, 1994.

Trotter, Joe William. *Black Milwaukee: The Making of the Industrial Proletariat, 1915–1945.* Urbana: University of Illinois Press, 1985.

Wright, George. *Life Behind a Veil: Blacks in Louisville, Kentucky, 1865–1930.* Baton Rouge: Louisiana State University Press, 1985.

### The Great Migration and the First World War

Adero, Malaika ed. *Up South: Stories, Studies, and Letters of the Century's Black Migrations.* New York: New Press, 1993.

Crew, Spencer R. *Field to Factory: Afro-American Migration 1915–1940.* Washington, D.C.: National Museum of American History, Smithsonian Institution, 1987.

Gottlieb, Peter. *Making Their Own Way: Southern Blacks' Migration to Pittsburgh, 1916–1930.* Urbana: University of Illinois Press, 1987.

Grossman, James R. *Land of Hope: Chicago, Black Southerners, and the Great Migration.* Chicago: University of Chicago Press, 1989.

Henri, Florette, and Arthur Barbeau. *The Unknown Soldiers: Black American Troops in the First World War.* Philadelphia: Temple University Press, 1974.

Trotter, Joe W., ed. *The Great Migration in Historical Perspective: New Dimensions of Race, Class and Gender.* Bloomington: Indiana University Press, 1991.

### Race Relations

Ayers, Edward L. *The Promise of the New South: Life After Reconstruction.* New York: Oxford University Press, 1993.

Dittmer, John. *Black Georgia in the Progressive Era, 1900–1920.* Urbana: University of Illinois Press, 1977.

Hair, William Ivy. *Carnival of Fury: Robert Charles and the New Orleans Race Riot of 1900.* Baton Rouge: Louisiana State University Press, 1976.

McMillen, Neil. *Dark Journey: Black Mississippians in the Age of Jim Crow.* Urbana: University of Illinois Press, 1989.

Tuttle, William M., Jr. *Race Riot: Chicago in the Red Summer of 1919.* New York: Atheneum, 1970.

Williamson, Joel. *A Rage for Order: Black/White Relations in the American South since Emancipation.* New York: Oxford University Press, 1986.

### Work and the Economy

Clark-Lewis, Elizabeth. *Living In, Living Out: African American Domestics in Washington, D.C., 1910–1940.* Washington, D.C.: Smithsonian Institution Press, 1994.

Harris, William H. *The Harder We Run: Black Workers since the Civil War.* New York: Oxford University Press, 1982.

Jones, Jacqueline. *The Dispossessed: America's Underclass from the Civil War to the Present.* New York: Basic Books, 1992.

Trotter, Joe William. *Coal, Class, and Color: Blacks in Southern West Virginia, 1915–32.* Urbana: University of Illinois Press, 1990.

Wright, Gavin. *Old South, New South: Revolutions in the Southern Economy since the Civil War.* New York: Basic Books, 1986.

## Chapter 3
### The Depression and the Second World War

Kusmer, Kenneth L., ed. *Depression, War, and the New Migration, 1930–1960.* Vol. 6 of *Black Communities and Urban Development in America, 1720–1960.* New York: Garland, 1991.

McElvaine, Robert S. *The Great Depression: America, 1929–1941.* New York: Times Books, 1984.

Nash, Gerald D. *The Crucial Era: The Great Depression and the Second World War, 1929–1945.* 2nd ed. New York: St. Martin's Press, 1992.

Sitkoff, Harvard. *A New Deal for Blacks: The Emergence of Civil Rights as a National Issue: The Depression Decade.* New York: Oxford University Press, 1978.

Sternsher, Bernard, ed. *The Negro in Depression and War: Prelude to Revolution, 1930–1945.* Chicago: Quadrangle, 1969.

Wright, Richard, and Edwin Rosskam. *12 Million Black Voices.* New York: Thunder's Mouth, 1941.

### African-American Culture and Institutions

Frazier, E. Franklin. *The Negro Church in America.* New York: Schocken, 1963.

Hazard-Gordon, Katrina. *Jookin': The Rise of Social Dance Formations in African-American Culture.* Philadelphia: Temple University Press, 1990.

Jones, LeRoi (Amiri Baraka). *Blues People: The Negro Experience in White America and the Music That Developed from It.* New York: Morrow, 1963.

Levine, Lawrence. *Black Culture and Black Consciousness: Afro-American Folk Thoughts from Slavery to Freedom.* New York: Oxford University Press, 1977.

Southern, Eileen. *The Music of Black Americans: A History.* 3rd ed. New York: Norton, 1997.

Tucker, Mark, ed. *The Duke Ellington Reader.* New York: Oxford University Press, 1993.

### *Black Community Studies*

Broussard, Albert S. *Black San Francisco: The Struggle for Racial Equality in the West, 1900–1954.* Lawrence: University Press of Kansas, 1993.

Daniels, Douglas Henry. *Pioneer Urbanites: A Social and Cultural History of Black San Francisco.* Philadelphia: Temple University Press, 1980.

Drake, St. Clair, and Horace R. Cayton. *Black Metropolis: A Study of Negro Life in a Northern City.* 2 vols. 1944. Reprint, New York: Harcourt, Brace & World, 1962.

Greenberg, Cheryl Lynn. *Or Does it Explode? Black Harlem in the Great Depression.* New York: Oxford University Press, 1991.

Lewis, Earl. *In Their Own Interests: Race, Class and Power in Twentieth Century Norfolk.* Berkeley: University of California Press, 1991.

Taylor, Quintard. *The Forging of a Black Community: Seattle's Central District from 1870 through the Civil Rights Era.* Seattle: University of Washington Press, 1994.

Trotter, Joe William, Jr. *Black Milwaukee: The Making of an Industrial Proletariat, 1915–45.* Urbana: University of Illinois Press, 1985.

### *Politics, Leadership, and Race Relations*

Anderson, Jervis. *A. Philip Randolph: A Biographical Portrait.* Berkeley: University of California Press, 1986.

Grant, Nancy L. *TVA and Black Americans: Planning for the Status Quo.* Philadelphia: Temple University Press, 1990.

Kelley, Robin D. G. *Hammer and Hoe: Alabama Communists during the Great Depression.* Chapel Hill: University of North Carolina Press, 1990.

Kirby, John B. *Black Americans in the Roosevelt Era: Liberalism and Race.* Knoxville: University of Tennessee Press, 1992.

Mintz, Sidney W., and Richard Price. *The Birth of African-American Culture: An Anthropological Perspective.* Boston: Beacon Press, 1992.

Myrdal, Gunnar. *An American Dilemma: The Negro Problem and Modern Democracy.* 2 vols. 1944. Reprint, New York: Pantheon, 1962.

Naison, Mark. *Communists in Harlem During the Depression.* Urbana: University of Illinois Press, 1983.

Nieman, Donald G. *Promises to Keep: African-Americans and the Constitutional Order, 1776 to the Present.* New York: Oxford University Press, 1991.

Plummer, Brenda Gayle. *Rising Wind: Black Americans and U.S. Foreign Affairs, 1935–1960.* Chapel Hill: University of North Carolina Press, 1996.

Shapiro, Herbert. *White Violence and Black Response: From Reconstruction to Montgomery.* Amherst: University of Massachusetts Press, 1988.

Urquhart, Brian. *Ralph Bunche.* New York: Norton, 1993.

von Eschen, Penny. *Race Against Empire: Black Americans and Anticolonialsim, 1937–1957.* Ithaca: Cornell University Press, 1997.

Wolters, Raymond. *Negroes and the Great Depression: The Problem of Economic Recovery.* Westport, Conn.: Greenwood, 1970.

### Work and Labor Relations

Dickerson, Dennis C. *Out of the Crucible: Black Steelworkers in Western Pennsylvania, 1875–1980.* Albany: State University of New York Press, 1986.

Foner, Philip S. *Organized Labor and the Black Workers, 1619–1981.* New York: International Publishers, 1982.

Harris, William H. *Keeping the Faith: A. Philip Randolph, Milton P. Webster, and the Brotherhood of Sleeping Car Porters, 1925–37.* Urbana: University of Illinois Press, 1977.

———. *The Harder We Run: Black Workers since the Civil War.* New York: Oxford University Press, 1982.

Meier, August, and Elliot Rudwick. *Black Detroit and the Rise of the UAW.* New York: Oxford University Press, 1979.

Painter, Nell Irvin. *The Narrative of Hosea Hudson: His Life as a Communist.* Cambridge: Harvard University Press, 1979.

Rosengarten, Theodore. *All God's Dangers: The Life of Nate Shaw.* New York: Knopf, 1975.

Trotter, Joe William, Jr. *Coal, Class, and Color: Blacks in Southern West Virginia, 1915–32.* Urbana: University of Illinois Press, 1990.

### African-American Women

Gray, Brenda Clegg. *Black Female Domestics during the Depression in New York City, 1930–1940.* New York: Garland, 1993.

Hawks, Joanne V., and Sheila L. Skemp, eds. *Sex, Race, and the Role of Women in the South.* Jackson: University Press of Mississippi, 1983.

Hine, Darlene Clark. *Black Women in White: Racial Conflict and Cooperation in the Nursing Profession, 1890–1950.* Bloomington: Indiana University Press, 1989.

Lerner, Gerda, ed. *Black Women in White America: A Documentary History.* New York: Vintage, 1973.

## Chapter 4

### The Civil Rights Era

Lincoln, C. Eric. *The Black Muslims in America.* Grand Rapids, Mich.: Eerdmans, 1994.

Patterson, James T. *Grand Expectations: The United States, 1945–1974.* New York: Oxford University Press, 1996.

Wofford, Harris. *Of Kennedys and Kings: Making Sense of the Sixties.* New York: Farrar Straus & Giroux, 1980.

### Civil Rights Movement

Archer, Jules. *They Had a Dream: The Civil Rights Struggle, from Frederick Douglass to Marcus Garvey to Martin Luther King, Jr. and Malcolm X.* New York: Viking, 1993.

Branch, Taylor. *Parting the Waters: America in the King Years, 1954–1963.* New York: Simon & Schuster, 1988.

———. *Pillar of Fire: America in the King Years, 1963–1965.* New York: Simon & Schuster, 1998.

Bullard, Sara. *Free at Last: A History of the Civil Rights Movement and Those Who Died in the Struggle.* New York: Oxford University Press, 1993.

Carawan, Guy, and Candie Carawan. *Freedom Is a Constant Struggle: Songs of the Freedom Movement.* New York: Oak Publications, 1968.

Carson, Clayborne. *In Struggle: SNCC and the Black Awakening of the 1960s.* Cambridge: Harvard University Press, 1981.

Carson, Clayborne, et al. *The Eyes on the Prize Civil Rights Reader.* New York: Penguin, 1991.

Chafe, William H. *Civilities and Civil Rights: Greensboro, North Carolina, and the Black Struggle for Freedom.* New York: Oxford University Press, 1980.

Cleghorn, Reese, and Pat Watters. *Climbing Jacob's Ladder: The Arrival of Negroes in Southern Politics.* New York: Harcourt, Brace & World, 1967.

Couto, Richard A. *Ain't Gonna Let Nobody Turn Me Round: The Pursuit of Racial Justice in the Rural South.* Philadelphia: Temple University Press, 1991.

Crawford, Vicki, Jacqueline Anne Rouse, and Barbara Woods, eds. *Women in the Civil Rights Movement: Trailblazers and Torchbearers, 1941–1965.* Bloomington: Indiana University Press, 1993.

Egerton, John. *Speak Now Against the Day: The Generation Before the Civil Rights Movement in the South.* New York: Knopf, 1994.

Fairclough, Adam. *To Redeem the Soul of America: The Southern Christian Leadership Conference and Martin Luther King, Jr.* Athens: University of Georgia Press, 1987.

Forman, James. *The Making of Black Revolutionaries.* New York: Macmillan, 1972.

Grant, Joanne, ed. *Black Protest: History, Documents, and Analyses, 1619 to the Present.* New York: St. Martin's Press, 1970.

Hampton, Henry, Steve Fayer, and Sarah Flynn. *Voices of Freedom: An Oral History of the Civil Rights Movement from the 1950s through the 1980s.* New York: Bantam, 1990.

Harding, Vincent. *Hope and History: Why We Must Share the Story of the Movement.* Maryknoll, N.Y.: Orbis, 1990.

Hughes, Langston. *Fight for Freedom: The Story of the NAACP.* New York: Berkley, 1962.

Kapur, Sudarshan. *Raising Up a Prophet: The African-American Encounter with Gandhi.* Boston: Beacon Press, 1992.

King, Martin Luther, Jr. *Stride toward Freedom.* New York: Harper & Row, 1958.

———. *Why We Can't Wait.* New York: Harper & Row, 1964.

———. *Where Do We Go from Here: Chaos or Community?* New York: Harper & Row, 1967.

———. *Trumpet of Conscience.* New York: Harper & Row, 1968.

Kluger, Richard. *Simple Justice: The History of Brown* v. *Board of Education and Black America's Struggle for Equality.* New York: Knopf, 1975.

Lawson, Stephen. *Running for Freedom: Civil Rights and Black Politics in America since 1941.* New York: McGraw-Hill, 1991.

Lewis, Anthony. *Portrait of a Decade: The Second American Revolution.* New York: Random House, 1964.

Lomax, Louis E. *The Negro Revolt.* New York: Harper & Row, 1962.

Lowery, Charles D., and John F. Marszalek, eds. *Encyclopedia of African-American Civil Rights.* New York: Greenwood, 1992.

Lyon, Danny. *Memories of the Southern Civil Rights Movement.* Chapel Hill: University of North Carolina Press, 1992.

Meier, August, and Elliot Rudwick. *CORE: A Study in the Civil Rights Movement, 1942–1968.* New York: Oxford University Press, 1973.

Morris, Aldon D. *The Origins of the Civil Rights Movement.* New York: Free Press, 1984.

O'Reilly, Kenneth. *"Racial Matters": The FBI's Secret File on Black America, 1960–1972.* New York: Free Press, 1989.

Payne, Charles M. *I've Got the Light of Freedom.* Berkeley: University of California Press, 1995.

Peck, James. *Freedom Ride.* New York: Simon & Schuster, 1962.

President's Committee on Civil Rights. *To Secure These Rights.* Washington: U.S. Government Printing Office, 1947.

Raines, Howell. *My Soul is Rested: The Story of the Civil Rights Movement in the Deep South.* New York: Viking Penguin, 1977.

Reiser, Bob, and Pete Seeger. *Everybody Says Freedom: A History of the Civil Rights Movement in Songs and Pictures.* New York: Norton, 1989.

Sitkoff, Harvard. *The Struggle for Black Equality.* New York: Hill & Wang, 1993.

Skolnick, Jerome. *The Politics of Protest.* New York: Ballantine, 1969.

Sugarman, Tracy. *Stranger at the Gates: A Summer in Mississippi.* New York: Hill & Wang, 1966.

Weisbrot, Robert. *Freedom Bound: A History of America's Civil Rights Movement.* New York: Norton, 1990.

Williams, Juan. *Eyes on the Prize: America's Civil Rights Years, 1954–1965.* New York: Penguin, 1988.

Young, Andrew. *An Easy Burden: The Civil Rights Movement and the Transformation of America.* New York: HarperCollins, 1996.

Zinn, Howard. *SNCC: The New Abolitionists.* Boston: Beacon Press, 1964.

### Autobiographies and Biographies

Anderson, Jervis. *Bayard Rustin: Troubles I've Seen, a Biography.* New York: HarperCollins, 1997.

Baraka, Amiri. *The Autobiography of LeRoi Jones/Amiri Baraka.* New York: Freundlich Books, 1984.

Bennett, Lerone, Jr. *What Manner of Man: A Biography of Martin Luther King, Jr.* Chicago: Johnson, 1964.

Burner, Eric. *And Gently He Shall Lead Them: Robert Parris Moses and Civil Rights in Mississippi.* New York: New York University Press, 1994.

Carmichael, Stokely. *Black Power: The Politics of Liberation in America.* New York: Vintage, 1992.

Carson, Clayborne. *Malcolm X, The FBI File.* New York: Carroll & Graf, 1991.

Carson, Clayborne, ed. *The Papers of Martin Luther King, Jr.* Berkeley: University of California Press, 1992, 1994.

Clark, Septima P. *Echo In My Soul.* New York: Dutton, 1962.

———. *Ready from Within.* Navarro, Calif.: Wild Trees Press, 1986.

Cone, James. *Martin and Malcolm and America.* Maryknoll, N.Y.: Orbis, 1991.

Farmer, James. *Lay Bare the Heart: An Autobiography of the Civil Rights Movement.* Forth Worth: Texas Christian University Press, 1998.

Garrow, David. *Bearing the Cross: Martin Luther King, Jr., and the Southern Christian Leadership Conference.* New York: Morrow, 1986.

Goldman, Peter. *The Death and Life of Malcolm X.* New York: Harper & Row, 1973.

Grant, Joanne. *Ella Baker: Freedom Bound.* New York: Wiley, 1998.

Hamilton, Charles V. *Adam Clayton Powell, Jr.* New York: Atheneum, 1991.

Harding, Vincent. *Martin Luther King: The Inconvenient Hero.* Maryknoll, N.Y.: Orbis, 1996.

King, Coretta Scott. *My Life with Martin Luther King, Jr.* New York: Holt, Rinehart & Winston, 1969.

King, Martin Luther, Sr., with Clayton Riley. *Daddy King.* New York: Morrow, 1980.

Lewis, David L. *King: A Critical Biography.* New York: Praeger, 1970.

Malcolm X, with the assistance of Alex Haley. *The Autobiography of Malcolm X.* New York: Grove Press, 1965.

Mills, Kay. *This Little Light of Mine: The Life of Fannie Lou Hamer.* New York: Dutton, 1993.

Oates, Stephen B. *Let the Trumpet Sound: The Life of Martin Luther King, Jr.* New York: Harper & Row, 1982.

Rowan, Carl Thomas. *Dream Makers, Dream Breakers: The World of Justice Thurgood Marshall.* Boston: Little, Brown, 1993.

Washington, James M. *A Testament of Hope: The Essential Writings of Martin Luther King, Jr.* New York: Harper & Row, 1986.

Wilkins, Roy, with Tom Mathews. *Standing Fast: The Autobiography of Roy Wilkins.* New York: Viking, 1982.

## Chapter 5
### *General Histories of the United States since 1970*

Amott, Teresa L., and Julie A. Matthaei. *Race, Gender, and Work: A Multicultural History of Women in the United States.* Boston: South End Press, 1991.

Carroll, Peter N. *It Seemed Like Nothing Happened: The Tragedy and Promise of America in the 1970s.* New York: Holt, Rinehart and Winston, 1982.

Coontz, Stephanie. *The Way We Never Were: American Families and the Nostalgia Trap.* New York: Basic Books, 1992.

Edsall, Thomas Byrne. *Chain Reaction: The Impact of Race, Rights, and Taxes on American Politics.* New York: Norton, 1991.

Evans, Sara M. *Born for Liberty: A History of Women in America.* New York: Free Press, 1989.

Omi, Michael, and Howard Winant. *Racial Formation in the United States: From the 1960s to the 1990s.* 2nd ed. New York: Norton, 2000.

Piven, Frances Fox. *The New Class War: Reagan's Attack on the Welfare State and its Consequences.* New York: Pantheon, 1982.

Siegel, Frederick F. *Troubled Journey: From Pearl Harbor to Ronald Reagan.* New York: Hill & Wang, 1984.

Stacey, Judith. *Brave New Families: Stories of Domestic Upheaval in Late Twentieth Century America.* New York: Basic Books, 1990.

### African-American Politics

Bell, Derrick. *And We Are Not Saved: The Elusive Quest for Racial Justice.* New York: Basic Books, 1987.

Collins, Sheila D. *The Rainbow Challenge: The Jackson Campaign and the Future of U.S. Politics.* New York: Monthly Review Press, 1986.

Davis, Angela. *Women, Culture, and Politics.* New York: Random House, 1989.

Harding, Vincent. *Hope and History: Why We Must Share the Story of the Movement.* Maryknoll, N.Y.: Orbis, 1990.

Hatch, Roger D., and Frank E. Watkins, eds. *Reverend Jesse L. Jackson: Straight from the Heart.* Philadelphia: Fortress Press, 1987.

Henry, Charles P. *Culture and African-American Politics.* Bloomington: Indiana University Press, 1990.

Horne, Gerald. *The Fire This Time: The Watts Uprising and the 1960s.* Charlottesville: University Press of Virginia, 1995.

James, Joy. *Transcending the Talented Tenth: Black Leaders and American Intellectuals.* New York: Routledge, 1997.

Kelley, Robin D. G. *Freedom Dreams: The Black Radical Imagination.* Boston: Beacon Press, 2002.

Lawson, Steven F. *Running for Freedom: Civil Rights and Black Politics in America since 1941.* Philadelphia: Temple University Press, 1991.

Lusane, Clarence. *African Americans at the Crossroads: The Restructuring of Black Leadership in the 1992 Elections.* Boston: South End Press, 1994.

Marable, Manning. *Race, Reform, and Rebellion: The Second Reconstruction in Black America, 1945–1990.* 2nd ed. Jackson: University Press of Mississippi, 1991.

Morrison, Toni, ed. *Race-ing Justice, En-gendering Power: Essays on Anita Hill, Clarence Thomas and the Construction of Social Reality.* New York: Pantheon, 1992.

West, Cornel. *Race Matters.* Boston: Beacon Press, 1993.

### African-American Social and Economic Conditions

Banner-Haley, Charles T. *The Fruits of Integration: Black Middle-Class Ideology and Culture, 1960–1990.* Jackson: University Press of Mississippi, 1994.

Billingsley, Andrew. *Climbing Jacob's Ladder: The Enduring Legacy of African-American Families.* New York: Simon & Schuster, 1992.

Bush, Rod. *We Are Not What We Seem: Black Nationalism and Class Struggle in the American Century.* New York: New York University Press, 1999.

Davis, Mike. *City of Quartz: Excavating the Future in Los Angeles.* London: Verso, 1990.

Feagin, Joe R., and Melvin P. Sikes. *Living with Racism: The Black Middle-Class Experience.* Boston: Beacon Press, 1994.

Gill, Gerald. *Meanness Mania: The Changed Mood.* Washington, D.C.: Howard University Press, 1980.

Glasgow, Douglas G. *The Black Underclass: Poverty, Unemployment, and Entrapment of Ghetto Youth.* New York: Vintage, 1981.

Jones, Jacqueline. *The Dispossessed: America's Underclasses from the Civil War to the Present.* New York: Basic Books, 1992.

Kasinitz, Philip. *Caribbean New York: Black Immigrants and the Politics of Race.* Ithaca, N.Y.: Cornell University Press, 1992.

Kelley, Robin D. G. *Race Rebels: Culture, Politics, and the Black Working Class.* New York: Free Press, 1994.

Landry, Bart. *The New Black Middle Class.* Berkeley: University of California Press, 1987.

Lusane, Clarence. *Pipe Dream Blues: Racism and the War on Drugs.* Boston: South End Press, 1991.

Madhubuti, Haki R., ed. *Why L.A. Happened: Implications of the '92 Los Angeles Rebellion.* Chicago: Third World Press, 1993.

Massey, Douglas S., and Nancy A. Denton. *American Apartheid: Segregation and the Making of the Underclass.* Cambridge: Harvard University Press, 1993.

Quandango, Jill. *The Color of Welfare: How Racism Undermined the War on Poverty.* New York: Oxford University Press, 1994.

Rank, Mark Robert. *Living on the Edge: The Realities of Welfare in America.* New York: Columbia University Press, 1994.

Simms, Margaret C., and Julianne Malveaux, eds. *Slipping through the Cracks: The Status of Black Women.* New Brunswick, N.J.: Transaction Books, 1986.

Wilson, William Julius. *The Truly Disadvantaged: The Inner City, the Underclass, and Public Policy.* Chicago: University of Chicago Press, 1987.

———. *When Work Disappears: The World of the New Urban Poor.* New York: Knopf, 1996.

### African-American Culture

Castleman, Craig. *Getting Up: Subway Graffiti in New York.* Cambridge: MIT Press, 1982.

Cross, Brian. *It's Not About a Salary . . . Rap, Race and Resistance in Los Angeles.* London: Verso, 1993.

Dates, Jannette L., and William Barlow, eds. *Split Image: African Americans in the Mass Media.* 2nd ed. Washington, D.C.: Howard University Press, 1993.

Dent, Gina, ed. *Black Popular Culture.* Seattle: Bay Press, 1992.

Eure, Joseph G., and James G. Spady. *Nation Conscious Rap.* Brooklyn, N.Y.: P.C. International Press, 1991.

Franklin, V. P. *Black Self-Determination: A Cultural History of African American Resistance.* Brooklyn, N.Y.: Lawrence Hill, 1992.

Gaines, Kevin. *Uplifting the Race: Black Leadership, Politics, and Culture in the Twentieth Century.* Chapel Hill: University of North Carolina Press, 1996.

George, Nelson. *The Death of Rhythm and Blues.* New York: Plume, 1988.

———. *Hip Hop America.* New York: Penguin, 1998.

Guerrero, Ed. *Framing Blackness: The African-American Image in Film.* Philadelphia: Temple University Press, 1993.

Hazzard-Gordon, Katrina. *Jookin': The Rise of Social Dance Formations in African-American Culture.* Philadelphia: Temple University Press, 1990.

Kelley, Robin D. G. *Yo' Mama's Disfunktional!: Fighting the Culture Wars in Urban America.* Boston: Beacon Press, 1994.

Lippard, Lucy R. *Mixed Blessings: New Art in a Multicultural America.* New York: Pantheon, 1990.

Lipsitz, George. *The Possessive Investment in Whiteness*. Philadelphia: Temple University Press, 1998.

MacDonald, J. Fred. *Blacks and White TV: Afro-Americans in Television since 1948*. Chicago: Nelson-Hall, 1983.

Rose, Tricia. *Black Noise: Rap Music and Black Culture in Contemporary America*. Middletown, Conn.: Wesleyan University Press, 1994.

Stuckey, Sterling. *Slave Culture: Nationalist Theory and the Foundations of Black America*. New York: Oxford University Press, 1987.

Tate, Greg. *Flyboy in the Buttermilk: Essays on Contemporary America*. New York: Simon & Schuster, 1992.

Van Deburg, William L. *New Day in Babylon: The Black Power Movement and American Culture, 1965–1975*. Chicago: University of Chicago Press, 1992.

Ward, Brian. *Just My Soul Responding: Rhythm and Blues, Black Consciousness, and Race Relations*. Berkeley: University of California Press, 1998.

### African-American Women and Politics

Carby, Hazel. *Reconstructing Black Womanhood*. New York: Oxford University Press, 1987.

Collins, Patricia Hill. *Fighting Words: Black Women and the Search for Justice*. Minneapolis: University of Minnesota Press, 1998.

Davis, Angela Y. *Blues Legacies and Black Feminism: Gertrude "Ma" Rainey, Bessie Smith and Billie Holiday*. New York: Pantheon, 1998.

Guy-Sheftall, Beverly, ed. *Words of Fire: An Anthology of African-American Feminist Thought*. New York: New Press, 1995.

hooks, bell. *Ain't I a Woman: Black Women and Feminism*. Boston: South End Press, 1983.

Hull, Gloria T., Patricia Bell Scott, and Barbara Smith, eds. *All the Women Are White, All the Blacks Are Men, But Some of Us Are Brave*. Old Westbury, N.Y.: Feminist Press, 1982.

Hunter, Tera. *To 'joy My Freedom: Southern Black Women's Lives and Labors After the Civil War*. Cambridge: Harvard University Press, 1997.

Smith, Barbara, ed. *Home Girls: A Black Feminist Anthology*. New York: Kitchen Table Press, 1983.

Steady, Filomina, ed. *The Black Woman Cross-Culturally*. Cambridge: Schenkman, 1981.

### Memoirs, Biographies, Autobiographies, Oral Histories

Carter, Stephen L. *Reflections of an Affirmative Action Baby*. New York: Basic Books, 1991.

Chisholm, Shirley. *The Good Fight*. New York: Harper & Row, 1973.

Delany, Samuel R. *The Motion of Light in Water*. New York: William Morrow, 1988.

Griffith, Farah Jasmine. *Who Set You Flowin'?: The African-American Migration Narrative*. New York: Oxford University Press, 1995.

Gwaltney, John Langston. *Drylongso: A Self-Portrait of Black America*. New York: Vintage, 1981.

Lanker, Brian. *I Dream a World: Portraits of Black Women Who Changed America*. New York: Stewart, Tabori, and Chang, 1989.

Lewis, Reginald, and Blair S. Walker. *Why Should White Guys Have all the Fun?* New York: Wiley, 1995.

Lorde, Audre. *Zami: A New Spelling of My Name.* Trumansberg, N.Y.: The Crossing Press, 1982.

McCall, Nathan. *Makes Me Wanna Holler: A Young Black Man in America.* New York: Random House, 1994.

Shakur, Sanyika ["Monster" Kody Scott]. *Monster: The Autobiography of an L.A. Gang Member.* New York: Penguin, 1993.

Tarpley, Natasha, ed. *Testimony: Young African Americans on Self-Discovery and Black Identity.* Boston: Beacon Press, 1994.

Terkel, Studs. *Race: How Blacks and Whites Think and Feel About the American Obsession.* New York: New Press, 1992.

Thomas, Arthur E. *Like It Is: Arthur E. Thomas Interviews Leaders on Black America.* Edited by Emily Rovetch. New York: Dutton, 1981.

Tyson, Timothy B. *Radio Free Dixie: Robert Williams and the Roots of Black Power.* Chapel Hill: University of North Carolina Press, 1998.

Williams, Patricia. *The Alchemy of Race and Rights: Diary of a Law Professor.* Cambridge: Harvard University Press, 1991.

Woodard, Komozi. *A Nation Within a Nation: Amiri Baraka (Leroi Jones) and Black Power Politics.* Chapel Hill: University of North Carolina Press, 1998.

### Fiction

Butler, Octavia E. *Imago.* New York: Warner Books, 1989.

Danticat, Edwidge. *Breath, Eyes, Memory: A Novel.* New York: Soho Press, 1994.

Delany, Samuel R. *Dahlgren.* New York: Bantam, 1975.

Guy, Rosa. *New Guys Around the Block.* London: Gollancz, 1983.

———. *And I Heard a Bird Sing.* New York: Delacorte Press, 1987.

Morrison, Toni. *Beloved.* New York: Random House, 1987.

———. *Jazz.* New York: Random House, 1992.

Mosley, Walter. *Devil in a Blue Dress.* New York: Norton, 1990.

Mowry, Jess. *Way Past Cool.* New York: Farrar, Straus & Giroux, 1992.

Shange, Ntozake. *For Colored Girls Who Have Considered Suicide, When the Rainbow is Enuf: A Choreopoem.* New York: Bantam, 1980.

———. *Sassafrass, Cypress & Indigo.* New York: St. Martin's Press, 1982.

Walker, Alice. *The Color Purple.* New York: Harcourt Brace, 1982.

Woodson, Jacqueline. *Between Madison & Palmetto.* New York: Delacorte, 1993.

# Picture Credits

Chicago Historical Society: 119, 302; Everett Collection: 160; Florida Photographic Collection, Florida State Archives: 70, 296; Courtesy of Hampton University Archives: 40; Library Company of Philadelphia: 46; Library of Congress: ii, 6, 9, 38, 63, 82, 85, 94, 103, 105, 129, 135, 140, 142, 147, 150, 156, 159, 200, 242, 278; Museum of Modern Art, Film Stills Archive: 266; Museum of the City of New York: 55; National Archives: 120, 162, 168, 291, 313; North Carolina State Archives: 132; Reuters/Corbis-Bettman: 330, 332; Schomburg Center for Research in Black Culture, New York Public Library, Astor, Lenox, and Tilden Foundations: 204 (Black Experience in America Collection), 231 (Black Experience in America Collection); Smithsonian Institution: 62; Courtesy Spelman College, Atlanta, Ga.: 43; Courtesy Tommy Boy Records: 306; University of Chicago Library: 29; University of Pittsburgh, Archives of Industrial Society, Urban League of Pittsburgh Collection: 116; UPI/Bettman Newsphotos: 283; UPI/Corbis-Bettman: 182, 197, 237, 256; Valentine Museum, Richmond, Va.: 16.

# Contributors

## The Editors

**Robin D. G. Kelley** is Professor of Anthropology and African-American Studies at Columbia University. Author of several prize-winning books, including *Race Rebels: Culture, Politics and the Black Working Class* and *Yo' Mama's DisFunktional!: Fighting the Culture Wars in Urban America*. His most recent publication is *Freedom Dreams: The Black Radical Imagination*. He lives in New York City.

**Earl Lewis** is Provost and Asa Griggs Candler Professor of History and African-American Studies at Emory University. He is the author or editor of seven books, among them *In Their Own Interests: Race, Class and Power in Twentieth-Century Norfolk, Virginia; Love on Trial: An American Scandal in Black and White* (with Heidi Ardizzone); and *Defending Diversity* (with Patricia Gurin and Jeffrey Lehman).

## The Authors

**Barbara Bair** is a historian at the Library of Congress. The author of several essays on black women's activism, she is an associate and contributing editor of *The Marcus Garvey and Universal Negro Improvement Association Papers* and a consultant and commentator for the PBS-American Experience documentary *Marcus Garvey: Look for Me in the Whirlwind*, produced and directed by Stanley Nelson. She received her Ph.D. from Brown University.

**James R. Grossman** is vice president for research and education at the Newberry Library and senior lecturer in history at the University of Chicago. He is the author of *Land of Hope: Chicago, Black Southerners, and the Great Migration*, editor of *The Frontier in American Culture*, and co-editor of the series "Historical Studies of Urban America."

**Vincent Harding** is professor of religion and social transformation at the Iliff School of Theology at the University of Denver. Harding has been director of the Martin Luther King, Jr., Memorial Center in Atlanta and the Institute of the Black World, which he helped to found. He was senior academic adviser to the PBS television series "Eyes on the Prize," about the Civil Rights movement, and he is author of many publications, including *There Is a River, Hope and History,* and *Martin Luther King: The Inconvenient Hero.*

**Joe William Trotter, Jr.,** is Mellon Professor of History and director of the Center for African-American Urban Studies and the Economy at Carnegie-Mellon University. He holds a Ph.D. from the University of Minnesota. In addition to other edited and co-edited volumes, Professor Trotter is the author of *River Jordan: African American Urban Life in the Ohio Valley; Coal, Class, and Color: Blacks in Southern West Virginia, 1915–1932;* and *Black Milwaukee: The Making of an Industrial Proletariat, 1915–1945.*

# Index